ON TARGET
70th Anniversary Special

The Battle of Britain
Camouflage & Markings 1940
By Peter Scott and Gary Madgwick

Introduction

As a hobby, running for about 12 years now, I have converted any worthwhile photographs that caught my fancy into the sort of illustrations contained in this book. I now have quite a considerable and eclectic collection, running to well over a thousand pages of artwork. A large proportion is of RFC and RAF aircraft, with much of the remainder being related to the Luftwaffe. So when The Aviation Workshop expressed interest in commissioning a book on the aircraft of the Battle of Britain and their markings for the 70th Anniversary of the event, I thought that I was quite well positioned to comply. However, it turned out that the job was only partially done... It was quickly established what had already been accomplished, so research for the remainder, which took over a year, was eased considerably by the assistance that I received from friends, in particular

Paul Lucas, the well known author and researcher. Heavy use was made of the essential 'Battle of France: Then and Now' and 'Battle of Britain: Then and Now', together with the seminal works on the 'Jagdfliegerverbände der Deutschen Luftwaffe' by Jochen Prien. The Air Ministry War Room 'Location of Enemy Aircraft Brought Down in the UK – Reports 1-124 August to December 1940' were also consulted throughout, since these were first-hand intelligence and often contained reference to camouflage and markings. The interpretation of colour from monochrome photographs taken using a variety of emulsions is an art, not a science – for me anyway. The following colour profiles and four-views are therefore based on a combination of known facts and my judgements, so any errors and omissions are mine, and mine alone. *Peter Scott, September 2010*

First published in Great Britain in 2010
by The Aviation Workshop Publications Ltd.
and Gary Madgwick
Watermill Studio, Unit 13/14A, Home Farm,
Ardington, Nr Wantage, Oxfordshire, OX12 8PD, UK
Tel: (01235) 861614   Fax: (01235) 861032
Email: sales@theaviationworkshop.co.uk
Website: www.theaviationworkshop.co.uk

© Copyright 2010
The Aviation Workshop Publications Ltd.

Managing Editor: Gary Madgwick
Authors: Peter Scott
and Gary Madgwick
Commissioning Editor: Andy J. Donovan
Technical Consultants: Paul Lucas
and Andy Scott
Layout Editor: James Lawrence, Gingercake Creative

Printed in England by PHP Litho Printers Ltd.
Hoyle Mill, Barnsley, South Yorkshire, S71 1HN

ISBN: 978-1-904643-36-1

Distribution and marketing in the UK by
The Aviation Workshop Publications Ltd.
Trade terms available on request.

The Globe is a registered trademark of
The Aviation Workshop Publications Ltd.

All enquiries regarding this publication, past publications or future projects and publications should be directed to the publishers.

1 Overview to the Battle of Britain
pages 3-15

2 The Phoney War
pages 16-49

3 Blitzkrieg! The invasion of France and the Low Countries
pages 50-75

4 Battle of Britain Phase 1:
The Channel Battles (Kanalkampf)
pages 76-89

5 Battle of Britain Phase 2: Adlerangriff
the initial assaults against the airfields
pages 90-105

6 Battle of Britain Phase 3:
Fight for survival
pages 106-115

7 Battle of Britain Phase 4:
The change of tactics
pages 116-135

8 Battle of Britain Phase 5:
Night Blitz
pages 136-141

9 The Regia Aeronautica in the Battle of Britain
pages 142-145

10 Bomber Command and Coastal Command in the Battle of Britain
pages 146-157

11 The Fleet Air Arm in the Battle of Britain
pages 158-161

12 Britain Alone
pages 162-168

THE AVIATION WORKSHOP PUBLICATIONS LTD

1 Overview to the Battle of Britain

'Never in the field of human conflict has so much been owed by so many to so few.'
Winston S. Churchill, 20 August 1940

In the summer of 1940, the Luftwaffe attempted to win air superiority over the English Channel and the south eastern part of the British Isles by destroying the Royal Air Force and the British aircraft industry. Victory over the RAF was absolutely essential to the Germans if they were to mount an invasion of the British Isles.

German ground and air forces had overrun Belgium, the Netherlands and northern France in May and June 1940, using the 'Blitzkrieg' (Lightning War) tactics that relied, amongst other things, upon close co-ordination between ground and air forces. Although the Luftwaffe had proved very competent in this tactical role, it was not trained, nor equipped, for longer-range strategic operations of the type that they were asked to fight during the summer and autumn of 1940. But, the Luftwaffe had to gain air superiority over the RAF, and Fighter Command in particular, if the planned amphibious and airborne forces invasion of Britain, code named 'Operation Sealion', (Unternehmen Seelöwe), stood any chance of success. However, even had the Germans succeeded in their aim of destroying the RAF, they would not necessarily have been able to invade Britain easily.

Athough the British fear of an imminent German invasion was real, it was perhaps to some extent a little exagerrated. Even though the country had just suffered a catastrophic defeat in the Battle of France, losing much of its Army's equipment, not to mention hundreds of aircraft, and was now the only European power still resisting Nazi Germany, she still enjoyed massive support from her Commonwealth partners.

Neither Adolf Hitler nor his High Command believed it was possible to carry out a successful amphibious assault on Britain until the RAF had been totally neutralised, however, when planning the air attacks, the Luftwaffe Generals appear to have made the mistake of regarding the English Channel as little more than a wide river crossing. There were also plenty of indications that they might face real problems in accomplishing their conquest of Britain during the evacuation of Allied troops from the Dunkerque (Dunkirk) beaches at the end of May, when they came up against determined, UK-based and controlled, Spitfire units for the first time.

But even if the Luftwaffe had achieved its aim of destroying the RAF, the Wehrmacht might still have failed to establish a foothold after any invasion as the British Royal Navy was still enormously strong, and very capable of intercepting any German invasion armada.

So, an important secondary consideration to this primary objective was not only the requirement to destroy British aircraft production and its ground infrastructure, but to attack areas of political significance forcing the British Government into seeking an armistice without Germany having the need to mount an invasion.

The generally accepted dates as far as the British are concerned for the Battle was from 10 July to 31 October 1940, for which a Campaign Medal was struck, and which represented the most intense period of daylight bombing. German historians tend to place the beginning of the Battle proper, (Luftschlacht um England), a little later, around mid-August 1940, a few weeks after the fighting in France had finally finished with the signing of the French Armistice on 22 June 1940 – during which period, the Luftwaffe had time to briefly rest, refit, and resupply its operational units – and end it in May 1941, which coincides with the major withdrawal of Luftwaffe bomber units from France and the Low Countries in preparation for 'Operation Barbarossa', (Unternehmen Barbarossa), the campaign against the Soviet Union, which was launched in June 1941.

The Battle of Britain was the first major campaign to be fought virtually entirely by opposing air forces and was to be the largest and most sustained aerial bombing campaign attempted up until that date. The RAF who were on the defensive, were mainly dependent on the fighter aircraft within Fighter Command, but Bomber Command aircraft were also very active during this period, bombing the accumulation of invasion barges in France and selected industrial targets in Germany.

The failure of the Luftwaffe, (and, later in the Battle, the token gesture by the Regia Aeronautica), to achieve its objectives of gainining air superiority over the British Isles, destroying Britain's air defences, breaking British morale and thereby forcing Britain to negotiate for an armistice or outright surrender, is now generally considered to be one of the crucial turning points in World War Two and one of Hitler's first major setbacks.

Phases of the Battle of Britain

The Battle went through a series of marked phases.

Phase 1: The Channel Battles (Kanalkampfkrieg) – from 10 July to 11 August 1940, in which coastal shipping, convoys and harbours, such as Portsmouth, were the main targets.

Phase 2: Adlerangriff – from 12 to 23 August 1940 when the Luftwaffe started to shift its attacks on to RAF airfields, the ground infrastructure and aircraft factories

Phase 3: Intensified Luftwaffe attacks on RAF airfields – from 24 August to 6 September 1940 and came very close to destroying Fighter Command and its bases.

Phase 4: Change of Luftwaffe tactics – from 7 September to 31 October 1940, when the Luftwaffe resorted to attacking areas of political significance such as London in daylight, using area bombing tactics.

Phase 5: Night Blitz – from late September 1940 through to the spring of 1941 when the Luftwaffe turned more and more on to a night bombing campaign against London and the UK's major cities.

RAF Fighter Command

The RAF had two main high performance, single-engined, single seat fighter designs in service during the Battle of Britain period. The Hawker Hurricane Mk.I, which was the most numerous fighter available to RAF Fighter Command with over thirty frontline squadrons equipped with the type, and the Supermarine Spitfire Mk.I, of which some nineteen frontline squadrons were so equipped.

There were two squadrons equipped with Boulton Paul Defiant Mk.Is, an outdated concept, turreted fighter, with no forward firing armament; and no less than seven squadrons equipped with Bristol Blenheim Mk.If twin-engined 'heavy' fighters – which were merely modified from the short-nosed bomber version fitted with a 'tray' of four 0.303 inch machine guns under the fuselage centreline. The first few examples of the Bristol Beaufighter Mk.I had also just been delivered but were not operational, and there was one squadron of Gloster Gladiator Mk.II biplanes for localised area defence.

The Luftwaffe

▲ In July 1940 a planning conference was held at the Berghof, Adolf Hitler's residence in the Bavarian Alps. The Führer can be seen in discussion with Admiral Erich Raeder as Field Marshal Walther von Brauchitsch, General Alfred Jodl, Field Marshal Wilhelm Keitel and a Kriegsmarine staff officer look on. Given the time period in which this photograph was taken it seems plausible that the subject under discussion may have been Operation Sealion. (Photo: Imperial War Museum)

The Messerschmitt Bf 109E was the Luftwaffe's principal single-engined fighter, and several sub-types were in service – E-1, E-3, E-4 and the first E-7s, with the Bf 109E-1/B, E-4/B and E-7 variants adapted for bomb-carrying. The Bf 109E had a maximum range of some 600km (360 miles). Even when operating from its forward bases in France during the Battle of France, which were still some way from the Dunkerque area, protection of German bombers proved difficult, making them vulnerable to interception by RAF fighters – which were then based just across the Channel. This was a foretaste of the problems that the Bf 109E would find itself facing over the British Isles – it only had enough fuel for 15 minutes 'loiter time' over Kent and was at the absolute limit of its range over London. The twin-engined Messerschmitt Bf 110 (Zerstörer) had a slightly longer range but was not as manouvreable as the Bf 109E. It came in the standard Bf 110C heavy fighter variant and the Bf 110D, long range fuel tank adapted and bomb-carrying sub-types. There was also the Messerschmitt Bf 110C-5 photo reconnaissance variant.

The four main bomber types were the Junkers Ju 88A-1 and A-5, Do 17Z-2 and Z-3 and Heinkel He 111H and He 111Ps (in various sub-types) – all 'medium' bombers – and the Junkers Ju 87B and R dive bombers.

Other types included the Ju 88C long range heavy escort fighter and Ju 88D reconnaissance bomber; Dornier Do 215, Do 17P and a few Do 17Ms for strategic reconnaissance; Dornier Do 18D for maritime reconnaissance and air sea rescue; Heinkel He 59C for air sea rescue; and Focke-Wulf Fw 200C for long range maritime reconnaissance.

Regia Aeronautica – Corpo Aero Italiano

An element of the Regia Aeronautica called the Corpo Aero Italiano (CAI), first saw action in late October 1940. It took part in the latter stages of the Battle, but achieved limited success. The unit was redeployed to the Mediterranean Theatre in early 1941. The main types of aircraft operated by the CAI were the Fiat BR.20M 'Cicogna' medium bomber; Fiat CR.42 'Falco' biplane fighter; and Fiat G.50 'Freccia' monoplane fighter.

Fighter design comparisons

Despite their success, German losses in the Battle of France had been heavy, some 30 per cent of the force committed, and the German aircraft industry was already falling behind the British in aircraft production.

The Spitfire was faster and more manoeuvrable than its stablemate but the Hurricane was a more stable gun platform and carried slightly more ammunition. The Bf 109E had a better climb rate and was between 10 to 30 mph faster than the Hurricane, depending on altitude. The performance of the Spitfire over Dunkerque came as a bit of a surprise to the Jagdwaffe, although the German pilots retained a strong belief that the Bf 109E was the superior fighter. However, the Bf 109E had a larger turning circle than either the Hurricane or the Spitfire.

The Bf 109E and the Spitfire were superior to each other in certain key areas; for example, at some altitudes, the Bf 109 could out-climb the British fighter. In general, though, the differences between the Spitfire Mk.I and the Bf 109E in performance and handling were only marginal, and in combat the advantage invariably went to whoever had seen the other first, or who was 'up sun', had higher altitude, was in greater numbers, the amount of fuel remaining, etc, and perhaps most important of all, pilot ability.

Both British single-seat fighters were equipped with eight Browning 0.303 inch machine guns as standard, although a small experimental batch of Spitfires was fitted with a pair of 20mm cannon – which were plagued by malfunctions due to poor manufacturing tolerances. Although many Bf 109E-1s were still armed with the original four 7.92mm MG 17 machine guns, (two in the wings and two above the nose), some of these earlier sub-types had been up-gunned, and most of the Bf 109Es equipping the Jagdgeschwadern were armed with two MG FF 20mm cannon in the wings and two 7.92mm machine guns over the nose.

The Bf 109E was also used as a fighter-bomber – the E-1/B, E-4/B and E-7 models had the ability to carry a 250kg bomb under the fuselage, and unlike the Stuka, the Bf 109E could fight on equal terms with RAF fighters after releasing its ordnance. At the time, these aircraft were the best the respective sides could produce, thus, in the struggle for air superiority, the two sides were about evenly matched.

At the start of the Battle, the twin-engined Messerschmitt Bf 110 long range fighter was expected to engage in air-to-air combat while escorting Luftwaffe bombers. Although the Bf 110 was faster than the Hurricane and almost as fast as the Spitfire, its lack of manoeuvrability and acceleration meant that it was something of a failure as an escort fighter. Between 13 and 15 August for example, over forty Bf 110s were lost – the equivalent of an entire Gruppe.

RAF Strategy

(Photo: Imperial War Museum)

The C-in-C RAF Fighter Command since 1937 was Air Chief Marshal Sir Hugh C T Dowding, who had overseen the procurement of both the Spitfire and the Hurricane, and was involved in the development of the Radio Direction Finding system (RDF – the original RAF name for radar). He had resisted demands by the then newly elected British Prime Minister Winston Churchill to send any more fighter aircraft to France in May 1940, holding them back for the forthcoming defence of the UK, and refused to commit Fighter Command in large numbers to defending sea convoys. Both decisions were subsequently proved to have been good ones. The keystone of the British defence was the complex infrastructure of detection, command, and control that ran the battle. The original air defence system had been set up in 1917, but Dowding built upon and modernised the system.

This trend continued with further losses on 16 and 17 August after which Göring ordered the Bf 110 units to operate only *"... where the range of the single-engined machines was not sufficient."*

The most successful role of the Bf 110 during the Battle was as a Schnellbomber (fast bomber). The Bf 110D-0s generally used a shallow dive to bomb the target and were able to escape at high speed. One unit, Erprobungsgruppe 210, (ErprGr 210) proved that the Bf 110 could be used to good effect in attacking specific or 'pinpoint' targets.

The Boulton Paul Defiant proved to be hopelessly outclassed. It lacked any form of forward firing armament and the heavy turret meant that it was unable to out-run or out-manoeuvre either the Bf 109 or the Bf 110. By the end of August, after disastrous losses, the aircraft was withdrawn from daylight service.

Bomber design comparisons

The German bomber fleet was relatively well equipped, with twin-engined 'medium' bombers. The Luftwaffe had no heavy four-engined strategic bombers of the type being developed by Britain and America, with the exception of the Focke-Wulf Fw 200 'Condor' – an ex-civil airliner design adapted for long-range maritime patrol operations. The three twin-engined bomber types differed in their capabilities. The Heinkel He 111H and Ps were the slowest but were used in greater numbers than the others; the Dornier Do 17Z was based upon a tried and tested design but was getting somewhat obsolete and carried the smallest bomb load; and the Junkers Ju 88A, which had recently started re-equipping several bomber Geschwadern, was the fastest, especially once its mainly externally carried bomb load had been dropped. All three bomber types suffered heavy losses from British fighters. Later in the conflict, when night bombing became more frequent, all three were put to use as night bombers. However, due to its reduced bomb load, the lighter Do 17Z was used less than the He 111 and Ju 88 for this purpose.

For pin-point accuracy strikes there was the Junkers Ju 87B 'Stuka', which was very effective in direct support of the army but proved extremely vulnerable in air-to-air combat. Although successful in previous campaigns, the 'Stukas' suffered heavy losses in the Battle of Britain, particularly on 18 August. These losses were due to its slow speed and vulnerability to fighter interception. As a result of combat losses and the limited payload and range it possessed, the Stukagruppen were largely removed from operations over mainland England and concentrated on attacking shipping instead until redeployed to the Eastern Front in 1941. They returned to targets on the British mainland on occasion, such as on the 13 September attack on Tangmere airfield.

On the British side, three bombers were mostly used on night operations against targets such as factories, invasion ports and railway centres. The Armstrong Whitworth Whitley, the Handley-Page Hampden and the Vickers Wellington – all of which were classed as heavy bombers by the RAF, although the Hampden was, in reality, a medium bomber comparable to the He 111. The twin-engined Bristol Blenheim Mk.IV and the obsolescent single-engined Fairey Battle were both classed as medium bombers. The Blenheim was the most numerous of the aircraft equipping RAF Bomber Command and was used in attacks against shipping, ports, airfields and factories on the continent by day and by night.

Fighter Command

The information from RDF and the Observer Corps was sent through to the main operations room of Fighter Command Headquarters at Bentley Priory. The plots were assessed to determine whether they were 'hostile' or 'friendly'. If 'hostile', the information was sent to the main operations room, which was in a large underground bunker.

▲ Oblique aerial view of RAF Bentley Priory, Stanmore, Middlesex: Headquarters Fighter Command, seen from the south west. (Photo: Imperial War Museum)

▲ The Royal Air Force Operations Room at Headquarters Fighter Command, located at Bentley Priory near Stanmore in Middlesex.
(Photo: Imperial War Museum)

Here the course information of each raid was plotted by Womens Auxilary Air Force (WAAFs) who received information via a telephone system. Additional intelligence was provided by the 'Y' Service radio posts, which monitored enemy radio transmissions, and the 'Ultra' decoding centre based at Bletchley Park.

Colour coded counters representing each raid were placed on a large table, which had a map of the UK overlaid and squared off with a British Modified Grid. The colour coding (red, yellow and blue) of each counter was changed every five minutes, conforming to a colour coded 24 hour sector clock. As the plots of the raiding aircraft moved, the counters were pushed across the map by magnetic 'rakes'. This system enabled the main Fighter Controller (usually of Squadron Leader rank) to see very quickly where each formation was heading and allowed an estimate to be made of possible targets. Because of the simplicity of the system, decisions could be made quickly and easily.

Chain Home Radio Direction Finding

Usually the first indications of incoming air raids were received by the Chain Home Radio Direction Finding facilities which were located around the coastlines of the UK. Each had a set of radar towers linked to a co-located control room. In most circumstances, RDF could pick up formations of Luftwaffe aircraft as they organised themselves over their own airfields in France. However, once the raiding aircraft moved inland over England, RDF contact was lost and the formations were then plotted by the Observer Corps.

(Photos: Imperial War Museum)

Apart from the controller, most of the room and map information was operated by members of the WAAF. Before the war, there was still a great deal of doubt about the ability of women to stand up to battle conditions with so many airwomen being employed on front-line RDF stations and aerodromes. Experience during the Battle proved that such doubts were unfounded and the contribution of the WAAFs became essential to the RAF in its control and communications systems, as well as in many other duties.

Fighter Command Groups

The UK's Fighter Command was divided up into four Groups;

▲ 10 Group defended Wales and the West Country and was commanded by Air Vice-Marshal Sir Quintin Brand. (Photo: via Donald Reeves)

▲ 11 Group covered the southeast of England and the critical approaches to London and was commanded by Air Vice-Marshal Keith Park, a New Zealander and World War One 'ace'. (Photo: Imperial War Museum)

▲ 12 Group defended the Midlands and East Anglia and was led by Air Vice-Marshal Trafford Leigh-Mallory. (Photo: Imperial War Museum)

▲ 13 Group covered the north of England, Scotland and Northern Ireland and was commanded by Air Vice-Marshal Richard Saul. (Photo: Imperial War Museum)

During the course of the Battle several Coastal Command and Fleet Air Arm units also came under Fighter Command control.

This 'possible target' information was simultaneously sent to the headquarters of each Group (for example, RAF Uxbridge for 11 Group), where it was 'filtered' through a filter room, (ie collated, cross-checked and simplified), before being sent through to another operations room, again housed in an underground bunker.

Because Group controlled the tactical control of the Battle, the operations room was different in layout to the one at Bentley Priory. The main map on the plotting table represented the Group command area and its associated airfields. Extensive radio and telephone equipment transmitted and received a constant flow of information from the various sector airfields as well as the Observer Corps, AA Command and the Navy. The Duty Fighter Controller's job was to control how and when each raid would be dealt with. He ordered the squadrons airborne and positioned them as he thought best. Timing was of the essence, because each minute of unnecessary delay waiting to make absolutely sure that the raid was coming in would cost the defenders some 2,000 feet of vital altitude.

Each Group room had a 'tote board' which showed each squadron available to that Group. The tote board had a system of lights which enabled the controllers to see the squadron status: Released (not available); Available (airborne in 20 minutes); Readiness (airborne in 5 minutes); Standby (pilots in cockpit, airborne in 2 minutes); Airborne and moving into position; Enemy sighted; Ordered to land; Landed and refuelling/rearming.

Next to the tote board, where it could be clearly seen, was a weather board which showed the state of the weather around each airfield. It was the responsibility of the WAAF plotters to continually update the tote and weather boards.

Despite appearances, the Groups were not 'mutually supporting'. Park, for instance, could only request, not demand, assistance from Brand (who usually co-operated), or from Leigh-Mallory (who sometimes didn't) This was because Dowding had never issued standing orders to assist, nor had he created a method to co-ordinate it.

There was a further problem in that the aircraft were not assigned equitably between the Groups. While the most effective RAF fighter was the Spitfire, 70% of 11 Group's aircraft were Hurricanes. Effectively, less than a third of Britain's best fighters were operating in the key sector.

Sectors

The Group areas were subdivided into Sectors; each Commanding Officer was assigned between two and four squadrons. Sector Stations, comprising an aerodrome with a Sector operations room, were the heart of this organisation, and they were also responsible for operating satellite aerodromes to which squadrons could be dispersed. The operations rooms duplicated those at the Group HQs, although they were on a smaller scale and most were still housed in brick, single-storey, tile-roofed structures above ground, where they were vulnerable to attack. By 1940, most were semi-protected by an earth bank or 'blast wall' surrounding them which reached as high as the eaves. Fortunately for Fighter Command, Luftwaffe Intelligence was unaware of the importance of these rooms and most were left alone.

The control rooms at Biggin Hill were completely destroyed by a raid on 31 August, but this was due to a chance bomb hit rather than a specifically targeted attack. Their vulnerability in time of war was appreciated and new airfields built during the expansion programme of the 1930s had new, bombproof structures. As a further precaution, emergency control rooms were set up in different locations away from the airfields, with small loss in efficiency. RAF Kenley, for example, used an alternative room housed in a vacant butcher's shop. The plotting table was laid out with a map of the sector and its airfields, and the tote and weather boards reflected this more localised information.

When ordered by their Group HQ, the Sector Stations would 'scramble' their squadrons into the air. Once airborne, the squadrons would be directed by radio-telephone (R/T) from their sector station. Squadrons could be ordered to patrol airfields or vital targets or be 'vectored' to intercept incoming raids. As well as directing the fighter squadrons, Sector stations

Map of the United Kingdom showing Group boundaries, Sector Stations and Fighter Command aerodromes

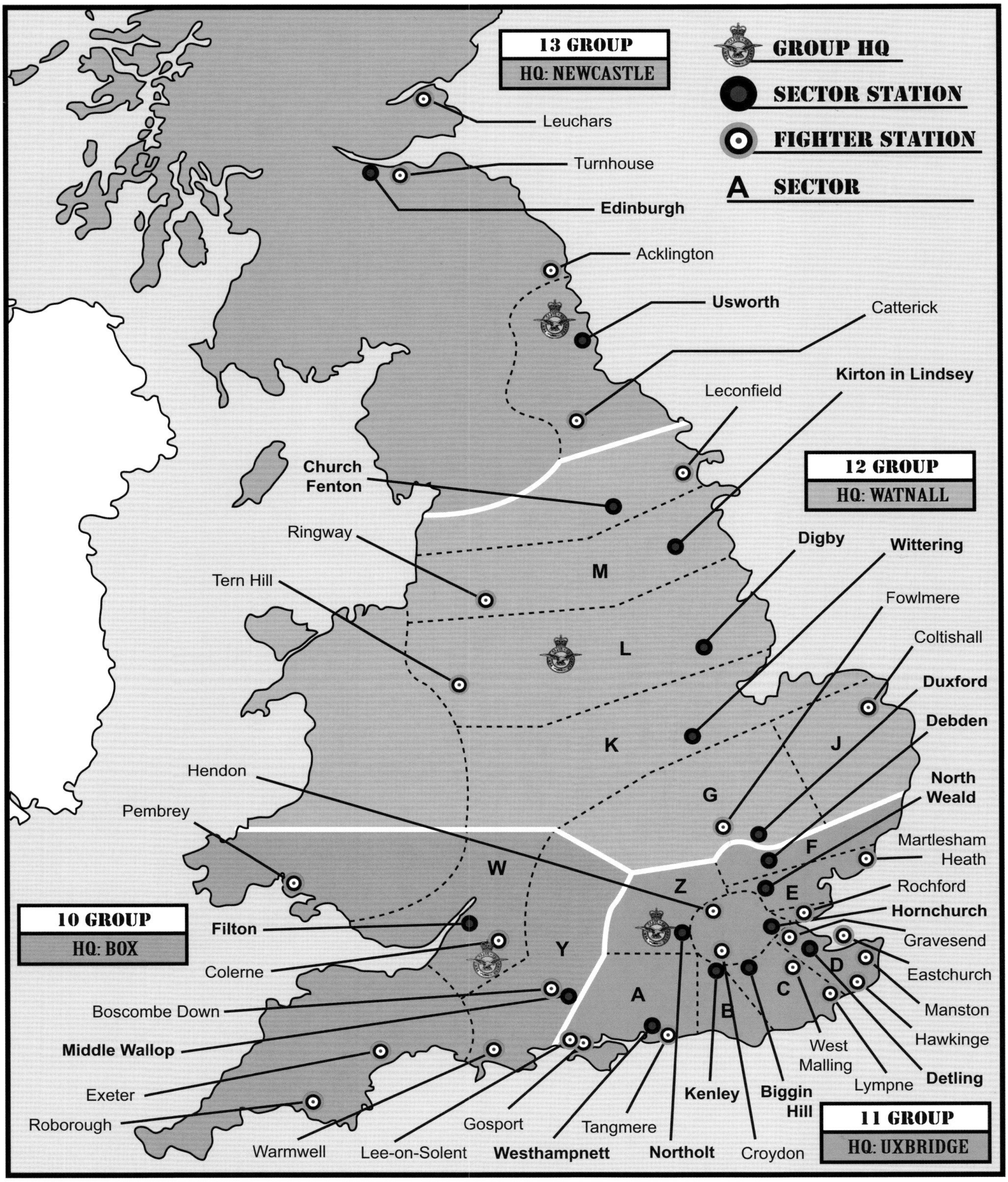

13 GROUP
HQ: NEWCASTLE

GROUP HQ
SECTOR STATION
FIGHTER STATION
A SECTOR

Leuchars
Turnhouse
Edinburgh
Acklington
Usworth
Catterick
Leconfield
Kirton in Lindsey
Church Fenton
12 GROUP
HQ: WATNALL
Ringway
Digby
Wittering
Tern Hill
M
Fowlmere
Coltishall
L
Duxford
Debden
K
J
North Weald
Hendon
G
Martlesham Heath
Pembrey
Rochford
F
W
Hornchurch
Z
E
Gravesend
10 GROUP
Filton
D
Eastchurch
HQ: BOX
Y
C
Colerne
Manston
Boscombe Down
A
B
Hawkinge
Middle Wallop
West Malling
Detling
Exeter
Kenley
Biggin Hill
Lympne
Roborough
Gosport
11 GROUP
Warmwell
Lee-on-Solent
Tangmere
HQ: UXBRIDGE
Westhampnett
Northolt
Croydon

(Artwork: Peter Scott and Andy J. Donovan)

also controlled the anti-aircraft batteries in their area. An Army Officer sat beside each Fighter Controller and directed the gun crews when to open fire and, if RAF aircraft flew into the gun-zones, ordered the guns to cease fire.

Although it was the most sophisticated air defence system in the world at that time, the 'Dowding System' had many limitations, including its need for qualified ground maintenance personnel, many of whom had received their training under the Aircraft Apprentice scheme instituted by Hugh Trenchard.

RDF was subject to errors and the Observer Corps had difficulty tracking raids at night or in bad weather. R/T communications with airborne fighters was restricted because of the RAF's use of High-Frequency (HF) radio sets. The TR9 HF radio used by RAF fighters was limited in range, and even with a network of relay stations the squadrons could not roam more than one or two sectors from their airfields. Distortion and interference

▲ The interior of the Sector 'G' Operations Room at RAF Duxford in Cambridgeshire. The callsigns of fighter squadrons controlled by this Sector can be seen on the wall behind the operator sitting third from left. The Controller can also be seen on the telephone to the right of the photograph, and on the extreme right, behind the Army Liaison Officer, are the R/T operators in direct touch with the aircraft. (Photo: Imperial War Museum)

often made communication difficult. It was also restricted to a single frequency per squadron, making inter-squadron communication impossible.

Finally, the system for tracking RAF fighters, known as HF/DF restricted sectors to a maximum of four squadrons in the air. The addition of Identification Friend or Foe (IFF), 'Pipsqueak', whilst a welcome help in identifying RAF aircraft, took up another radio channel.

Starting in late September 1940, Very High Frequency (VHF) T/R Type 1133 radios started replacing the HF TR9 sets. These had first been fitted to Spitfires of Nos 54 and 66 Squadrons starting in October 1939, but production delays with these improved sets meant the bulk of Spitfires and Hurricanes were not fitted with this equipment until October 1940. Whilst it

also had faults, these provided much clearer reception over a longer range, and controllers and pilots had a wider range of communications channels to choose from.

In spite of these radio transmission problems, Fighter Command at times achieved interception rates of over 80% as the RAF's system of ground control continued to direct its fighters to where they were needed. The Luftwaffe, with no similar system, was always at a disadvantage.

RAF Fighter Command Tactics

The weight of the Battle fell upon 11 Group. Air Vice-Marshal Keith Park's tactics were to despatch individual squadrons to intercept raids. The intention was to subject attackers to continual attacks by relatively small numbers of aircraft and try to break up the tight formations of bombers. Once formations had fallen apart, stragglers could be picked off one by one.

Where multiple squadrons reached a raid, the ideal procedure was to try to get the slower Hurricanes to tackle the bombers whilst the more agile Spitfires engaged the fighter escort. This ideal was not always achieved however, and sometimes the Spitfires and Hurricanes reversed roles.

During the Battle, 12 Group's Air Vice-Marshal Trafford Leigh-Mallory proposed that squadrons be formed into 'Big Wings', consisting of at least three squadrons, to attack the enemy en masse – a method then being pioneered by the CO of 242 Squadron, the legendary Squadron Leader Douglas Bader.

▲ Squadron Leader Douglas Bader is seen here with fellow pilots, Flight Lieutenant Ball and Pilot Officer McKnight DFC, standing next to his Hurricane Mk.I, V7467/LE-D of 242 Squadron, RAF Duxford. The fighter is adorned with an emblem of Hitler receiving the welcome they all hoped to give him should they ever get the chance! Bader was instrumental in the development of the 'Big Wing' concept. (Photo: Imperial War Museum)

Proponents of this tactic claimed interceptions in large numbers caused greater enemy losses whilst reducing their own casualties. Opponents pointed out the 'Big Wings' would take too long to form up, and the strategy ran a greater risk of fighters being caught on the ground refuelling. The 'Big Wing' idea also caused over-claiming by pilots, due to the confusion of a more intense and congested battle zone. This led to the belief 'Big Wings' were far more effective than they actually were.

The issue caused intense friction between Park and Leigh-Mallory, as 12 Group was tasked with protecting 11 Group's airfields whilst Park's squadrons intercepted incoming raids.

The Fighter Control System

```
Radar          Radar          Radar
Station        Station        Station
                  │
                  ▼
          RAF STANMORE
           Filter Room
        Fighter Command
        Operations Room

Group                              Group
Operations                         Operations
Room                               Room

              Group
           Operations
              Room

Sector                             Sector
Operations                         Operations
Room                               Room

Radio          Sector            Gun
D/F          Operations        Defences
Station         Room
                              Barrage
                              Balloons

                              Observer
                               Centre

Airborne       Fighter
Fighter        Airfield
Squadron
                         Obs.   Obs.   Obs.
                         Post   Post   Post
```

However, the delay in forming up 'Big Wings' meant the formations often did not arrive until after German bombers had hit 11 Group's airfields or on occasions not at all.

In an effort to highlight the problem of the 'Big Wing's performance, Dowding submitted a report compiled by Park to the Air Ministry on 15 November 1940. In the report, he highlighted the fact that during the period of 11 September to 31 October, the extensive use of the 'Big Wing' had resulted in just ten interceptions and one German aircraft destroyed, but his report was ignored.

Post-war analysis agrees that Park's approach was probably best for 11 Group. Dowding's removal from his post in November 1940 has been partially blamed on this struggle between Park and Leigh-Mallory's strategy. However, the intensive raids and destruction wrought during the night Blitz also damaged Dowding, and Park in particular, for the failure to produce an effective night-fighter defence system – something for which the influential Leigh-Mallory had long criticised them.

▲ Air Marshal Sir W. Sholto Douglas, Air Officer Commanding, RAF Fighter Command, pictured at his desk at Fighter Command Headquarters at Bentley Priory, Stanmore, Middlesex on 24 February 1942. Douglas replaced Hugh Dowding in the post in November 1940 and was himself replaced by Leigh-Mallory almost exactly two years later. (Photo: Imperial War Museum)

Luftwaffe structure

The Luftwaffe was originally devised to provide tactical support for the army on the battlefield. During the 'Blitzkrieg' offensives against Poland, Denmark and Norway, and France and the Low Countries, the Luftwaffe had co-operated fully with the Wehrmacht. For the Battle of Britain however, the Luftwaffe had to operate in a strategic role, something for which it was unsuited. Its main task was to ensure air supremacy over southeast England, to pave the way for an invasion fleet.

The basic Luftwaffe tactical operational unit was the Geschwader, broadly equivalent to an RAF Group. The Geschwader were split in to the roles their aircraft were designed for and their crews trained for.

Jagdgeschwader (JG): Fighter Group
Kampfgeschwader (KG): Bomber Group (literally Battle Group)
Zerstörergeschwader (ZG): Heavy twin-engined/long-range Fighter Group (literally Destroyer Group)
Stukageschwader (StG): Dive Bomber Group

Luftwaffe strategy

Reichsmarschall Hermann Göring (Photo: Imperial War Museum)

For the Luftwaffe, the Battle of Britain effectively began on 30 June 1940. Reichsmarschall Hermann Göring, head of the Luftwaffe, ordered his force to draw the RAF into battle by attacking coastal convoys and bombing radar stations along the south coast, installations of the British aircraft industry, and RAF airfields. This dilution of effort, which became more marked as the battle progressed, was one of the principal reasons why the Luftwaffe eventually failed to gain air superiority over Britain.

The limited range of the German aircraft and the fact that they were fighting over enemy territory were two major disadvantages for the Germans. A downed German airman was lost to Germany, and a damaged aircraft was likely to ditch in the sea; whereas damaged RAF aircraft could limp home, or land somewhere friendly, and downed RAF pilots parachuted onto their home territory and were returned to their units almost immediately.

Lehrgeschwader (LG): Operational Training Group, but in fact LGs were extremely efficient specialist units operating a variety of aircraft types such as Bf 109Es, Bf 110s, Ju 87s and Ju 88s.

Additional ancillary units were formed on the Gruppe (broadly equivalent to an RAF Wing), comprising one or two Gruppen with some three or six Staffeln:

Kampfgruppe (KGr): Bomber Wing, usually semi-autonomous specialised units such as KGr 100's pathfinders or KGr 126's minelayers.

Erprobungsgruppe 210 (ErprGr 210): Operational Experimental Wing 210, which was originally formed to introduce the new Messerschmitt Me 210 twin-engined 'Zerstörer' in to service, but due to that type's delayed development, was turned in to another extremely efficient specialist unit operating Bf 109Es and Bf 110s in the fighter-bomber role.

Aufklärungsgruppe (AufklGr): Reconnaissance Wing. Although generally abbreviated to AufklGr, the type and/or range of reconnaissance the unit was undertaking was indicated by a prefix. For example Fernaufklärungsgruppe (FAGs) was long range/strategic reconnaissance Wing; Nahaufklärungsgruppe (NAGr) was short range/tactical reconnaissance Wing; and Heeresaufklärungsgruppe (HAGr) was Army cooperation reconnaissance Wing. When written down, the type and/or range of the unit was simply indicated as (F), (N) or (H) respectively. For example 3(F)./22 was the designation for 3 Staffel, I Gruppe, Fernaufklärungsgruppe 22 – (ie 3rd squadron of No I long range/strategic reconnaissance Wing 22.)

Küstenfliegergruppe (KüFlGr): Coastal Reconnaissance Wing.

One additional and very important unit which was frequently operational over the British Isles during the summer and autumn of 1940, was Wettererkundungsstaffel (Wekusta): Meteorological Reconnaissance Squadron!

In the summer of 1940, a Jagdgeschwader, generally consisted of three Gruppen (Wings), which in turn was made up of three Staffeln (Squadrons). Some Jagdgeschwadern, especially towards the end of the Battle of Britain, added a fourth Staffel to some of its Gruppen, which caused some re-adjustments in the Staffel numbering procedure, (as might be deduced from the accompanying tables on page 34 and 35 in Chapter 2).

Each Gruppe had a Stabsschwarm (Staff Flight), ostensibly of four aircraft which included the Gruppen Kommandeur, and usually the unit Adjutant and Technical Officer, who were generally pilots. However, not all members of the Gruppe staff were necessarily pilots, and often non-staff rank pilots, including experienced NCOs flew with the Stabsschwarm.

The Geschwader also had a Stabsschwarm, the Geschwaderstab, led by the Geschwader Kommodore, which again invariably consisted of four aircraft and generally included the Geschwader Adjutant and Geschwader Technical Officer, plus experienced pilots, that could be drawn from any of the Staffeln within the Geschwader.

With some twelve to sixteen aircraft in a fully up-to-strength Staffel, the total strength of an average Jagdgeschwader could have been anything been between 100 to 150 or so aircraft, including the Stabsschwarme – on paper. Actual operational strength varied considerably, and the average serviceable figure would have been somewhat lower. (see Chapter 4 for further details)

Kampfgeschwadern, Zerstörergeschwadern and Stukageschwardern also generally consisted of three or four Gruppen (Wings), which in turn were each made up of three Staffeln (Squadrons), with some nine to twelve aircraft in a fully up-to-strength Staffel. Again each Gruppe had a Stab flight, usually of three aircraft ('kette') as did the Geschwader, the Geschwaderkette.

Underestimating the strength of the RAF

A plan to use the Luftwaffe as the prelude to the invasion of the UK had been discussed in 1939, and was at first rejected. However, in view of the strength of the Royal Navy, it was eventually decided that the RAF had to be eliminated first. The Germans had won convincingly in the Polish campaign in 1939, and the Scandinavian and French campaigns in 1940, but they were now up against a well-organised air defence system, and things were going to be more difficult. Furthermore, they were operating at the limit of the range of the fighters needed to protect their vulnerable bombers.

Another factor counting against a German success was the Luftwaffe's underestimation of the strength of the RAF and the British aviation industry's production capacity. Göring believed that 'his' Luftwaffe could eliminate RAF Fighter Command in four days and the British aviation industry in four weeks. The British, on the other hand, somewhat overestimated German strength and competence.

The Luftwaffe had regrouped after the Battle of France into three Luftflotten (Air Fleets). Luftflotte 2, commanded by Generalfeldmarschall Albrecht Kesselring, was responsible for covering the southeast of England and the London area. Luftflotte 3, under Generalfeldmarschall Hugo Sperrle, covered the West Country, Midlands, and northwest England. Luftflotte 5, led by Generaloberst Hans-Jürgen Stumpff from his headquarters in Norway, covered the north of England and Scotland. As the battle progressed, command responsibility shifted, with Luftflotte 3 taking more responsibility for the nightime attacks whilst the main daylight operations fell upon Luftflotte 2's shoulders.

▲ Generalfeldmarschall Albrecht Kesselring. (Photo: Imperial War Museum)

▲ Generalfeldmarschall Hugo Sperrle. (Photo: Imperial War Museum)

Initial Luftwaffe estimates were that it would take four days to defeat RAF Fighter Command in southern England. This would be followed by a four-week offensive during which the bombers and long-range fighters would destroy all military installations throughout the country and wreck the British aircraft industry. The campaign was planned to begin with attacks on airfields near the coast, gradually moving inland to attack the ring of airfields defending London.

Later reassessments gave the Luftwaffe five weeks, from 8 August to 15 September, to establish temporary air superiority over England. To achieve this goal, Fighter Command had to be destroyed, either on the ground or in the air, yet the Luftwaffe had to be able to preserve its own strength in order to be able to support the invasion. This meant that the Luftwaffe had to maintain a high 'kill' ratio over the RAF fighters.

The Luftwaffe kept broadly to this scheme, but its commanders also had differences of opinion on strategy. Sperrle wanted

The Luftwaffe also tried using small formations of bombers as bait, covering them with large numbers of escorts. This was more successful, but escort duty tied the fighters to the bombers' slow speed and made them more vulnerable. The Ju 87 units, which had suffered heavy casualties, were only to be used under particularly favourable circumstances.

In early September, due to increasing complaints from the bomber crews about RAF fighters seemingly being able to get through the escort screen, Göring ordered an increase in close escort duties. This decision shackled many more of the Bf 109s to the bombers and, although they were more successful at protecting the bomber forces, casualties amongst the fighters mounted – primarily because they were forced to fly and manoeuvre at reduced speeds

By mid-September, tactics for raids had become an amalgam of techniques. Generally, a Freie Jagd would precede the main attack formations. The bombers would fly in at altitudes between 16,000 feet (4,900m) and 20,000 feet (6,100m), closely escorted by more fighters, which were divided into two parts (usually of Gruppen strength), some operating in close contact with the bombers, and others a few hundred yards away and a little above.

The biggest disadvantage faced by Bf 109 pilots was that without the benefit of long-range drop tanks, (which were only introduced in very limited numbers in the later stages of the Battle, usually of 300 litre capacity), the Bf 109s had a 600km (360 mile) range and an endurance of just over an hour. Once over Britain, a Bf 109E pilot had to keep an awareness for the red 'low fuel' light on the instrument panel. Once this was illuminated, he was forced to turn back and head for France. With the prospect of two long, over-water flights, and knowing their range was substantially reduced when escorting bombers or in the event of combat, the Jagdflieger soon coined the term Kanalkrankheit or 'Channel sickness'.

▲ Luftwaffe flying ace Major Adolph 'Dolfo' Joseph Ferdinand Galland enjoys some canine company during one of his quieter moments in WWII. Galland was a Gruppenkommandeur of Jagdgeschwader 26 (JG 26) and flew Messerschmitt 109s during the Battle of Britain. (Photo: Imperial War Museum)

to eradicate the air defence infrastructure by bombing it. His counterpart, Kesselring, championed attacking London directly – either to bombard the British government into submission or to draw RAF fighters into a decisive battle. Göring did nothing to resolve this disagreement between his commanders, and only vague directives were set down during the initial stages of the battle, with Göring seemingly unable to decide upon which strategy to pursue. He seemed at times obsessed with maintaining his own power base within the Luftwaffe and indulging his outdated beliefs on air fighting, which were later to lead to tactical and strategic errors.

Luftwaffe Tactics

Luftwaffe tactics were influenced by their fighters. The Bf 110 proved too vulnerable to the more nimble single-engined RAF fighters. This meant the bulk of fighter escort duties fell on the Bf 109E. Fighter tactics were then complicated by bomber crews who demanded closer protection. After the hard-fought battles of 15 and 18 August, Göring met with his unit leaders. During this conference, the need for the fighters to meet up on time with the bombers was stressed. It was also decided that one bomber Gruppe could only be properly protected by several Gruppen of Bf 109s. In addition Göring stipulated that as many fighters as possible were to be left free for Freie Jagd (free hunts). This fighter sweep would precede a raid to try to draw up RAF fighters and knock any defenders out of the raid's path. However, RAF fighter controllers were often able to detect these and position squadrons to avoid them, keeping to Dowding's plan to preserve fighter strength for intercepting the bomber formations.

Luftwaffe Intelligence

The Luftwaffe was ill-served by its lack of military intelligence about the British defences. The German intelligence services were fractured and plagued by rivalries and their overall performance was somewhat 'amateurish'. By 1940, there were few if any German agents operating in the UK and a handful of bungled attempts to insert spies into the country were foiled.

As a result of intercepted radio transmissions, the Germans began to realise that the RAF fighters were being controlled from ground facilities. In July and August 1939, for example, the airship 'Graf Zeppelin', which was packed with equipment for listening in on RAF radio and RDF transmissions, flew around the coasts of Britain. Although the Luftwaffe correctly interpreted the purpose of these new ground control procedures, they were incorrectly assessed as being rigid and ineffectual.

The existence of a British radar system was well known to the Luftwaffe from intelligence gathered before the war, but the highly developed Chain Home RDF system linked with fighter control had been a well kept secret. Even when good information existed, it was ignored if it did not match conventional preconceptions.

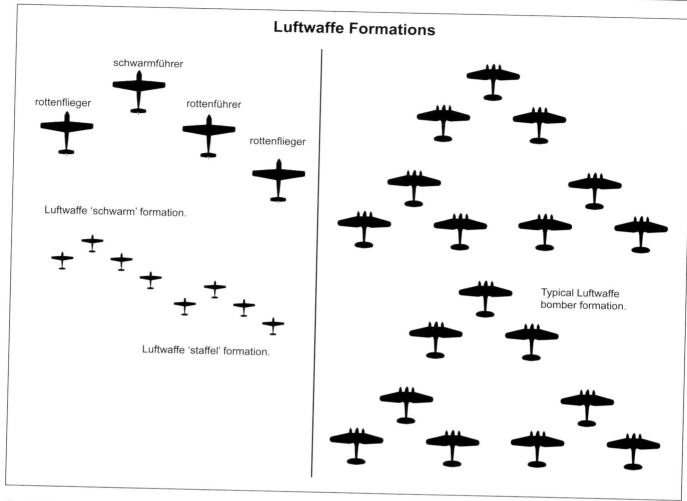

Luftwaffe Formations

schwarmführer

rottenflieger

rottenführer

rottenflieger

Luftwaffe 'schwarm' formation.

Luftwaffe 'staffel' formation.

Typical Luftwaffe bomber formation.

On 16 July 1940, Abteilung V, commanded by Oberstleutnant 'Beppo' Schmidt, produced a report on the RAF and on Britain's defensive capabilities which was adopted by the frontline commanders as a basis for their operational plans. One of the most conspicuous failures of the report was the lack of any information on the RAF's RDF network and control systems capabilities; it was assumed that the system was rigid and inflexible, with the RAF fighters being 'tied' to their home bases.

The optimistic and, as it turned out, erroneous conclusion reached was that the British aircraft industry only produced about 180 to 200 frontline fighters and 140 frontline bombers a month and due to difficulties in the procurement of raw materials and the disruption and breakdown of production at factories due to air attacks, output would decrease rather than increase. An intensification of the air war was therefore expected to cause the strength of the RAF to fall, with the decline further aggravated by the continued decrease in production.

Another more detailed report, issued on 10 August 1940, suggested that the RAF would eventually run out of frontline fighters. The Luftwaffe believed it was weakening Fighter Command at three times the actual attrition rate. Many times, the Luftwaffe leadership believed Fighter Command's strength had collapsed, only to discover that the RAF were seemingly able to send up defensive formations at will.
Throughout the Battle, the Luftwaffe had to use numerous reconnaissance sorties to make up for the poor intelligence. Reconnaissance aircraft (at first mostly Dornier Do 17Ps and

Do 215s, but increasingly Bf 110C-5s and Ju 88Ds) proved relatively easy prey for British fighters, as it was seldom possible for them to be escorted by Bf 109s. Thus, the Luftwaffe operated 'blind' for much of the Battle, unsure of its enemy's true strengths, capabilities, and deployments.

Many of Fighter Command's airfields were never attacked, whilst raids against supposed fighter airfields fell instead on Bomber or Coastal Command stations. The results of bombing and air fighting were consistently exaggerated, due to over-enthusiastic claims and the difficulty of effective confirmation over enemy territory. In the euphoric atmosphere of perceived victory, the Luftwaffe leadership became increasingly disconnected from reality. This lack of leadership and solid intelligence meant the Germans did not adopt any consistent strategy – even when Fighter Command had its back to the wall. Moreover, there was never a systematic focus on any one type of target (such as air bases, radar stations, or aircraft factories), so the already haphazard effort was further diluted.

It is unclear how much the British intercepts of the 'Enigma' cipher, used for high-security German radio communications, affected the Battle. Ultra, the information obtained from 'Enigma' intercepts, gave the highest echelons of the UK's command a view of German intentions but it seems little of this material filtered down to Hugh Dowding's desk. It would probably have had little tactical value in any case. However, the radio listening service (known as the Y Service), monitoring the patterns of Luftwaffe radio traffic, contributed considerably to the early warning of raids.

Fighter formations

In the late 1930s, Fighter Command was not expecting to be facing single-engine fighters over Britain, only bombers. With this in mind, a series of 'Fighting Area Tactics' were formulated – and rigidly adhered to. These involved a series of manoeuvres designed to concentrate a squadron's firepower to bring down bombers. With no apparent prospect of escorting fighters to worry about, RAF fighter pilots flew in tight, V-shaped sections (vics) of three. These restricted squadrons to tight twelve aircraft formations, composed of four sections, in another tight 'V'. With this formation, only the squadron leader at the front was free to actually watch for the enemy; the other pilots had to concentrate on keeping station.

RAF fighter training also emphasised 'by-the-book' attacks by sections breaking away in sequence. Fighter Command recognised the weaknesses of this rigid structure early in the Battle, but it was felt too risky to change tactics in the midst of the campaign, because replacement pilots, often with only minimal actual flying time, could not be readily retrained and it was decided that inexperienced RAF pilots needed the firm leadership in the air that only these rigid formations could provide. German pilots dubbed the RAF formations 'Idiotenreihen' (rows of idiots) because they left squadrons vulnerable to attack.

By contrast Luftwaffe fighters employed a loose section of two aircraft, (Rotte), based on a leader (Rottenführer) followed at a distance of about 180 metres (200 yards) by his wingman (Rottenhund or Katschmarek), who also flew slightly higher and stayed with his leader at all times. Whilst the leader was free to search for enemy aircraft, and concentrate on getting the 'kills', his wingman was able to concentrate on searching the airspace in the leader's blind spots, behind and below. Any attacking aircraft could be sandwiched between the two '109s.

Two Rotten usually teamed up to create a four aircraft Schwarm, where all of the pilots could watch what was happening around them, and two or three Schwarme made up a Staffel. Each Schwarm within a Staffel flew at staggered heights and with 180 metres (200 yards) of room between them, making the formation difficult to spot at longer ranges and allowing for a great deal of flexibility. By utilising a tight 'cross-over' turn, a Schwarm could quickly change direction.

The Bf 110 fighters adopted the same Schwarm formation as the Bf 109s, but were seldom able to use it to the same advantage. When attacked, Zerstörergruppen increasingly resorted to forming large 'defensive circles', in which each Bf 110 guarded the tail of the aircraft ahead of it. Göring ordered that they be renamed 'offensive circles' in a vain bid to improve rapidly declining morale within the Zerstörergruppen. The Bf 110's most successful method of attack was the 'bounce' from above.

Experienced frontline RAF pilots were acutely aware of the inherent deficiencies of their own tactics, and in some of the more enlightened squadrons, a compromise was adopted whereby squadron formations used much looser formations. One or two 'weavers' flew above and behind the main

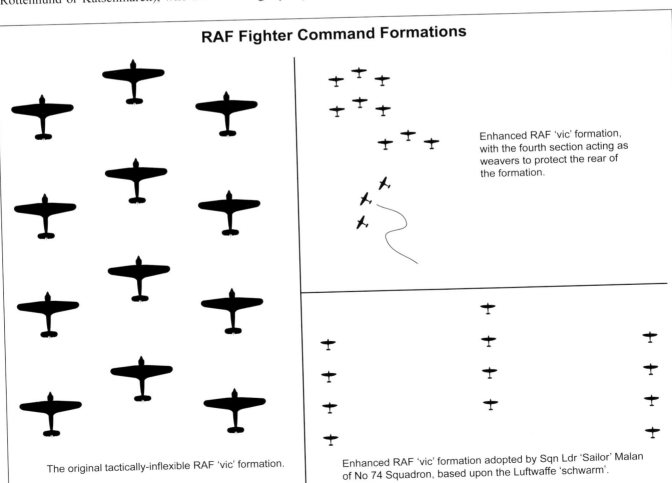

RAF Fighter Command Formations

Enhanced RAF 'vic' formation, with the fourth section acting as weavers to protect the rear of the formation.

The original tactically-inflexible RAF 'vic' formation.

Enhanced RAF 'vic' formation adopted by Sqn Ldr 'Sailor' Malan of No 74 Squadron, based upon the Luftwaffe 'schwarm'.

formation to provide increased observation and rear protection. However, these tended to be the least experienced pilots and were often the first to be shot down often without the other pilots even noticing that they were under attack!

During the Battle, 74 Squadron under Squadron Leader Adolph 'Sailor' Malan adopted a variation of the German Schwarm formation called the 'fours in line astern', which was a vast improvement on the old three aircraft 'vic'. Malan's formation was later generally used by Fighter Command.

Air-sea rescue

One of the biggest oversights of the entire system was the lack of a proper air-sea rescue organisation. The RAF had started organising a system in 1940 with High Speed Launches (HSLs) being based around flying boat bases and at a number of overseas locations, but it was still believed that the amount of cross-Channel traffic meant that there was no need for a dedicated rescue service to cover these areas. Downed pilots and aircrew, it was hoped, would be picked up by any boats, trawlers or ships which happened to be passing by. Otherwise the local life boat would be alerted, assuming of course someone had seen the pilot going into the water.

RAF aircrew were issued with a life jacket, (nicknamed 'Mae West' after a well-endowed American film star of the period), but in 1940 it still required manual inflation – which was almost impossible for someone who was injured or in shock. The waters of the English Channel and Dover Straits are cold, even in the middle of summer, and clothing issued to RAF aircrew did little to insulate them against these freezing conditions.

In 1939 air-sea rescue had been placed under the control of Coastal Command, but because a number of pilots had been lost at sea during the 'Channel Battles', on 22 August control of RAF rescue launches was passed to the local naval authorities and twelve Lysanders were given to Fighter Command to help look for pilots at sea. In all some 200 pilots and aircrew were lost at sea during the Battle. No proper air-sea rescue service was formed until 1941.

The Luftwaffe was much better prepared for the task of air-sea rescue than the RAF, with one unit, the Seenotdienst equipped with Heinkel He 59 floatplanes, specifically tasked with picking up downed aircrew from the North Sea, English Channel and the Dover Straits.

'The Few...'
Pilots of the Royal Air Force

▲ Pilots and gunners of 264 Squadron pass the time with a game of draughts while waiting at readiness outside their dispersal tent at Kirton-in-Lindsey, Lincolnshire. (Photo: Imperial War Museum)

For these reasons, the RAF had fewer experienced pilots at the start of the Battle, and it was the lack of trained pilots in the fighter squadrons, rather than the lack of aircraft, that became the greatest concern for Air Vice-Marshal Dowding. Drawing from regular RAF forces as well as the Auxiliary Air Force and the Volunteer Reserve, the British could muster a total of some 1,103 fighter pilots on 1 July 1940. Replacement pilots, with little actual flight training and often no gunnery training whatsoever, suffered high casualty rates.

Due mostly to more efficient training, the Luftwaffe could muster a larger number (1,450) of more experienced fighter pilots. Drawing from a cadre of Spanish Civil War veterans, they had comprehensive courses in aerial gunnery, as well as instructions in tactics suited for fighter-versus-fighter combat. Luftwaffe training manuals also stressed the utmost importance of attacking only when the odds were in the pilot's favour.

Prior to World War Two, the RAF's processes for selecting potential candidates were more concerned with social standing than actual aptitude, and by the summer of 1940, there were just over 9,000 pilots in the RAF and approximately 5,000 aircraft, albeit the majority of which were bombers.

The problem of pilot shortage was somewhat self-inflicted, due to inefficiencies in training and assignment. Aircraft production was running at 300 each week, but only 200 pilots were being trained in the same period. Another problem was that only about 30% of these 9,000 pilots were assigned to operational squadrons; 20% of the pilots were involved in conducting pilot training, and a further 20% were undergoing further instruction. The rest were assigned to staff positions. At the height of fighting, and despite Churchill's insistence, only thirty pilots were released to the front line from administrative duties.

▲ Czech pilots of 310 (Czechoslovak) Squadron RAF and their British flight commanders are seen here grouped in front of Hawker Hurricane Mk.I, P3143/NN-D at RAF Duxford, Cambridgeshire. (Photo: Imperial War Museum)

In addition, Luftwaffe aircraft were equipped with life rafts and the aircrew were provided with sachets of a chemical called fluorescein which, on reacting with water, created a large, easy-to-see, bright green patch.

In accordance with the Geneva Convention, the He 59s were unarmed and painted white overall, with civilian registration markings and red crosses. Nevertheless, RAF aircraft attacked these aircraft, particularly as some were escorted by Bf 109s. A controversial order was issued to the RAF on 13 July which stated that as of 20 July, Seenotdienst aircraft were to be shot down.

One of the reasons given was that the British didn't recognise the rescue of enemy pilots so they could come and bomb the British civil population again, and all German air ambulances were to be forced down or shot down on definite orders approved by the War Cabinet. It was also suggested that these enemy aircraft in civilian markings and marked with the red cross had flown over British ships at sea and in the vicinity of the British coast, and were being employed for purposes which couldn't be regarded as being consistent with the privileges generally accorded to the Red Cross.

The white He 59s were soon repainted in camouflage colours and armed with defensive machine guns. Although another four He 59s were shot down by RAF aircraft, the Seenotdienst continued to pick up downed Luftwaffe and RAF aircrew throughout the Battle, earning well deserved praise for their gallantry.

Bomber and Coastal Command contributions

It must never be forgotten that Bomber Command and Coastal Command aircraft continued to fly offensive sorties against targets in Germany and France throughout the period of the Battle of Britain – and beyond of course. After the initial disasters of the war, with Wellington bombers shot down in large numbers attacking Wilhelmshaven and the slaughter of the AASF Fairey Battle squadrons sent to France, it became clear that Bomber Command would have to operate mainly at night to achieve any results without incurring very high losses. From 15 May, 1940, a night bomber campaign was launched against the German oil industry, communications, and forests/crops, mainly in the Ruhr area.

As the threat mounted, Bomber Command changed its targeting priority, on 3 June 1940, to attack the German aircraft industry. On 4 July, the Air Ministry gave Bomber Command orders to attack ports and shipping. By September, the build up of invasion barges in the Channel ports had become a top priority target.

On 7 September, the government issued a warning that an invasion could be expected within the next few days and that night, Bomber Command attacked the Channel ports and supply dumps. On 13 September, they carried out another large raid on the Channel ports, sinking some eighty large barges in the port of Ostend. Eighty-four barges were sunk in Dunkerque after another raid on 17 September and by 19 September, almost 200 barges had been sunk. The loss of these barges may well have contributed to Hitler's decision to postpone 'Operation Sealion' indefinitely.

The success of these raids was in part due to the fact that the Germans had few Freya radar stations set up in France, so that air defences of the French harbours were not nearly as good as the air defences over Germany. Bomber Command had directed some 60% of its strength against the Channel ports.

The Blenheim Mk.IV light bomber units also raided German-occupied airfields throughout July to December 1940, both during daylight hours and at night. Although most of these raids were unproductive, there were some successes. For example on 1 August, five out of twelve Blenheims sent to attack Haamstede and Evere (Brussels) were able to destroy or heavily damage three Bf 109s of II./JG 27. Two other Bf 109s were claimed by Blenheim gunners. Another successful raid on Haamstede was made by a single Blenheim on 7 August which destroyed one Bf 109E of 4./JG 54, heavily damaged another and cause lighter damage to four more.

However, there were some missions which produced an almost 100% casualty rate amongst the Blenheims. One such operation was mounted on 13 August 1940 against a Luftwaffe airfield near Aalborg in north-eastern Denmark by twelve aircraft of 82 Squadron. One Blenheim returned early, but the other eleven, which reached Denmark, were shot down, five by flak and six by Bf 109s. Of the thirty-three crewmen who took part in the attack, twenty were killed and thirteen captured.

As well as the bombing operations, Blenheim-equipped units had been formed to carry out long-range strategic reconnaissance missions over Germany and German-occupied territories. In this role, the Blenheims once again proved to be too slow and vulnerable against Luftwaffe fighters, and they took constant casualties.

Coastal Command directed its attention towards the protection of British shipping, and the destruction of enemy shipping. As invasion became more likely, it participated in the strikes on French harbours and airfields, laying mines, and mounting numerous reconnaissance missions over the enemy-held coast. In all, some 9,180 sorties were flown by bombers from July to October 1940. Although this was much less than the 80,000 sorties flown by fighters, bomber crews suffered about half the total number of casualties borne by their fighter colleagues. The bomber contribution was therefore much more dangerous on a loss-per-sortie comparison.

It is a testament to the courage of the men in these Bomber, Reconnaissance and Coastal Command units that they continued to operate throughout these months with little respite and with little of the publicity accorded to Fighter Command.

In his famous 20 August 1940 speech about 'The Few', praising Fighter Command, Churchill also made a point to mention Bomber Command's contribution, adding that bombers were even then striking back at Germany. This part of the speech is often overlooked. The Battle of Britain Chapel in Westminster Abbey lists in a Roll of Honour 718 Bomber Command crew members, and 280 from Coastal Command who were killed between 10 July and 31 October.

The Phoney War - 3 September 1939 to 9 May 1940

▲ Pilots of 87 Squadron practicing a scramble to their Hawker Hurricane Mk.Is at Lille-Seclin. (Photo: Imperial War Museum)

The Phoney War – also called the 'der Sitzkrieg' (the sitting war) by the Germans – a play on the word Blitzkrieg and 'La Drôle de Guerre' (the joke war) by the French – is generally considered to be the period in the months following the German (and Russian) invasion of Poland in September 1939 and preceding the Battle of France in May 1940; a period that was marked by a lack of major military operations in Continental Europe.

Despite Great Britain and France declaring war on Germany on 3 September 1939 following the invasion of Poland – under the terms of the Anglo-Polish Military Alliance and Franco-Polish Military Alliance, which obliged the United Kingdom and France to assist Poland in the event of a hostile act by another country – neither Britain nor France made any effort to actually commit forces to any specific physical response. However, a British Expeditionary Force of four Divisions, comprising some 158,000 men with 25,000 vehicles, left for France on 11 September 1939.

Whilst most of the German army and air force was still engaged in Poland, a small force covered the Siegfried Line, a fortified defensive line along the French border. At the Maginot Line on the other side of the border, French and the newly arrived British, troops stood facing them, but there were only some local, minor skirmishes.

In fact during the Polish Campaign, in which Poland was overrun in just twenty-eight days, despite heroic, often suicidal defence of their homeland by the Polish armed forces,

approximately 110 French and British Divisions in the West were completely inactive against the twenty-three German Divisions facing them.

The British and French Governments, amongst others, tried a number of political solutions to prevent the spread of war, all the while reinforcing their positions in Northern France with land and air forces from Britain. France's strategy was dominated by the Maginot line, a defensive super-trench along the border, which French generals believed would keep France safe from German attack, whilst the British dropped propaganda leaflets on Germany. Western Europe settled in to a strange calm for seven months.

The Advanced Air Striking Force

Mobilised on 24 August 1939, the Advanced Air Striking Force (AASF), of the British Expeditionary Force (BEF) was actually despatched to France on 2 September. Ten Fairey Battle squadrons, Nos 12, 15, 40, 88, 103, 105, 142, 155, 218 and 226, (some 160 aircraft), were flown to bases in metropolitan France.

A token force of four squadrons of Hurricanes, Nos 1, 73, 85 and 87, known as the Air Component, arrived in France on 8 and 9 September, and initially formed 60 Wing. By the middle of September further RAF squadrons, made up of Blenheim bombers and Lysander tactical reconnaissance and Army Co-operation aircraft, started arriving.

Over the autumn and winter, the rotation of squadrons around

Vickers Wellington Mk.Ia, N2944/OJ-L, 149 Squadron, RAF Mildenhall, Suffolk, December 1939.

Standard Temperate Land Scheme of Dark Earth and Dark Green upper surfaces, to the A Scheme pattern, with Night under surfaces. Note the dimensions of the fuselage roundel which had probably been converted from the Red/Blue style applied on the production line, and lack of underwing roundels.

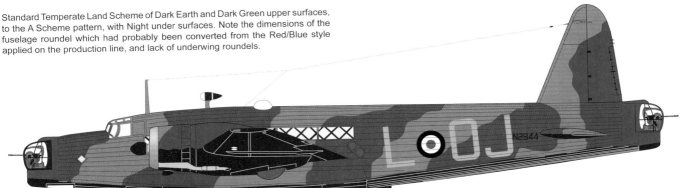

Vickers Wellington Mk.Ia, N3000/WS-L, 9 Squadron, RAF Honington, Suffolk, April 1940.

Standard Temperate Land Scheme of Dark Earth and Dark Green upper surfaces, to the A Scheme pattern, with Night under surfaces. In this instance the Red/White/Blue fuselage roundels were applied as such on the production line at the time of the aircraft's manufacture. Note the Red/White/Blue underwing roundels.

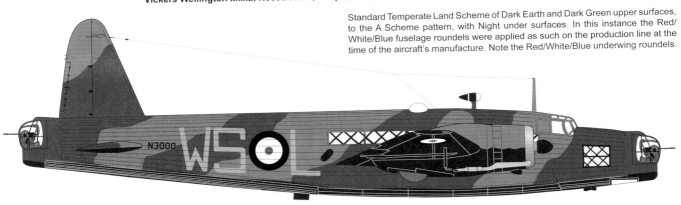

Not to any scale

various bases occurred and more RAF aircraft and squadrons arrived. During the winter, 1 and 73 Squadrons were detached from the Air Component control to form 67 Fighter Wing attached directly to the AASF.

Luftwaffe air raids on Britain began on 16 October 1939 when British warships were attacked at Rosyth on the Firth of Forth. Spitfires of Nos 602 and 603 Squadrons succeeded in shooting down two Ju 88s and a Heinkel He 111 over the Firth. Then in a raid on Scapa Flow the next day, a Ju 88 was downed by anti-aircraft fire, crashing on the island of Hoy. The first Luftwaffe aircraft to be brought down on the British mainland proper in World War Two was a He 111 of KG 26 at Haddington, East Lothian, on 29 November 1939, with both Nos 602 and 603 Squadrons involved in this victory.

There was also some sporadic activity over France during this period, mainly reconnaissance flights and minor bombing raids to probe the defences. The RAF also conducted a large number of combined reconnaissance and propaganda leaflet flights over Germany. These leaflet flights were jokingly termed 'Pamphlet raids' or 'Confetti War' in the British press.

Few in the British High Command would have opted for an immediate attack via northern France on Germany, despite the fact they considered Germany was in no position to wage a war on two fronts, and with hindsight they would have been right. However French over-caution and British War Cabinet nervousness held any idea of attack in abeyance, and brought about a military power vacuum.

Although having declared war on Germany, the French High Command forbade any strategic bombing attacks on Germany from French bases by the Advanced Air Striking Force, until Germany actually attacked France, and at the same time made it more than clear they were to be in total command of any aerial operations. The British opinion was that Germany would strike only when it was ready, and by then it would probably be too late!

From day to night

Bomber Command's initial hopes of daylight bombing were literally shot down in flames when twelve out of twenty-two Wellingtons on an armed reconnaissance of the Wilhelmshaven area, were lost and three more made forced landings on their return. This caused the Air Staff to acknowledge that even with the much vaunted power operated turrets, RAF bombers could not survive in daylight over Germany.

When such losses were compared with the negligible casualties inflicted on No 4 Group's Whitleys which operated entirely by night, mainly due to their low performance, turning to night bombing became very attractive, especially when the then C-in-C Bomber Command, Sir Edgar Ludlow-Hewitt, suggested that it might be possible to carry out precision bombing by night.

On 28 January 1940 he wrote to the Air Ministry suggesting that a role be found for Bomber Command which did not involve it suffering 50% casualties on each operation. This set in motion not only a change in target policy but also the method by which the bombing was carried out. Thus began the conversion of Bomber Command from a predominantly day flying, to a predominantly night flying, force.

However, during most of 1940, Bomber Command found itself diverted from what it considered true strategic bombing by the extenuating circumstances of the war situation.

The Winter War

One notable event during the 'Phoney War' was the so called 'Winter War', which started with the Soviet Union's assault on Finland on 30 November 1939. Public opinion, particularly in France and Britain, found it easy to side with democratic Finland, and demanded from their governments effective action in support of the Finns against their much larger aggressor, particularly since the Finns' defence seemed so much more successful than that of the Poles' during September.

Change of British Prime Minister

(Photo: Imperial War Museum)

The debacle of the Allied campaign in Norway, forced a debate in the House of Commons during which the British Prime Minister Neville Chamberlain was under constant attack. After a vote of confidence in his government was only narrowly won, with many of Chamberlain's supporters either voting against him or abstaining, Chamberlain found it impossible to continue to lead.

On 10 May 1940 Chamberlain resigned the premiership. Winston Churchill, who had been a consistent opponent of Chamberlain's policy of appeasement, was appointed as his successor and formed a new coalition government that included members of the Conservative Party, the Labour Party and the Liberal Party as well as several ministers from non-political backgrounds.

That same day German troops marched into Belgium, the Netherlands and Luxembourg. A short eight months after Britain and France had declared war on Germany – the 'Phoney War' was well and truly over...

As a consequence, the Soviet Union was expelled from the League of Nations and a proposed Franco-British expedition to northern Scandinavia was debated. In the event, the British forces that began to be assembled to send to Finland's aid were not despatched before the Winter War ended – and were eventually sent to Norway instead. On 20 March, after the end of the Winter War, Édouard Daladier was forced to resign as Prime Minister of France, due to his failure to aid Finland.

The German invasion of Denmark and Norway

Secret information leaked to the Germans about the debate over the proposed Franco-British expedition to northern Scandinavia alarmed Hitler to such an extent that he decided the country's iron ore supplies might be compromised, which gave him the reason for Germany 'to secure' the Norwegian coast.

Codenamed 'Unternehmen Weserübung' ('Operation Weserübung'), the German invasion of Denmark and Norway commenced on 9 April 1940. The Wehrmacht crossed the Danish border around 4.15am in a coordinated operation. German troops disembarked at the Langelinie docks in the Danish capital, Copenhagen, and began occupying the city. German Fallschirmjäger (paratroops) also captured Aalborg airport. Simultaneously, an ultimatum was presented by the German ambassador to King Christian X. The Danish army was small, ill-prepared and used obsolete equipment but resisted in several parts of the country.

By 6.00am, the small Danish Air Force had been all but destroyed and German bombers were threatening to drop their bombs over Copenhagen. King Christian X, having consulted with his Prime Minister, Foreign Minister and the commanders of the army and the navy, decided to capitulate, believing that further resistance would only result in a useless loss of Danish lives. The Danish public was taken completely by surprise by the occupation, and was instructed by the government to cooperate with the German authorities. Germany's occupation of Denmark was completed on 10 April and lasted until 5 May 1945.

Norway

On 9 April, the first day of the invasion of Norway, German Fallschirmjäger airborne troops landed at Norway's Oslo airport Fornebu, Kristiansand airport Kjevik, and Sola Air Station – the latter constituting the first opposed paratrooper attack in history. The Jagevingen (Fighter Flight) of the Norwegian Army Air Service, based on Fornebu resisted with their seven serviceable Gloster Gladiator biplane fighters and managed to shoot down five German aircraft – two Messerschmitt Bf 110s, two Heinkel He 111s and one Junkers Ju 52 transport. One Gladiator was shot down during the air battle and two were strafed and destroyed whilst refuelling and rearming at Fornebu airport. The remaining four operational fighters were ordered to land wherever they could on whatever secondary airfields were available away from the base, on frozen lakes around Oslo.

The ground personnel of the Fighter Flight soon ran out of ammunition for their anti-aircraft machine guns as well. In the general confusion and stress to make the fighters ready for action no one had had the presence of mind, or the time, to issue small-arms ammunition for the personal weapons of the ground personnel

▲ Three Fairey Battle Mk.Is, K9353/HA-J, K9324/HA-B and K9325/HA-D, of 218 Squadron RAF, based at Auberives-sur-Suippes, in flight over northern France. K9325 went missing during an attack on enemy troops near St Vith on 11 May 1940, and K9353 was shot down north of Bouillon the following day. K9324 survived the Battle of France to serve with the RAAF until 1944. (Photo: Imperial War Museum)

On 14 April Allied troops were landed in Norway, but by the end of the month, the southern parts of the country were in German hands. The fighting continued in northern Norway until the Allies evacuated the country in early June 1940 – during the German invasion of France. Norwegian forces in mainland Norway laid down their arms at midnight on 9 June 1940, but the King, Parliament, and the national treasury fled to the north and eventually escaped to Great Britain. As a result, Norway never officially surrendered to the Germans.

Camouflage and Markings

RAF aircraft

By the outbreak of war in September 1939, the standard RAF camouflage scheme adopted for all home-based, monoplane, operational aircraft types had been settled on Dark Earth and Dark Green upper surfaces, known as the Temperate Land Scheme. Essentially, this Temperate Land Scheme was devised to conceal the aircraft whilst either at rest on the ground or whilst flying at an altitude of 10,000 feet or less over land.

The relatively few, frontline operational, biplane aircraft left in service, such as the Gloster Gladiator, were finished in a variation of the Temperate Land Scheme, with the upper surfaces of the top mainplane, the upper surfaces of the fuselage/cowling and the upper surfaces of the tailplanes finished in Dark Earth and Dark Green, with a Shadow Compensating scheme of Light Earth and Light Green on the upper surfaces of the lower mainplanes and on the sides of the fuselage/cowling.

Camouflage scheme drawings were prepared in June 1936 on Air Diagrams for all the main aircraft types: eg AD 1157 'Camouflage Scheme for Twin Engine Monoplanes - Heavy Bombers'; AD 1158, 'Camouflage Scheme for Single Engine Monoplanes - Medium Bombers'; AD 1159, 'Camouflage Scheme for Twin Engine Monoplanes - Medium Bombers; and AD 1160 for Single Engine Monoplanes'. (see pp18 & 19)

These illustrated two disruptive camouflage patterns to be applied to the upper surfaces which were known as the 'A Scheme' and the 'B Scheme'. The intention was that these schemes, which were the mirror image of each other, would be applied to alternate aircraft on the production line.

The demarcation line between the Dark Earth/Dark Green Temperate Land Scheme on the upper surfaces and the under surfaces followed a line at a tangent of 60 degrees to the horizontal, low down on the fuselage side to what would later become known as Pattern No 1. A higher upper/under surface demarcation was introduced later, known as Pattern No 2.

Fighters, Army co-operation aircraft, and light bombers would be camouflaged on the upper surfaces in the Dark Green and Dark Earth Temperate Land Scheme but retain Aluminium (silver painted) under surfaces; whilst medium and heavy bombers would also be camouflaged on the upper surfaces in the Dark Green and Dark Earth Temperate Land Scheme, but with a colour called 'Night', (a very dark blue grey) on the under surfaces. This same 'Night' shade had also been adopted for the serial number identification lettering and as an overall finish on the airscrews in June 1936.

Markings

The basic RAF roundel was based upon that of the RAF's Ensign, proportioned in a ratio of 1-3-5. With the adoption of camouflage in 1936, the only RAF aircraft not to use the Red, White and Blue roundel were night flying types which used a Red and Blue roundel with a red centre 2/5ths the diameter of the whole roundel.

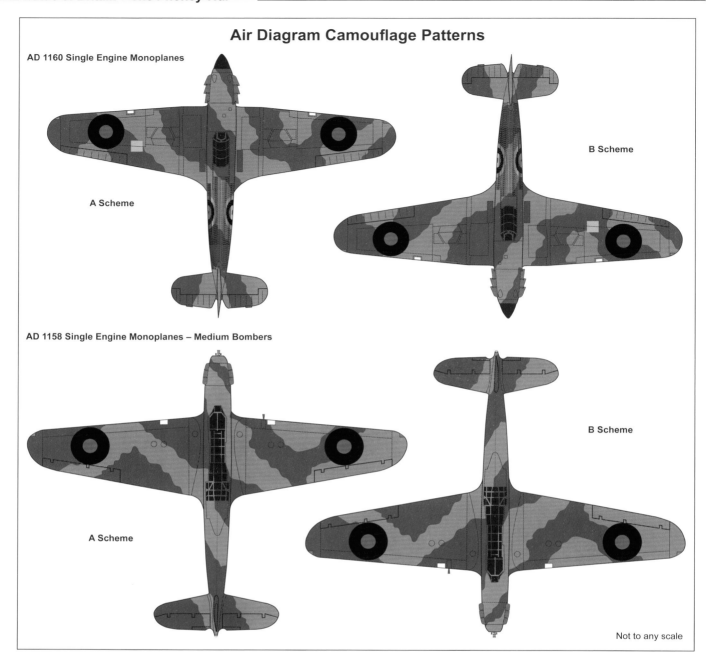

Air Diagram Camouflage Patterns

AD 1160 Single Engine Monoplanes

A Scheme

B Scheme

AD 1158 Single Engine Monoplanes – Medium Bombers

A Scheme

B Scheme

Not to any scale

Following the introduction of camouflage, some changes were made to the National Markings. Firstly, the traditional bright Red and Blue shades were replaced by duller shades of Red and Blue; and secondly, a Yellow outer ring was added to the Red, White and Blue roundels, perversely, to make the camouflaged aircraft more visible, as concern was raised with regard to the risk of collision. The Yellow outer ring was to be equal in width to the other rings of the roundel.

When the camouflage trials had begun in 1933, it was quickly established that the White ring in the roundel tended to compromise the camouflage finish, so trials aircraft were flown with a Red and Blue roundel in the dull shades, and the Air Ministry decided to adopt this Red/Blue roundel as the standard National Marking for use on camouflaged machines in wartime. Thus, when the Munich crisis of September 1938 led to the majority of the RAF's front line aircraft adopting camouflage finishes, they also adopted the Red and Blue roundel on wings and fuselage as their wartime National Marking.

With little improvement in the international situation in

the closing months of 1938, a conference held at the Air Ministry on 20 December 1938 decided to adopt wartime markings in peacetime. Thus on 27 April 1939, AMO A.154 – 'Identification Markings on Aircraft of Operational Units and Marking of Unit Equipment' was issued.

This AMO stated that it had been decided to adopt a standard system of identification markings on aircraft of operational squadrons throughout the whole of the RAF, both at home and overseas. As regards the National Markings, these were defined as, *"(i) a blue ring surrounding a red centre which was to be located on both sides of the fuselage and on the upper surfaces of the wing tips; and, (ii) a blue ring surrounding a white ring with the latter surrounding a red centre which was to be located on the lower surface of the wing tips."*

Fighter aircraft however were not to carry the National Marking on the lower surface of the wing tips as the lower surfaces were to carry the special 'half black and half white' scheme as an identification marking (see later). An exception was made for fighters operating over France which were to

Air Diagram Camouflage Patterns

AD 1159 Twin Engine Monoplanes – Medium Bombers

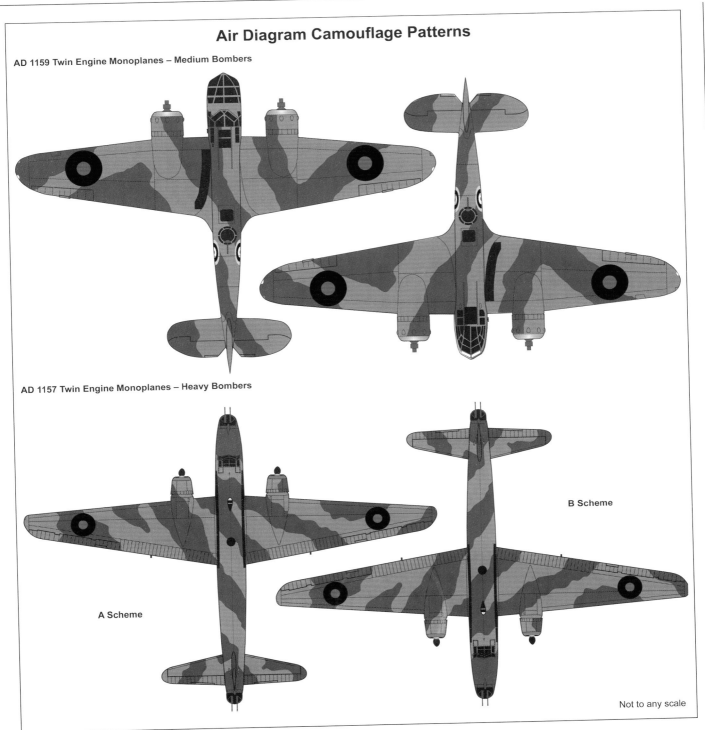

AD 1157 Twin Engine Monoplanes – Heavy Bombers

B Scheme

A Scheme

Not to any scale

carry Red, White and Blue roundels on the under surfaces of their wings.

The onset of war however quickly revealed problems with these Red/Blue national markings. On 24 October 1939 a section of Spitfires of 602 Squadron was despatched on patrol following receipt of information that a convoy off St Abbs Head was being bombed. On reaching the reported position, the section found that a twin-engined monoplane was flying low over the front of the convoy. It required close inspection to reveal that this aircraft was in fact an Anson as no national recognition markings were easily visible.

Following this encounter, the 602 Squadron Section Leader put forward the suggestion that Coastal Reconnaissance aircraft on patrol over a convoy should be marked in some way which made

them easily recognisable for what they were from a distance.

Whilst waiting for some comment to emerge from the Air Ministry, Coastal Command conducted some experiments of its own which would appear to have consisted of applying Red, White and Blue roundels to the fuselage sides of at least one aircraft at Bircham Newton. The results of the trial were sent to Fighter Command on 7 November. It had been found that whilst these markings aided recognition, they did not prove sufficient for fighter pilots during either an approach from astern or during circling manoeuvres. It was therefore recommended that...
(a) red, white, and blue roundels be applied on the upper surface of the mainplanes of all General Reconnaissance aircraft in lieu of the present red and blue roundels;
(b) similar roundels were to be applied to the sides of the fuselage;

(c) the red, white, and blue roundels then in use on the silver under surfaces of General Reconnaissance aircraft were to be continued; and

(d) if after a period during which these new markings were to be considered 'on trial', difficulties in recognition were still being experienced, a narrow yellow band on the upper surface of the mainplanes and the fuselage sides might be tried.

These changes were evidently forwarded to the Air Ministry where they met with approval as, on 21 November 1939, the Air Ministry wrote to all Air Officers Commanding to advise them that war experience had shown that some of the recognition markings set out in AMO A.154/39 had been found to be unsuitable. So, all British aircraft were now to have Red, White and Blue roundels on the sides of the fuselage; General Reconnaissance aircraft were to have Red, White and Blue roundels on top of their wings; and all British aircraft, (except fighters operating over Great Britain and night bombers), were to carry Red, White and Blue roundels on the under surfaces of the wings.

These changes in the National Markings were incorporated in AMO A.520 which was issued on 7 December 1939, and remained in use, unchanged, until May 1940, when they were again revised. These revisions will be dealt with in Chapter 3.

Coastal Command continued to conduct trials to improve the recognition markings carried by British aircraft and part of these trials involved reapplying the Yellow outer ring to the fuselage roundel, which had been abandoned circa September 1938, and which was found to be very successful in making the marking more visible. At about the same time, it had also been found that the application of Red, White and Blue rudder stripes, similar to those carried by French aircraft and by the Hurricanes of the Air Component in France, had proved a very effective identification feature and the Air Ministry therefore decided to utilise both of these markings for the identification of British aircraft.

As a result, on 1 May 1940 the Air Ministry sent signal X485 to all Commands at Home and Overseas amending the markings carried by RAF aircraft. Fuselage roundels were now to be encircled with an outer Yellow ring the same width of the existing Blue ring. Vertical stripes of Red, White and Blue, (Red leading) each of the same width, were to be painted on the fins – see Chapter 3 for more details.

Serial Numbers

Contemporary documents refer to this marking by the terms 'Aircraft number', 'Registration number' or 'Serial number'. Whatever the term used, it refers to the number allotted to each individual aircraft by the Air Ministry, which served to give the airframe its individual identity. This marking was applied by the manufacturer on the production line and stayed with the aircraft throughout its active service life. As there was no standard set of characters for this marking, the aircraft manufacturers went their own way.

Initially the serial number was applied to the rear of the fuselage, the under surfaces of the mainplanes, and on the rudder, although the outbreak of war saw the removal of the underwing serial numbers from all types except training aircraft. Serial numbers on the rudder were also removed (or overpainted) on many aircraft as indeed was sometimes the

case with the fuselage serial number.

These fuselage serial numbers were to be 8 inches high, with individual characters not more than 5 inches wide and made up of brush strokes of 1 inch in width. As mentioned earlier, this was to be marked on the fuselage of camouflaged aircraft in Night.

Black and White undersides for fighters

One of the most prominent identification markings carried by any British military aircraft during the opening stages of World War Two was the black and white identification marking carried on the undersides of fighter aircraft.

One of the major problems encountered in building the world's first integrated air defence system lay in finding some means of identifying friendly fighter aircraft, (a) to avoid them being shot at by anti-aircraft gunners, and (b) to allow them to be tracked by the Observer Corps. The need to have friendly fighters easily identifiable by anti-aircraft gunners was fairly obvious, but the need for the Observer Corps to be able to do the same thing was less so.

The requirement lay in the fact that the early Chain Home Radio Location system transmitted its signals through 360 degrees, and in order for the operators to tell from which direction any returns were coming, the inland 180 degrees had to be blocked out electronically. This meant that there was no radar coverage inland, and all the plotting information which was required for a successful interception, such as the location of the fighters in relation to the raiders once they had crossed the coast, had to be obtained visually by the Observer Corps.

On 10 May 1937, Dowding wrote a letter to the Air Ministry in which he outlined an idea as to how friendly fighter aircraft could be easily identified by anti-aircraft gunners and the Observer Corps. Dowding considered it essential that the undersides of fighter aircraft should be painted in such a way as to make them most easily identifiable from the ground. His recommendation was that the underside of one of the lower mainplanes (of the mainly biplane aircraft then in service) should be finished in silver dope and the other in black. Accordingly, on 28 July 1937, the Air Ministry wrote to HQ Fighter Command giving permission for the painting of one wing of fighter aircraft black so that the idea could be tried out.

The experimental work with this form of marking was carried out at North Weald on biplane fighters and consisted of having the underside of one lower mainplane painted black and the other white. The ailerons were not to be painted due to the risk of the application of the new finish upsetting their balance.

On 28 October 1937, Dowding wrote to the Air Ministry to inform them of the results of the experiment. At the same time he suggested that with production of the Hawker Hurricane gathering pace, the undersides of the wings of these aircraft, including the flaps and ailerons, should be finished black on the port side and white on the starboard. He also suggested that to make the marking as clear as possible, the serial numbers should be omitted from the wing under surfaces.

The Air Ministry agreed that some Hurricanes could be

Hurricane Night/White under surface schemes

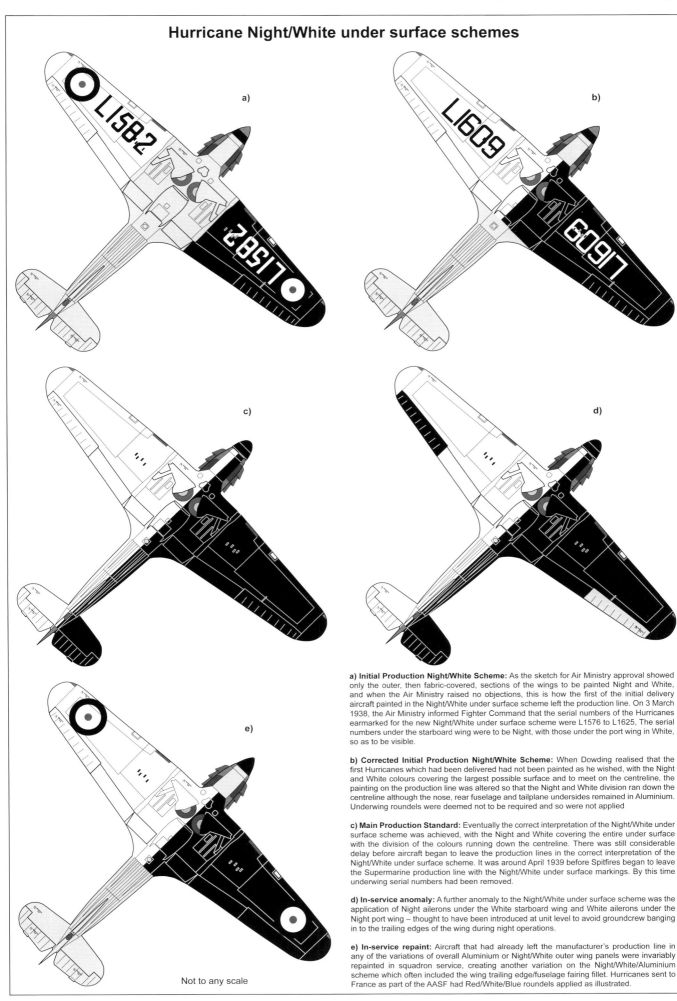

a) **Initial Production Night/White Scheme:** As the sketch for Air Ministry approval showed only the outer, then fabric-covered, sections of the wings to be painted Night and White, and when the Air Ministry raised no objections, this is how the first of the initial delivery aircraft painted in the Night/White under surface scheme left the production line. On 3 March 1938, the Air Ministry informed Fighter Command that the serial numbers of the Hurricanes earmarked for the new Night/White under surface scheme were L1576 to L1625, The serial numbers under the starboard wing were to be Night, with those under the port wing in White, so as to be visible.

b) **Corrected Initial Production Night/White Scheme:** When Dowding realised that the first Hurricanes which had been delivered had not been painted as he wished, with the Night and White colours covering the largest possible surface and to meet on the centreline, the painting on the production line was altered so that the Night and White division ran down the centreline although the nose, rear fuselage and tailplane undersides remained in Aluminium. Underwing roundels were deemed not to be required and so were not applied

c) **Main Production Standard:** Eventually the correct interpretation of the Night/White under surface scheme was achieved, with the Night and White covering the entire under surface with the division of the colours running down the centreline. There was still considerable delay before aircraft began to leave the production lines in the correct interpretation of the Night/White under surface scheme. It was around April 1939 before Spitfires began to leave the Supermarine production line with the Night/White under surface markings. By this time underwing serial numbers had been removed.

d) **In-service anomaly:** A further anomaly to the Night/White under surface scheme was the application of Night ailerons under the White starboard wing and White ailerons under the Night port wing – thought to have been introduced at unit level to avoid groundcrew banging in to the trailing edges of the wing during night operations.

e) **In-service repaint:** Aircraft that had already left the manufacturer's production line in any of the variations of overall Aluminium or Night/White outer wing panels were invariably repainted in squadron service, creating another variation on the Night/White/Aluminium scheme which often included the wing trailing edge/fuselage fairing fillet. Hurricanes sent to France as part of the AASF had Red/White/Blue roundels applied as illustrated.

Not to any scale

Hawker Hurricane Mk.I, L1833/NO-J, 85 Squadron, RAF Debden, Essex, early 1939.

Typical of the Hurricanes of the first production batches, finished in the standard Temperate Land Scheme of Dark Earth and Dark Green upper surfaces, to the A Scheme pattern, with Night/White under surfaces divided down the centreline. The white areas of the fuselage roundel have also been overpainted and toned down, as would have the white and yellow rings on the upper wing roundels. This aircraft remained with No 85 Squadron throughout its service life and was lost in France in May 1940.

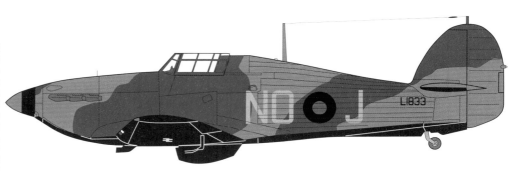

Hawker Hurricane Mk.I, L1934/OP-D, 3 Squadron, RAF Biggin Hill, Kent, mid-1939.

Illustrated as L1934 looked immediately prior to the outbreak of war, in the standard Temperate Land Scheme of Dark Earth and Dark Green upper surfaces, to the B Scheme pattern, with Night/White under surfaces divided down the centreline. The fuselage roundel has either been modified at unit level or applied on the production line in the Red/Blue style. A small (25 inch diameter?) Red/Blue roundel was carried on the port wing upper surface only, that on the starboard wing having been painted out. The unit's code letters, OP, were changed to QO in September 1939.

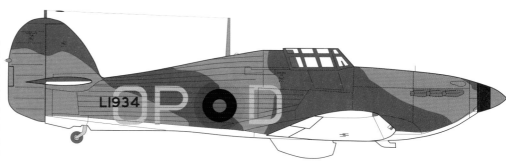

Hawker Hurricane Mk.I, L1662/KT-A, 32 Squadron, RAF Biggin Hill, Kent, mid-1939.

Standard Temperate Land Scheme of Dark Earth and Dark Green upper surfaces, to the B Scheme pattern, with Night/White under surfaces divided down the centreline. Note the fuselage serial number appears to have been overpainted, a regular feature following the Munich Crisis of September 1938. No 32 Squadron was involved in night exercises immediately prior to the outbreak of war, and had contrasting Aluminium and Night ailerons under the Night and White wings. The unit's code letters, KT, were changed to GZ in September 1939.

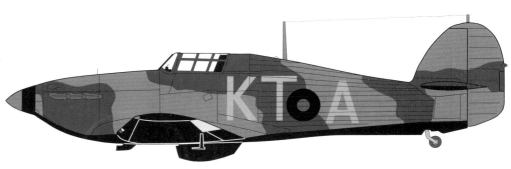

Hawker Hurricane Mk.I, L1800/LR-R, 56 Squadron, RAF North Weald, Essex, mid-1939.

Standard Temperate Land Scheme of Dark Earth and Dark Green upper surfaces, to the B Scheme pattern, with Night/White/Aluminium under surfaces. Note the de Havilland/Hamilton propeller unit and the replacement panel over the exhaust manifolds – which had presumably come from an aircraft in the A Scheme! The unit's code letters, LR, were changed to US in September 1939.

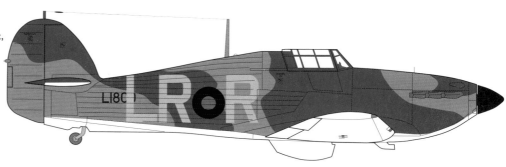

Hawker Hurricane Mk.I, L1659/SD-V, 501 Squadron, RAF Filton, Gloucestershire, September 1939.

Standard Temperate Land Scheme of Dark Earth and Dark Green upper surfaces, to the A Scheme pattern, with Night/White under surfaces divided down the centreline. The aircraft has the recently applied unit 'war codes' (SD) applied. Note the early war standard Red/White/Blue fuselage roundel (of approximately 25 inches diameter) possibly modified from the previous Red/Blue roundel. Upper wing roundels were Red/Blue and no under wing roundels were carried.

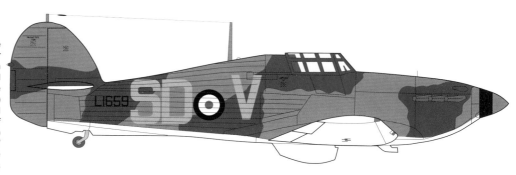

Not to any scale

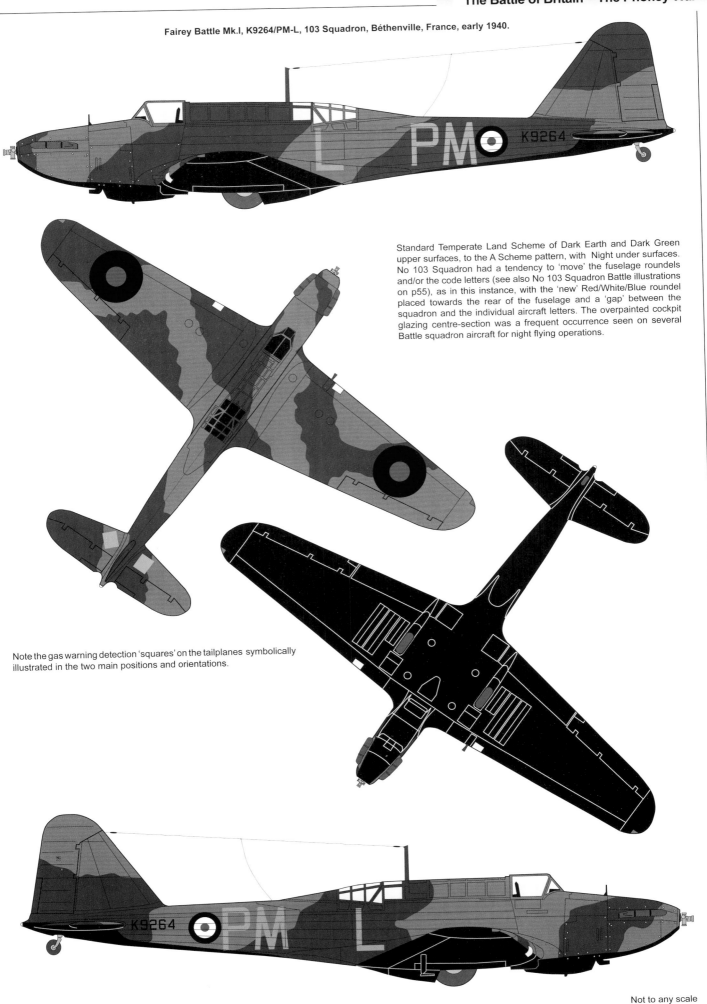

Fairey Battle Mk.I, K9264/PM-L, 103 Squadron, Béthenville, France, early 1940.

Standard Temperate Land Scheme of Dark Earth and Dark Green upper surfaces, to the A Scheme pattern, with Night under surfaces. No 103 Squadron had a tendency to 'move' the fuselage roundels and/or the code letters (see also No 103 Squadron Battle illustrations on p55), as in this instance, with the 'new' Red/White/Blue roundel placed towards the rear of the fuselage and a 'gap' between the squadron and the individual aircraft letters. The overpainted cockpit glazing centre-section was a frequent occurrence seen on several Battle squadron aircraft for night flying operations.

Note the gas warning detection 'squares' on the tailplanes symbolically illustrated in the two main positions and orientations.

Not to any scale

finished in this way for the purpose of a large scale service trial, although as production of the Hurricane was well advanced by this time, it had not been found possible to apply the marking to early production aircraft, but it was to be instituted as soon as possible without delaying production.

Whilst agreeing to the introduction of this marking, the Air Ministry however did not agree to the omission of the aircraft serial number from the under surfaces of the wings. It was felt that these markings should be retained because where disciplinary action had been found necessary in cases of unauthorised low flying, the offending aircraft was almost always identified by these numbers.

The decision was made to apply the black and white undersurface marking to a batch of fifty Hawker-built Hurricanes in January 1938. The Air Ministry informed Hawkers that it was desired that the under surface of the port wing was to be finished in Night, and the under surface of the starboard wing in White, with the flaps and ailerons included in this colour scheme. The identification serial numbers under the starboard wing of the aircraft were to remain as they were at present, but those under the port wing were to be applied in White so as to be visible. The rest of the camouflage scheme was to remain unchanged.

However, it had not been made clear whether the outer wings only were to be black and white or whether the dividing line between the two colours should be on the centre line of the centre section. A sketch for Air Ministry approval showed only the outer, then fabric-covered, sections of the wings to be so coloured, and when the Air Ministry raised no objections, this is how the aircraft left the production line.

On 3 March 1938, the Air Ministry informed Fighter Command that the serial numbers of the Hurricanes earmarked for the new under surface colour scheme were L1576 to L1625, and delivery was expected to commence before the end of the month.

Once these aircraft began to go into service, during early April 1938, Fighter Command expressed a wish that all Spitfires and Hurricanes should be finished in this manner. Dowding complained that the Hurricanes which had been delivered by that time had not been properly painted, as he wished the black and white colours to cover the largest possible surface and to meet on the centreline. The Hurricanes supplied thus far had not been painted on the fuselage at all, leaving a 'silver band' between the black and white which caused the colours to blend into one another when seen from a distance, destroying the contrast.

He then went on to suggest that the National Markings on the underside of Home Defence fighter aircraft were no longer necessary, as the black and white finish would act as sufficient identification from below and the National Markings only served to break up the clean expanse of black and white which was being relied upon for recognition.

This latter suggestion was considered by the Air Ministry which concluded that there was no legal reason why this could not be done and, on 30 August 1938, the Director of Operations and Intelligence wrote to Fighter Command to inform them of the decision. It was however stated that the National Markings must continue to be used on the 'Field Force' fighter squadrons.

With September 1938 came the Munich crisis, and on 23 September, Fighter Command wrote to the Air Ministry to obtain permission to paint the undersides of the mainplanes of all fighters, with the exception of 'Field Force' fighters, black and white up to the centre line of the aircraft. This appears to have been granted as the black and white scheme spread very quickly amongst the Home Defence squadrons.

Once the decision had been made that fighter aircraft were to have the undersides of their wings painted Night and White with the division between the colours running down the centreline of the aircraft, there was still considerable delay before aircraft began to leave the production lines in these new markings. At Supermarine for example, it was around April 1939 before Spitfires began to leave the production line with the Night/White under surface markings.

This left the problem of those aircraft already delivered to the service which had originally been finished with their under surfaces in Aluminium. The wings of these aircraft, (but not their ailerons), were to be repainted in squadron service. By 11 April, it appears to have been decided that as the silver ailerons did not appear to detract greatly from the black and white scheme, their continued use would be accepted for the time being. However, arrangements were to be made to paint spare ailerons held in store in the correct Night or White colours so that they would gradually replace the incorrectly finished ones in units. Ultimately it was decided that the painting of the under surfaces of the ailerons would be undertaken by the manufacturers at their service depots.

The exception to the Night/White rule was made for fighter aircraft stationed in France, in AMO A.520 dated 7 December 1939, which stated that Fighter aircraft stationed in France were to carry Red, White and Blue roundels under the mainplanes.

Code letters

Following the Munich Crisis in 1938, it had been decided to adopt a standard system of identification markings on aircraft of operational squadrons throughout the whole of the RAF, both at home and overseas and the system was to be adopted forthwith. Squadron badges could still be carried if desired, but were to be removable at short notice without leaving any trace.

A system of code letters was introduced to identify squadrons and individual aircraft within a squadron which were to consist of two letters to identify the squadron, to be placed either forward or aft of the roundel on the side of the fuselage; whilst a letter, to indicate the individual aircraft within the squadron, was placed on the other side of the fuselage roundel.

These code letters were to be applied at squadron level, using Medium Sea Grey paint and to be 48 inches high with 6 inch wide strokes, with letters smaller than this only being used when lack of space made the use of the specified dimensions impossible – eg on the likes of 'smaller' fighter aircraft such as the Spitfire. As there was no set style for these markings considerable variation could be seen in how they were actually applied to the aircraft. Despite the instructions as regards size, much variation could be seen, as well as in the exact shade of grey paint used to apply them.

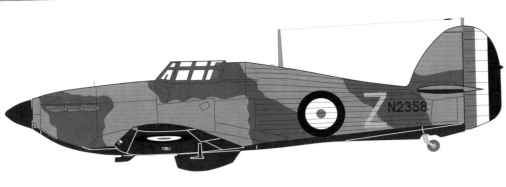

Hawker Hurricane Mk.I, N2358/(TP)-Z, 73 Squadron, Rouvres, France, late 1939.

Standard Temperate Land Scheme of Dark Earth and Dark Green upper surfaces, to the B Scheme pattern, with Night/White under surfaces divided down the centreline. To comply with Armée de l'Air practice, with whom the RAF aircraft of 67 Wing were in close cooperation, the squadron's codes (TP) were painted out. French-style rudder stripes were also added, albeit with the Red leading and Red/White/Blue under wing roundels which were applied to all French-based RAF aircraft. De Havilland/Hamilton propeller unit.

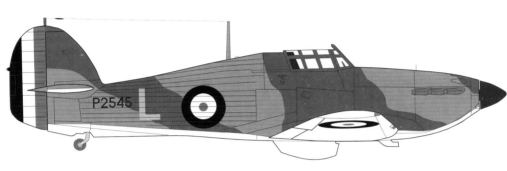

Hawker Hurricane Mk.I, P2545/(TP)-L, 73 Squadron, Rouvres, France, late 1939.

Standard Temperate Land Scheme of Dark Earth and Dark Green upper surfaces, to the B Scheme pattern, with Night/White under surfaces divided down the centreline. Squadron codes (TP) painted out to comply with Armée de l'Air practice, as was the addition of French-style rudder stripes, with the Red leading. Red/White/Blue under wing roundels. De Havilland/Hamilton propeller unit.

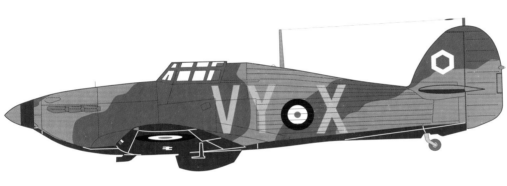

Hawker Hurricane Mk.I, (serial overpainted)/VY-X, 85 Squadron, Lille-Seclin, France, December 1939.

Standard Temperate Land Scheme of Dark Earth and Dark Green upper surfaces, to the A Scheme pattern, with Night/White under surfaces divided down the centreline. Squadron hexagon marking placed on the fin – orientated with 'points' up/down which might have indicated B Flight? Red/White/Blue under wing roundels. Watts two-blade wooden propeller unit.

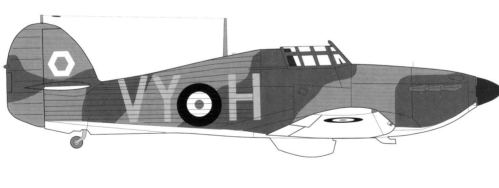

Hawker Hurricane Mk.I, (serial overpainted)/VY-H, 85 Squadron, Lille-Seclin, France, March 1940.

Standard Temperate Land Scheme of Dark Earth and Dark Green upper surfaces, to the B Scheme pattern, with Night/White/Aluminium under surfaces. Note the de Havilland/Hamilton propeller unit and the replacement panel over the exhaust manifolds – which had presumably come from an aircraft in the A Scheme! The unit's code letters, LR, were changed to US in September 1939.

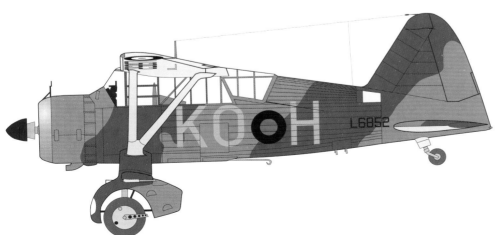

Westland Lysander Mk.II, L6852/KO-H, 2(AC)Squadron, Abbeville, France, April 1940.

Standard Temperate Land Scheme of Dark Earth and Dark Green upper surfaces, to the A Scheme pattern for Single Engine Monoplanes, with Aluminium under surfaces. 2 Squadron retained its pre-war codes KO, (but changed them to XV in April 1942 possibly to avoid confusion with No 115 Squadron.) Red/Blue roundels were retained on fuselage sides. Serial number and Red/White/Blue roundels under the wings.

The Battle of Britain – The Phoney War

Bristol Blenheim Mk.I, K7045/114, 114 Squadron, RAF Wyton, Huntingdonshire, June 1937.

This is how Blenheims looked in the 18 months or so prior to the outbreak of war – in the Standard Temperate Land Scheme of Dark Earth and Dark Green upper surfaces, in this instance to the A Scheme pattern, with Night under surfaces. Red/White/Blue/Yellow roundels were applied above the wings and on the fuselage sides with the serial number, in white, under the wings, reading from the front under the port wing and from the rear under the starboard wing. The squadron number positioned on the fuselage sides, (in the colour – in this case green?) and the serial positioned on the rear fuselage and on

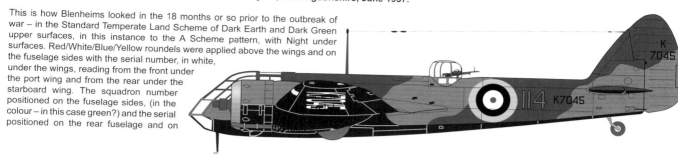

Bristol Blenheim Mk.I, L1206/FD-H, 114 Squadron, RAF Wyton, Huntingdonshire, April 1939.

By the beginning of 1939 with the war clouds looming, Blenheim squadrons, including 114 Squadron, adopted toned-down Red/Blue roundels above the wings and on the fuselage sides and had the newly introduced Medium Sea Grey squadron code letters applied. Underwing serial numbers were being removed too, but otherwise the aircraft looked much the same as before with standard Temperate Land Scheme of Dark Earth and Dark Green upper surfaces, in L1206's instance to A Scheme pattern, with Night under The serial number was retained on fuselage sides and on the rudder.

Bristol Blenheim Mk.IV, N6155/FD-F, 114 Squadron, RAF Wyton, Huntingdonshire, May 1939.

114 Squadron began re-equipping with Blenheim Mk.IVs in April 1939 and continued to apply toned-down Red/Blue roundels above the wings and on the fuselage sides together with Medium Sea Grey squadron code letters to its new mounts. Underwing serial numbers were supposed to have been removed, but the photograph of N6155 upon which this illustration is based shows them still in place together with Red/White/Blue underwing roundels. Temperate Land Scheme Dark Earth and Dark Green upper surfaces, in N6155's instance to the B Scheme pattern, with Night under surfaces. The serial number was retained on the rear fuselage sides and on the rudder and note the squadron badge in a standard Bomber Frame on the fin.

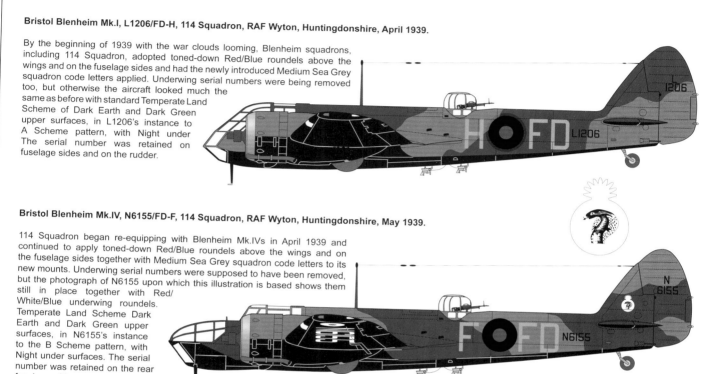

Bristol Blenheim Mk.IV, L4841/TE-N, 53 Squadron, RAF Odiham, Hampshire, October 1939.

Other than the deletion of any squadron badges and underwing serial numbers, the RAF's Blenheims went to war in essentially the same Temperate Land Scheme of Dark Earth and Dark Green upper surfaces, in L4841's instance to the B Scheme pattern, with Night under surfaces. Red/Blue roundels were carried above the wings and on the fuselage sides together with Medium Sea Grey squadron code letters. No underwing markings were carried. The serial number was retained on the rear fuselage but was starting to be removed from aircrafts' rudders.

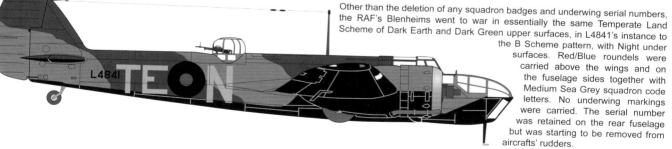

Bristol Blenheim Mk.IV, L8793/TR-M, 59 Squadron, Poix, France, April 1940.

Even by early 1940, many of the Blenheims sent to France with the AASF, retained the same Temperate Land Scheme of Dark Earth and Dark Green upper surfaces, in L8793's instance to the B Scheme pattern, with Night under surfaces. Red/Blue roundels were carried above the wings and on the fuselage sides together with Medium Sea Grey squadron code letters. Although they were promulgated for aircraft operating over France, no underwing roundels were carried on L8793 at the time it was photographed upon which this illustration is based. The serial number was retained on the rear fuselage but was removed from the rudder. Note the fuselage roundel which appears to have had the Yellow outer ring painted out in black.

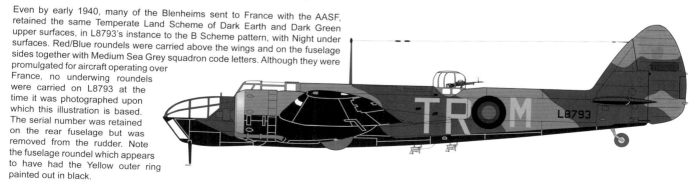

Not to any scale

Fairey Battle Mk.I, K7578/105F, 105 Squadron, RAF Harwell, Berkshire, 1937.

Soon to bear the brunt of the German 'Blitzkrieg' offensive, this is how Battles looked some two years earlier, in the Standard Temperate Land Scheme of Dark Earth and Dark Green upper surfaces, in this instance to the A Scheme pattern, with Night under surfaces. Red/White/Blue/Yellow roundels were applied above the wings and on the fuselage sides with the serial number, in white, under the wings, reading from the front under the port wing and from the rear under the starboard wing. Underwing roundels were also

carried. The squadron number was positioned on the fuselage sides under the cockpit glazing together with an individual aircraft letter 'F' on the rear fuselage, in K7578's case both in white, and the serial number was positioned on the rear fuselage and on the rudder.

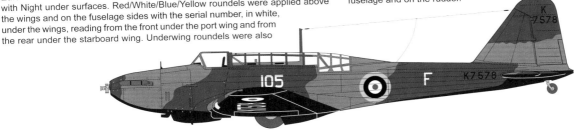

Fairey Battle Mk.I, K9176/G, 226 Squadron, RAF Harwell, Berkshire, August 1939.

Following the Munich Crisis, all RAF units toned down their upper wing and fuselage National Markings in to the Red/Blue style, generally by overpainting the Yellow outer ring in matching camouflage colours and by expanding the Blue ring and the Red centre over the White ring. Squadron codes, in Medium Sea Grey, had also been introduced by this time but K9176 only had the individual aircraft letter applied at the time it was photographed in August 1939. Standard Temperate Land Scheme of Dark Earth

and Dark Green upper surfaces, in this instance to the B Scheme pattern, with Night under surfaces. The serial number was applied to the rear fuselage and the rudder but deleted from under the wings.

Fairey Battle Mk.I, K9244/RH-L, 88 Squadron, Mourmelon-le-Grande, France, September 1939.

Many of the the first Battles sent to France upon the outbreak of war in September 1939 modified their fuselage roundels back in to the Red/White/Blue style and applied Red/White/Blue underwing roundels. Standard Temperate Land Scheme of Dark Earth and Dark Green upper surfaces, in

this instance to the A Scheme pattern, with Night under surfaces. Medium Sea Grey codes, with the serial number positioned on the rear fuselage and on the rudder.

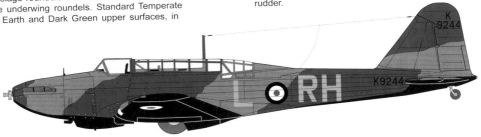

Fairey Battle Mk.I, (serial overpainted)/QT-F, 142 Squadron, Berry-au-Bac, France, late 1939.

Variations in the proportions of fuselage roundels abounded, as in the case of QT-F's with a larger Red centre. Serial numbers were also frequently painted over, as was the centre section of the canopy glazing, for night operations. Red/White/Blue underwing roundels. Standard Temperate Land

Scheme of Dark Earth and Dark Green upper surfaces, in this instance to the A Scheme pattern, with Night under surfaces. Medium Sea Grey codes.

Fairey Battle Mk.I, (serial overpainted)/MQ-R, 226 Squadron, Rheims, France, winter 1939/1940.

It was relatively rare for RAF aircraft of this period to carry artwork of any kind, so it is all the more frustrating that MQ-R's serial number was overpainted, denying us the opportunity of identifying the airframe. Medium Sea Grey codes and Red/

White/Blue underwing roundels. Standard Temperate Land Scheme of Dark Earth and Dark Green upper surfaces, to the A Scheme pattern, with Night under surfaces.

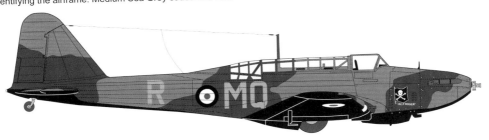

"JOLLY ROGER"

Not to any scale

The codes allocated to every active squadron, and a large number of squadrons which might form in the future, were given in a list which ran to some 650 squadrons.

Upon the outbreak of war, all RAF squadrons were to have their squadron code allocation changed, presumably as a security measure to confuse the enemy, although, almost inevitably, a number did not, which created several anomalies. An example of such being with 92 Squadron and 616 Squadron; both equipped with Spitfires. The code letters QJ were originally allocated to 616 pre-war and 92 was allocated the codes GR. After the outbreak of war, 92's codes were duly changed from GR to QJ, (although photographs of 92 Squadron Spitfires operating over France in the spring of 1940 still show them to be using GR codes), and 616 was allocated the codes YQ. However, for some reason, which has never been properly explained, 616 continued to use QJ well into mid-1941!

Squadron badges

The squadron badge was to be that approved by H M The King and was to be located as laid down in Air Ministry Orders. Such badges were to be removable at short notice without leaving any trace.

RAF aircraft in France

The pre-war Anglo-French Defence Plans had never been a straightforward matter. The Principal RAF Liaison Officer with the French Army and Armée de l'Air, Air Marshal Arthur Barratt, had faced many difficulties over how the RAF was going to operate from, and over, France, and later, after becoming Air Officer Commanding-in-Chief, British Air Forces in France, the situation had worsened.

Matters put through his HQ by the French High Command, for Air Staff consideration, had asked that all British aircraft operating from or over France must have 'Gris Bleu Ciel' (grey blue sky) under surfaces with roundels at each wingtip, and should carry vertical striping on rudders. Fighters in particular were to delete the squadron code letters and only show the individual aircraft letter, in the French style, otherwise the authorities could not be held responsible for any recognition errors.

From the RAF's first arrival in France in September 1939 there had been 'friendly fire' incidents from both ground and air, in spite of the Hurricanes carrying the distinctive Night and White under surfaces, and in January 1940 the French reiterated their demand several times for the adoption by the RAF of Armée de l'Air style colours and markings.

A Directorate of Operational Requirements (DOR), Minute (dated 16 April 1940) ruled that, *"The adoption of any form of blue under surface colouring is entirely out of the question as this is far too near that of enemy aircraft. The addition of underwing red, white and blue roundels has been sanctioned. The complication of adopting striping on rudders as already carried out by some Air Component fighter units cannot be further tolerated, and this marking must be applied to the fin."*

It would appear that the exception to this rule continued to be the two Hurricane squadrons of No 67 Wing (Nos 1 and 73 Squadrons), who were attached to the AASF, and operated in very close liaison with Armée de l'Air aircraft. Not only had

they dropped the use of squadron code letters, simply retaining the individual aircraft letter, but retained the rudder striping as mentioned in DOR Minute above.

1 Squadron went even further and applied pale blue paint to the under surfaces of some of its Hurricanes during early April 1940, possibly created by mixing the White and Blue roundel paint or maybe using Armée de l'Air colours?

However, the Directorate of Operational Requirements continued to resist any general use of 'blue' under surfaces for RAF fighters and light/medium day bombers, although consideration was allowed of 'camouflage tints' of some kind for the proposed high altitude reconnaissance fighter flights, with the full knowledge of the workings of the secret Photographic Development Unit at Heston.

The development of a camouflage finish for the under surface of day flying aircraft had already begun in 1936 as a follow-on from work done on Sea Camouflage schemes. The RAE was asked to prepare a quantity of some suitable camouflage colours in December 1936, which included a colour called Sky Grey. Trials with this colour were successful and Sky Grey was later adopted as the standard under surface camouflage colour for Fleet Air Arm aircraft.

Day Bomber under surface scheme

Work on a suitable camouflage colour for the undersides of day flying aircraft for the RAF however seems to have been given a much lower priority, although by July 1939, some concern was being felt at Bomber Command about the under surface colouring of its aircraft. The Night under surfaces were felt to make them conspicuous by day against a sky background, and it was by day that most of the flying over enemy territory was envisaged as being carried out. It therefore seemed that all bombers not definitely allocated to night operations should be painted a colour, or combination of colours, which would make them as inconspicuous as possible against various forms of sky background. If any of these aircraft were required for operations at night, it was thought that the under surfaces could easily be blacked over with a temporary finish. It was also thought that a suitable under surface colour might be silver, light blue, or grey, or some other colour or combination of colours.

Despite these feelings of unease by Bomber Command, no further work on camouflage finishes for the under surfaces of day flying aircraft seems to have been done, until the outbreak of war in September brought the activities of F S (Sidney) Cotton and the Photographic Development Unit (PDU) at Heston to the attention of higher authority. This unit had been set up to form an experimental unit for the purpose of testing and developing, what were then considered novel techniques for making photo reconnaissance sorties over enemy territory. The basis of the scheme proposed was the use of high speed and invisibility, with the originator of the scheme, Sidney Cotton in charge.

The unit's initial equipment was the Bristol Blenheim which was soon found to be too slow and, with Night under surfaces, too visible from below. The cure for the first problem was to make a determined attempt to clean-up the airframe as much as possible, and the cure for the second problem was to apply a different, lighter, colour to the under surfaces.

Bristol Blenheim Mk.I, L1410/WV-B, 18 Squadron, Méharicourt, France, January 1940.

On 3 January 1940, L1410 managed to evade an attack by Hurricanes but then fell to an attack by Bf 109Es and crash-landed at Eynatten, Belgium, where the surviving crew were interned. Dark Earth and Dark Green upper surfaces, in this instance to the A Scheme pattern, with Night under surfaces. Note the pre-war 'bright' Red/White/Blue fuselage roundels. Medium Sea Grey codes. Serial number was positioned on the rear fuselage and on the rudder.

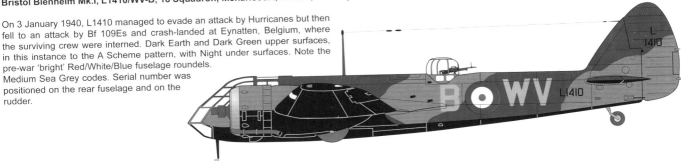

Bristol Blenheim Mk.IV, N6216/XD-B, 139 Squadron, Pivot, France, late 1939.

This may well have been one of the Blenheims finished in the Glossy Sky Camotint or BS 381 Eau-de-Nil duck egg green shade on the under surfaces that operated over France in the late 1939/early 1940 period. Upper surfaces were the standard Temperate Land Scheme of Dark Earth and Dark Green, in this instance to the A Scheme pattern. Medium Sea Grey codes. Serial number only on the rear fuselage. N6216 was

Bristol Blenheim Mk.IV, N6190/OM-D, 107 Squadron, RAF Wattisham, Lincolnshire, January 1940.

The other 'non-standard' under surface colour applied to several Blenheim Mk.IVs during this period was an unidentified 'light blue/blue grey' colour which is thought might have been Air ministry Sky Blue. Note the undulating fuselage demarcation. Upper surfaces were the standard Temperate Land Scheme of Dark Earth and Dark Green, in this instance to the B Scheme pattern. Medium Sea Grey codes. Serial number only on the rear fuselage. N6190 was reported 'missing' on 12 May 1940.

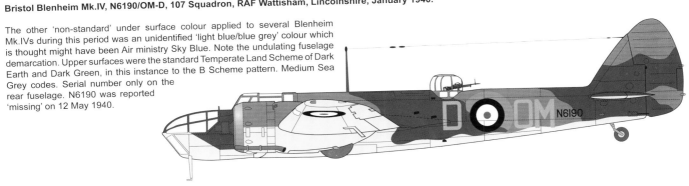

Bristol Blenheim Mk.IV, L8875/WV-S, 18 Squadron, Méharicourt, France, April 1940.

During early 1940, 18 Squadron started re-equipping with Blenheim Mk.IVs whilst still operating from its base at Méharicourt, France. Upper surfaces were the standard Temperate Land Scheme of Dark Earth and Dark Green, in this instance to the A Scheme pattern, with Night under surfaces. Medium Sea Grey codes. Serial number only on the rear fuselage. Note the narrow yellow outer ring to the fuselage roundel. L8875 force-landed at Brussels-Evere on 30 April 1940, following a compass failure, where the crew were interned, as Belgium was still neutral – albeit just for another 11 days!

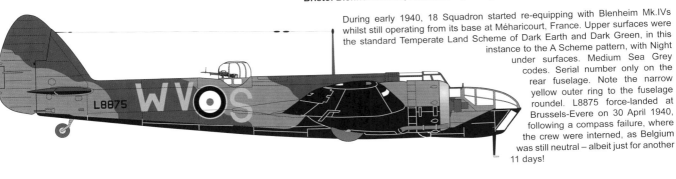

Bristol Blenheim Mk.IV, L9332/PZ-Z, 53 Squadron, Poix, France, May 1940.

L9332 is typical of the Blenheims operating over France immediately prior to the German Blitzkrieg offensive – several of which still did not have the Yellow outer ring added to the fuselage roundel, although in L9932's case, did have fin stripes applied! Upper surfaces were the standard Temperate Land Scheme of Dark Earth and Dark Green, in this instance to the B Scheme pattern, with Night under surfaces. Medium Sea Grey codes. Serial number only on the rear fuselage. L9332 crash-landed at Vitry-en-Artois, on 10 May 1940, and was abandoned when the airfield was evacuated.

Not to any scale

Supermarine Spitfire Mk.I, K9911/YT-E, 65 Squadron, RAF Hornchurch, Essex, late February 1940.

By the beginning of 1940, Spitfires were equipping a growing number of frontline RAF Fighter Squadrons, finished in the standard Temperate Land Scheme of Dark Earth and Dark Green upper surfaces, in this instance to the B Scheme pattern, with the official production Night/White under surfaces divided down the aircraft's centreline. Note the 25 inch diameter Red/White/ Blue fuselage roundel probably created by painting over the original Yellow outer ring. Small Red/Blue roundels were carried above wings. Note also the pole type radio aerial mast and strakes over cowling for fitting anti-glare exhaust shields.

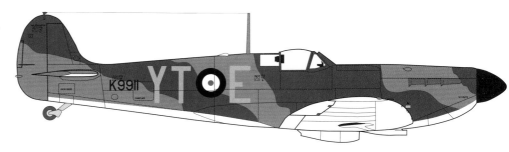

Supermarine Spitfire Mk.I, P9444/ RN-A, 72 Squadron, RAF Acklington, Northumberland, May 1940.

Finished in the standard Temperate Land Scheme of Dark Earth and Dark Green upper surfaces, to the A Scheme pattern, with the official production Night/ White under surfaces divided down the aircraft's centreline. Note the slightly larger diameter Red/White/Blue fuselage roundel probably created by painting over the original Yellow outer ring. Small 40 inch Red/Blue roundels were carried above wings. Note also the pole type radio aerial mast and 5 inch wide Red/ White/Blue fin stripes,

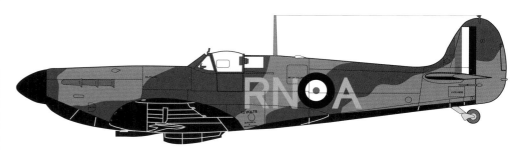

Supermarine Spitfire Mk.I, (serial unknown, overpainted)/PR-Q, 609 Squadron, RAF Drem, East Lothian, April 1940.

Several squadrons were still painting out the fuselage serial numbers and applying them in very small characters at the top of the fin, making identification from photographs very difficult, as in PR-Q's case. Standard Temperate Land Scheme of Dark Earth and Dark Green upper surfaces, to the B Scheme pattern, with Night/White/Aluminium under surfaces. Small 40 inch Red/Blue roundels were carried above wings. Note also the pole type radio aerial mast.

Hawker Hurricane Mk.I, L1931/TM-O, 504 Squadron, RAF Wattisham, Suffolk, April 1940.

Standard Temperate Land Scheme of Dark Earth and Dark Green upper surfaces, to the A Scheme pattern, with Night/White under surfaces divided down the centreline. Note also the pole type radio aerial mast, de Havilland spinner. Codes read O-TM on port side. L1931 was shot down by Bf 109Es near Abbeville on 7 June 1940.

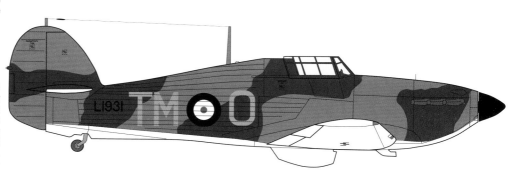

Hawker Hurricane Mk.I, P2617/AF-F, 607 Squadron, Croydon, mid-May 1940.

Standard Temperate Land Scheme of Dark Earth and Dark Green upper surfaces, to the A Scheme pattern, with Night/White/Aluminium under surfaces. De Havilland spinner. P2617 survived the Battle of France, (and the Battle of Britain), and after its operational life with No 607 Squadron ended served with several Flying Training Schools, eventually being preserved in these markings and is currently on display in the Battle of Britain Hall at the RAF Museum, Hendon.

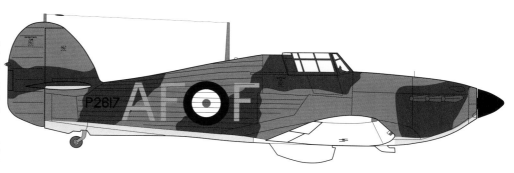

Not to any scale

Bristol Blenheim Mk.If, L1503/YB-E, 29 Squadron, RAF Debden, Essex, early 1939.

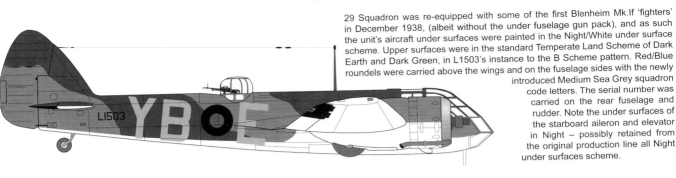

29 Squadron was re-equipped with some of the first Blenheim Mk.If 'fighters' in December 1938, (albeit without the under fuselage gun pack), and as such the unit's aircraft under surfaces were painted in the Night/White under surface scheme. Upper surfaces were in the standard Temperate Land Scheme of Dark Earth and Dark Green, in L1503's instance to the B Scheme pattern. Red/Blue roundels were carried above the wings and on the fuselage sides with the newly introduced Medium Sea Grey squadron code letters. The serial number was carried on the rear fuselage and rudder. Note the under surfaces of the starboard aileron and elevator in Night – possibly retained from the original production line all Night under surfaces scheme.

Bristol Blenheim Mk.If, (serial unknown, overpainted)/YP-Q, 23 Squadron, RAF Wittering, Cambridgeshire, early 1940.

Sporting its new 'wartime' codes, this aircraft from 23 Squadron still appears to have the all Night under surfaces, although it is difficult to be certain from the angle of the reference photo. Upper surfaces were in the standard Temperate Land Scheme of Dark Earth and Dark Green, in the A Scheme pattern. Red/Blue roundels above the wings and Red/White/Blue on the fuselage sides. The Medium Sea Grey squadron code letters were somewhat smaller than those of the aircraft above. The serial number was carried on the rear fuselage only.

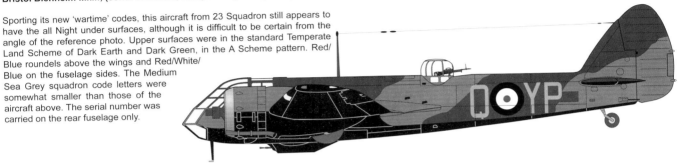

Bristol Blenheim Mk.If, L8685/FK-N, 219 Squadron, RAF Catterick, North Yorkshire, February 1940.

Standard Temperate Land Scheme of Dark Earth and Dark Green, in the B Scheme pattern, with Night/White under surface scheme divided down the fuselage centreline. Red/Blue roundels above the wings and Red/White/Blue on the fuselage sides. The serial number was carried on the rear fuselage only.

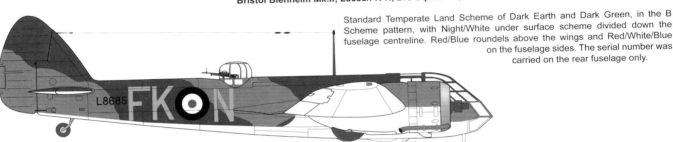

Bristol Blenheim Mk.If, L1257/ZK-I, 25 Squadron, RAF North Weald, Essex, February 1940.

Standard Temperate Land Scheme of Dark Earth and Dark Green, in the B Scheme pattern, with Night/White under surface scheme divided down the fuselage centreline. Red/Blue roundels above the wings and Red/White/Blue on the fuselage sides. The serial number was carried on the rear fuselage only.

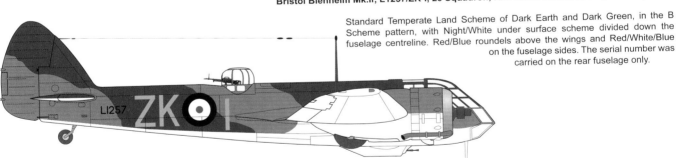

Bristol Blenheim Mk.If, K7181/RE-P, 229 Squadron, RAF Digby, Lincolnshire, March 1940.

Standard Temperate Land Scheme of Dark Earth and Dark Green, in the B Scheme pattern, with Night/White under surface scheme divided down the fuselage centreline. Red/Blue roundels above the wings and Red/White/Blue on the fuselage sides. The serial number was carried on the rear fuselage only.

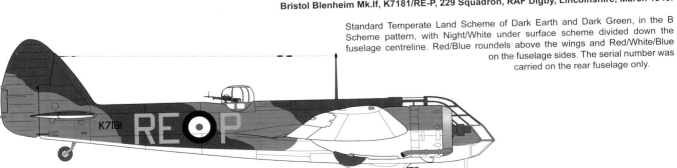

Not to any scale

The Battle of Britain – The Phoney War

Hawker Hurricane Mk.I, L1679/JX-G, 1 Squadron, Vassincourt, France, late 1939/early 1940.
Pilot: Plt Off Paul Richey

One of the two RAF Fighter Squadrons attached to the AASF as part of 67 Wing was 1 Squadron, who applied French-style rudder stripes, (Red leading) and Red/White/Blue underwing roundels to conform with Armée de l'Air practice, with whom the were operating in close proximity. Squadron codes were retained for a period, but were later overpainted, as was the fuselage serial number. Standard Temperate Land Scheme of Dark Earth and Dark Green upper surfaces, to the A Scheme pattern. Note the Night/White under surfaces were overpainted in "a pale blue colour" and the red cap to the Watts two-blade wooden propeller.

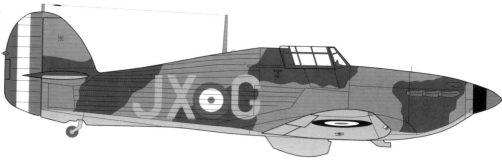

Hawker Hurricane Mk.I, P2647/(TP)-X, 73 Squadron, Rouvres, France, early May 1940.

The other RAF Fighter Squadron attached to the AASF as part of 67 Wing was 73 Squadron, which, immediately prior to the Blitzkrieg offensive, had applied Yellow outer rings to its fuselage roundels, but retained the French-style rudder stripes. Standard Temperate Land Scheme of Dark Earth and Dark Green upper surfaces, to the A Scheme pattern, with Night/White/Aluminium under surfaces. De Havilland propeller unit.

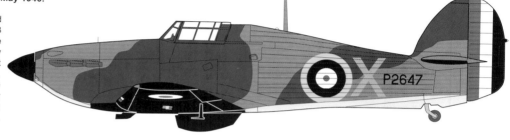

Hawker Hurricane Mk.I, (serial unknown, overpainted)/VY-C, 85 Squadron, Merville, France, early May 1940.

One of the two RAF Fighter Squadrons initially sent to France in 1939, but which continued with 60 Wing as part of the BEF's Air Component was 85 Squadron, which retained its historic hexagon squadron marking – on the fin. Again, immediately prior to the Blitzkrieg offensive, this unit had applied Yellow outer rings to its fuselage roundels, in this instance in a narrow style. Red/White/Blue fin stripes, approximately 5 inches wide, had also been applied. Standard Temperate Land Scheme of Dark Earth and Dark Green upper surfaces, to the A Scheme pattern, with Night/White under surfaces divided down the centreline. De Havilland propeller unit.

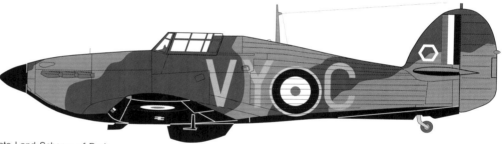

Hawker Hurricane Mk.I, L1619 (overpainted)/LK-P, 87 Squadron, Merville France, November 1939.

The other RAF Fighter Squadron retained by 60 Wing as part the BEF's Air Component was 87 Squadron, which also adopted Armée de l'Air style rudder stripes like the aircraft of 67 Wing. Standard Temperate Land Scheme of Dark Earth and Dark Green upper surfaces, to the A Scheme pattern, with Night/White under surfaces divided down the centreline. Note the Watts two-blade wooden propeller unit has a white spinner cap.

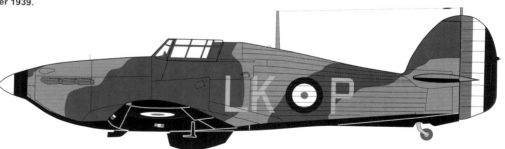

Gloster Gladiator Mk.II, (possibly N2306 – overpainted)/KW-T, 615 Squadron, St Inglevert, France, April 1940.
Pilot: Flg Off Anthony Eyre

615 Squadron was the last frontline operational Gladiator unit left in France immediately prior to the Blitzkrieg offensive. The squadron's aircraft were finished in the Shadow Compensating scheme of Dark Earth and Dark Green upper surfaces of the top mainplane, the upper surfaces of the fuselage/cowling and the upper surfaces of the tailplanes the upper surfaces of the lower mainplanes and the sides of the fuselage/cowling were in Light Earth and Light Green. Under surfaces were Night/White divided down the centreline although the under surface of the upper wing remained in Aluminium. Note the red wheel hubs (Flight colour?) trimmed in white (?) and the area of fresh paint under the squadron's 'KW' code where the previous owner's codes (No 605's 'HE') had been painted over.

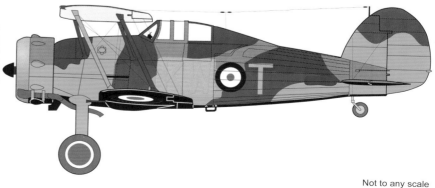

Not to any scale

Gloster Gladiator Mk.II, '427', Jagevingen (Fighter Flight), Norwegian Army Air Service, Fornebu Airport, Norway, April 1940.

Pilot: Sergeant Pilot Kristian Fredrik Schye

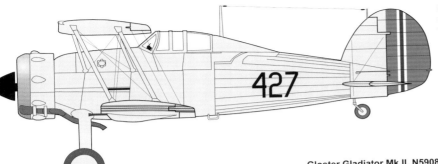

Six Gladiator Mk.Is were delivered to the Fighter Flight of the Norwegian Army Air Service in August 1937, followed by the last six Gladiator Mk.IIs ever built, diverted from the RAF, and delivered in 1939. The Norwegian Gladiators were numbered 413, 415, 417, 419, 421, 423, 425, 427, 429, 431, 433 and 435. They were finished in overall painted Aluminium with Norway's national colours in bands across the upper surface of the upper wing and the under surface of the lower wing and on the rudder. Three-digit black numerals were applied to the fuselage. '427' was the sole Norwegian air-to-air Gloster Gladiator combat loss, shot down by the future 'Experte' Ltn Helmut Lent, on 9 April 1940.

Gloster Gladiator Mk.II, N5908/HE-F, 263 Squadron, Bardufoss, Norway, June 1940,

263 Squadron was reformed in October 1939, not only taking over some, 605's Gladiators, but also the Auxiliary Air Force squadron's code letters, 'HE' too. Gladiators were used by the squadron during the last two months of the Norwegian Campaign, arriving on HMS Glorious on 24 April, and operating from the frozen lake Lesjaskogsvatnet.

After less than a week, all the squadron's aircraft were unserviceable and it was evacuated back to the UK to re-equip. 263 Squadron resumed its operations in Norway when the squadron returned on 21 May, reinforced by the Hurricanes, 46 Squadron. On 7 June the ten surviving Gladiators landed on HMS Glorious but she was intercepted by the German battlecruisers Gneisenau and Scharnhorst the next day and sunk. 263 Squadron lost its CO and nine other pilots. N5908, one of the aircraft lost on board HMS Glorious, was finished in the Shadow Compensating scheme of Dark Earth and

Dark Green upper surfaces of the top mainplane, the upper surfaces of the fuselage/cowling and the upper surfaces of the tailplanes the upper surfaces of the lower mainplanes and the sides of the fuselage/cowling were in Light Earth and Light Green. Under surfaces were Night/White divided down the centreline.

Blackburn Skua, L2963/F, 803 NAS, operating off HMS Ark Royal, June 1940.

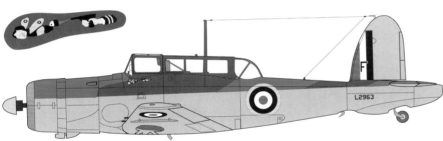

Fleet Air Arm monoplane aircraft were camouflaged in Extra Dark Sea Grey and Dark Slate Grey on the upper surfaces, in L2963's case to the A Scheme pattern, and Sky Grey on the under surfaces, with the upper/under demarcation being half way up the fuselage. The fin and rudder were also to be Sky Grey. A Yellow outer ring to the fuselage roundel had been applied by this time and fin stripes covering the whole of the fin. Note the 'cartoon' under the cockpit. L2963 force landed at Trondheim, Norway, on 13 June 1940 following an attack on the German battlecruiser Scharnhorst.

Junkers Ju 87R, A5+IH, 1./StG 1, Trondheim-Vaernes, Norway, April 1940.

Finished in the standard two-tone green RLM 70 Schwarzgrün and RLM 71 Dunkelgrün upper surfaces in a straight-edged 'splinter' pattern with RLM 65 Hellblau undersides. Codes were black with a white individual aircraft letter 'I' in the staffel colour. Note the Staffel's 'diving raven' badge under the windscreen.

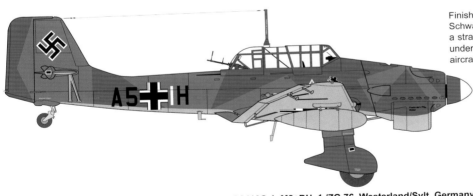

Messerschmitt Bf 110C-1, M8+DH, 1./ZG 76, Westerland/Sylt, Germany, April 1940.

Typical of most Luftwaffe aircraft of this period this Bf 110C was finished in the standard two-tone green RLM 70 Schwarzgrün and RLM 71 Dunkelgrün upper surfaces in a straight-edged 'splinter' pattern with RLM 65 Hellblau undersides. Codes were black with a white individual aircraft letter 'D' in the staffel colour.

Flown by Ltn Helmut Lent, M8+DH was hit by ground fire and crash landed during the attack on Oslo-Fornebu on 9 April 1940. Note the four 'kill' bars on the fin. Ltn Lent had five victories at the time, having shot down a Norwegian Gladiator (see above) earlier in the mission.

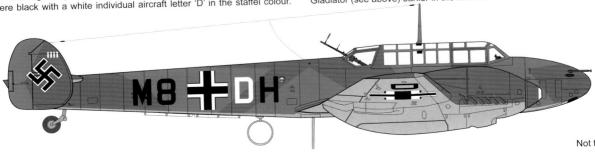

Not to any scale

Prior to the outbreak of war, Sidney Cotton was involved in carrying out clandestine photography flights over Germany on behalf of the Secret Intelligence Service. The aircraft used on these flights are said to have been painted a 'very pale green colour' which did not look out of place on a 'civil' aircraft, but at the same time happened to be very good at concealing the aircraft from observers on the ground. It would appear that it was this 'very pale green colour' which was applied to the under surfaces of the Blenheims at Heston.

Bomber Command evidently heard something of the PDU's work on modifying the Blenheim as, during October, a Blenheim from 139 Squadron was sent to Heston to be modified in a similar manner. As part of these modifications, the aircraft received the glossy camouflage paints then in use at Heston, consisting of the normal Dark Earth and Dark Green colours applied in the usual disruptive pattern on the upper surfaces, and what was apparently described as a 'light sea green' colour on the under surfaces.

This new camouflage seems to have been reported in some detail to the Air Ministry as two representatives from the Royal Aircraft Establishment (RAE) at Farnborough travelled to Heston on 18 November 1939. They found that a Blenheim Mk.IV had been extensively worked upon to eliminate gaps in the skin joints and had been given a very smooth, glossy, paint finish with a colour described in the subsequent RAE report as *"... Duck Egg Green termed Camotint..."* on its under surfaces. It was claimed that this 'Duck Egg Green' finish rendered the aircraft practically invisible at heights of 10,000ft and upwards.

As it was thought that the glossiness of the new smooth paint could compromise the camouflage effect, it was requested that the RAE supply Heston with a suitable paint which would match the Dark Earth, Dark Green and the 'Duck Egg Green' in colour, and would be smoother than the standard camouflage finishes but without the glossiness.

As soon as Bomber Command learned of this new colour they began to press for its adoption as soon as possible, especially on the Blenheim. The problem was that the paint manufacturers were faced with sudden demands for comparatively large quantities of a new colour to an entirely new technical specification. Sufficient supplies of such paint could not be made available at short notice so compromise was inevitable. The first compromise to be made was with the technical specification of the paint. Instead of the new smooth Type S finish it was agreed that paint could be supplied to a pre-war standard, DTD 63A which bestowed a smooth glossy finish.

However, in order to try to cut down the glossiness it was agreed that steps would be taken to reduce the degree of gloss. This appears to have been done as a letter sent from the Air Ministry to Bristols on 20 April 1940 states that *"It is agreed that you should call on the schedule for Mod 864 on the Blenheim IV for Laquer to DTD 63 with reduced gloss... As regards colour, the pale blue green which has been called Camotint is now defined as Standard Sky and this description should be given in your Schedule"*.

The second compromise appears to have been with the accuracy of colour match to the standard for the new colour Sky. Whilst it is thought that Bristol-built Blenheims were finished in the correct shade of Sky, physical evidence appears to show that in the early part of 1940 Rootes-built Blenheims were finished in a somewhat different colour which might subjectively be described as a 'rich duck egg green' – which may have been BSS 381 (1930) No 16 Eau-de-Nil. The surface finish appears to be very smooth and glossy, apparently once again indicating the use of materials to 'DTD 63A with reduced gloss'.

Bomber Command meanwhile, was apparently most impressed with its 'streamlined' 139 Squadron Blenheim and wrote to both the Air Ministry and HQ Fighter Command, to inform them of their experiments. The letter then went on to state

Table A
Luftwaffe bombers, transports, twin-engined fighters, maritime and reconnaissance aircraft identification code system

	Fourth code letter	Colour of aircraft letter
Geschwaderstab I Gruppe stab II Gruppe stab III Gruppe stab IV Gruppe stab V Gruppe stab	A B C D E F	Blue or green

Gruppe colour	I white	II red	III yellow	IV blue	V green	Staffel colour
Staffel Last letter	1 H	4 M	7 R	10 U	13 X	white
Staffel Last letter	2 K	5 N	8 S	11 V	14 Y	red
Staffel Last letter	3 L	6 P	9 T	12 W	15 Z	yellow

that coincident with this process a change had been made in the under surface colour of these Blenheims which were now painted what was described as 'Grey-Blue' (sic), to merge into the background of the sky when viewed from below.

Bomber Command wanted this change of colouring to be brought to the attention of all concerned as it was being progressively introduced into the Blenheim bomber squadrons. It would also be necessary to inform the French authorities as two of these squadrons of repainted Blenheims were to replace two Fairey Battle squadrons in France in the very near future.

Accordingly, on 29 November 1939, signals A399 and A432 informed No 1 Mission for onward transmission to the French, and all home based forces respectively, that a 'light blue' colour was being introduced for the under surfaces of Blenheim bombers instead of the present black finish.

Whether this was yet another colour being applied to Blenheims, possibly the ones already in squadron service, or a description of the factory-applied Sky or Eau-de-Nil shades, is not clear, but it is certainly described in the official correspondence as 'blue-grey' (and also 'light blue'). This unidentified 'blue-grey' cannot be found in any Standard which has yet come to light, but there is certainly the documented use of such a colour in late 1939 when Bomber Command employed a colour described as being a 'blue-grey' on Blenheim bombers despatched to France as day flying camouflage on the under surfaces. Red, White and Blue roundels were also to be carried on the under surfaces of the wings of aircraft painted in the 'blue-grey' under surface colour scheme.

This 'blue-grey' colour might well have been an existing colour, eg Air Ministry Sky Blue, which had originally been produced as a 'Camouflage Scheme for Target Aircraft', for

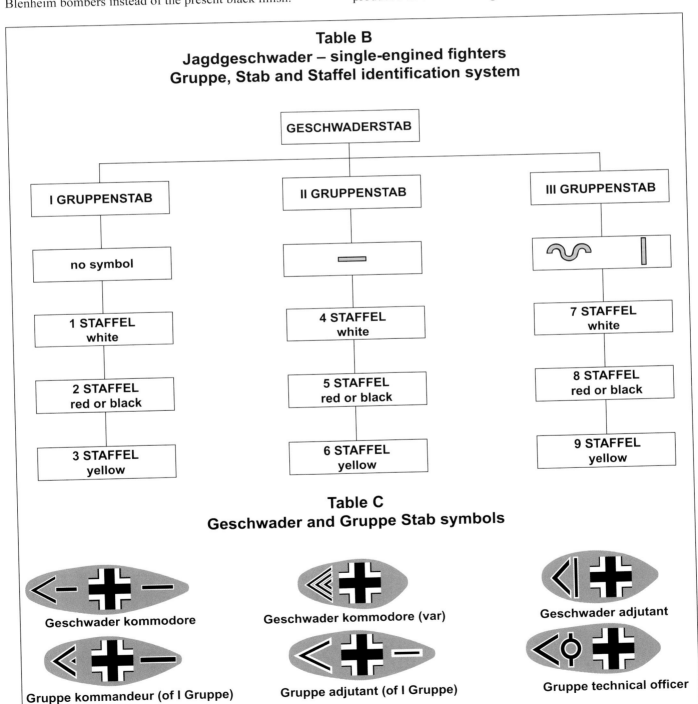

Table B
Jagdgeschwader – single-engined fighters
Gruppe, Stab and Staffel identification system

GESCHWADERSTAB

I GRUPPENSTAB — II GRUPPENSTAB — III GRUPPENSTAB

no symbol

1 STAFFEL white — 4 STAFFEL white — 7 STAFFEL white

2 STAFFEL red or black — 5 STAFFEL red or black — 8 STAFFEL red or black

3 STAFFEL yellow — 6 STAFFEL yellow — 9 STAFFEL yellow

Table C
Geschwader and Gruppe Stab symbols

Geschwader kommodore

Geschwader kommodore (var)

Geschwader adjutant

Gruppe kommandeur (of I Gruppe)

Gruppe adjutant (of I Gruppe)

Gruppe technical officer

Messerschmitt Bf 110C, M8+DB, Stab I/ZG 76, Olmütz, Germany, August 1939.
Pilot: The Gruppe Kommandeur, Hptm Günther Reinecke

This is how the Luftwaffe's Bf 110Cs looked immediately prior to the outbreak of war in the summer of 1939, finished in the then relatively new standard two-tone green RLM 70 Schwarzgrün and RLM 71 Dunkelgrün upper surfaces in a straight-edged 'splinter' pattern with RLM 65 Hellblau undersides. Codes were

black with a green individual aircraft letter 'D' in the Gruppe Stab colour. Note the black with narrow white outline chevron used by Hptm Reinecke as a Stab symbol.

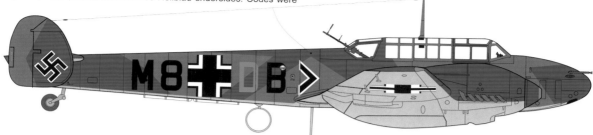

Messerschmitt Bf 109D-1, 'Yellow 5', 3./JG 144, Gablingen, Germany, August 1939.

On the eve of war, many Luftwaffe fighter units were still equipped with the Bf 109D, like this one – with a striking 'sharkmouth' design on the nose. Two-tone green RLM 70 Schwarzgrün and RLM 71 Dunkelgrün upper surfaces in a straight-edged 'splinter' pattern with RLM 65 Hellblau undersides. Yellow (RLM 04 Gelb) spinner and numeral. Note the (early) central position of the swastika across the fin and rudder.

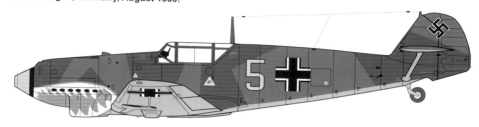

Messerschmitt Bf 109D-1, 'Yellow 12', 3./JGr 152, Biblis, Germany, September 1939.
Pilot: Ltn Karl Rosenkranz

Two-tone green RLM 70 Schwarzgrün and RLM 71 Dunkelgrün upper surfaces in a straight-edged 'splinter' pattern with RLM 65 Hellblau undersides. RLM 70 spinner and yellow (RLM 04 Gelb) numeral. Note the later position of the swastika only on the fin. Ltn Rosenkranz force-landed 'Yellow 12' near Saarbrücken, following combat with Armée de l'Air Morane MS 406s on 24 September 1939.

Messerschmitt Bf 109D-1, 'Yellow 3', 6./JG 51, Eutingen, Germany, late 1939.

Two-tone green RLM 70 Schwarzgrün and RLM 71 Dunkelgrün upper surfaces in a straight-edged 'splinter' pattern with RLM 65 Hellblau undersides. RLM 70 spinner and yellow (RLM 04 Gelb) numeral. Note the 'weeping woodpecker' unit badge and the (early) central position of the swastika across the fin and rudder.

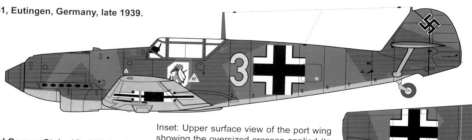

Inset: Upper surface view of the port wing showing the oversized crosses applied (to the upper and under surfaces), following the Polish Campaign.

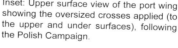

Messerschmitt Bf 109D-1, 'White chevron' of I Gruppe Stab, JGr 102, Lachen-Speyerdorf, Germany, October 1939.
Pilot: The Gruppenkommandeur, Hptm Johannes Gentzen

Two-tone green RLM 70 Schwarzgrün and RLM 71 Dunkelgrün upper surfaces in a straight-edged 'splinter' pattern with RLM 65 Hellblau undersides. RLM 70 spinner and yellow (RLM 04 Gelb) numeral. Note the 'weeping woodpecker' unit badge and the (early) central position of the swastika across the fin and rudder.

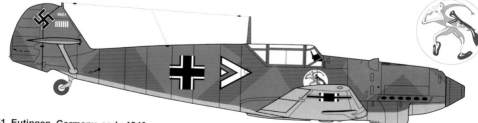

Messerschmitt Bf 109D-1, 'White 15', 4./JG 51, Eutingen, Germany, early 1940.

By the beginning of 1940, Bf 109s were being recorded with the RLM 65 Hellblau undersides extended up the fuselage sides as in this example. The RLM 70 Schwarzgrün and RLM 71 Dunkelgrün upper surfaces of the wing, tailplane and fuselage spine were retained, with the remainder of the under surfaces in RLM 65 Hellblau undersides. White spinner with RLM 70 back plate, and white, thinly outlined in black, numeral. Note the central position of the swastika across the fin and rudder and the unit's 'weeping woodpecker' badge.

Inset: II/JG 51's 'weeping woodpecker' badge had the words 'Gott strafe England' added following Britain's declaration of war against Germany in September 1939. Note the umbrella and spectacles on the 'woodpecker' which is thought to be a reference to the British Prime Minister at the time, Neville Chamberlain.

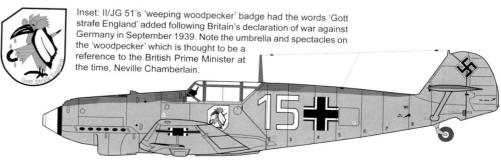

Not to any scale

Messerschmitt Bf 109E-1, 'Red 15', 2./JG 77, Juliusburg-Nord, Germany, August 1939.

Inset: 2./JG 77's 'clog' emblem.

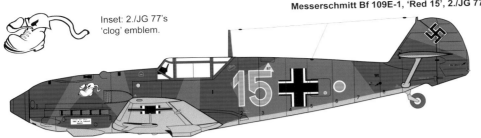

Two-tone green RLM 70 Schwarzgrün and RLM 71 Dunkelgrün upper surfaces in a straight-edged 'splinter' pattern with RLM 65 Hellblau undersides and RLM 70 spinner. Red (RLM 23 Rot) numeral '15' and 'red dot' Gruppe marking, both thinly outlined in white. Note the (early) central position of the swastika across the fin and rudder.

Messerschmitt Bf 109E-1, 'Black Chevron', Stab JGr 101, Lichtenau, Germany, September 1939.

Inset: JagdGruppe 101's white cross on a red shield emblem later adopted by the Geschwaderstab of StG 2.

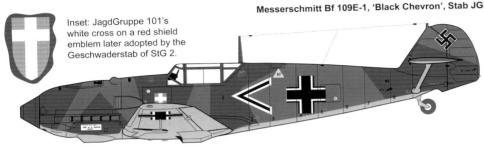

JagdGruppe 101 was the temporary redesignation of II/ZG 1 for the Polish Campaign. Two-tone green RLM 70 Schwarzgrün and RLM 71 Dunkelgrün upper surfaces in a straight-edged 'splinter' pattern with RLM 65 Hellblau undersides and RLM 70 spinner. Black Gruppe Adjutant chevron thinly outlined in white. Note the (early) central position of the swastika across the fin and rudder.

Messerschmitt Bf 109E-1, 'Yellow 1', 4./JG 53, Mannheim-Sandhofen, Germany, November 1939.

Inset: 4 Staffel's 'zylinder hut' (top hat) emblem (awaiting completion with the black areas?) and JG 53's 'Pik As' (Ace of Spades) emblems.

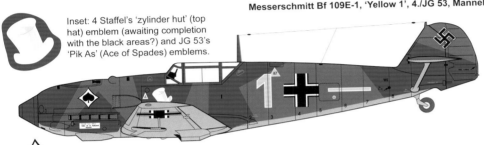

Two-tone green RLM 70 Schwarzgrün and RLM 71 Dunkelgrün upper surfaces in a straight-edged 'splinter' pattern with RLM 65 Hellblau undersides and RLM 70 spinner. Yellow (RLM Gelb 04) numeral '1' and horizontal II Gruppe bar to the rear of the fuselage balkenkreuz, both thinly outlined in white. Note the (early) central position of the swastika across the fin and rudder.

Messerschmitt Bf 109E-3, 'Black Chevron and bars', Stab III/JG 20, Brandenburg-Briest, Germany, October 1939.

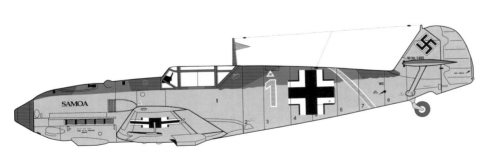

Two-tone green RLM 70 Schwarzgrün and RLM 71 Dunkelgrün upper surfaces in a straight-edged 'splinter' pattern with RLM 65 Hellblau undersides and RLM 70 spinner. Black chevron and vertical bars and 'wavy' III Gruppe bar to the rear of the fuselage balkenkreuz, both thinly outlined in white. Note the (early) central position of the swastika across the fin and rudder.

Messerschmitt Bf 109E-1, 'Red 1', 2./JG 27, Krefeld, Germany, spring 1940.
Pilot: the Staffelkapitän Oblt Gerd Framm

Two-tone green RLM 70 Schwarzgrün and RLM 71 Dunkelgrün upper surfaces in a straight-edged 'splinter' pattern with the RLM 65 Hellblau under surfaces extended up the fuselage sides, and over the fin and rudder. RLM 70 spinner. Red (RLM Rot 23) numeral '1' and diagonal bar around the rear of the fuselage, (denoting the Staffelkapitän?), both thinly outlined in white. Note the name 'Samoa' on the cowling, red Staffelkapitän pennant on the radio mast and the later position of the swastika only on the fin.

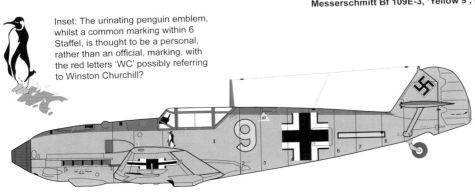

Messerschmitt Bf 109E-3, 'Yellow 9', 6./JG 77, Westerland, Germany, March 1940.

Inset: The urinating penguin emblem, whilst a common marking within 6 Staffel, is thought to be a personal, rather than an official, marking, with the red letters 'WC' possibly referring to Winston Churchill?

Either the original two-tone green RLM 70/71 upper surfaces have been overpainted in service – the original RLM 70 in RLM 71 Dunkelgrün and the original RLM 71 in RLM Grau 02 – or this aircraft was one of the first to be finished in the 'new' RLM 71/02 scheme on the production line. The RLM 65 Hellblau under surfaces have also been extended up the fuselage sides, and over the fin and rudder. RLM 70 spinner. Yellow (RLM Gelb 04) numeral '9' and horizontal bar, both thinly outlined in black. Note the 'urinating penguin' emblem and the later position of the swastika only on the fin.

Not to any scale

Dornier Do 17P, F6+FM, 4./(F) 122, Goslar, Germany, November 1939.

Finished in the standard two-tone green RLM 70 Schwarzgrün and RLM 71 Dunkelgrün upper surfaces in a straight-edged 'splinter' pattern with RLM 65 Hellblau undersides. Codes were black with a yellow individual aircraft letter 'F' (in a stylised form) in the staffel colour. Note the early central placing of the swastika across the fin and rudder. This aircraft was shot down over northern France by Hurricanes, 1 Squadron on 23 November 1939.

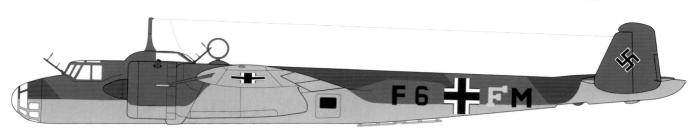

Dornier Do 17P, 4N+TL, 3./(F) 22, operating over Belgium and France in early 1940.

Finished in the standard two-tone green RLM 70 Schwarzgrün and RLM 71 Dunkelgrün upper surfaces in a straight-edged 'splinter' pattern. Note how the RLM 65 Hellblau undersides have been brought up the fuselage sides and a light mottle of what appears to be RLM 71/02 had been applied. Codes were all black without the individual aircraft letter 'T' in the staffel colour.

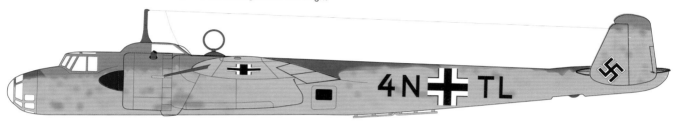

Dornier Do 17Z, F1+BH, 4./(F) 122, Goslar, Germany, November 1939.

Finished in the standard two-tone green RLM 70 Schwarzgrün and RLM 71 Dunkelgrün upper surfaces in a straight-edged 'splinter' pattern with RLM 65 Hellblau undersides. Codes were black with a white individual aircraft letter 'B' in the staffel colour. Note the early narrow-bordered balkenkreuze yet later placing of the swastika on the fin only. White spinners and narrow white mid-fuselage band.

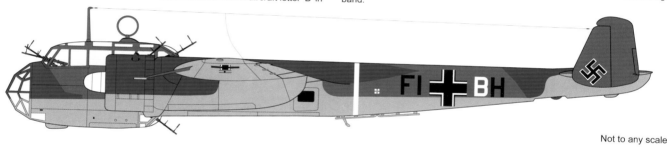

Not to any scale

use on de Havilland Queen Wasp target aircraft. However, as far as is known, this scheme was never applied to any Queen Wasp aircraft as, by the time the type finally entered service, the camouflage requirements for target aircraft had changed.

By mid-December 1939, the Air Ministry was trying to get all these improvements incorporated into Blenheims on the production line. There were however problems thrown up by the introduction of these new under surface camouflage materials. The PDU at Heston seems to have been in the habit of obtaining its materials direct from the manufacturer, Titanine. Therefore, when Bomber Command began submitting demands for this same material to the Air Ministry for use on its day-flying Blenheims, nothing was known about it by the Directorate of Engineering. Not being able to obtain supplies of this material might have been the reason why Bomber Command squadrons used the 'light blue/blue-grey' (ie Sky Blue?) colour instead.

Whilst all of this had been going on, work had been put in hand at the RAE to produce a finish employing a very finely ground pigment which it was hoped would give a smooth matt finish.

Sky Type S was the name given by the RAE to the 'duck egg green' colour known at Heston as 'Camotint'. The suffix 'Type S' given by the RAE identified the new smooth paint which featured a more finely ground pigment which resulted in a smaller particle size and thus a smoother finish.

Thus, by the end of January 1940, the only Sky 'Type S' available was in the hands of the PDU at Heston, having been supplied in very small quantities by the RAE. In February however, Bristol appear to have modified the camouflage scheme of the Blenheims they were producing to have what was described as 'light green' under surfaces. This is understood to have been the first use of Sky on a production aircraft, but this was almost certainly not to the new improved 'Type S' standard; more than likely being the same material that Titanine had been supplying to the PDU which appears to have been to DTD specification 63A with reduced gloss' from April 1940 onwards.

However, the overriding concern was still one of provisioning the new under surface colour. The initial problem being that it needed to be determined exactly what quantities of this new material were required for maintenance purposes on such

Junkers Ju 87B-1, S2+AC '10', Stab II/StG 77, Breslau-Schongarten, Germany, August 1939.
Pilot: Maj Alfond Orthofer

Finished in the standard two-tone green RLM 70 Schwarzgrün and RLM 71 Dunkelgrün upper surfaces in a straight-edged 'splinter' pattern with RLM 65 Hellblau undersides. Codes were black with a green individual aircraft letter 'A' (in the Stab colour) outlined in white, and green (RLM 25?) tip to the RLM 70 propeller spinner. Note the large sharkmouth and eye and numeral '10 on the outer faces of the wheel spats

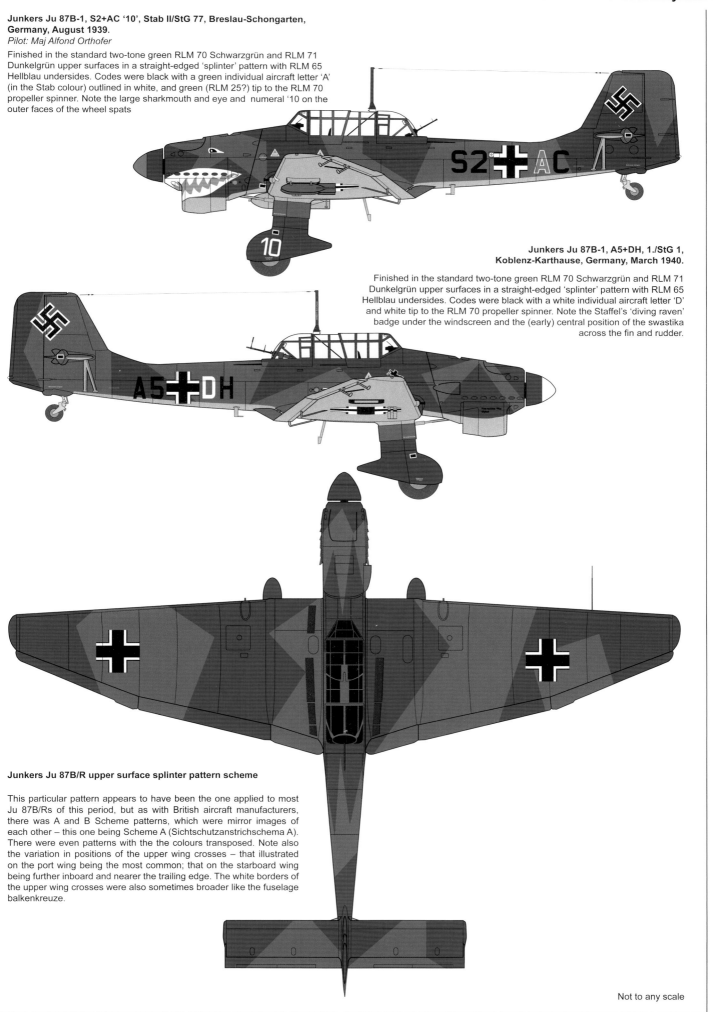

Junkers Ju 87B-1, A5+DH, 1./StG 1, Koblenz-Karthause, Germany, March 1940.

Finished in the standard two-tone green RLM 70 Schwarzgrün and RLM 71 Dunkelgrün upper surfaces in a straight-edged 'splinter' pattern with RLM 65 Hellblau undersides. Codes were black with a white individual aircraft letter 'D' and white tip to the RLM 70 propeller spinner. Note the Staffel's 'diving raven' badge under the windscreen and the (early) central position of the swastika across the fin and rudder.

Junkers Ju 87B/R upper surface splinter pattern scheme

This particular pattern appears to have been the one applied to most Ju 87B/Rs of this period, but as with British aircraft manufacturers, there was A and B Scheme patterns, which were mirror images of each other – this one being Scheme A (Sichtschutzanstrichsschema A). There were even patterns with the the colours transposed. Note also the variation in positions of the upper wing crosses – that illustrated on the port wing being the most common; that on the starboard wing being further inboard and nearer the trailing edge. The white borders of the upper wing crosses were also sometimes broader like the fuselage balkenkreuze.

Not to any scale

Junkers Ju 52/3mg4e, CH+BP, KGrzbV 107, Norway, April 1940.

KGrzbV 107 was a composite unit created especially for 'Operation Weserübung' ('Unternehmen Weserübung'), the invasion of Denmark and Norway. The aircraft is still finished in the pre-war three-tone RLM 61 Dunkelbraun, RLM 62 Grün

and RLM 63 Hellgrau, upper surfaces applied in a straight-edged 'splinter' scheme. The original RLM 65 Hellblau under surfaces appear to have been overpainted in a temporary black distemper. The factory radio call sign codes, (stammkennzeichen), were all black. Note the position of the swastika across the fin and rudder where the original red band and white disc had been painted over. This aircraft crash-landed at Fornebu during the invasion.

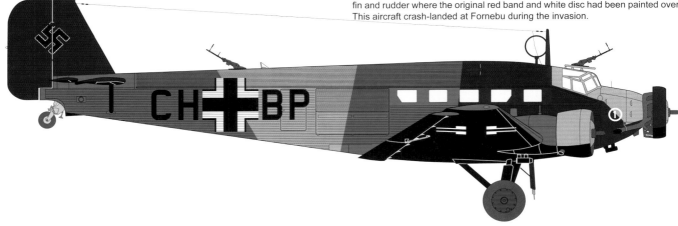

Junkers Ju 88A-1, U4+TK, Erprobungsgruppe/KG 26, Lake Jonsvatnet, Norway, April 1940.

Finished in the standard two-tone green RLM 70 Schwarzgrün and RLM 71 Dunkelgrün upper surfaces in a straight-edged 'splinter' pattern with RLM 65 Hellblau undersides. Codes were black with a white individual aircraft letter 'T' in the staffel colour. Note the blue (RLM 24?) tips to the propeller spinners. Several bombers from various units used the frozen lake near trondheim as an advanced

base during 'Unternehmen Weserübung' in April 1940. This particular machine was damaged there and was unable to be recovered before the ice melted. It was finally recovered for restoration and display in 2004.

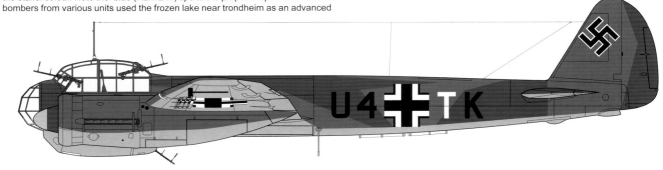

Heinkel He 111H, 5J+HP, 6./KG 4, 'General Wever', Fassberg, Germany, April 1940.

Finished in the standard two-tone green RLM 70 Schwarzgrün and RLM 71 Dunkelgrün upper surfaces in a straight-edged 'splinter' pattern with RLM 65

Hellblau undersides. Codes were black with a yellow individual aircraft letter 'H' in the staffel colour. Note the yellow (RLM 04?) tips to the propeller spinners. This machine crash-landed on to Oslo-Fornebu airfield on 9 April 1940, during the initial stages of the attack on Norway.

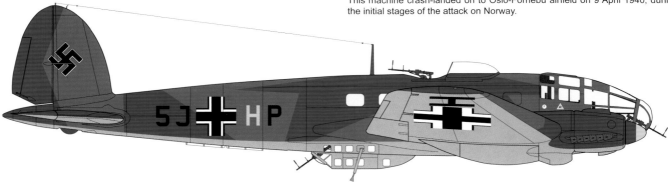

Focke-Wulf Fw 200C-1, F8+EH, 1./KG 40, home-based at Bremen, Germany, on detachment to Aalborg, then Copenhagen, Denmark, May/June 1940.

For their long-range maritime role, Fw 200's were finished in the 'maritime greens' of RLM 72 Grün and RLM 73 Grün on the upper surfaces, in a straight-edged

'splinter' pattern, with RLM 65 Hellblau undersides. Codes were black with a white individual aircraft letter 'E' in the staffel colour. Note the application of the full code F+8 and E+H under the wings positioned either side of the underwing balkenkreuze.

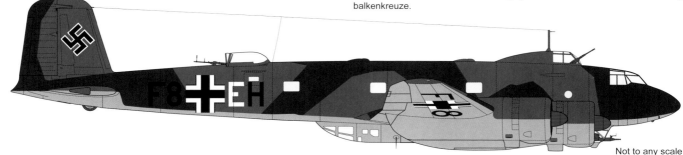

Not to any scale

Junkers Ju 52/3mg4e, D-TABX, unknown Seenotgruppe, based in France, circa June 1940.

This particular aircraft was operating in the air-sea rescue role in support of ditched aircrew in the English Channel. The aircraft was painted white (RLM 21 Weiss) overall with Red Cross markings in place of military balkenkreuze. The civil registration, D-TABX, was black and repeated under the wings. Note the red (Rot 23) band across the fin and rudder with 'civil' style swastika orientated 'square' at right angles to the rudder line.

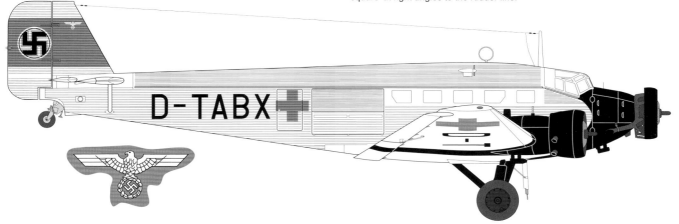

aircraft as were already finished in 'Camotint', (ie Sky and/or Eau-de-Nil) and for repainting Blenheims held by the Aircraft Storage Units awaiting issue. At that time, samples of Camotint were being prepared by Cellon as an alternative supply to Titanine, but no difficulties were envisaged in obtaining supplies of the new materials from any of the approved paint manufacturers.

Luftwaffe aircraft

At the time of the German invasion of Poland in September 1939, Luftwaffe camouflage was virtually through a transitional period, which included the introduction of new aircraft types and improved sub-types of existing designs.

Camouflage

By September 1939, multi- and single-engined bomber and transport aircraft were changing over from the previous three-tone upper surface scheme of RLM 61 Dunkelbraun (dark brown), RLM 62 Grün (green) and RLM 63 Hellgrau (light grey), applied in a straight-edged 'splinter' scheme. This scheme was applied at factory production level using a pre-determined pattern based upon a grid, and which allowed for mirror images of the pattern and for the colours to be transposed. Under surfaces were RLM 65 Hellblau (light blue).

The new scheme which was introduced in 1938 and deemed more suitable for a continental European conflict than the earlier RLM 61/62/63 combination, comprised just two colours, both greens, RLM 70 Schwarzgrün (black green) and RLM 71 Dunkelgrün (dark green); again in a straight-edged 'splinter' pattern. Applied using factory paint charts that were also based upon a grid, it also allowed the two colours to be mirrored and transposed. The under surfaces remained in RLM 65 Hellblau (light blue).

Fighter aircraft such as the relatively new monoplane Messerschmitt Bf 109 and Bf 110 were manufactured and delivered in the new RLM 70 Schwarzgrün and RLM 71 Dunkelgrün upper surfaces with RLM 65 Hellblau under surfaces from the outset.

The majority of the Luftwaffe aircraft involved in the Polish

Campaign had either been repainted, in part or wholly, or manufactured from new, in the new two-tone RLM 70/71 upper surface scheme by September 1939, although some of the older bomber types such as the Do 17Es of KG 77 and Do 17Fs of AufklGr 124, and some of the Ju 52 transports of the KGzbV units, were still in the earlier three-tone 'splinter' RLM 61/62/63 upper surface camouflage which had been introduced in 1936.

Some of the previous generation biplane fighters and ground attack aircraft that were still in service in September 1939, such as the Heinkel He 51 and Arado Ar 68 which had been delivered in RLM 01 Silber (silver) or RLM 02 Grau (grey – in fact a green-grey shade), and the Henschel Hs 123s, of II(S)/LG 2 for example still in the RLM 61/62/63 straight-edged 'splinter' upper surface scheme with RLM 65 Hellblau under surfaces, were gradually repainted in the new two-tone green RLM 70 Schwarzgrün and RLM 71 Dunkelgrün 'splinter' upper surface scheme.

National markings

Luftwaffe national markings of this period consisted of a narrow, white-bordered black cross, (balkenkreuz), which was itself thinly outlined in black, laid down to specific proportions and dimensions for individual aircraft types, applied above and below the mainplanes and on the fuselage sides of all operational aircraft.

A swastika, (hakenkreuz), also in black, bordered by a narrow white outline which was then bordered by a thin black outline, again laid down to specific proportions and dimensions for individual aircraft types, was applied on both sides of the vertical flying surfaces, invariably placed centrally across the fin and rudder, overlapping the hinge line – this central position being a left-over from when the hakenkreuz was placed on a white disk on a broad red (RLM 23 Rot) band, which was discontinued in 1938.

The horizontal red band and white circle on the original RLM 61/62/63 finished aircraft was generally painted out, usually in RLM 61 Dunkelbraun, merely leaving a thin white outline to the 'arms' of the swastika.

▲ Formation of Heinkel He III bombers. (Photo: Imperial War Museum)

Luftwaffe code system

The identification coding system, generally applied to the fuselage sides and wing under surfaces of Luftwaffe bombers and transports, twin-engined fighters and reconnaissance/communications aircraft, was also changed in the spring of 1939 – from the previous five-character code to a somewhat more simplified four-character system.

The first two characters invariably positioned to the left of the fuselage balkenkreuz, comprised a letter/number or number/letter combination, which identified the parent unit – usually the Geschwader (Group), or in smaller units the Gruppe (Wing). The next character immediately to the right of the fuselage balkenkreuz, and invariably painted in the Staffel (squadron) or Stab (Staff) colour, identified the individual aircraft within the staffel, whilst the fourth and last character identified the Staffel within the Gruppe.

Typical examples to illustrate this practice include:-
Junkers Ju 87B-1 of 1./StG 1, coded A5+DH.
A5 = Stukageschwader 1.
D = individual aircraft letter painted in the staffel colour in this instance, white.
H = 1 Staffel/I Gruppe identification letter,
or
Heinkel He 111H-1 of 6./KG 4, coded 5J + HP.
5J = Kampfgeschwader 4.
H = individual aircraft letter painted in the Staffel colour in this instance, yellow.
P = 6 Staffel/III Gruppe identification letter.
(see table A on page 36)

Single-engined fighters, such as the Bf 109, sported an individual Staffel coloured numeral system initially introduced on the He 51 and Ar 68 biplanes in 1936. These coloured numerals, in white, red or yellow, to reflect the Staffel within the Gruppe, and often outlined in a contrasting colour, were generally placed in front of the fuselage balkenkreuz on both sides. On the rear fuselage, to the rear of the balkenkreuz, appeared a system of 'bars' which identified the Gruppe within the Geschwader

Stab (Staff) machines sported a system of chevrons and bars in the same place as the Staffel numerals in front of the fuselage balkenreuze.
(see tables B and C on page 37)

Tactical markings

The use of specific tactical markings does not appear to have been widely used by Luftwaffe aircraft during the invasion of Poland or the subsequent Phoney War period. However several Do 17Es of KG 77 and Do 17Zs of KG 3 appear to have sported a fairly broad yellow (Gelb 04?) band around their noses in September 1939, but this 'marking' may have been a left-over from manoeuvres undertaken in the weeks leading up to the outbreak of war.

L'Armée de l'Air

The Armée de l'Air was formed as an independent service In April 1933. The command covered the four major regions of France, with HQs in Dijon, Paris, Aix-en-Provence and Tunis, North Africa. The command control centred on the bases rather than the units, which created an inflexibility that showed up during the 'Blitzkrieg'.

The Armée de l'Air's operational unit structure was based upon World War One style Escadres, (ie Air Divisions, broadly equivalent to an RAF Group), which generally comprised two or sometimes three Groupes, (equivalent to RAF Wings), which in turn were made up of two or three Escadrilles (Squadrons). The Escadres generally operated a mix of Fighter, Bomber and Reconnaissance Groupes.

The Groupes themselves were based upon the type and role of the aircraft, for instance...
Groupe de Chasse (GC) – Fighter Wing
Groupe de Bombardement (GB) – Bomber Wing
Groupe de Reconnaissance (GR) – Reconnaissance Wing
Groupe de Bombardement d'Assault (GBA) – Ground Attack Bomber Wing
Groupe Aérien d'Observation (GAO) – General Observation/Army Cooperation Wing
Groupe de Chasse de Nuit (GCN) or Escadrille de Chasse de Nuit (ECN) – Night Fighter Wing or Night Fighter Squadron
The Groupes were numbered 1e, 2e, 3e etc, followed by their role designation, ... de Chasse, ... de Bombardement,... de Reconnaissance etc. When written down, the Groupes were identified by arabic numerals, (1, 2, 3 etc) and the Escadrilles within the Groupes were numbered in roman numerals, (I, II, III).

For example, 6e Groupe de Chasse comprised I Escadrille, II Escadrille and III Escadrille, (ie GC I/6, II/6 and III/6) and 11e Groupe de Bombardement comprised I Escadrille and II Escadrille (ie GB I/11 and II/11).

Aircraft complements and strengths varied. Single engine fighter Groupes de Chasse generally had between twenty and thirty aircraft on strength – individual Escadrilles comprising some ten to fifteen aircraft, which were further split in to Patrouilles (Flights) of three or four aircraft. Similarly, Groupes de Bombardement comprised around twenty or so bombers and Groupes de Reconnaissance around ten to fifteen aircraft.

Shortly after war was declared in September 1939, the French Air Ministry reorganised the regions in to zones, to cover the French Army's land forces, which was always the Armée de l'Air's primary function, and as such were responsible to the Army Group commander. Each zone contained an Escadre (Air Division), with various Groupes forming together to create Groupements of various strengths. Individual Army formations also had their own Groupes Aérien d'Observation (GAOs), General Observation/Army Cooperation Wings.

Camouflage

Just before the outbreak of war, Armée de l'Air Fighters were generally finished in either overall Vert Emaillite (dark green) with polished natural metal cowlings and fuselage side panels or were simply left in overall natural metal with silver painted fabric areas. Day bombers were invariably the same overall Vert Emaillite (dark green), and night bombers overall Chocolat, (chocolate/dark brown), both types often sporting polished natural metal engine cowlings.

On 6 December 1938, following the Munich Crisis in the September, the French Air Ministry issued an official circular, Instruction 1422, calling for the immediate camouflaging of all land-based operational aircraft.

Initially, the order only specified the application of Kaki (khaki – a yellowish/brown olive green shade) for the mainplane upper and fuselage side surfaces. A little later Gris Bleu Clair (light blue grey) was added for the undersides. Both these Kaki and Gris Bleu Clair colours had a matt finish and were applied in a undulating soft-edged demarcation line along the fuselage sides and the wing leading edges.

However, this measure was deemed insufficient, and it was stipulated that one or more of three additional colours, mixed from a range of available shades including Vert Foncé (dark green), Ombre Calcinee (ivory), Terre de Sienne (sienna/light earth), Blanc (white), Noir (black) and even Rouge (red) and Bleu (blue) in order to obtain various camouflage colours, were to be applied to the upper surfaces in large soft-edged 'patches', with no particular geometrical shape. As can be imagined, the resulting variations in tone and shade could be described as almost infinite!

A certain degree of standardisation was attained however, following the issue of standard colour charts by the paint manufacturers during 1939, which included the following colours:-
Chocolat (dark brown), Vert Emaillite (dark green), Gris Bleu Foncé (dark blue grey) , Vert (green) , Vert Foncé (dark green), Terre Foncé or Brun Foncé (dark earth), Terre de Sienne (sienna/light earth), Kaki (khaki), Sable (sand) and Gris Bleu Clair (light blue grey).

It was during this period that Gris Bleu Foncé (dark blue

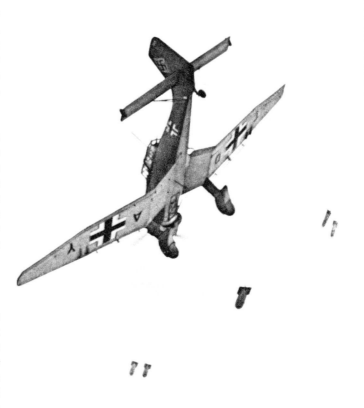

▲ Bombs falling away from a Junkers Ju 87 Stuka dive-bomber. The photograph appears to have been taken from a following aircraft. (Photo: Imperial War Museum)

grey) and Terre Foncé/Brun Foncé (dark earth) made their appearance and were used almost universally thereafter in combination with Kaki on the upper surfaces of Armée de l'Air aircraft, with Gris Bleu Clair (light blue grey) undersides. In May 1939, the camouflage scheme was further 'standardised' with Vert (green) replacing Kaki on the production line of new build aircraft.

Aircraft already in service were progressively camouflaged by their units during 1939, while the new production machines were camouflaged accordingly on the production lines at the factories. The painting of production line aircraft was made following the instructions issued by the Direction Technique et Industrielle (DTI), which with typical Gallic panache, gave them, if not perfect instructions, at least a guide to follow.

In general, the camouflage scheme was applied without following any precise camouflage patterns, unlike the British Air Ministry and German Reichluftministerium (RLM) aircraft painting instructions, although certain factories did at least follow a certain degree of uniformity of 'style' of camouflage pattern, according to aircraft type.

Some types such as the MB 174 and LeO 451 received a more or less 'standard' scheme, but the best that can be said about the application of the French 'multi-colour' upper surface scheme is that it remained fairly random throughout the Phoney War and Battle of France period – and beyond, in to the rest of the war.

National markings

National markings comprised three-colour roundels, in Bleu (blue), Blanc (white) and Rouge (red) outer, positioned

Dewoitine D.501, No 234, R-264, '1', 5 Escadrille, Groupe de Chasse GC III/3, Dijon, France, May 1939.

Finished in the overall natural metal/silver paint finish of the period, the upper surface of the cowling in front of the cockpit has an application of what appears to be Vert Emaillite (dark green) in a stylised form of anti-glare panel. This aircraft was flown by Capt Roger Trouillard, the unit's Commandant.

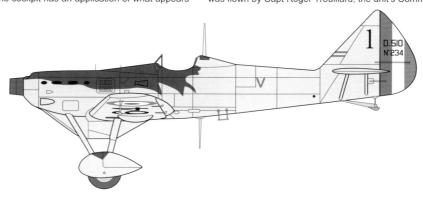

Mureaux 117R-2, No 174, X-398, '2', GAO 1/551, Malmaison, France, mid-1939.

GAO 151 was one of several reconnaissance units 'watching' the Franco-German border immediately prior to and following the outbreak of war. The aircraft were camouflaged in a three-tone upper surface scheme of Gris Bleu Foncé (dark blue grey) and Terre Foncé (dark earth) and either Kaki (Khaki) or Vert (Green) on the upper surfaces with Gris Bleu Clair (light blue grey) undersides. Note the undulating soft-edged demarcation line along the fuselage sides.

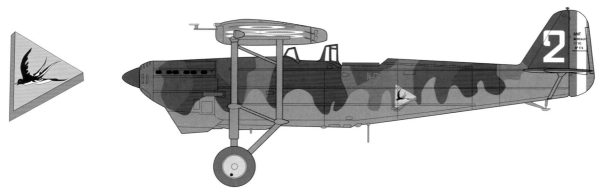

Morane-Saulnier MS.406, No 272, 2 Escadrille, Groupe de Chasse (GC) I/3, Velaine-en-Haye, France, September 1939.

The MS.406 was the most widely-used Armée de l'Air single-seat fighter in service at the outbreak of war and GC I/3 was amongst the first Groupes de Chasse to be re-equipped with the type. Camouflaged in the three-tone upper surface scheme of Gris Bleu Foncé (dark blue grey) and Terre Foncé (dark earth) and either Kaki (Khaki) or Vert (Green) on the upper surfaces with Gris Bleu Clair (light blue grey) undersides. This particular aircraft was flown by Capt Bernard Challe, CO of 2 Escadrille. Note the emblem of SPA 69 on the fuselage side and the blank white disc awaiting the individual aircraft number.

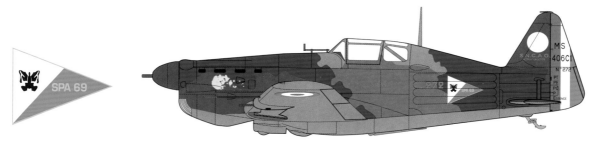

Bloch MB.151, No 66, '5', GC II/10, Rouen-Boos, France, early 1940.

One of the other main fighter types operated by the Armée de l'Air, was the Bloch MB.151, which was soon found to be underpowered and was rapidly replaced by the improved MB.152. Camouflaged in the three-tone upper surface scheme of Gris Bleu Foncé (dark blue grey) and Terre Foncé (dark earth) and either Kaki (Khaki) or Vert (Green) on the upper surfaces with Gris Bleu Clair (light blue grey) undersides. Note the large roundel on the fuselage.

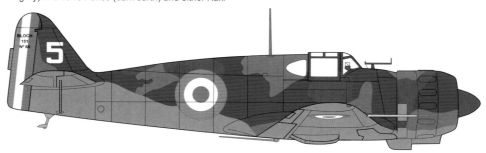

Not to any scale

Curtiss Hawk 75A-1, No 99, X-898 '9', 1 Escadrille, GC I/4, Norrent-Fontes, France, April 1940.

The Armée de l'Air ordered several hundred of the American designed and manufactured Hawk 75 in several variants, which proved to be amongst one of the best fighters in Armée de l'Air service in 1940. Camouflaged in the three-tone upper surface scheme of Gris Bleu Foncé (dark blue grey) and Terre Foncé (dark

earth) and either Kaki (Khaki) or Vert (Green) on the upper surfaces with Gris Bleu Clair (light blue grey) undersides. Note the large roundel on the fuselage and the Matricule Militaire, X-898, in black under the wings.

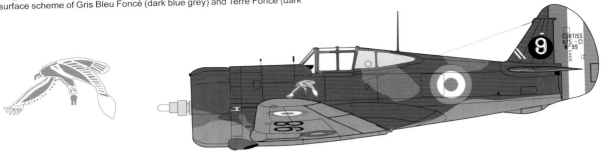

Morane-Saulnier MS.406, No 1000, L-590, the Centre d'Instruction de la Chasse, Etampes, France, February 1940.

MS.406s also equipped several other Armée de l'Air units, units, such as this Fighter Pilot's School which served as an Operational Training Unit. Camouflaged in the three-tone upper surface scheme of Gris Bleu Foncé (dark blue grey) and Terre Foncé (dark earth) and either Kaki (Khaki) or Vert (Green) on the upper

surfaces with Gris Bleu Clair (light blue grey) undersides. Note the enormous size of the fuselage roundel and the Matricule Militaire, L-590, in white under the wings.

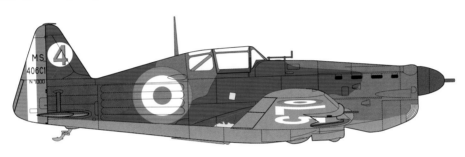

Morane-Saulnier MS.406, No 449, L-9xx (full MM unknown), GC I/2, Xaffévilliers, France, March 1940.

Camouflaged in the three-tone upper surface scheme of Gris Bleu Foncé (dark blue grey) and Terre Foncé (dark earth) and either Kaki (Khaki) or Vert (Green) on the upper surfaces with 'panels' of what appear to be either pale grey or

silver on the fuselage side and nose. Gris Bleu Clair (light blue grey) undersides. Matricule Militaire in white under the wings. This aircraft was flown by Capt R Patureau-Mirand.

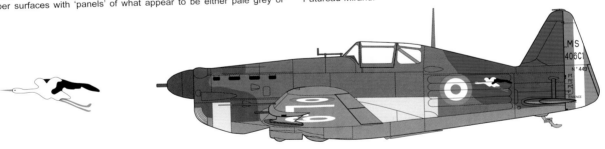

Morane-Saulnier MS.406, No 989, L-579, GC II/3, Connantre, France, April 1940.

Camouflaged in the three-tone upper surface scheme of Gris Bleu Foncé (dark blue grey) and Terre Foncé (dark earth) and either Kaki (Khaki) or Vert (Green) on the upper surfaces with Gris Bleu Clair (light blue grey) undersides. Note the

diagonal red and blue 'ribbon' down the fuselage side and the Matricule Militaire, L-579, in white under the wings.

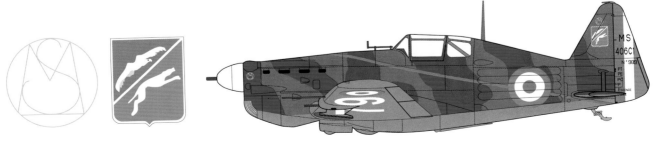

Not to any scale

above and below the mainplanes and generally, (although not invariably) on the fuselage sides. These roundels were usually of a 1-2-3 ratio and varied in size depending upon the date of manufacture – (during early 1939 the roundels were smaller, but were then increased is diameter to improve visibility) – and aircraft manufacturer. Bleu, Blanc and Rouge vertical stripes, Bleu leading, were applied to the rudder which was standard practice for all French aircraft.

Aircraft markings

French aircraft could carry up to three different sets of aircraft numbers. On the rudder there usually appeared a three line Constructor's number applied over the rudder stripes. The first line was the name of the manufacturer. The second line was the aircraft type which also contained the configuration of the aircraft. For example all French single seat fighters carried a C1 suffix – C for Chasse (fighter) and 1 indicating a single-seater. The serial number below this was a simple register of the aircraft's number within the production run and could be viewed as the equivalent of the RAF's serial number or Luftwaffe's werknummer.

The Matricules Militaire, was a single letter and three number code applied, and to be read from underneath and to the rear of the aircraft, in large white or occasionally large black characters under the wings. However, by the late spring of 1940, new production aircraft were being delivered without Matricules Militaire markings and those on 'in service' aircraft were starting to be painted out.

Numerals identified the individual aircraft within the Escadrille. Pre- and early war practice had the numerals 1-12 for the first Escadrille of a Groupe and 14-25 for the second, but

this practice wasn't always adhered to. These numerals were generally applied to the fin, although they could also be applied to the fuselage sides. There was also considerable variation in the system, with many colours and sizes of numerals, and even the use of Roman or Arabian (as opposed to Arabic) numerals to further confuse. After April 1940, an attempt was made to standardise on large white individual aircraft numbers placed on the fuselage sides next to the roundel, with the numerals 1-20 for the first Escadrille and 21-40 for the second.

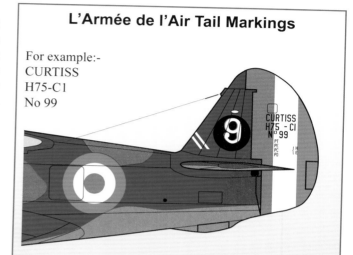

L'Armée de l'Air Tail Markings

For example:-
CURTISS
H75-C1
No 99

...identified this aircraft as a Curtiss-built Hawk 75A, single-seat fighter, with the Construction Number, 99, further revealing that it was from the first production Hawk 75A-1 batch. The white numeral 9 within the black disc on the fin was the individual aircraft identifiction number within the Escadrille

Breguet Br.693, No 91, Groupe de Bombardement d'Assault (Attack Bomber Group) GBA I/51, Toulouse-Francazal, France, April/May 1940.

Despite the great things that the Armée de l'Air expected from the type, which had not long been in service, the tadpole-shaped attack bomber tragically suffered a similar fate to that of the RAF's Fairey Battles – and were decimated in disastrous low-level ground attack operations. Camouflaged in the three-tone

upper surface scheme of Gris Bleu Foncé (dark blue grey) and Terre Foncé (dark earth) and either Kaki (Khaki) or Vert (Green) on the upper surfaces with Gris Bleu Clair (light blue grey) undersides.

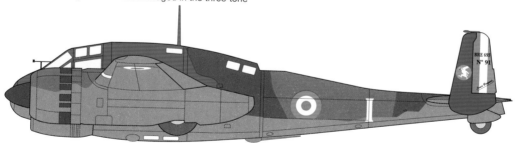

Breguet Br.693, No 23 of GBA I/54, Bessay, France, April/May 1940.

Immediately prior to the German invasion, two Groupes de Bombardment, GBA 51 and GBA 54, were in the process of re-equipping with the type together with GBA II/35 and by 10 May some fifty or so Br.693s were operational. Camouflaged in the three-tone upper surface scheme of Gris Bleu Foncé (dark blue grey) and Terre Foncé (dark earth) and either Kaki (Khaki) or Vert (Green)

on the upper surfaces with Gris Bleu Clair (light blue grey) undersides. Note the differing positions of the fuselage roundel of this aircraft and the Br.693 illustrated above, not to mention the variations in camouflage demarcations, typifying the lack of any specific camouflage and markings orders given to the French aircraft manufacturers at this time.

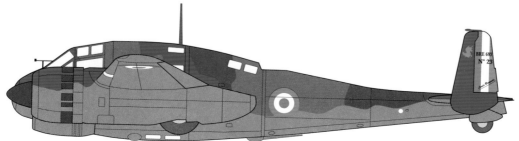

Not to any scale

Amiot 143, No 95, E-329, '12', Groupe de Bombardement II/22, Orléans, France, 1939/40.

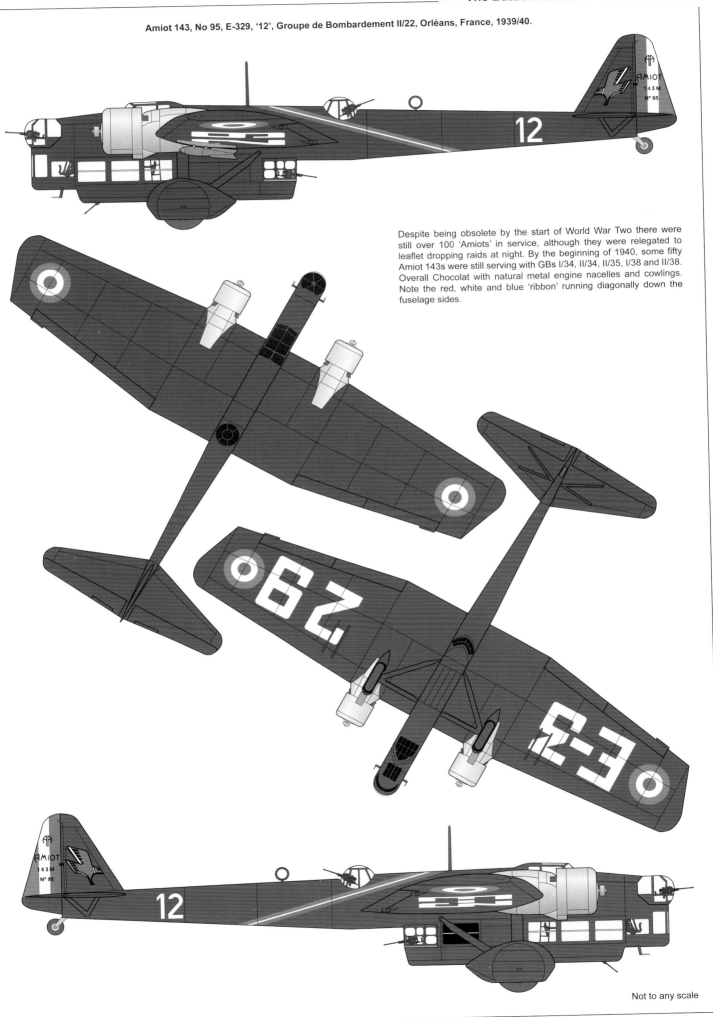

Despite being obsolete by the start of World War Two there were still over 100 'Amiots' in service, although they were relegated to leaflet dropping raids at night. By the beginning of 1940, some fifty Amiot 143s were still serving with GBs I/34, II/34, II/35, I/38 and II/38. Overall Chocolat with natural metal engine nacelles and cowlings. Note the red, white and blue 'ribbon' running diagonally down the fuselage sides.

Not to any scale

▲ A group of journalists from Dominions newspapers watch a flight of 56 Squadron Hawker Hurricane Mk.Is departing North Weald for a sortie over France in May 1940. In the foreground another Hurricane, P2764/US-P, stands at its dispersal point near the perimeter track on the south-western edge of the Essex airfield. (Photo: Imperial War Museum)

Fall Gelb, (Case Yellow), the German invasion of France, Belgium and the Netherlands started in the early hours of 10 May 1940, and ended the so called 'Phoney War'.

The invading German Army was divided into three Army Groups. Army Group A, commanded by Gerd von Rundstedt, Army Group B, under Fedor von Bock, and Army Group C under Wilhelm Ritter von Leeb. The invasion consisted of two main features. The first was when German armoured units pushed through the heavily wooded Ardennes area, which contained a poor road network, making it implausible as a route for invasion, to cut off and surround the Allied units that had advanced into Belgium. In the second operation, Fall Rot, (Case Red), executed from 5 June, German forces outflanked the Maginot Line to attack the greater French territory.

The air forces

The Luftwaffe divided its forces into two groups. 1,815 combat, 487 transport and fifty glider aircraft were deployed to support Army Group B, whilst a further 3,286 combat aircraft were deployed to support Army Groups A and C.

The French Armée de l'Air had some 1,560 aircraft, and RAF Fighter Command some 680 machines, whilst RAF Bomber Command could contribute another 390 or so aircraft to operations. Most of the allied aircraft were obsolete types – amongst the fighter force only the British Hawker Hurricane and the French Dewoitine D.520 could contend with the German Messerschmitt Bf 109E on something approaching equal terms.

The French aviation industry had reached a considerable output, with an estimated reserve of nearly 2,000 aircraft. However, a chronic lack of vital parts, such as propellers, crippled this stock fleet. Only 29% (some 600) of the aircraft were serviceable, of which 170 were bombers.

Battle of the Netherlands

The Luftwaffe was guaranteed air superiority over the Netherlands. They allocated 247 medium bombers, 147 fighter aircraft, 424 transports and twelve seaplanes to direct operations over the Netherlands. The Dutch Air Force, the LuchtVaartAfdeling Militaire (LVA/ML), had a strength of

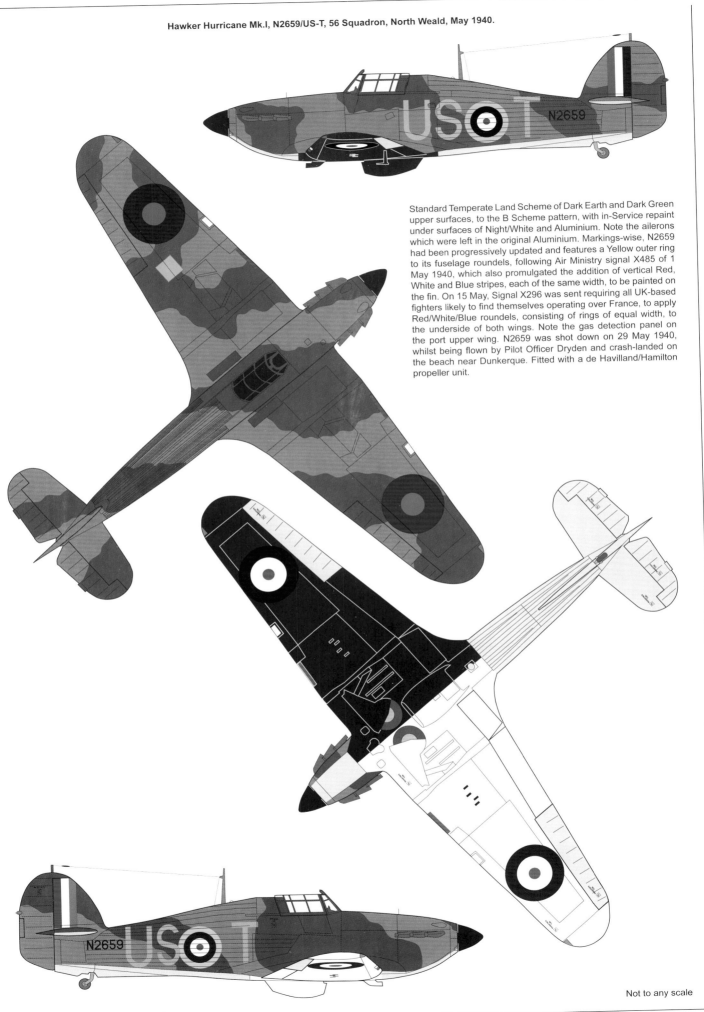

Hawker Hurricane Mk.I, N2659/US-T, 56 Squadron, North Weald, May 1940.

Standard Temperate Land Scheme of Dark Earth and Dark Green upper surfaces, to the B Scheme pattern, with in-Service repaint under surfaces of Night/White and Aluminium. Note the ailerons which were left in the original Aluminium. Markings-wise, N2659 had been progressively updated and features a Yellow outer ring to its fuselage roundels, following Air Ministry signal X485 of 1 May 1940, which also promulgated the addition of vertical Red, White and Blue stripes, each of the same width, to be painted on the fin. On 15 May, Signal X296 was sent requiring all UK-based fighters likely to find themselves operating over France, to apply Red/White/Blue roundels, consisting of rings of equal width, to the underside of both wings. Note the gas detection panel on the port upper wing. N2659 was shot down on 29 May 1940, whilst being flown by Pilot Officer Dryden and crash-landed on the beach near Dunkerque. Fitted with a de Havilland/Hamilton propeller unit.

Not to any scale

The Battle of Britain – Blitzkrieg!

Hawker Hurricane Mk.I, (serial unknown, overpainted but in the L-range)/UF-B, 601 Squadron, RAF Tangmere, May 1940.

UF-B is illustrated as she looked in early May 1940 prior to moving to France on detachment to Merville, St Valery. Standard Temperate Land Scheme of Dark Earth and Dark Green upper surfaces, to the A Scheme pattern, with Night/White under surfaces divided down the centreline. Note the lack of Yellow outer ring to the fuselage roundel and lack of fin stripes, which would have been added a few days later. Similarly the lack of underwing Red/White/Blue roundels, which would have also been added after the Air Ministry Signal X296 of 15 May. In June 1940 the squadron moved back to the UK to RAF Middle Wallop. Fitted with a de Havilland/Hamilton propeller unit.

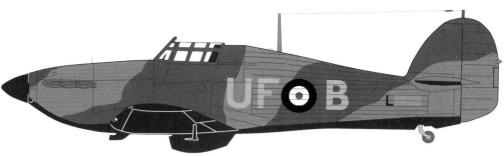

Hawker Hurricane Mk.I, L1774/LK-D, 87 Squadron, Lille/Seclin, France, May 1940.

L1774 is typical of the Hurricanes operating from the French mainland immediately after the start of the 'Blitzkrieg', with service applied Yellow outer ring to the fuselage roundels and narrow fin stripes. Standard Temperate Land Scheme of Dark Earth and Dark Green upper surfaces, to the A Scheme pattern, with Night/White under surfaces divided down the centreline. L1774 was shot down by a Bf 110 on 19 May 1940. Note the aircraft is still fitted with the Watts two-blade wooden propeller unit.

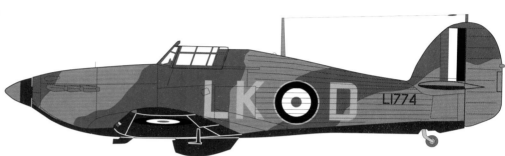

Supermarine Spitfire Mk.I, P9317/ZD-A, 222 Squadron, RAF Hornchurch, Essex, May 1940.

This profile is dated to a two week period between 1 May 1940, as it has had the Yellow outer ring added to the fuselage roundel and narrow fin stripes, but immediately prior to the 15 May introduction of underwing roundels for UK-based fighters likely to find themselves operating over France, as 222 Squadron did. Standard Temperate Land Scheme of Dark Earth and Dark Green upper surfaces, to the B Scheme pattern, with Night/White under surfaces divided down the centreline. Fitted with a de Havilland/Hamilton propeller unit.

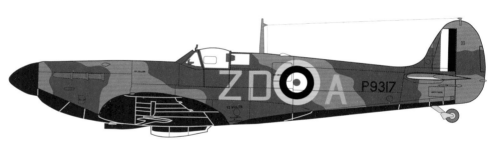

Boulton Paul Defiant Mk.I, L6977/PS-U, 264 Squadron, RAF Martlesham Heath, Suffolk, but temporarily operating out of RAF Duxford, Essex, May 1940.

Standard Temperate Land Scheme of Dark Earth and Dark Green upper surfaces, to the B Scheme pattern, with Night/White and Aluminium under surfaces. Note the fuselage roundels in the pre-war bright Blue and Red shades, and although the Yellow outer ring has not been added, the fin stripes have. Red/White/Blue roundels under the wings. On 13 may 1940, L6977 was one of five Defiants from B Flight to be shot down, with the pilot, Pilot Officer P E J Greenhouse and gunner Sergeant F D Greenhalgh both captured after baling out.

Hawker Hurricane Mk, L1754/DZ-E, 151 Squadron, RAF Martlesham Heath, Suffolk, May 1940.

Standard Temperate Land Scheme of Dark Earth and Dark Green upper surfaces, to the B Scheme pattern, with Night/White under surfaces divided down the centreline. Note how the Yellow outer ring has been added to the fuselage roundel but is truncated along the lower fuselage longeron and the style of fin flash with 9 inch wide Blue and White stripes with the whole of the remainder of the fin in Red. Red/White/Blue roundels under the wings. Fitted with a Rotol propeller unit.

Not to any scale

▲ The Junkers Ju 88A-1. The original bomber version of the highly adaptable Junkers 88 aircraft. (Photo: Imperial War Museum)

some 144 combat aircraft, half of which were destroyed within the first day of operations. The remainder was dispersed and accounted for only a handful of Luftwaffe aircraft shot down. In total the Militaire Luchtvaartafdeling flew a mere 332 sorties losing 110 of its aircraft.

The Luftwaffe's Transportgruppen also suffered heavily. Transporting the German paratroops had cost it 125 Ju 52s destroyed and forty-seven damaged, representing 50% of the fleet's strength. Most of these transports were destroyed on the ground, and some whilst trying to land under fire, as German forces had not properly secured the airfields and landing zones.

German armoured forces from the 9th Panzer Division reached Rotterdam on 13 May, and the Dutch Army surrendered in the evening of 14 May after the bombing of Rotterdam by Heinkel He 111s of KG 54. The capitulation document was signed on 15 May 1940. However, the Dutch troops in Zeeland and the overseas colonies continued the fight and Queen Wilhelmina established a government-in-exile in Britain.

The Battle for Belgium

The Germans were able to establish air superiority in Belgium with ease. Having completed thorough photographic reconnaissance missions, they destroyed eighty-three of the 179 aircraft of the Aeronautique Militaire within the first 24 hours. The Belgians flew seventy-seven operational missions but contributed little to the air campaign.

The Luftwaffe was assured air superiority over the Low Countries.

The German breakthrough at Sedan

On 13 May, Lieutenant-General Heinz Guderian's XIXth Army Corps' elite armoured formation forced three crossings near Sedan. The Luftwaffe concentrated most of its tactical bomber force to smash a hole in a narrow sector of the French lines by carpet bombing punctuated by dive bombing. Luftflotte 3, supported by Luftflotte 2, executed the heaviest

air bombardment the world had yet witnessed. The Luftwaffe committed two Stukageschwader to the assault, flying 300 sorties against French positions, with StG 77 alone flying 201 individual missions. A total of 3,940 sorties were flown by nine Kampfgeschwader, often in Gruppe strength.

Air battles over the Meuse

General Gaston-Henri Billotte, commander of the First Army Group whose right flank pivoted on Sedan, urged that the bridges across the Meuse River be destroyed by air attack. That day every available Allied light bomber was employed in an attempt to destroy the three bridges, but failed to hit them whilst suffering heavy losses.

The RAF's Advanced Air Striking Force (AASF) under the command of Air Vice-Marshal P H L Playfair, bore the brunt of these attacks. The plan called for the RAF to commit its bombers for the attack whilst receiving protection from French fighter Groupes. The British bombers received insufficient air cover and as a result some twenty-one French fighters and forty-eight British bombers, (44% of the AASF's strength), was destroyed.

The Armée de l'Air also tried to halt the German armoured columns, but the small French bomber force had been so badly mauled in the previous days, that only two dozen or so aircraft could be committed and several French bombers were shot down. The German anti-aircraft defences accounted for half of the Allied bombers destroyed. In just one day the Allies lost ninety bombers!

The French collapse

On 16 May, both Guderian and Rommel broke out of their bridgeheads and moved their Divisions many kilometres to the west as fast as they could push them. Guderian reached Marle, 80km from Sedan, while Rommel crossed the river Sambre at Le Cateau, 100km from his bridgehead at Dinant.

The Panzer Corps were now well stretched out, exhausted, low

▲ German Dornier 17Zs of II./KG77 being serviced on Freux auxiliary airfield in Belgium, circa May/June 1940. The type was successful in the campaigns against Poland and France but subsequently suffered heavy losses over Britain during the autumn of 1940. (Photo: Imperial War Museum)

on fuel, (many tanks had broken down), and had put themselves in a very vulnerable position. There was a dangerous gap between them and the infantry. A determined attack by a fresh and large enough allied mechanised force would have cut the Panzers off and wiped them out.

However, the French High Command was reeling from the shock of the sudden offensive and was infected by a sense of defeatism. On the morning of 15 May French Prime Minister Paul Reynaud telephoned the new Prime Minister of the United Kingdom, Winston Churchill, and said, "We have been defeated."

Churchill flew to Paris on 16 May and immediately recognised the gravity of the situation when he observed that the French government was already burning its archives and was preparing for an evacuation of the capital.

The German advance to the Channel

The Panzer troops used 17 and 18 May to refuel, eat, sleep, and return more tanks to working order. On 18 May, Rommel caused the French to give up Cambrai by merely feinting an armoured attack toward the city.

The Allies seemed incapable of coping with such events. On 19 May the Germans started to cut off the Allies' escape. The Panzer Corps started moving again and smashed through the weakened British 18th and 23rd Territorial Divisions, occupied Amiens and secured the westernmost bridge over the river Somme at Abbeville which isolated the British, French, Dutch and Belgian forces in the north and that evening, a reconnaissance unit from 2nd Panzer Division reached Noyelles-sur-Mer, 100 kilometres (62 miles) to the west. From there they were able to see the Somme estuary and the English Channel.

VIII Fliegerkorps under the command of Wolfram von Richthofen committed the Ju 87s of StG 77 and StG 2 to cover this 'dash' to the channel coast. Heralded as the Stukas' 'finest hour', these units responded via an extremely efficient ground-to-air communications system to the Panzer Divisions' every request for support, which effectively blasted a path for the Army. The Ju 87s were particularly effective at breaking up attacks along the flanks of the German forces, destroying

fortified positions, and disrupting rear-area supply chains.

The Weygand plan

On 20 May French Prime Minister Paul Reynaud dismissed Maurice Gamelin and replaced him with Maxime Weygand. Weygand immediately attempted to devise new tactics to contain the Germans – what was to be known as the 'Weygand Plan'. He ordered his forces to pinch off the German armoured spearhead by combining attacks from the north and the south. On the map this seemed like a feasible mission. However, the condition of the Allied Divisions was far worse than envisaged. Both in the south and the north they could only muster only a handful of tanks.

On 22 May the German High Command ordered Guderian's XIXth Panzer Corps to press north and push onto the Channel ports of Boulogne and Calais. This position was to the rear of the British and Allied forces to the north. The French tried to attack south to the east of Arras with infantry and tanks, but by now the German infantry had begun to catch up, and the attack was stopped by the German 32nd Infantry Division.

The Dunkirk evacuation

In the early hours of 23 May, Gort ordered a retreat from Arras. By now he had no faith in Weygand's proposal to try to hold a pocket on the Flemish coast. Gort knew that the ports needed to supply such a foothold were already being threatened. That same day the 2nd Panzer Division had assaulted Boulogne. The British garrison there surrendered on 25 May, although 4,368 troops were evacuated. This British decision to withdraw was much criticised by the French.

The 10th Panzer Division attacked Calais on 24 May. British reinforcements (the 3rd Royal Tank Regiment equipped with Cruiser tanks and the 30th Motor Brigade) had been hastily landed 24 hours before the Germans attacked. The Siege of Calais lasted for four days. The British defenders were finally overwhelmed and surrendered at approximately 4.00pm on 26 May whilst the last French troops were evacuated in the early hours of 27 May.

The 1st Panzer Division was ready to attack Dunkerque on 25 May, but Hitler ordered it to halt the day before. This remains

Supermarine Spitfire Mk.I, P9434/GR-W, 92 Squadron, RAF Northolt, May/June 1940.

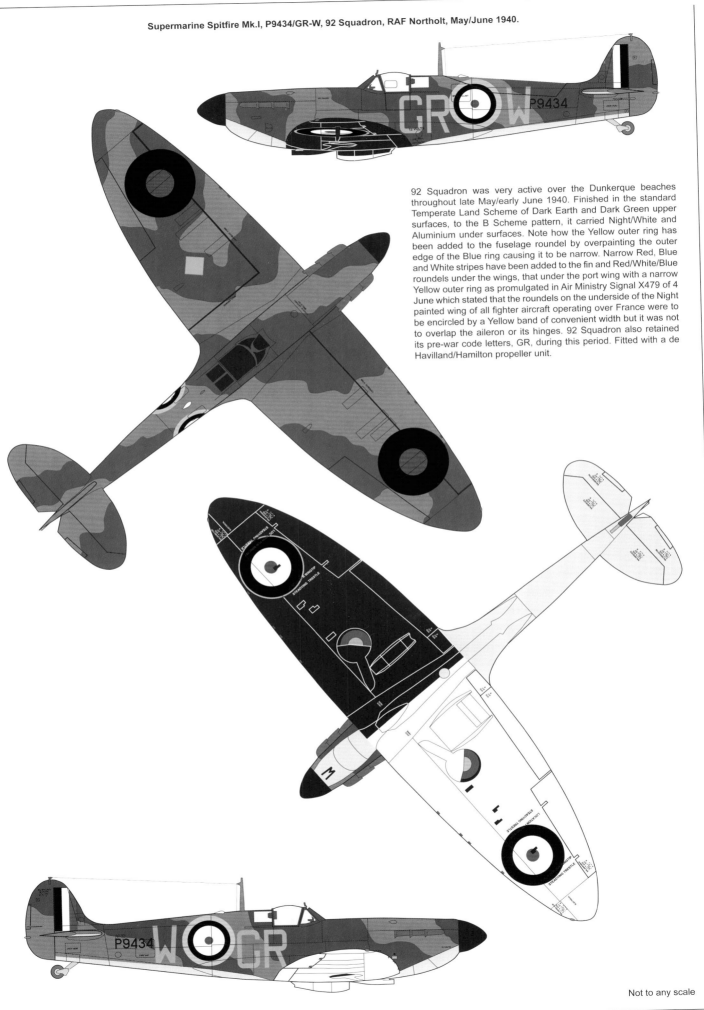

92 Squadron was very active over the Dunkerque beaches throughout late May/early June 1940. Finished in the standard Temperate Land Scheme of Dark Earth and Dark Green upper surfaces, to the B Scheme pattern, it carried Night/White and Aluminium under surfaces. Note how the Yellow outer ring has been added to the fuselage roundel by overpainting the outer edge of the Blue ring causing it to be narrow. Narrow Red, Blue and White stripes have been added to the fin and Red/White/Blue roundels under the wings, that under the port wing with a narrow Yellow outer ring as promulgated in Air Ministry Signal X479 of 4 June which stated that the roundels on the underside of the Night painted wing of all fighter aircraft operating over France were to be encircled by a Yellow band of convenient width but it was not to overlap the aileron or its hinges. 92 Squadron also retained its pre-war code letters, GR, during this period. Fitted with a de Havilland/Hamilton propeller unit.

Not to any scale

The Battle of Britain – Blitzkrieg!

Hawker Hurricane Mk.I, N2319/VY-P, 85 Squadron, Lille-Seclin, France, May 1940.

Pilot: Sergeant Geoffrey 'Sammy' Allard

As part of the Air Component of the BEF from the outbreak of war, 85 Squadron was at the forefront of the fighting in France following the German attack on 10 May. Standard Temperate Land Scheme of Dark Earth and Dark Green upper surfaces, to the A Scheme pattern, with Night/White under surfaces divided down the centreline. On 10 May Sergeant Allard destroyed two He 111s plus a 'probable' in this machine, which was itself lost on 17 May 1940.

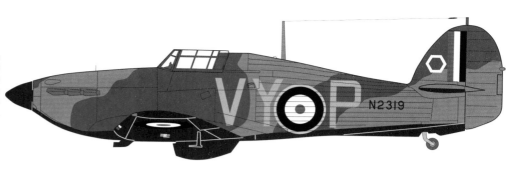

Hawker Hurricane Mk.I, L2045/SD-A, 501 Squadron, Béthienville, France, May 1940.

No 501 was one of the first UK-based squadrons sent to France immediately following the German attack on 10 May. Standard Temperate Land Scheme of Dark Earth and Dark Green upper surfaces, to the A Scheme pattern, with Night/White under surfaces divided down the centreline. This particular machine was damaged on 15 May when Sergeant Proctor force landed it safely, after which it was returned by rail and sea to the UK, eventually ending its service career in the FAA in May 1943.

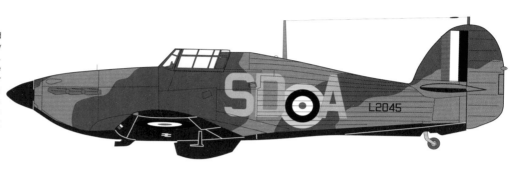

Supermarine Spitfire Mk.I, N3200/QV-, 19 Squadron, RAF Hornchurch, Essex, May 1940.

Pilot: Squadron Leader G D Stephenson

For some reason this particular machine never had an individual aircraft letter applied, despite having the Yellow outer ring to the fuselage roundels and fin stripes added by the squadron. Finished in the standard Temperate Land Scheme of Dark Earth and Dark Green upper surfaces, to the B Scheme pattern, with Night/White and Aluminium under surfaces, N3200 crash landed on the beach near Calais on 26 May 1940, where the pilot, Squadron Leader G D Stephenson, was captured.

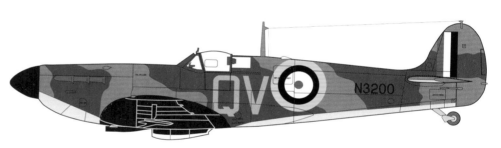

Supermarine Spitfire PR Mk.IB, P9331, 212 Squadron, Lille-Seclin, France, May 1940.

212 Squadron was reformed at Heston in February 1940 as a strategic photographic reconnaissance unit working closely with the Photographic Development Unit (PDU – which became the Photographic Reconnaissance Unit (PRU) in July 1940). It briefly operated Spitfire Mk.Is that were modified to carry cameras and a few camera-equipped Blenheims, before being absorbed in to the PDU in June 1940. Three-aircraft detachments were rotated to operate from the French mainland, and when they were forced to evacuate their base at Lille-Seclin on 14 June, P9331 was abandoned and captured by the Germans. Finish is thought to have been overall Cosmic, (later named PRU Blue), with Red/White/Blue roundels, those on the fuselage outlined in white. Note the white spinner and Medium Sea Grey serial number.

Boulton Paul Defiant Mk.I, L7036/TW-H, 141 Squadron, RAF Turnhouse, Scotland, May/June 1940.

141 was the second Defiant squadron to form, receiving its aircraft in April and becoming operational at the beginning of June 1940. Standard Temperate Land Scheme of Dark Earth and Dark Green upper surfaces, to the A Scheme pattern, with Night/White under surfaces divided down the centreline. Note the thin Yellow outline to the fuselage roundel added at unit level as was the fin flash.

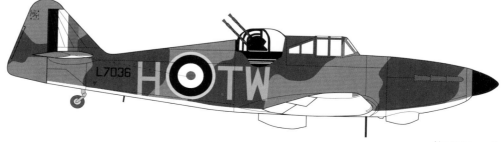

Not to any scale

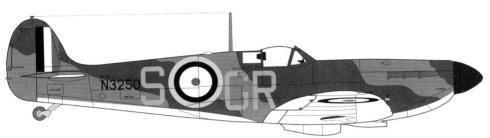

Supermarine Spitfire Mk.I, P9377/ZD-U, 222 Squadron, RAF Hornchurch, Essex, May/June 1940.
Pilot: Pilot Officer Roy Morant

One of the many victims of 'Operation Dynamo', the evacuation of the Dunkerque area beaches, P9377 was shot down on 1 June, whilst being flown by Pilot Officer Roy Morant, who set fire to it on the beach. he returned to the UK on a cross-Channel steamer. Standard Temperate Land Scheme of Dark Earth and Dark Green upper surfaces, to the B Scheme pattern, with Night/White under surfaces divided down the centreline. Note the Yellow thin outline to the port underwing roundel introduced from 4 June 1940. De Havilland/Hamilton propeller unit.

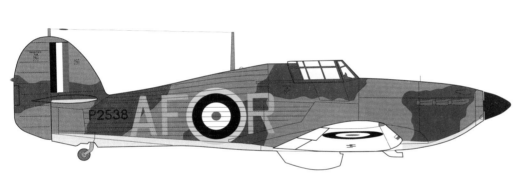

Supermarine Spitfire Mk.I, N3250/GR-S, 92 Squadron, RAF Hornchurch, Essex, May/June 1940.
Pilot: Pilot Officer Alan Wright

Another Spitfire squadron operating out of Hornchurch and covering the 'Dunkirk Evacuation' was 92. N3250, which was damaged on 2 June, was finished in the standard Temperate Land Scheme of Dark Earth and Dark Green upper surfaces, to the B Scheme pattern, with Night/White under surfaces divided down the centreline. Red/White/Blue roundels under the wings, that under the port wing with a narrow Yellow outer ring. Note how the Yellow outer ring has been added to the fuselage roundel by overpainting the outer edge of the Blue ring causing it to be narrow. Fitted with a de Havilland/Hamilton propeller unit. (see also 4-view on p51)

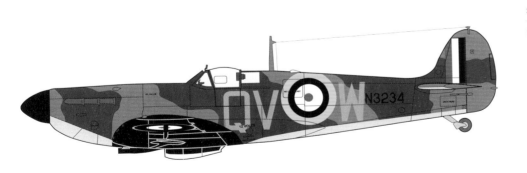

Hawker Hurricane Mk.I, P2538/AF-R, 607 Squadron, RAF Croydon, May/June 1940.

Following their evacuation from the French mainland on 20 May, the remnants, 607 Squadron reformed at Croydon before transferring to Usworth in Northumberland where it recouped until sent south again in early September. Standard Temperate Land Scheme of Dark Earth and Dark Green upper surfaces, to the A Scheme pattern, with Night/White and Aluminium under surfaces. Red/White/Blue roundels under the wings, the one under the port wing with a narrow Yellow outer ring. Note the narrow fin stripes, probably 5 inches wide. Fitted with a de Havilland/Hamilton propeller unit.

Supermarine Spitfire Mk.I, N3234/QV-W, 19 Squadron, Hornchurch, Essex, May/June 1940.

19 Squadron was also temporarily, Hornchurch for a brief spell during late May/early June 1940, whilst covering the evacuation of the Dunkerque area beaches, before returning to Duxford. Standard Temperate Land Scheme of Dark Earth and Dark Green upper surfaces, to the B Scheme pattern, with Night/White and Aluminium under surfaces. Red/White/Blue roundels under the wings, that under the port wing with a narrow Yellow outer ring. Fitted with a de Havilland/Hamilton propeller unit.

Bristol Blenheim Mk.IV, N6232/RT-P, 114 Squadron, Vraux, France, May 1940.

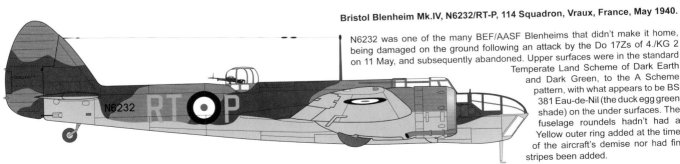

N6232 was one of the many BEF/AASF Blenheims that didn't make it home, being damaged on the ground following an attack by the Do 17Zs of 4./KG 2 on 11 May, and subsequently abandoned. Upper surfaces were in the standard Temperate Land Scheme of Dark Earth and Dark Green, to the A Scheme pattern, with what appears to be BS 381 Eau-de-Nil (the duck egg green shade) on the under surfaces. The fuselage roundels hadn't had a Yellow outer ring added at the time of the aircraft's demise nor had fin stripes been added.

Not to any scale

Fairey Battle Mk.I, L5145/PH-D, 12 Squadron, Amifontaine, France, May 1940.

Standard Temperate Land Scheme of Dark Earth and Dark Green upper surfaces, to the A Scheme pattern, with Night under surfaces. Note the narrow

Yellow outline to the fuselage roundel and the Red/White/Blue stripes covering the whole of the fin area.

Fairey Battle Mk.I, L5190/PH-P, 12 Squadron, Amifontaine, France, May 1940.

Standard Temperate Land Scheme of Dark Earth and Dark Green upper surfaces, to the A Scheme pattern, with Night under surfaces. Note the broader Yellow outline to the fuselage roundel and the 'block' of Red/White/Blue stripes

on the fin. Flown by Pilot Officer A W Mathews, L5190 force-landed on 10 May during an attack on a German column near Junglister, Luxemburg.

Fairey Battle Mk.I, P2204/PH-K, 12 Squadron, Amifontaine, France, May 1940.
Crewed by: Flg Off D E Garland, Sergeant T Gray and LAC L Reynolds

Standard Temperate Land Scheme of Dark Earth and Dark Green upper surfaces, to the A Scheme pattern, with Night under surfaces. Note the broad Yellow outline to the fuselage roundel and the 'angled' Red/White/Blue stripes on the fin. P2204 was shot down in flames in a low-level attack on the Veldwezelt

Bridge over the Albert Canal on Sunday 12 May 1940. Only Garland and Gray got the VC, their gunner Leadind Aircraftsman Lawrence Reynolds was not decorated although all three share the same grave.

Fairey Battle Mk.I, P2332/PH-F, 12 Squadron, Amifontaine, France, May 1940.
Pilot: Flg Off N M Thomas

Standard Temperate Land Scheme of Dark Earth and Dark Green upper surfaces, to the A Scheme pattern, with Night under surfaces. Note the broad Yellow outline to the fuselage roundel and the 'angled' Red/White/ lue stripes on the fin. P2332 was shot down and force-landed largely intact on the same

mission as P2204/PH-K above, although Thomas' target was the Vroenhoven bridge at Maastricht. The aircraft came down in the target area.

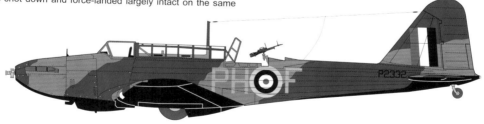

Fairey Battle Mk.I, N2150/PH-Y, 12 Squadron, Sougé, France, June 1940.

Standard Temperate Land Scheme of Dark Earth and Dark Green upper surfaces, to the B Scheme pattern, with Night under surfaces. Note the narrower

Yellow outline to the fuselage roundel and the 'angled' Red/White/Blue stripes covering the whole of the fin area. N2150 was abandoned at Nantes on 15 June when the squadron evacuated back to the UK.

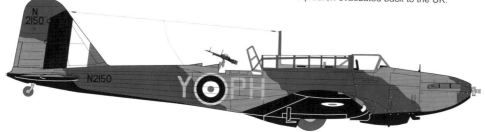

Not to any scale

Fairey Battle Mk.I, (serial unknown – overpainted)/RH-L, 88 Squadron, Mourmelon, France, May 1940.

Standard Temperate Land Scheme of Dark Earth and Dark Green upper surfaces, to the B Scheme pattern, with Night under surfaces. Note the Yellow outline added to the fuselage roundel and the Red/White/Blue stripes angled to match the rudder hinge line. RH-L was one of four damaged 88 Squadron Battles that were abandoned when the airfield was evacuated on 16 May.

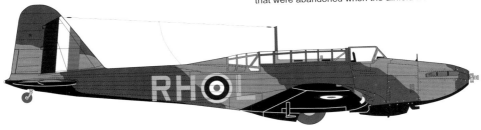

Fairey Battle Mk.I, P2191/PM-K, 103 Squadron, Bétheniville, France, May 1940.

Standard Temperate Land Scheme of Dark Earth and Dark Green upper surfaces, to the A Scheme pattern, with Night under surfaces. Note the position of the fuselage roundel, the placing of the code letters and the Red/White/Blue stripes angled to match the rudder hinge line and taking up the whole of the fin area. The serial number was painted over on the rudder but kept on the fuselage. P2191 crash-landed on 14 May 1940, following an attack on a pontoon bridge near Cauroy.

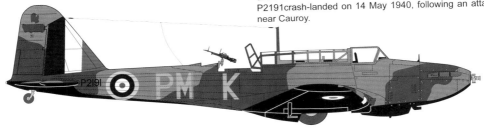

Fairey Battle Mk.I, L5234/PM-B, 103 Squadron, Bétheniville, France, May 1940.

Standard Temperate Land Scheme of Dark Earth and Dark Green upper surfaces, to the A Scheme pattern, with Night under surfaces. Note again the position of the fuselage roundel, the placing of the code letters and the Red/White/Blue stripes angled to match the rudder hinge line and taking up the whole of the fin area. L5234 crashed on take off on 16 May 1940, as the airfield was being evacuated and was abandoned.

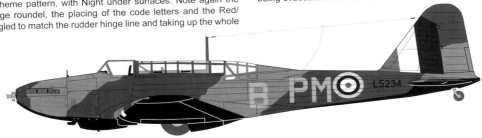

Fairey Battle Mk.I, L5446/PM-N, 103 Squadron, Bétheniville, France, May 1940.

Standard Temperate Land Scheme of Dark Earth and Dark Green upper surfaces, to the B Scheme pattern, with Night under surfaces. Note the narrower presentation of the Red/White/Blue fin stripes and 'correctly' positioned code letters. Red/White/Blue roundels were applied above the wings.

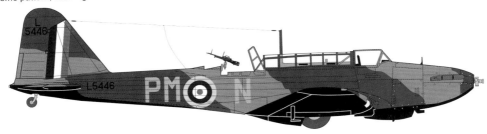

Fairey Battle Mk.I, (serial unknown – overpainted)/PM-L, 103 Squadron, Bétheniville, France, May/June 1940.

Standard Temperate Land Scheme of Dark Earth and Dark Green upper surfaces, to the B Scheme pattern, with Night under surfaces. As illustrated above, 103 Squadron had a tendency to 'move' the fuselage roundels and/or the code letters around, in this instance, with very small codes grouped together on the rear fuselage. Note also the fuselage roundel still hasn't had the Yellow outer ring added, there are no fin stripes and the cockpit glazing centre-section has been overpainted for night flying operations.

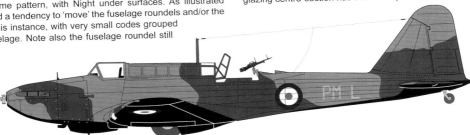

Not to any scale

Fairey Battle Mk.I, K9342/GB-V, 105 Squadron, Villeneuve, France, May 1940.

Standard Temperate Land Scheme of Dark Earth and Dark Green upper surfaces, to the A Scheme pattern, with Night under surfaces. Note the non-standard proportions of the fuselage roundel, with the broad Yellow outline slightly overlapping on to the 'G' of the squadron code and the name 'Nicki' in between the roundel and the individual aircraft letter 'V'. Narrow Red/White/Blue stripes on the fin following the angle of the rudder hinge. K9342 crash-landed on 14 May 1940 near Villamontry, Sedan – one of seven Battles from a formation of eleven to be shot down.

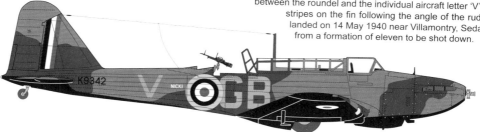

Fairey Battle Mk.I, (serial unknown – overpainted)/GB-O, 105 Squadron, Villeneuve, France, May 1940.

Standard Temperate Land Scheme of Dark Earth and Dark Green upper surfaces, to the A Scheme pattern, with Night under surfaces. Note again how the Yellow outline of the fuselage roundel slightly overlaps on to the 'B' of the squadron code and the smaller presentation of the individual aircraft letter 'O'.

Narrow Red/White/Blue stripes on the fin following the angle of the rudder hinge. GB-O was abandoned when the airfield was evacuated on 18 May 1940.

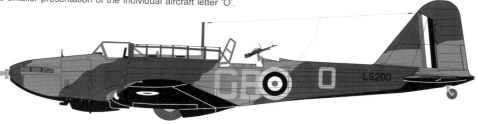

Fairey Battle Mk.I, L5231/QT-G, 142 Squadron, Berry-au-Bac, France, May 1940.

Standard Temperate Land Scheme of Dark Earth and Dark Green upper surfaces, to the B Scheme pattern, with Night under surfaces. Note the wide Red/White/Blue stripes angled to match the rudder hinge line and taking up the whole of the fin area and the cockpit glazing centre-section overpainted for night flying operations. L5231 crash-landed on 10 May 1940 during an attack on an enemy column in the vicinity of Dippach, Luxemburg.

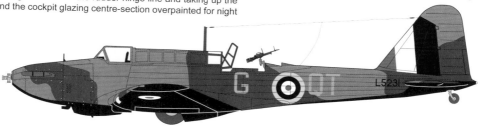

Fairey Battle Mk.I, L5226/QT-Q, 142 Squadron, Faux-Villecerf, France, May 1940.

Standard Temperate Land Scheme of Dark Earth and Dark Green upper surfaces, to the B Scheme pattern, with Night under surfaces. Note the wide Red/White/Blue stripes angled to match the rudder hinge line and taking up the whole of the fin area and parts of the cockpit glazing centre-section overpainted for night flying operations. L5226 crash-landed on 19 May 1940 during an attack on an enemy column in the vicinity of Dagny-Lambercy, near Laon, France.

Fairey Battle Mk.I, K9390/JN-I, 150 Squadron, Ecury-sur-Coole, France, May 1940.

Standard Temperate Land Scheme of Dark Earth and Dark Green upper surfaces, to the A Scheme pattern, with Night under surfaces. Note the narrow Red/White/Blue fin stripes of varying widths angled to match the rudder hinge line and lack of underwing roundels. K9390 crash-landed on 10 May 1940 at Gosselles, Belgium, following an attack on an advancing German column.

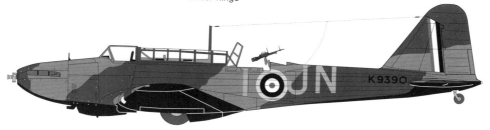

Not to any scale

Fairey Battle Mk.I, L5540/JN-C, 150 Squadron, Ecury-sur-Coole, France, May 1940.

Standard Temperate Land Scheme of Dark Earth and Dark Green upper surfaces, to the A Scheme pattern, with Night under surfaces. Note the narrow Red/White/Blue fin stripes angled to match the rudder hinge line and lack of underwing roundels. L5540 crash-landed on 10 May 1940 near Grevenmascher, Luxemburg, following an attack on an advancing German column.

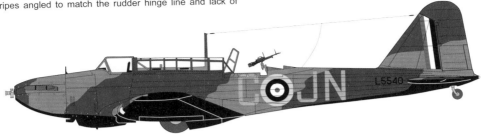

Fairey Battle Mk.I, K9273/HA-R, 218 Squadron, Auberive-sur-Suippes, France, May 1940.

Standard Temperate Land Scheme of Dark Earth and Dark Green upper surfaces, to the A Scheme pattern, with Night under surfaces. Note the fuselage roundels still without the Yellow outer ring and the narrow Red/White/Blue fin stripes angled to match the rudder hinge line. K9273 was abandoned in France in May 1940.

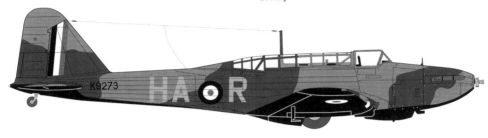

Fairey Battle Mk.I, L5235/HA-W, 218 Squadron, Auberive-sur-Suippes, France, May 1940.

Standard Temperate Land Scheme of Dark Earth and Dark Green upper surfaces, to the B Scheme pattern, with Night under surfaces. Note the narrow Red/White/Blue fin stripes angled to match the rudder hinge line and lack of underwing roundels. L5235 crash-landed on 14 May 1940 during an attack on bridges in the Sedan area.

Fairey Battle Mk.I, L5468/MQ-, 226 Squadron, Rheims, France, May 1940.

Standard Temperate Land Scheme of Dark Earth and Dark Green upper surfaces, to the B Scheme pattern, with Night under surfaces. Note the lack of an individual aircraft letter and underwing roundels. The wide Red/White/Blue fin stripes were angled to match the rudder hinge line and took up the whole of the fin area. L5468 survived the Battle of France and eventually served in Canada as a trainer, re-serialled as 2137.

Fairey Battle Mk.I, P2255/MQ-O, 226 Squadron, Rheims, France, May 1940.

Standard Temperate Land Scheme of Dark Earth and Dark Green upper surfaces, to the B Scheme pattern, with Night under surfaces. Note the fuselage roundels still without the Yellow outer ring, the rear positioning of the individual aircraft letter and the narrow Red/White/Blue fin stripes angled to match the rudder hinge line plus the lack of underwing roundels. The serial number has been painted over on the rudder but retained on the fuselage. P2255 was one of seven airframes abandoned at Rheims on 16 May 1940 when the airfield was evacuated.

Not to any scale

The Battle of Britain – Blitzkrieg!

Henschel Hs 126B-1, T1+KH, 1.(H)/10 'Tannenberg', Choiselle, France, June 1940.

The Hs 126 was the Luftwaffe's army-cooperation tactical reconnaissance workhorse, getting valuable information about the Allies' dispositions back to the Wehrmacht's commanders in the field. Finished in the standard two-tone green RLM 70 Schwarzgrün and RLM 71 Dunkelgrün upper surfaces in a straight-edged 'splinter' pattern with RLM 65 Hellblau undersides. Codes were black including the individual aircraft letter 'K' which would normally be in the staffel colour white. Note the angled white stripes radiating down from the observer's cockpit which helped to line up the hand-held camera.

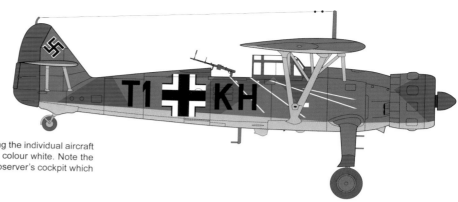

Henschel Hs 123A-1, 'Black 12', 5.(S)/LG 2, operating from various temporary forward airstrips in France in support of German ground forces in May/June 1940.

II Gruppe of Lehrgeschwader 2 was still operating the Hs 123 in the ground attack role for the 'Blitkrieg' offensive. Many of their Hs 123s were still finished in the pre-war three-tone RLM 61 Dunkelbraun, RLM 62 Grün and RLM 63 Hellgrau, upper surfaces applied in a straight-edged 'splinter' scheme, such as the aircraft illustrated here, with RLM 65 Hellblau under surfaces. Note the 'fighter-style' numeral 'Black 12' and the II Gruppe horizontal bar, both thinly outlined in white.

Henschel Hs 123A-1, (L2+??), 4.(S)/LG 2, operating from various temporary forward airstrips in France in support of German ground forces in May/June 1940.

This Hs 123 was also finished in a variation of the pre-war three-tone RLM 61 Dunkelbraun, RLM 62 Grün and RLM 63 Hellgrau, upper surfaces applied in a straight-edged 'splinter' scheme with RLM 65 Hellblau under surfaces. Note the pre-war central position of the swastika and the painted-out codes in front of the fuselage balkenkreuz.

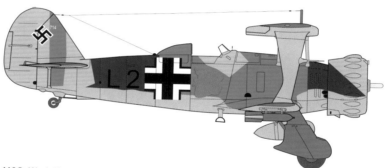

Messerschmitt Bf 110C, Werk Nummer 3011, U8+DL, 3./ZG 26, Niedermendig, Germany, May 1940.
Flown by: Fw Hannes Reimann and Ogefr Heinrich Röwe

Finished in the standard two-tone green RLM 70 Schwarzgrün and RLM 71 Dunkelgrün upper surfaces in a straight-edged 'splinter' pattern with RLM 65 Hellblau undersides. Codes were black with the individual aircraft letter 'D' in the 3 Staffel colour yellow. Note the Werk Nummer 3011 in white on the rear fuselage. Fw Reimann and his bordfunker Gfr Röwe were shot down in U8+DL at Beaumont-en-Argonne, east of Rethel, France on 10 May 1940

Inset: 3./ZG 26's blackbird holding a gunsight emblem.

Messerschmitt Bf 110C, A2+AH, 1./ZG 2, Neufchateau, France, May 1940.

Finished in the new camouflage scheme of RLM 71 Dunkelgrün and RLM 02 Grau upper surfaces in a soft-edged 'splinter' pattern with RLM 65 Hellblau undersides which have been extended up the fuselage sides in a soft edged demarcation. Codes were black with the individual aircraft letter 'A' in the 1 Staffel colour white. Note the upper/under colour demarcation on the fin/rudder.

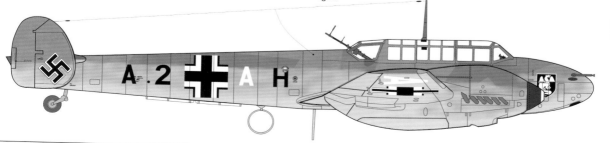

Inset: 1./ZG 2's dragon emblem.

Not to any scale

Messerschmitt Bf 109E-4, 'Yellow 15', 3./JG 1, Guise, France, May 1940.

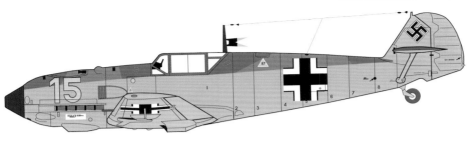

By the opening stages of the Battle of France the majority of front-line Bf 109Es had been repainted in the 'new' RLM 71 Dunkelgrün and RLM Grau 02 upper surface scheme, either on the production line or whilst in staffel service. The RLM 65 Hellblau under surfaces were also extended up the fuselage sides and over the fin and rudder. Note the position of the yellow (RLM Gelb 04) numeral '15' thinly outlined in black on the cowling, the RLM 70 spinner and the 'command' pennant on the radio mast.

Messerschmitt Bf 109E-1, 'Black chevron and vertical bars', Stab I/JG 1, Charleville, France, May 1940.

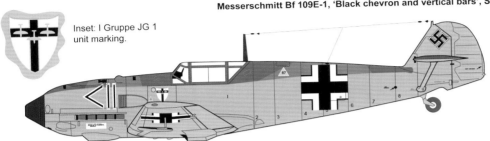

Inset: I Gruppe JG 1 unit marking.

RLM 71 Dunkelgrün and RLM Grau 02 upper surfaces with RLM 65 Hellblau under surfaces extended up the fuselage sides and over the fin and rudder. Note the position of the black chevron and bars Stab marking, thinly outlined in white, on the cowling and the RLM 70 spinner.

Messerschmitt Bf 109E-1, 'Red 11', 2./JG 2, Beaulieu-en-Aronne, France, May 1940.

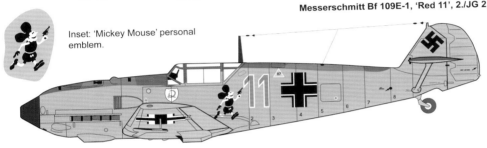

Inset: 'Mickey Mouse' personal emblem.

RLM 71 Dunkelgrün and RLM Grau 02 upper surfaces in a soft-edged semi-splinter pattern with RLM 65 Hellblau under surfaces extended high up on the fuselage sides and over the fin and rudder. Note the small, narrow-bordered fuselage balkenkreuz, 'Mickey Mouse' emblem and the JG 2 'Red R in a shield' badge under the cockpit. RLM 70 spinner.

Messerschmitt Bf 109E-3, 'White 5', 1./JG 2, Beaulieu-en-Aronne, France, May 1940.
Pilot: Lt Paul Temme

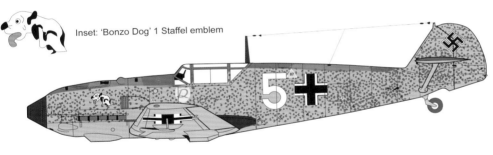

Inset: 'Bonzo Dog' 1 Staffel emblem

RLM 71 Dunkelgrün and RLM Grau 02 upper surfaces in a soft-edged semi-splinter pattern with RLM 65 Hellblau under surfaces. The RLM 65 Hellblau fuselage sides, extended high up on the fuselage and over the fin and rudder was stippled with a mix of RLM 70 and RIM 71. Note the small, narrow-bordered fuselage balkenkreuz, the 'Bonzo Dog' 1 Staffel emblem on the cowling, and JG 2 'Red R in a shield' badge under the cockpit. RLM 70 spinner.

Messerschmitt Bf 109E-4, 'double chevron', Stab III/JG 2, Signy-le-Petit, France, May 1940,
Pilot: Major Dr Erich Mix, the Gruppe Kommandeur

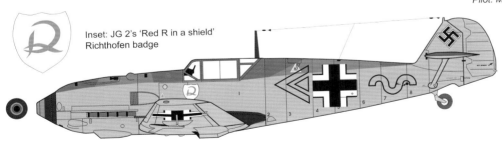

Inset: JG 2's 'Red R in a shield' Richthofen badge

RLM 71 Dunkelgrün and RLM Grau 02 upper surfaces in a soft-edged semi-splinter pattern with RLM 65 Hellblau under surfaces and fuselage sides, fin and rudder. Note the Stab chevron and III Gruppe wavy bar in outline only and the JG 2 'Red R in a shield' badge under the cockpit. The RLM 70 spinner had a red tip. Major Dr Mix was shot down in this aircraft on 21 May 1940, near Compiégne, but evaded capture.

Messerschmitt Bf 109E-4, 'Black 3', 8./JG 26, Chiévres, Belgium, May 1940.

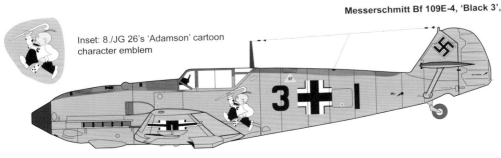

Inset: 8./JG 26's 'Adamson' cartoon character emblem

RLM 71 Dunkelgrün and RLM Grau 02 upper surfaces in a soft-edged semi-splinter pattern with RLM 65 Hellblau under surfaces extended high up on the fuselage sides and over the fin and rudder. Note the small, broad-bordered, fuselage balkenkreuz. The black numeral '3' and vertical III Gruppe bar were without any outline. A famous German cartoon character 'Adamson' was drawn under the cockpit as the 8 Staffel emblem.

Not to any scale

The Battle of Britain – Blitzkrieg!

Junkers Ju 87B-1, L1+HU, 10 Staffel, IV Gruppe/LG 1, operating from forward bases in northern France, May 1940.

The Stuka Geshwader spearheaded the German attack on France and the Low Countries and the period is now universally accepted as being the type's 'finest hour'. Finished in the standard two-tone green RLM 70 Schwarzgrün and RLM 71 Dunkelgrün upper surfaces in a straight-edged 'splinter' pattern with RLM 65 Hellblau undersides. Codes were black with a white (for 10 Staffel) individual aircraft letter 'H' and white band around the RLM 70 propeller spinner. Note the Staffel's 'devil riding a bomb' badge under the windscreen and propellers on the wheel spat legs.

Inset: 10./LG 1's 'devil riding a bomb' badge

Junkers Ju 87B-1, T6+HN, 5./StG 2, operating from forward bases in northern France, May 1940.

There were almost 400 Stukas involved in the invasion of France and the Low Countries including the aircraft of I and II Gruppen StG 2. T6+HN of II Gruppe, is finished in the standard two-tone green RLM 70 Schwarzgrün and RLM 71 Dunkelgrün upper surfaces in a straight-edged 'splinter' pattern with RLM 65 Hellblau undersides. Codes were black with a red (for 5 Staffel) individual aircraft letter 'H' and a thin white band around the RLM 70 propeller spinner. Note the Staffel's 'angry penguin' badge under the windscreen and individual aircraft letter 'H' on the front of the wheel spats. This particular aircraft was fitted with B-2 style 'ejector' exhausts.

Inset: 5./StG 2's 'angry penguin' badge

Junkers Ju 87B-2, 6G+AR, 7./StG 51, operating from forward bases in northern France, May 1940.

There were two variants of the Ju 87B sub-type operating side-by-side during this period, the original B-1 and the improved B-2 as illustrated here. Finished in the standard two-tone green RLM 70 Schwarzgrün and RLM 71 Dunkelgrün upper surfaces in a straight-edged 'splinter' pattern with RLM 65 Hellblau undersides, codes were black with a white (for 7 Staffel) individual aircraft letter 'A' and a broad white band around the RLM 70 propeller spinner. Note the swastika in the earlier position across the fin and rudder and the Staffel's yellow 'comet' design under the cockpit.

Inset: 7./StG 51's 'leaping bull in comet' badge

Junkers Ju 87B-2, 6G+FR, 7./StG 51, operating from forward bases in northern France, May 1940.

To illustrate the point of the two Ju 87B sub-types operating side-by-side during this period, this is an original B-1 of the same Staffel as the aircraft above. Finished in the standard two-tone green RLM 70 Schwarzgrün and RLM 71 Dunkelgrün upper surfaces in a straight-edged 'splinter' pattern with RLM 65 Hellblau undersides, codes were black with a white (for 7 Staffel) individual aircraft letter 'F' and a broad white band around the RLM 70 propeller spinner. Note the swastika in the earlier position across the fin and rudder and the Staffel's yellow 'comet' design under the cockpit.

Inset: 8./StG 51's 'coat of arms' badge

Junkers Ju 87B-2, 6G+FS, 8./StG 51, operating from forward bases in northern France, May 1940.

Finished in the standard two-tone green RLM 70 Schwarzgrün and RLM 71 Dunkelgrün upper surfaces in a straight-edged 'splinter' pattern with RLM 65 Hellblau undersides, codes were black with a red (for 8 Staffel) individual aircraft letter 'F' and a broad red band around the RLM 70 propeller spinner. Note the Staffel's badge in front of the cockpit and the propellers on the wheel spat legs.

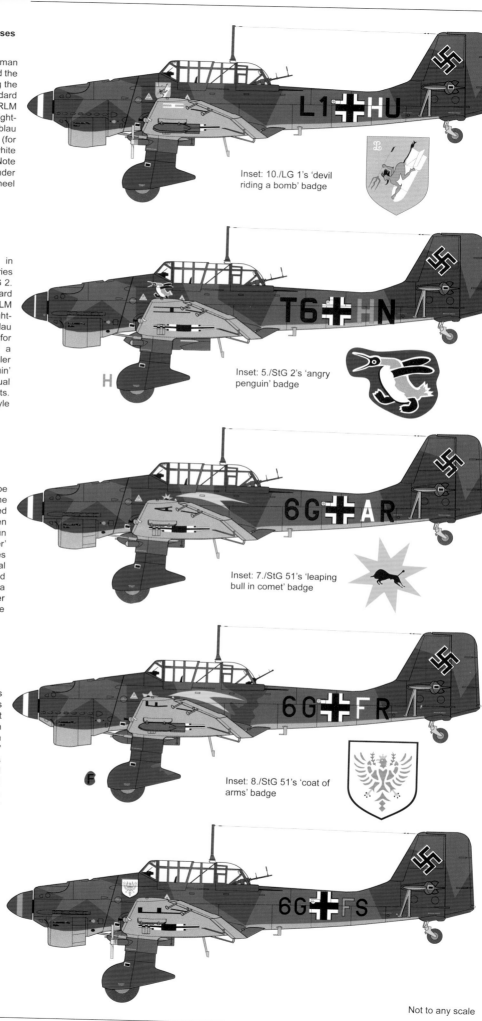

Not to any scale

Heinkel He 111H-1, 1H+BN, 5./KG 26, Westerland, Germany, April 1940.

The He 111 was also produced in several variants, 1H+BN illustrated here being the first sub-type of the H-range. Finished in the standard two-tone green RLM

70 Schwarzgrün and RLM 71 Dunkelgrün upper surfaces in a straight-edged 'splinter' pattern with RLM 65 Hellblau undersides, codes were black with a red (for 5 Staffel) individual aircraft letter 'B' and red propeller spinners. Note the Staffel's red and black 'Vestigum Leonis' badge under the cockpit partially hidden by the engine cowling.

Heinkel He 111P-2, G1+AN, 5./KG55, Schwaighofen, Germany, April/May 1940.

The other major variant of the He 111 was the P, powered by Daimler Benz DB 601 engines, which was produced in limited numbers due to the high demand of DB 601 engines for fighter aircraft. Finished in the standard two-tone green RLM 70 Schwarzgrün and RLM 71 Dunkelgrün upper surfaces in a straight-edged 'splinter' pattern with RLM 65 Hellblau undersides, codes were black with a red

(for 5 Staffel) individual aircraft letter 'A' and red propeller spinners. Note the Staffel's red and black 'Greif' (Griffon) badge to the rear of the cockpit.

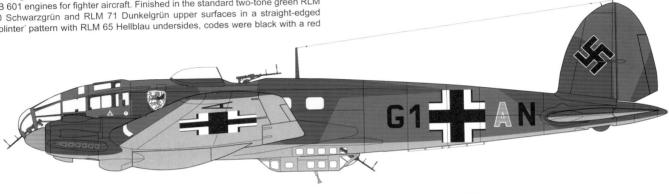

Heinkel He 111H-2, V4+IP, 6./KG 1, Kirtorf, Germany, April/May 1940.

The He 111H-series was powered by Jumo 211 engines, which, whilst not quite as powerful as the He 111P's DB 601 engines, were in less demand. Finished in the standard two-tone green RLM 70 Schwarzgrün and RLM 71 Dunkelgrün upper surfaces in a straight-edged 'splinter' pattern with RLM 65 Hellblau undersides, codes were black with a yellow (for 6 Staffel) individual aircraft letter

'I' and yellow propeller spinners. Note the Staffel's white diamond with red cross at the top of the fin/rudder.

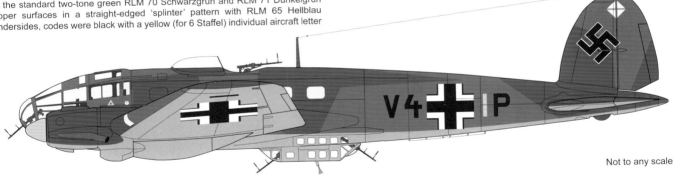

Not to any scale

one of the most controversial decisions of the war. Hermann Göring had convinced Hitler that the Luftwaffe could prevent an evacuation and von Rundstedt warned him that any further effort by the Armoured Divisions would lead to a much longer refitting period.

Encircled, the British, Belgian and French forces launched 'Operation Dynamo' which evacuated Allied troops from the northern pocket in Belgium and the Pas-de-Calais, beginning on 26 May. About 198,000 British, along with nearly 140,000 French soldiers were evacuated in 'Dynamo'. Belgium surrendered on 28 May.

During the 'Dunkirk Battle' the Luftwaffe flew 1,882 bombing and 1,997 fighter sorties. British losses included sixty precious

fighter pilots. Although the Luftwaffe failed in its task of preventing the evacuation, it inflicted serious losses on the Allied forces. A total of eighty-nine ships were lost; the Royal Navy lost twenty-nine of the forty destroyers committed – sunk or seriously damaged.

The French pressed the British to commit more RAF fighters to the battle. The C-in-C of RAF Fighter Command, Hugh Dowding, refused, arguing that if France collapsed, the British fighter force would be severely weakened. The RAF's force of 1,078 aircraft had been reduced to some 475 – RAF records show just 179 Hurricanes and 205 Spitfires were serviceable on 5 June 1940.

After the evacuation at Dunkerque and while Paris was under

Junkers Ju 52/3m, 1Z+EU, 10./KGzbV 1, Stendal, Germany, May 1940.

The transport workhorse of the Luftwaffe, the Ju 52 operated in every Theatre of Operations from the beginning of hostilities until the end of the Second World War and was heavily involved in the invasion of France and the Low Countries. Finished in the standard two-tone green RLM 70 Schwarzgrün and RLM 71 Dunkelgrün upper surfaces in a straight-edged 'splinter' pattern this particular machine had its RLM 65 Hellblau undersides overpainted with a temporary coat of matt black. Codes were black with a black individual aircraft letter 'E' outlined in white (for 10 Staffel). Note the Staffel's 'Berlin Bear' in a red shield on the nose in front of the cockpit.

Junkers Ju 52/3m, 3U+MT, III./ZG 26, Yvrench/St Omer, France, May 1940.

Many front-line units had Ju 52s attached to them for the essential supply, unit transport and 'hack' duties, such as this example operated by the Bf 110-equipped III./ZG 26. Finished in the standard two-tone green RLM 70 Schwarzgrün and RLM 71 Dunkelgrün upper surfaces in a straight-edged 'splinter' pattern, note how the RLM 65 Hellblau undersides have been extended up the fuselage sides leaving the image of a snake down the length of the fuselage. Unit codes were black, but in this instance, the individual aircraft letter 'M' was also black whilst the 9 Staffel letter 'T' was painted yellow. Note the swastika in the earlier position across the fin and rudder.

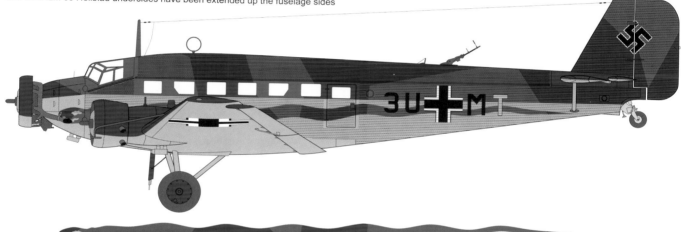

Not to any scale

siege, part of the 1st Canadian Infantry Division was sent to Brittany (Brest) and moved 320 kilometres (200 miles) inland towards Paris before they heard that Paris had fallen and France had capitulated. They withdrew and re-embarked for England. The British 1st Armoured Division, under General Evans, (without its infantry, which had been re-assigned to keep the pressure off the BEF at Dunkirk), arrived in France in June 1940. It was joined by the 51st (Highland) Division and was forced to fight a rearguard action. Other British battalions were later landed at Cherbourg, waiting to form a second BEF.

At the end of the campaign Erwin Rommel praised the staunch resistance of the British forces, despite being under-equipped and without ammunition for much of the fighting.

'Fall Rot'

The best and most modern French armies had been lost; the French had also lost much of their heavy weaponry and their best armoured formations. Weygand was faced with the prospect of defending a long front stretching from Sedan to the Channel with a greatly depleted French Army now lacking significant Allied support. Unlike the Germans, he had no significant reserves to counter a breakthrough or to replace frontline troops, should they become exhausted from a prolonged battle. If the frontline was pushed further south, it would inevitably get too long for the French to man. Some elements of the French leadership had openly lost heart, particularly as the British were evacuating. The 'Dunkirk Evacuation' was a blow to French morale because it was seen as an act of abandonment.

The Italian invasion of France

Adding to this grave situation, on 10 June, Italy declared war on France and Britain. However, the country was not prepared for war and made little impact during what was to be the last twelve days of fighting. Italian dictator Benito Mussolini was aware of this and sought to profit from German successes. Mussolini's immediate aim was the expansion of the Italian colonies in North Africa by taking land from the British and French in that region.

▲ An RAF officer examines the wreckage of a crashed Luftwaffe Dornier Do 17 bomber which crashed in a French field during fighting in June 1940. Presumably it had attempted to limp home after taking damage inflicted by RAF fighters. (Photo: Imperial War Museum)

The fall of Paris

The Germans renewed their offensive on 5 June on the Somme. An attack broke through the scarce reserves that Weygand had put between the Germans and the capital. On 10 June the French government fled to Bordeaux, declaring Paris an open city.

Churchill returned to France on 11 June and met the French War Council in Briare. The French requested that Churchill supply all available fighter squadrons to aid in the battle. With only twenty-five squadrons remaining, Churchill refused, believing at this point that an upcoming 'Battle for Britain' could be decisive. At the meeting, Churchill obtained assurances from Admiral François Darlan that the French fleet would not fall into German hands. On 14 June Paris fell to the Wehrmacht.

German air supremacy

By this time the situation in the air had grown critical. The Luftwaffe had established total air supremacy (as opposed to air superiority) as the French air arm was on the verge of collapse. Between 5 and 9 June, the Armée de l'Air had undertaken just over 1,815 missions, of which 518 were by bombers, but the number of sorties flown declined as losses were now becoming impossible to replace.

The RAF attempted to divert the attention of the Luftwaffe with some 660 sorties flown against targets over the Dunkirk area but their losses were heavy too; on 21 June alone thirty-seven Blenheims were destroyed. After 9 June, French aerial resistance virtually ceased, and some of the surviving aircraft withdrew to French North Africa. The Luftwaffe now 'ran riot'.

Its attacks were focused on the direct and indirect support of the Wehrmacht. The Luftwaffe subjected any areas of resistance to ferocious assault, which then quickly collapsed under armoured attack.

The Luftwaffe virtually destroyed the Armée de l'Air during the campaign and inflicted heavy losses on the RAF contingent that was deployed. It is estimated the French lost 1,274 aircraft during the campaign, the British suffered losses of some 959, of which 477 were fighters, mainly Hurricanes. The Battle for France had cost the Luftwaffe 1,428 aircraft destroyed (1,129 to enemy action, 299 in accidents). A further 488 were damaged (225 to enemy action, 263 in accidents), but the campaign had been a spectacular success for the Luftwaffe.

The second BEF evacuation

Most of the remaining British troops in the field had arrived at Saint-Valery-en-Caux for evacuation, but the Germans took the heights around the harbour making this impossible and on 12 June, General Fortune and the remaining British forces surrendered to Rommel. The evacuation of the second BEF took place during 'Operation Ariel' between 15 June and 25 June. The Luftwaffe, with complete mastery of the French skies, was determined to prevent more Allied evacuations after the Dunkerque debacle.

I Fliegerkorps was assigned to the Normandy and Brittany sectors, and on 9 and 10 June the port of Cherbourg was subjected to heavy bombing, whilst Le Havre received ten bombing attacks which sank many Allied ships attempting to escape. On 17 June, Ju 88s, mainly from KG 30, sank the 'Lancastria' off St Nazaire, killing over 5,000 Allied personnel. Nevertheless, the Luftwaffe failed to prevent the mass evacuation of most of the Allied personnel.

Surrender and Armistice

Prime Minister Paul Reynaud was forced to resign and was succeeded by Marshal Philippe Pétain, who delivered a radio address to the French people announcing his intention to ask

Potez 63-11, No 636, GAO 2/506, based at Chambley- Bussiéres, France, spring 1940.

This aircraft, which was devoid of unit markings, may have been attached to a particular individual Army formation which operated its own Groupe Aérien d'Observation (GAO), General Observation/Army Cooperation Wing. Camouflage was the 'standard' (sic) three-tone upper surface scheme of Gris Bleu Foncé (dark blue grey) and Terre Foncé (dark earth) with either Kaki (Khaki) or Vert (Green) on the upper surfaces and Gris Bleu Clair (light blue grey) undersides. Note the aircraft's construction number '636' repeated in white on the rear fuselage and that no Matricule Militaire was carried under the wings.

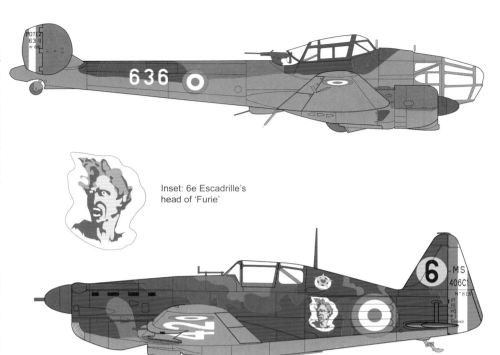

Inset: 6e Escadrille's head of 'Furie'

Morane-Saulnier MS.406, No 813, '6', L-842, 6e Escadrille, GC III/7, Vitry-en-Francois, France, May 1940.

Camouflaged in the three-tone upper surface scheme of Gris Bleu Foncé (dark blue grey) and Terre Foncé (dark earth) and either Kaki (Khaki) or Vert (Green) on the upper surfaces with Gris Bleu Clair (light blue grey) undersides. Note the large roundel on the rear fuselage with the head of 6e Escadre's 'Furie' in front, the numeral '6' in a yellow disc on the fin and the Matricule Militaire, L-842, in white under the wings. This aircraft was lost in combat on 10 May 1940.

Morane-Saulnier MS.406, No 287, '1', N-699, GC II/2, Clermont les Fermes, France, May 1940.
Pilot: Capt Baudoinne de Calonne d'Avesnes,

Camouflaged in the three-tone upper surface scheme of Gris Bleu Foncé (dark blue grey) and Terre Foncé (dark earth) and either Kaki (Khaki) or Vert (Green) on the upper surfaces with Gris Bleu Clair (light blue grey) undersides. Note the lack of fuselage roundel on the rear fuselage, 'red Griffon' (SPA 65 marking usually painted in black), the numeral '1' in a black disc on the fin and the Matricule Militaire, N-699, in white under the wings.

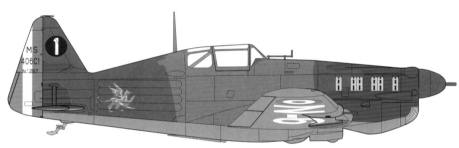

Curtiss Hawk 75A-1, No 258, '1', X-857, 3e Escadrille, GC II/5, Toul-Croix-de-Metz, France, May 1940.
Pilot: Capt Marie Monraisse

Camouflaged in the three-tone upper surface scheme of Gris Bleu Foncé (dark blue grey) and Terre Foncé (dark earth) and either Kaki (Khaki) or Vert (Green) on the upper surfaces with Gris Bleu Clair (light blue grey) undersides. Note the lack of fuselage roundel on the rear fuselage, 3e Escadrille's (Escadrille Lafayette) 'Sioux' Indian's head, the white numeral '1' on the fin and the Matricule Militaire, X-857, in black under the wings.

Inset: 3e Escadrille's (Escadrille Lafayette) 'Sioux' Indian's head,

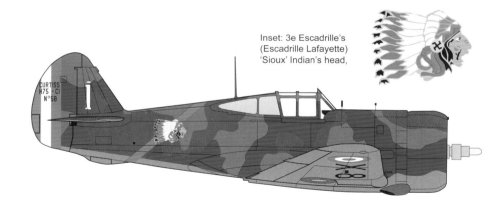

Caudron-Renault C.714 'Cyclone', No 85-49, '13', I-209, 1e Escadrille, GC I/145, Villacoublay, France, May 1940.
Pilot: Lt Alexsy Zukowsky

Groupe de Chasse 1/145 was the only all-Polish pilot unit in the Armée de l'Air and the only unit to operate the Caudron C.714. Camouflaged in the three-tone upper surface scheme of Gris Bleu Foncé (dark blue grey) and Terre Foncé (dark earth) and either Kaki (Khaki) or Vert (Green) on the upper surfaces with Gris Bleu Clair (light blue grey) undersides. Note the Polish national insignia on the fuselage, the white numeral '13' on the fin and the Matricule Militaire, I-209, in black under the wings.

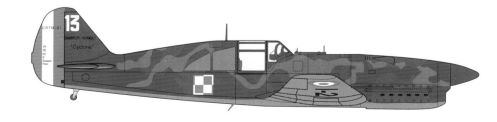

Not to any scale

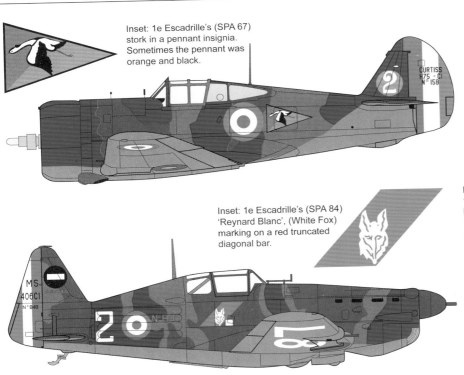

Inset: 1e Escadrille's (SPA 67) stork in a pennant insignia. Sometimes the pennant was orange and black.

Curtiss Hawk 75A-1, No 158, '2', 1e Escadrille, GC I/5, St Dizier, France, May 1940.
Pilot: Lt Marin le Meslée

Camouflaged in the three-tone upper surface scheme of Gris Bleu Foncé (dark blue grey) and Terre Foncé (dark earth) and either Kaki (Khaki) or Vert (Green) on the upper surfaces with Gris Bleu Clair (light blue grey) undersides. Note the forward position of the fuselage roundel, 1e Escadrille's (SPA 67) stork in a pennant insignia, the white numeral '2' within an orange disc on the fin and lack of a Matricule Militaire under the wings.

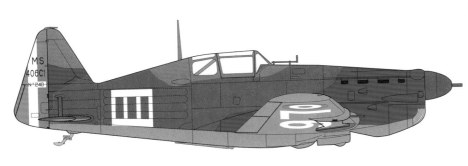

Inset: 1e Escadrille's (SPA 84) 'Reynard Blanc', (White Fox) marking on a red truncated diagonal bar.

Morane-Saulnier MS.406, No 846, '2', L-875, 1e Escadrille, GC III/1, Rozay-en-Brie, France, May/June 1940.
Pilot: Adjt Edgard Gagnaire

Camouflaged in the three-tone upper surface scheme of Gris Bleu Foncé (dark blue grey) and Terre Foncé (dark earth) and either Kaki (Khaki) or Vert (Green) on the upper surfaces with Gris Bleu Clair (light blue grey) undersides. Note the small fuselage roundel on the rear fuselage, 1e Escadrille's (SPA 84) 'Reynard Blanc' (White Fox) marking, the white numeral '2' on the fuselage and the black disc with a white horizontal bar on the fin which was probably a Patrouille (Flight) marking. The Matricule Militaire, L-875, is in white under the wings.

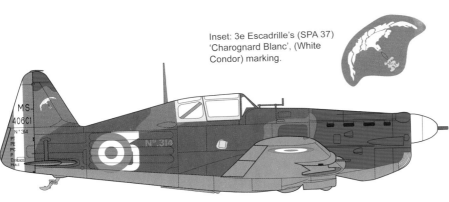

Morane-Saulnier MS.406, No 240, 'III', L-652, DAT Patrouille Tchéque, Chartres, France, June 1940.
Pilot: Cpl Rudolf Ptacek

This aircraft was attached to one of the twenty or so Défense Aérienne du Territoire (DAT) units stationed around Metropolitan France which were specifically charged with protecting strategically important targets such as military bases, armament factories, aircraft assembly plants etc. Camouflaged in the three-tone upper surface scheme of Gris Bleu Foncé (dark blue grey) and Terre Foncé (dark earth) and either Kaki (Khaki) or Vert (Green) on the upper surfaces with Gris Bleu Clair (light blue grey) undersides. Note the three 'bars' on the fuselage which was probably an aircraft in Patrouille (Flight) marking. The Matricule Militaire, L-652, is in white under the wings. Cpl Rudolf Ptacek, a Czech national, crashed in this aircraft on 1 June 1940.

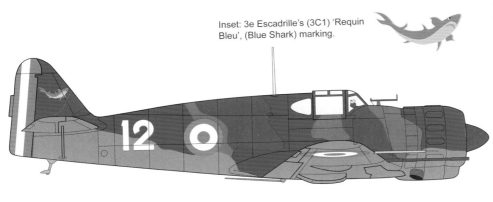

Inset: 3e Escadrille's (SPA 37) 'Charognard Blanc', (White Condor) marking.

Morane-Saulnier MS.406, No 314, '3', 3e Escadrille, GC II/3, Connantre, France, April/May 1940.

GC II/3 was one of the MS.406 units in the process of converting over to the Dewoitine D.520 immediately prior to the 'Blitzkrieg'. Camouflaged in the three-tone upper surface scheme of Gris Bleu Foncé (dark blue grey) and Terre Foncé (dark earth) and either Kaki (Khaki) or Vert (Green) on the upper surfaces with Gris Bleu Clair (light blue grey) undersides. Note the numeral '3' overlapped by the fuselage roundel, the 3e Escadrille (SPA 37) white 'Condor' on the fin which was usually in black and the natural metal framing to the canopy. No Matricule Militaire was carried under the wings.

Inset: 3e Escadrille's (3C1) 'Requin Bleu', (Blue Shark) marking.

Bloch 152, '12', 3e Escadrille, GC II/8, Marseille-Marignane, France, May/June 1940.

Camouflaged in the three-tone upper surface scheme of Gris Bleu Foncé (dark blue grey) and Terre Foncé (dark earth) and either Kaki (Khaki) or Vert (Green) on the upper surfaces with Gris Bleu Clair (light blue grey) undersides. Note the lack of aircraft technical details on the rudder stripes and Matricule Militaire under the wings. 3e Escadrille's (Esc 3C1, previously an Aéronavale unit) 'Requin bleu', (blue Shark) marking was carried on the fin on this particular aircraft but was positioned on the fuselage to the rear of the cockpit on other Bloch 152s of this ex-Aéronavale unit.

Not to any scale

The Battle of Britain – Blitzkrieg!

Morane-Saulnier MS.406, No 636, 'III', 5e Escadrille, GC III/1, Rozay-en-Brie, France, June 1940.
Pilot: Lt Kazimierz Bursztyn

Kazimierz Bursztyn was one of several Polish nationals to fly with 5e Escadrille of GC III/1. Camouflaged in the three-tone upper surface scheme of Gris Bleu Foncé (dark blue grey) and Terre Foncé (dark earth) and either Kaki (Khaki) or Vert (Green) on the upper surfaces with Gris Bleu Clair (light blue grey) undersides. Note the large Polish national insignia on the fuselage and 5e Escadrille's 'Reynard Clignotant' (winking fox) variation of SPA 84's 'Reynard Blanc' (white fox) marking. This Escadrille used white roman numerals to identify its individual aircraft within the 'Polskie Patrouille' (Polish Flight). No Matricule Militaire was carried under the wings.

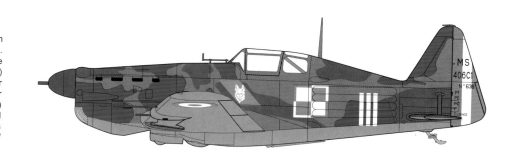

Morane-Saulnier MS.406, No 969, 'VII', L-998, 1e Escadrille, GC I/2, Nimes-Courbessac, France, June 1940.

GC I/2 was another unit to use roman numerals to identify its individual aircraft. Camouflaged in the three-tone upper surface scheme of Gris Bleu Foncé (dark blue grey) and Terre Foncé (dark earth) and either Kaki (Khaki) or Vert (Green) on the upper surfaces with Gris Bleu Clair (light blue grey) undersides. Note the roundel on the rear of the fuselage, the red nose area and spinner and red band across the fin on which was placed the famous 1e Escadrille 'Cigogne' (Stork née SPA 3) marking – with wings in the 'down' position; 2e Escadrille (née SPA 103) had a Stork with the wings in the 'up' position. The Matricule Militaire, L-998, was carried under the wings in white.

Inset: 1e Escadrille 'Cigogne' (Stork) née SPA 3 marking.

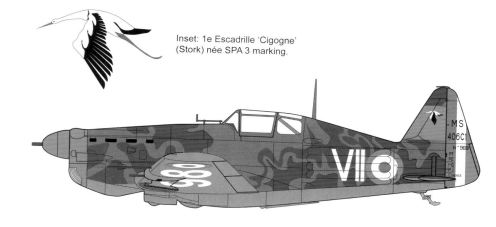

Bloch 152, No 499, '45', GC II/9, Toulouse-Francazal, France, June 1940.

Camouflaged in the three-tone upper surface scheme of Gris Bleu Foncé (dark blue grey) and Terre Foncé (dark earth) and either Kaki (Khaki) or Vert (Green) on the upper surfaces with Gris Bleu Clair (light blue grey) undersides. Note the lack of any Groupe/Escadrille/SPA marking and Matricule Militaire under the wings.

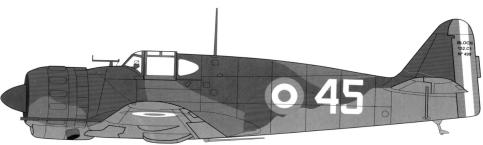

Dewoitine D.520, No 131, '3' of GC II/3, Betz- Bouillancy, France, May 1940.
Pilot: Sous/Lt Prayer

No 131 was amongst the first D.520s to be delivered to GC II/3 which had previously been equipped with MS.406s (see opposite page). Camouflaged in the three-tone upper surface scheme of Gris Bleu Foncé (dark blue grey) and Terre Foncé (dark earth) and either Kaki (Khaki) or Vert (Green) on the upper surfaces with Gris Bleu Clair (light blue grey) undersides. Note the lack of any Groupe/Escadrille/SPA marking and Matricule Militaire under the wings. This aircraft was shot down near Abbeville on 31 May 1940. Sous/Lt Prayer was wounded.

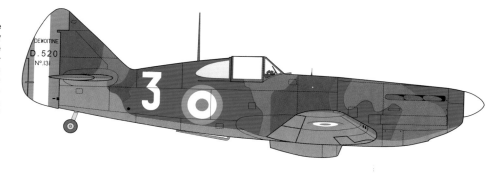

Dewoitine D.520, No 397, GC II/6, Avignon-Pujaut, France, June 1940.

GC II/6 was another unit that re-equipped with the Dewoitine D.520 immediately before the Armistice, having previously operated MS.406s and MB 152s. Camouflaged in the three-tone upper surface scheme of Gris Bleu Foncé (dark blue grey) and Terre Foncé (dark earth) and either Kaki (Khaki) or Vert (Green) on the upper surfaces with Gris Bleu Clair (light blue grey) undersides. Note the construction number '397' roughly painted on the fin in red and lack of any Groupe/Escadrille/SPA marking or Matricule Militaire number.

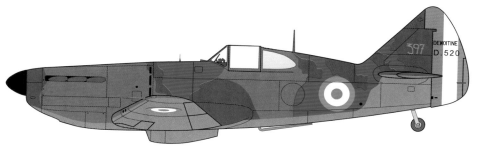

Not to any scale

for an Armistice with Germany. When Hitler received word from the French government that they wished to negotiate an armistice, he selected the Compiègne Forest as the site for the negotiations – the site of the 1918 Armistice, which had ended World War One with a humiliating defeat for Germany. Hitler viewed the choice of location as a supreme moment of revenge for Germany over France.

The armistice was signed on 22 June in the very same railway carriage in which the 1918 Armistice was signed (it was removed from a museum building and placed on the precise spot where it was located in 1918). Hitler sat in the same chair in which Marshal Foch had sat when he faced the defeated German representatives. After listening to the reading of the preamble, Hitler, in a calculated gesture of disdain to the French delegates, left the carriage, leaving the negotiations to his OKW Chief, General Wilhelm Keitel. The French Second Army Group, under the command of General Pretelat, surrendered the same day as the armistice and the cease-fire went into effect on 25 June 1940.

The British began to doubt Admiral Darlan's promise to Churchill not to allow the French fleet to fall into German hands, and acted upon the assumption that his promises were insufficient guarantees. On 3 July 1940, in an engagement off the coast of French Algeria, a British Royal Navy task force under the code name 'Operation Catapult' attacked the French Fleet at Mers-el-Kébir, near Oran, destroying or damaging much of it and killing over 1,290 French sailors. The attack demonstrated to the world, and to the United States in particular, Britain's determination to continue the war with Germany, but led to more feelings of animosity and mistrust between the former French and British allies.

Camouflage and Markings

RAF National Markings changes

Despite the issue of AMO A.520/39 in November 1939 re-introducing higher visibility Red/White/Blue roundels, Coastal Command had continued to conduct trials to further improve the visibility of recognition markings carried by British aircraft. During February 1940, an Anson of 16 Group was marked up with a Yellow band around the fuselage roundel and a Yellow band around the fin, and observation tests were made. In its report to HQ Coastal Command on 6 March 1940, 16 Group reported that the narrow band of Yellow which had been applied around the fuselage roundel was remarkably conspicuous and greatly facilitated recognition. Because the Yellow band around the roundel was visible some distance before the Yellow band around the fin, the latter was considered superfluous.

The Air Ministry meanwhile was considering the implications of putting recognition markings on the tails of RAF aircraft. At a meeting on 8 March 1940, held at the Air Ministry, the question of recognition markings arose and mention was made that the markings applied to the rudders of Air Component Hurricanes in France were proving a very effective identification feature. The Coastal Command representative then mentioned the work being done by 16 Group with regard to this matter.

After some discussion it was agreed that a Yellow ring around the fuselage roundel and Red/White/Blue stripes applied to the fixed part of the fin found widespread approval within the Service, and on 1 May 1940, the Air Ministry sent signal X485 to all Commands, at Home and Overseas, amending the markings carried by RAF aircraft.

On operational aircraft, the existing Red/White/Blue (officially known as National marking ii) fuselage roundels were to be encircled with an outer Yellow band, the same width of the existing Blue band, and vertical stripes of Red, White and Blue, each of the same width, were to be painted on the fins, 'at Squadron level' or at the MUs, and on the manufacturers' production line as soon as was practical after 1 May 1940.

Although 1 and 73 Squadrons based in France had set a precedent of applying Red/White/Blue vertical stripes on their Hurricanes' rudders, it was thought that this might cause problems with the rudder's mass balance, and in the Air Ministry signal X485, it was stressed that the new striped marking, of vertical Red, White and Blue stripes, were only to be painted on the fin. The only further detail given in the signal was that the Blue stripe should be nearest the rudder, but clear of the hinge.

The changes were implemented fairly rapidly, but because no detail on the size of the new marking was given, many different interpretations were made by the units themselves as they tried to comply with the new instructions. Roundels were modified with Yellow bands of many different widths to suit the size of the aircraft they were being applied to, whilst the fin flash was also applied in many different variations.

Such was the confusion that, on 11 May, a further signal, X740, was sent to amplify Signal X485. The new signal stated that the fin markings of three vertical stripes need not necessarily occupy the whole surface of the fin. It was sufficient that the width of the marking was to be such that it was to be clearly visible. On no account were the hinge points or surfaces of the rudder to be painted.

The instructions for modifying the fuselage roundels were also amplified. Aircraft with slim fuselages were to have the whole roundel reduced in size in order to accommodate the new Yellow outer ring and prevent it encroaching on the upper or under surfaces of the fuselage. As a temporary measure, in order to obviate excessive work on operational aircraft, the existing roundels could be outlined with a narrower band of Yellow where the space available made the application of a Yellow band the same width as the Blue band impractical.

Whilst this change was in the process of being made, the German offensive in the West opened on 10 May and the war entered a new phase.

With many more British-based fighters now likely to find themselves operating over France, on 15 May, the underwing markings of all home based fighter aircraft were revised by Signal X296. Red/White/Blue roundels, consisting of rings all of equal width, were to be applied to the underside of both wings forthwith. The roundels were to be as large as possible but were to be kept clear of the ailerons.

Following the fighting which ultimately led to the beaches of Dunkerque, Signal X479 of 4 June made reference to Signal

X296 of 15 May, before going on to state that the roundels on the underside of the port Night painted wing of all fighter aircraft were to be encircled by a Yellow band of convenient width but not less than one quarter, or greater than the full width, of the Blue band. It was permissible to 'break' the new Yellow band in order to keep the aileron and its hinges free from paint. This new marking was to be applied at the earliest possible moment.

Scarcely had this marking instruction had time to be assimilated by the fighter squadrons then they were assailed by a much more troublesome requirement, that of removing all undersurface identification markings and replacing them with a new camouflage colour – Sky!

Luftwaffe camouflage changes

At the end of 1939, the predominant colour scheme for Luftwaffe fighters was still the RLM 70 Schwarzgrün/RLM 71 Dunkelgrün upper surfaces in the hard-edged splinter pattern with RLM 65 Hellblau under surfaces – ideal camouflage for aircraft dispersed within a woodland background.

However, following the Polish Campaign field trials were undertaken to devise a camouflage scheme which was more suitable for concealment for single and twin-engined fighters in the air. As the Luftwaffe confronted French and British aircraft over a winter landscape, it was found that the dark green upper surfaces actually compromised the aircraft. As a result of these trials two changes were made to fighter camouflage – although the bombers remained in the RLM 70 Schwarzgrün/RLM 71 Dunkelgrün upper surfaces with RLM 65 Hellblau undersides

The first of these changes to fighters was to extend the pale grey-blue RLM 65 Hellblau under surface colour up the fuselage sides on to a line level with the canopy sill, (or even higher) and entirely covering the fin and rudder. The second change was the replacement of RLM 70 Schwarzgrün with RLM 02 Grau on the upper surfaces of the main and tailplanes and the fuselage spine. Spinners generally remained in Schwarzgrün 70, or were partially or entirely, repainted in the Staffel or Gruppe colour(s).

These camouflage scheme changes are thought to have been made on the production line, together with a new simplified, softer demarcation, camouflage pattern, sometime around the end of 1939/beginning of 1940. Aircraft already in service appear to have been totally repainted in the new upper surface scheme in the new simplified camouflage pattern by their parent units, (and did not simply apply RLM 02 Grau over the existing RLM 70 Schwarzgrün in the original 'splinter' pattern). This mix of production line and 'on unit' painting methods resulted in the inevitable variations of the basic scheme. (see Chapter 5, 'Messerschmitt Bf 109E upper surface camouflage patterns' diagram on p99)

Fokker D.XXI, No 237, 1e JaVa II-1 (1-II-1 LvR), Nederlandse LuchtVaartAfdeling Militaire, De Kooy, Netherlands, November 1939.

Following the outbreak of war in September 1939, the LuchtVaartAfdeling Militaire adopted large orange triangles outlined in a broad black border, in six positions, above and below the wings and on the fuselage sides. The rudder was also orange with a broad black border. These so called neutrality markings replaced the earlier red, white and blue equally segmented roundels with a small orange centre spot and horizontal red/white/blue rudder bands, to avoid confusion with British and French aircraft. Camouflage was the three-colour scheme of Camouflagebruin (Camouflage Brown) overall, including the under surfaces, with disruptive patterns of Camouflagebeige (Camouflage Beige) and Camouflagegroen (Camouflage Green) on the upper surfaces applied in one of two distinct patterns, in this instance to Pattern 2. This particular aircraft was destroyed in a crash on 22 November 1939.

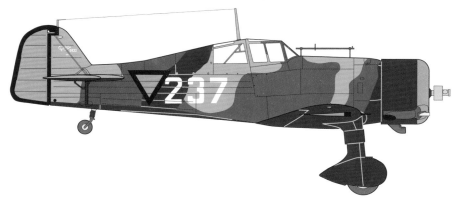

Fokker D.XXI, No 228, 1e JaVa V-2 (1-V-2 LvR), Nederlandse LuchtVaartAfdeling Militaire, Ypenburg, Netherlands, May 1940.

Camouflaged in the three-colour scheme of Camouflagebruin overall, including the under surfaces, with disruptive patterns of Camouflagebeige and Camouflagegroen on the upper surfaces applied in Pattern 2. Flown by Tlt Droste, this machine, in which he shot down a Ju 88, landed at Ockenburg to refuel and rearm after its first combat flight, but was damaged in an air strike and abandoned.

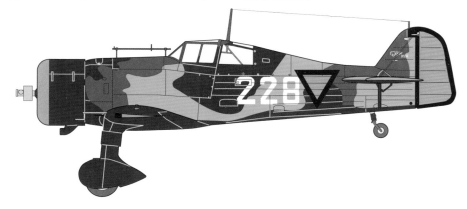

Not to any scale

Of course none of these changes were effected overnight, although there is evidence to suggest that RLM 71/02/65 finished Bf 109Es were operational shortly before the fighting in Poland had ceased, and certainly the scheme appears to have been in widespread use before the 1940 'Blitzkrieg' offensive, as contemporary photographs taken in the rather cold, early spring, show.

However, both the original and the new styles continued in use until the fall of France in June 1940, which, by that stage, some units had found that the large areas of light grey-blue Hellblau 65 was actually too conspicuous and that a greater degree of camouflage was required. They therefore applied soft paint-gun mottling or rag-applied stippling over the fuselage sides in a mix of the basic RLM 70/71/02 camouflage colours. Some of the earlier applications of RLM 65 up the fuselage sides had also eroded sufficiently for the original two-tone 70/71 dark greens to show through, which had a similar effect.

National insignia had also gone through a change in late 1939/early 1940. The fuselage and underwing crosses (Balkenkreuze) received wider white borders, and the swastika (Hakenkreuz) was repositioned fully on to the fin from its previous location centrally across the fin and rudder hinge line.

Armée de l'Air

The main change within the Armée de l'Air was the introduction of the Dewoitine D.520 in to service. Developed as a private venture in late 1936, the first production examples didn't enter Groupes de Chasse service until April 1940, with GC I/3 based at Cannes-Mandelieu.

Although the unit was still working up on the type at the start of the Blitzkrieg on 10 May 1940, they were sent north to help stop the German invasion, and on 13 May in their first combat, claimed three Henschel Hs 126s and a Heinkel He 111 for no

loss. The following day, GC I/3 claimed three Bf 110s, two Bf 109s, two He 111s and two Do 17s over Sedan for the loss of two pilots.

By the time of the Armistice on 22 June 1940, GC II/3 and III/3, GC III/6 and GC II/7 had begun re-equipping with the Dewoitine D.520, but what effect the fighter would have had against the Luftwaffe had it been available in larger numbers is unknown. With a top speed of some 330mph (530km/h), similar to that of the RAF's Hurricane, it was certainly an improvement on most of the other Armée de l'Air fighters such as the Morane MS.406, Bloch MB.151/152 and Curtiss Hawk 75A, but it was still of inferior performance to the Spitfire and more importantly the Bf 109E, and in any event, was a case of too few too late...

Netherlands

The Nederlandse LuchtVaartAfdeling Militaire, LVA/ML, (Netherlands Air Force), consisted of three Aviation Regiments, (LuchtVaartRegimenten, LvR). The 1st Regiment, (1 LvR), was split in to two Groups (Groep), with I Groep/1 LvR (I-1 LvR), comprising a strategic reconnaissance squadron (Strategische VerkenningsVliegtuigAfdeling, VerVA) equipped with Fokker C.Xs and a BombardementsVliegtuigAfdelingen, BomVa, (Bomber squadron) equipped with Fokker T.Vs.

II-1 LvR, (II Groep/1 LuchtVaartRegimenten), was essentially an air defence fighter group operating Fokker D.XXIs and Fokker G.1As in four JachtVliegtuigAfdelingen, JaVA, (Fighter squadrons) – 1e and 2e JaVA with Fokker D.XXIs and 3e and 4e JaVA with Fokker G.1As.

The 2nd Regiment, (2 LvR), was basically an Army Cooperation force, of five Groepen; I-2 to IV-2 LvR equipped with a mix of Fokker C.X, Fokker C.V and Koolhoven FK-51s and the fifth Groep, V-2 LvR, of two JachtVliegtuigAfdelingen

Fokker G.1A, No 301, 4e JaVA II-1 (4-II-1 LvR), Nederlandse LuchtVaartAfdeling Militaire, Bergen, Netherlands, May 1940.

Two JaVa (Fighter Squadrons), were operational with the twin-engined, twin-boom, Fokker G-1A, 3e and 4e JaVA. Camouflage was the three-colour scheme of Camouflagebruin (Camouflage Brown) overall, including the under surfaces, with disruptive patterns of Camouflagebeige (Camouflage Beige) and

Camouflagegroen (Camouflage Green) on the upper surfaces applied in one of two distinct patterns, in this instance to Pattern 2. This machine was severely damaged in the first Luftwaffe strike on 10 May and was abandoned and later captured.

Fokker T.V, No 864, 2e BomVa, (2-I-1 LvR), Nederlandse LuchtVaartAfdeling Militaire, Schipol, Netherlands, April 1940.

The Fokker T.V was the LVA/ML's only medium bomber and equipped just one VliegtuigAfdelingen, (squadron), the 2e BombardementsVliegtuigAfdelingen (BomVa). Camouflaged in the standard LVA/ML three-colour scheme of Camouflagebruin overall, including the under surfaces, with disruptive patterns of Camouflagebeige and Camouflagegroen on the upper surfaces applied in

one of two distinct patterns, in this instance to Pattern 2. This machine was damaged in a forced landing and was returned to Fokkers for repair. It therefore avoided the fate of most of its contemporaries, which were generally destroyed or captured by 11 May 1940.

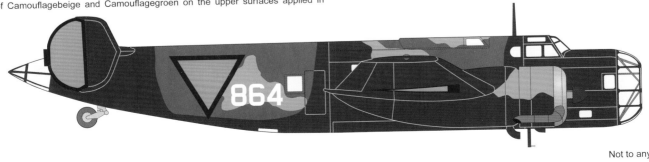

Not to any scale

(Fighter squadrons, ie 1-V-2 LvR and 2-V-2 LvR) with Fokker D.XXIs. A third squadron was added to V-2 LvR, (3-V-2 LvR), equipped with American Douglas DB 8-A-3Ns, (Douglas-built A-17A light bombers) just prior to the Blitzkrieg, which were pressed into use as fighters as they had four forward-firing machine guns.

The 3rd Regiment, (3 LvR) provided training and support with Fokker S.IVs, S.IXs and C.Vs, and there was the naval arm, Marine Luchtvaart Dienst, equipped with various floatplanes such as Fokker C.VIIs, C.VIIIs, C.XIVs and T.VIIIs.

LvR colour schemes and markings

Prior to the outbreak of war, Luchtvaartafdeling Militaire aircraft carried a red, white and blue equally segmented roundel with a small orange centre spot in six positions, above and below the wings and on the fuselage sides. The rudder(s) had red (uppermost), white, blue horizontal bands. However, in mid-January 1939, the LVA/ML dropped the red, white, blue horizontal bands on the rudder.

After some brief experiments with various designs, following the outbreak of war in September 1939, the Luchtvaartafdeling Militaire adopted large orange triangles outlined in a broad black border, in six positions, above and below the wings and on the fuselage sides. The rudder(s) were similarly painted in orange with a broad black border.

Camouflage carried by all LVA/ML aircraft comprised a three-colour scheme of Camouflagebruin (Camouflage Brown – a dark chocolate brown similar to FS 20059) overall, including the under surfaces, with disruptive patterns of Camouflagebeige (Camouflage Beige – a light tan colour similar to FS 206360) and Camouflagegroen (Camouflage Green – a medium blue-green similar to FS 24077) on the upper surfaces.

The two colours of the disruptive camouflage pattern were applied in one of two distinct patterns, (Pattern 1 or Pattern 2), specifically designed for each aircraft type, which appears to have been strictly adhered to despite the intricate nature of the scheme.

Hawker Hurricane Mk.I, H-25, 2 Escadrille 'Le Chardon' 2/I./2 Aé, Belgian Aéronautique Militaire, Beauvechain, Belgium, April 1940.

This Hawker-built Hurricane Mk.I was finished in the standard RAF Temperate Land Scheme of Dark Earth and Dark Green upper surfaces, to the A Scheme pattern, with Aluminium under surfaces. Note the 'thistle' unit marking on the rear fuselage, numeral 25 on the rudder and full 'H-25' code under the wings. Watts two-blade wooden propeller. This aircraft was damaged in an accident on 27 April 1940 and doesn't feature in subsequent casualty lists.

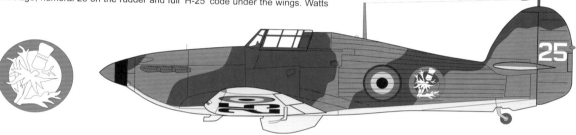

Fairey Fox Mk.VI, A-F-6144, O-175, 7 Escadrille, 'Fleche Ailée' 7/IV./1 Aé, Belgian Aéronautique Militaire, Lonzée, Belgium, May 1940.

This Fairey-built Fox VI was finished in an unrecorded shade of dark green on the upper surfaces with silver under surfaces, applied by the manufacturer. This machine was hit by ground fire during a reconnaissance of enemy road columns on 12 May 1940, and nosed over on landing so it was abandoned.

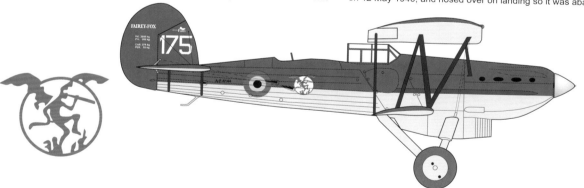

Fairey Battle Mk.I, T-69, 5 Escadrille, 'Aigle Egyptien' 5/III./3 Aé, Belgian Aéronautique Militaire, Brussels-Evere, Belgium, May 1940.

Fairey-built Battles for the Belgian Aéronautique Militaire, featured an enlarged radiator fairing that covered the carburettor intake that was visible on RAF-operated machines. Temperate Land Scheme of Dark Earth and Dark Green upper surfaces, to the B Scheme pattern, with Aluminium under surfaces. Note the pale grey '69' on the fin, black, yellow and red rudder stripes, and the full 'T-69' code under the wings. This machine was damaged on the ground at its war station at Belsele, in the initial attack on 10 May 1940, and was destroyed whilst being repaired in a further attack on 18 May.

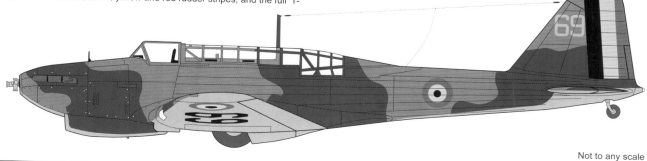

Not to any scale

Ju 88A-1, 9K+HM, 4./KG 51, München-Riem, Germany, June 1940.

Finished in the standard two-tone green RLM 70 Schwarzgrün and RLM 71 Dunkelgrün upper surfaces in a straight-edged 'splinter' pattern with RLM 65 Hellblau undersides. Codes were black with a white individual aircraft letter 'H'

in the staffel colour. Note the white tips to the propeller spinners. This machine was shot down by MS.406s of GC 1/2 on 5 June 1940, whilst on a mission to bomb Tours airfield.

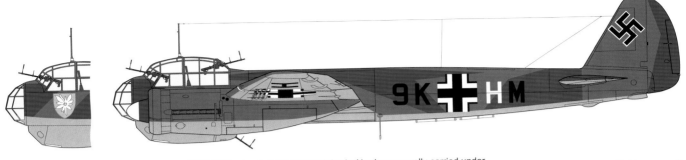

Inset: II/KG 51's 'Eidelweiss' badge generally carried under the front cockpit glazing, (obscured by the engine cowling on the side view) of most of the unit's Ju 88.

Not to any scale

Individual aircraft identification comprised of a three digit number, the first numeral identifying the role of the aircraft, (eg 2xx for single-engined fighter, 3xx for heavy fighters, 7xx for reconnaissance aircraft and 8xx for bombers).

Belgium

Unlike the Nederlandse LuchtVaartAfdeling Militaire, the Belgian Aéronautique Militaire, (Belgian Air Force), was equipped with a mix of imported machines, such as the Gloster Gladiator, Fairey Fox and Fairey Battle from the UK and Fiat CR.42 from Italy, and licensed-built aircraft such as the Hawker Hurricane and French Renard R.31.

By the outbreak of war in September 1939, the Aéronautique Militaire consisted of three operational combat Régiments d'Aéronautique/Luchtmacht Regiments, (Aviation Regiments) – 1.Aé, 2.Aé and 3.Aé, organised in to Groupes (Squadrons) generally operating a particular aircraft type and/or role, which were then further split in to Escadrilles (Flights).

For example, 2/I./2 Aé = No 2 Escadrille (Flight), I Groupe (Squadron) of No 2 Aé (Aviation Regiment) operated a mix of Gladiators and Hurricanes out of Schaffen and 4/III./2 Aé = No 4 Escadrille (Flight), III Groupe (Squadron) of No 2 Aé (Aviation Regiment) flew single seat fighter Fairey Fireflies out of Nivelles. The six Fairey Battles attached to II./3 Aé (II Groupe/3 Aviation Regiment) at Evere were transferred to 5/III./3 Aé, also equipped with Fairey Battles at Belcele, on 10 May, and 4/II./2 Aé from Nivelles but which moved to its wartime base of Brustem, flew Fiat CR.42s; and 7/III/3 Aé operated two-seater Fairey Fox VIs from Evere.

On the day of the invasion, the Aéronautique Militaire had twelve Groupes (Squadrons) comprising some seventy-three Escadrilles (Flights) stationed at their wartime bases. Prior to the outbreak of the war Belgium sought to equip its Aéronautique Militaire with foreign designs, ordering production licenses in Poland and France and aircraft from the USA. However, the acquired licenses could not be used until May 1940 and the aircraft produced in the USA were eventually delivered to France and to the United Kingdom.

Ateliers Renard in Evere, built ten R.31 parasol monoplanes, and twenty-six others were built by SABCA between 1935-

37. Some twenty-two Gloster Gladiator Mk.Is were bought from Britain in 1938. In the same year twenty Hawker-built Hurricane Mk.Is were delivered. Then in March 1939 a license to build a further eighty Hurricanes was granted. The Belgian-built Hurricanes were to be armed with four .50 calibre (12.65mm) Browning machine guns, whilst the original British manufactured machines retained the eight .303 calibre machine guns, but few of these were operational in May 1940.

The Aéronautique Militaire used a black, yellow and red roundel, in six positions, above and below the wings and on the fuselage sides. Occasionally, national colour black/yellow/red tail markings were carried in vertical bands on the rudder. Individual aircraft numbers (serials) were applied to the fin, or rudder, usually in white numerals, with the full serial, prefixed by a letter – eg H for Hurricane, G for Gladiator, O for Fairey Fox, T for Fairey Battle and R for Fiat CR.42 – applied in large black characters under the wings, the letter under one wing and the numerals under the other.

Aéronautique Militaire aircraft colour schemes invariably retained those of the country of origin and manufacture – Dark Earth and Dark Green upper surfaces with Aluminium (silver) undersides, on the Hurricanes and Battles, in the standard 'A' and 'B' Scheme patterns. The Belgian manufactured Hurricanes had very similar 'dark brown/dark green' upper surfaces, in the same standard MAP 'A' and 'B' Scheme patterns, but the shades may have been slightly different.

The Fiat CR.42s of 3/II/2 and 4/II/2 retained their Italian three-tone camouflage scheme of a light tan Giallo Mimetico 3 (Camouflage Yellow No 3) upper surface base with soft-edged dark olive green Verde Mimetico 3 (Camouflage Green No 3) and reddish brown Marrone Mimetico 2 (Camouflage Brown No 2) mottling. Under surfaces were in the medium grey Grigio Mimetico (Camouflage Grey).

The Gladiators, Fairey Foxes and Renard R.31s had dark green upper surfaces, with silver under surfaces, applied by their respective manufacturers, which would have resulted in slightly varying shades of dark green.

Battle of Britain Phase 1:
The Channel Battles (Kanalkampf) 10 July - 11 August 1940

▲ Supermarine Spitfire Mk.Is P9495/DW-K and R6595/DW-O, of 610 Squadron, based at Biggin Hill, Kent, are seen here flying in three 'vic' formations on 24 July 1940. (Photo: Imperial War Museum)

Following the evacuation of British and French soldiers from Dunkerque and the French surrender on 22 June 1940, a few short weeks passed whilst the Luftwaffe replaced its losses from the French Campaign and took over airfields in the countries they had captured. In Britain the time was spent putting as many new fighters and trained pilots into service as possible, to guard against the attack everyone knew was coming.

The lull as the German forces consolidated their position was vital to the RAF, as it allowed it to prepare. By the beginning of July 1940, the RAF had built up its strength to some 640 fighters, but the Luftwaffe had 2,600 bombers and fighters.

The stage was set – in the skies above southeast England, the future of Britain was about to be decided. As the Prime Minister, Winston Churchill put it, *"What General Weygand called the Battle of France is over, the Battle of Britain is about to begin"*

As for Hitler, he believed the war was practically over. He also believed that the British, defeated on the continent and now without European allies, would quickly come to terms.

Although the Foreign Secretary, Lord Halifax, and an element of the British public and some politicians favoured a negotiated peace with Germany, Winston Churchill, newly installed as Prime Minister, and the majority of his Cabinet refused to consider an armistice with Hitler. Instead Churchill used his skillful rhetoric to harden public opinion against capitulation, and to prepare the British for a long war.

On 11 July 1940, Grossadmiral Erich Raeder, Commander-in-Chief of the Kriegsmarine (German Navy), told Hitler that an invasion could only be contemplated as a last resort, and only then with full air superiority. The Kriegsmarine had been nearly crippled by the Norwegian Campaign, with many of its ships having been sunk or damaged, whilst the Royal Navy still had over fifty destroyers, twenty-one cruisers and eight battleships in the British Home Fleet. There was little the weakened Kriegsmarine could do to stop the Royal Navy from intervening. The only alternative was to use the Luftwaffe's dive bombers and torpedo bombers, which required air superiority in order to operate effectively.

Although he agreed with Raeder, on 16 July, Hitler ordered the preparation of a plan to invade Britain. He hoped that news of the preparations would frighten Britain into negotiating for peace. The plan, under Hitler's 'Directive No 16: The Preparation of a Landing Operation against England' was code-named 'Unternehmen Seelöwe' (Operation Sealion). It was submitted by the OKW (Oberkommando der Wehrmacht – High Command of the Armed Forces). All preparations were to be made by mid- August and it was scheduled to take place in mid-September 1940.

Operation Sealion called for landings on the south coast of England, backed by an airborne assault. Neither Hitler nor the OKW believed it would be possible to carry out a successful amphibious assault on Britain until the RAF had been neutralised. Raeder believed that air superiority might make a successful landing possible although it would be a very risky operation and required absolute mastery over the Channel by the Luftwaffe.

Hawker Hurricane Mk.I, P3522/GZ-V, 32 Squadron, RAF Hawkinge, July 1940.

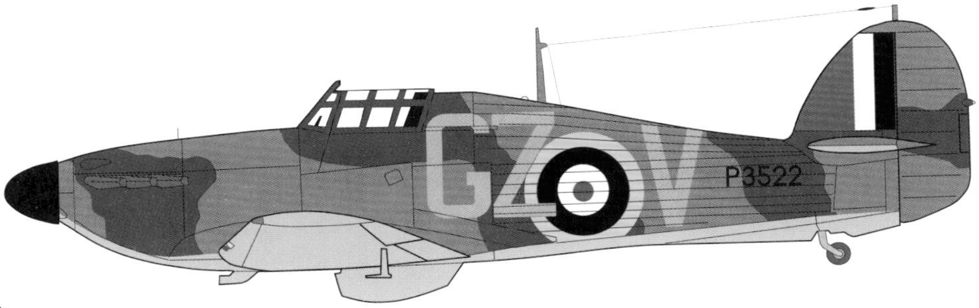

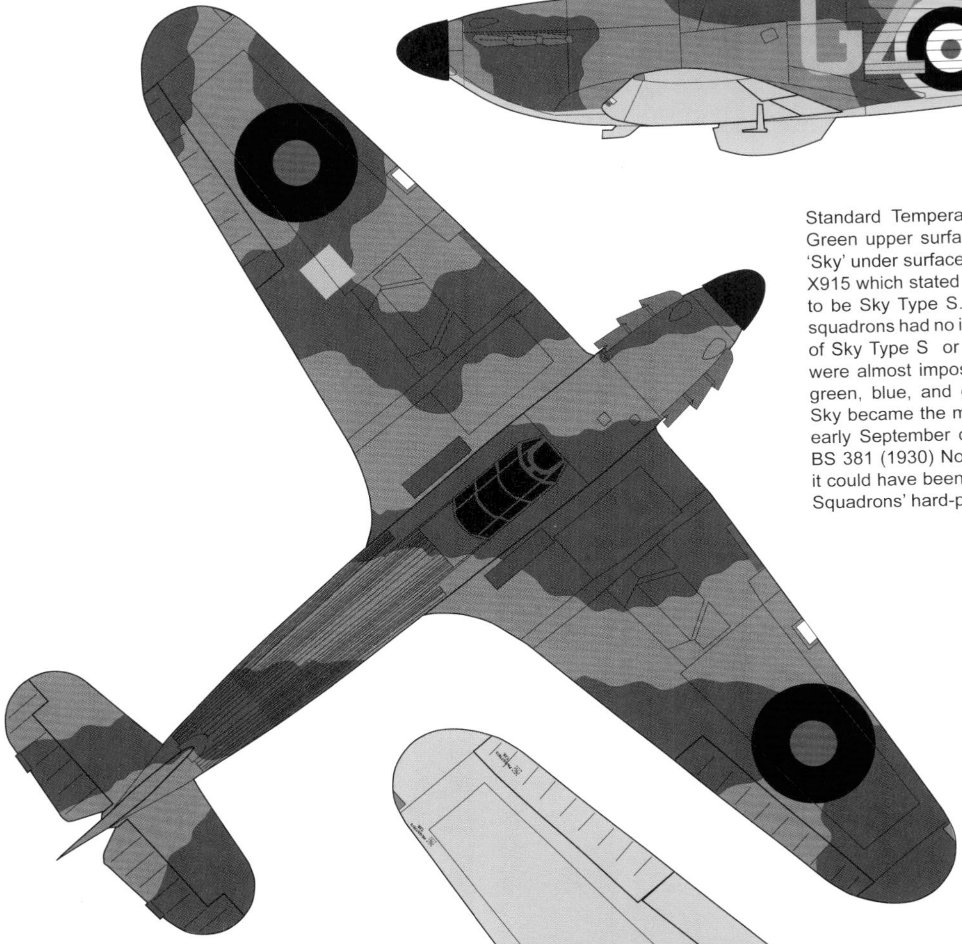

Standard Temperate Land Scheme of Dark Earth and Dark Green upper surfaces, to the B Scheme pattern, with the new 'Sky' under surfaces introduced on 7 June 1940 following Signal X915 which stated that all under surfaces of fighter aircraft were to be Sky Type S. The problem was, at that time most fighter squadrons had no idea what colour Sky was and anyway supplies of Sky Type S or indeed Sky to DTD 63A with reduced gloss, were almost impossible to obtain. Therefore various shades of green, blue, and grey were used before the official shade of Sky became the more commonly seen colour from late-August/ early September onwards. P3522 has been illustrated here in BS 381 (1930) No 16 Eau-de-Nil, a duck-egg green shade, but it could have been any one of the other alternatives used by the Squadrons' hard-pressed ground crews.

This particular aircraft shows how the various markings changes had been implemented, with the addition of the Yellow outer ring to the original Red/White/Blue fuselage roundel, truncated along the lower longeron upper/under surface colour demarcation line, the fin stripes with approximately 9 inch wide Blue and White bands and the whole of the forward fin in Red, and the large Medium Sea Grey code letters overlapping on to the fuselage roundel. P3522 was fitted with a Rotol propeller unit.

Not to any scale

▲ N1536/PS-R can be seen at the head of this line of Defiant Mk.Is of 264 Squadron from Kirton-in-Lindsey during August 1940. (Photo: Imperial War Museum)

Conversely Grossadmiral Karl Dönitz believed air superiority alone was not enough. The massive superiority of the Royal Navy over the Kriegsmarine could have made 'Sealion' a disaster and even the mighty Luftwaffe might have been unable to prevent intervention by British cruisers and destroyers, even with air superiority.

Despite all these doubts, the opening stages of the Battle of Britain began with a series of running fights over convoys in the English Channel and occasional attacks on the convoys by Ju 87 Stuka dive bombers. These attacks were launched partly because Kesselring and Sperrle needed to keep the pressure on the RAF and partly because it gave German aircrews some training and a chance to probe the British defences.

In general, these battles off the coast of southeast England tended to favour the Germans, whose bomber escorts massively outnumbered the RAF's airborne convoy patrols. The need for constant patrols over the convoys put a severe strain on Fighter Command's pilots and machines, wasting fuel, engine hours and exhausting the pilots, but eventually the number of ship sinkings became so great that the British Admiralty cancelled all further convoys through the Channel.

However, these early combat encounters provided both sides with a degree of combat experience. They also gave the first indications that some of the aircraft types, such as the Defiant and Bf 110, were not up to the intense dog-fighting that would characterise the rest of the Battle.

One other worrying aspect, (that was not made public at the time) was that RAF fighter losses had been much higher than had been anticipated, (including losses of Spitfires), and with intelligence reports overestimating Luftwaffe numbers, any means of improving the performance of Home Defence Fighter Units was to be urgently sought.

Realisation that the existing two-position (coarse and fine) de Havilland/Hamilton variable pitch propellers on Hurricanes and Spitfires was seriously limiting their performance, prompted the instigation of a major operation which saw the conversion over to Rotol constant speed propellers just as the Battle of France was in its final critical phase.

Camouflage and Markings

Sky under surfaces for Fighters

With France expected to fall whilst the evacuation at Dunkerque was taking place, there was a call for a new under surface scheme for Home Defence fighters, especially in light of the anticipated ground based Radio-location and airborne Identification Friend or Foe (IFF) equipment that would soon be fitted in to RAF aircraft, thus negating the need for the special Night and White under surface recognition marking scheme.

If the supply situation was difficult with 'Sky' being applied to Bomber Command's Blenheims, (see previous chapter), the

▲ An air-gunner of 264 Squadron about to enter the gun-turret of his Boulton Paul Defiant Mk.I at at Kirton-in-Lindsey, Lincolnshire, in early August 1940. He is wearing the GQ Parasuit, supplied exclusively to Defiant gunners, which incorporates a parachute harness and life-saving jacket within a smock overall. Four .303 Browning machine-guns are mounted in the Boulton Paul power-operated turret. (Photo: Imperial War Museum)

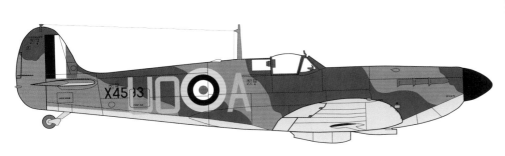

Supermarine Spitfire Mk.I, X4593/ UO-A, 266 Squadron, RAF Wittering, Cambridgeshire, July/August 1940.

Finished in the standard Temperate Land Scheme of Dark Earth and Dark Green upper surfaces, to the B Scheme pattern, with 'Sky' under surfaces – illustrated in a pale duck egg green shade – X4593 was one of the Spitfires which featured the large 7 inch diameter Red centre to the fuselage roundel, thought to be a Supermarine draughtsman's error on the revised camouflage drawings of 16 May 1940. Fitted with a de Havilland/ Hamilton propeller unit.

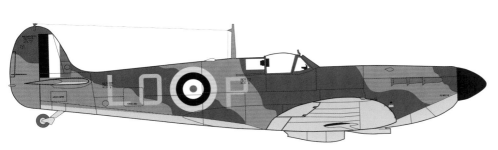

Supermarine Spitfire Mk.I, (serial unknown – overpainted)/LO-P of 602 Squadron, RAF Westhampnett, West Sussex, August 1940.

602 Squadron moved south from its base at Drem in Scotland at the beginning of August to Westhampnett, a satellite airfield near the Sector Station at Tangmere, and stayed there in the thick of the fighting throughout the Battle. LO-P, whose serial number appears to have been overpainted, (still a frequent occurrence during this period), is finished in the standard Temperate Land Scheme of Dark Earth and Dark Green upper surfaces, to the B Scheme pattern, with 'Sky' under surfaces – illustrated in BS 381 (1930) No 16 Eau-de-Nil, a rich duck egg green shade. Fitted with a de Havilland/Hamilton propeller unit.

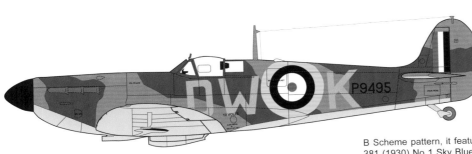

Supermarine Spitfire Mk.I, P9495/ DW-K, 610 Squadron, RAF Biggin Hill, Kent, August 1940.

Featured in one of the most iconic photos taken during the Battle of Britain of a formation, 610 Squadron Spitfires, the lead aircraft coded DW-K is thought to have been P9495, which may have been painted over. Finished in the standard Temperate Land Scheme of Dark Earth and Dark Green upper surfaces, to the B Scheme pattern, it featured 'dark' Sky under surfaces – possibly BSS 381 (1930) No 1 Sky Blue, a duck egg blue shade. P9495 was damaged by Bf 109s at Romney near Dover in Kent on 12 August 1940 and was subsequently Struck Off Charge. Note the large fuselage roundel and narrow fin stripes. Fitted with a de Havilland/Hamilton propeller unit.

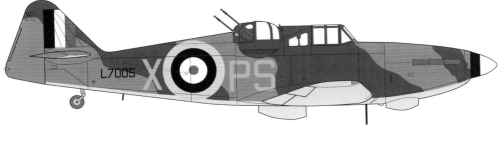

Boulton Paul Defiant Mk.I, L7005/PS-X, 264 Squadron, RAF Kirton-in-Lindsey, Lincolnshire, August 1940.

L7005 was 264 Squadron's top-scoring Defiant which saw action over Dunkerque as well as in the Battle of Britain proper, (including at least three night patrols), before it was written-off after a forced landing following combat with Bf 109Es over Hearne Bay on 26 August 1940, crewed by the top-scoring team of Sergeants R Thorn and F Barker. Finished in the standard Temperate Land Scheme of Dark Earth and Dark Green upper surfaces, to the B Scheme pattern, with 'Sky' under surfaces – illustrated here in a pale duck-egg green shade.

Hawker Hurricane Mk.I, P2946/VK-A, 238 Squadron, RAF Middle Wallop, Hampshire, August 1940.

Standard Temperate Land Scheme of Dark Earth and Dark Green upper surfaces, to the A Scheme pattern, with 'Sky' under surfaces – illustrated here in a duck-egg blue shade, possibly BSS 381 (1930) No 1 Sky Blue. Note the bright pre-war Red and Blue shades of the fuselage roundel, which was still being applied by some manufacturers and the broad (approx 12 inch wide) fin stripes. Fitted with a Rotol propeller unit.

Not to any scale

Supermarine Spitfire Mk.I, P9503/DW-D, 610 Squadron, RAF Gravesend, Kent, early/mid June 1940.

610 Squadron were at the forefront of the early clashes over the Channel between the Luftwaffe and RAF Fighter Command following the fall of France. P9503 was finished in the standard Temperate Land Scheme of Dark Earth and Dark Green upper surfaces, to the B Scheme pattern, with 'Sky' under surfaces introduced on 7 June 1940 – in this instance illustrated in Sky DTD 63A with reduced gloss. P9503 was damaged on 29 July 1940, was repaired and allocated to 609 Squadron at RAF Warmwell, Dorsetshire. It was damaged again on 15 October, and was finally lost on 27 October 1940, although its pilot, Pilot Officer P A Baillon, baled out successfully. Fitted with a de Havilland/Hamilton propeller unit.

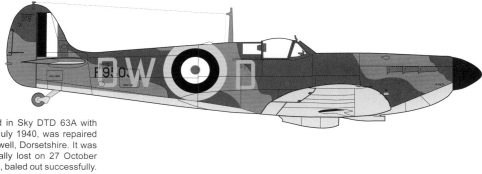

Hawker Hurricane Mk.I, (serial unknown – overpainted)/SO-E, 145 Squadron, RAF Croydon, June 1940.

Standard Temperate Land Scheme of Dark Earth and Dark Green upper surfaces, to the A Scheme pattern, with the new 'Sky' under surfaces – illustrated here in BS 381 (1930) 16 Eau-de-Nil, a duck-egg green shade. Note the narrow Yellow outer ring to the fuselage roundel, the truncated Red/White/Blue fin flash not quite reaching the top of the fin, the painted out serial number and the relatively small code letters. Fitted with a de Havilland/Hamilton propeller unit.

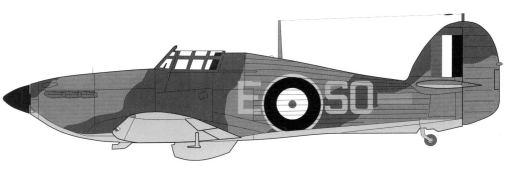

Hawker Hurricane Mk.I, N2359/YB-J, 17 Squadron, RAF Debden, North Essex, June 1940.

Standard Temperate Land Scheme of Dark Earth and Dark Green upper surfaces, to the A Scheme pattern, with 'Sky' under surfaces – illustrated here in a pale duck-egg green shade. Note the 'Sky' spinner, a non-standard anomaly at this time applied to several 17 Squadron Hurricanes, and the winged Popeye cartoon, (another rarity; as any form of 'artwork' on RAF aircraft at this time was rare), who appears to be holding a gun or perhaps a screwdriver? Fitted with a de Havilland/Hamilton propeller unit.

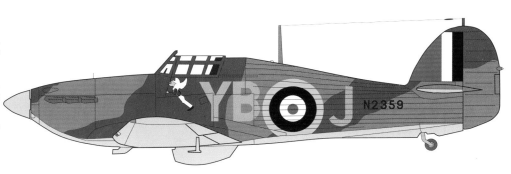

Supermarine Spitfire Mk.I, R6799/YT-D, 65 Squadron, RAF Hornchurch, Essex, early July 1940.
Pilot: Squadron Leader H C Sawyer

Finished in the standard Temperate Land Scheme of Dark Earth and Dark Green upper surfaces, to the B Scheme pattern, with 'Sky' under surfaces – in this instance illustrated in a duck egg green shade, possibly BS 381 (1930) No 16 Eau-de-Nil. Note the 'East India Fund Flight' stencil below the canopy on the starboard side. R6799 stalled on take-off for a night patrol at Rochford on 2 August 1940, tragically killing the pilot, Squadron Leader H C Sawyer. Fitted with a de Havilland/Hamilton propeller unit.

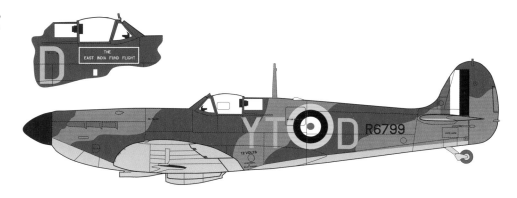

THE EAST INDIA FUND FLIGHT

Supermarine Spitfire Mk.I, (possibly K9953 – overpainted)/ZP-A, 74 Squadron, RAF Hornchurch, Essex, July 1940.
Pilot: Flt Lt Adolph G 'Sailor' Malan

74 was another of the 'Hornchurch Wing' squadrons operating out of that famous RAF airfield in July 1940. Flown by an equally famous pilot, Adolph G 'Sailor' Malan, who was promoted Squadron Leader of the unit in August 1940, ZP-A, (possibly K9953) was finished in the standard Temperate Land Scheme of Dark Earth and Dark Green upper surfaces, to the A Scheme pattern, with 'Sky' under surfaces – in this instance illustrated in a duck egg blue shade, possibly BSS 381 (1930) No 1 Sky Blue. Fitted with a de Havilland/Hamilton propeller unit.

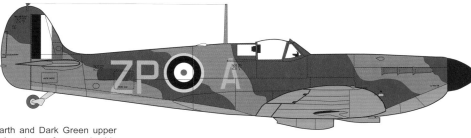

Not to any scale

Heinkel He 111P, G1+FA, Geschwaderstab/KG 55 'Greif', Villacoublay, France, July 1940.

Finished in the standard two-tone green RLM 70 Schwarzgrün and RLM 71 Dunkelgrün upper surfaces in a straight-edged 'splinter' pattern with RLM 65 Hellblau undersides, codes were black with a black individual aircraft letter 'F' outlined in the Geschwaderstab colour green, and green propeller spinners. Note the central position of the swastika across the fin and rudder and the Geschwader's red and black 'Griffon' on a white shield to the rear of the cockpit.

Heinkel He 111P, G1+FA, Geschwaderstab/KG 55 'Greif', Villacoublay, France, July 1940.

The Luftwaffe operated several floatplane He 59-equipped maritime reconnaissance units based around the country's Baltic coastline, typified by this Küstenfliegergruppe 506 example finished in the two-tone 'maritime greens' RLM 72 Grün and RLM 73 Grün upper surfaces, in a straight-edged 'splinter' pattern, with RLM 65 Hellblau undersides. Codes were all black with without the individual aircraft letter 'V' being painted in, or even outlined in, the usual Staffel colour yellow. Note the central position of the swastika across the fin and rudder and the unit's 'Ram's Skull' badge on the forward fuselage.

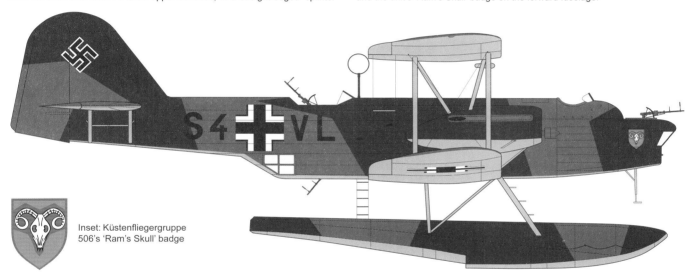

Inset: Küstenfliegergruppe 506's 'Ram's Skull' badge

Heinkel He 59B-2, D-ASUO, Seenotflugkommando 1, Boulogne, France, July 1940.

The Luftwaffe was much better prepared for the task of air-sea rescue than the RAF, with one unit, Seenotflugkommando 1 equipped with Heinkel He 59 floatplanes, specifically tasked with picking up downed aircrew from the North Sea, English Channel and the Dover Straits. In accordance with the Geneva Convention, the He 59s were unarmed and painted white overall, with civilian registration markings and red crosses. Nevertheless, RAF aircraft attacked them, particularly as some were escorted by Bf 109s. A controversial combat occurred on on 9 July 1940 when this machine was forced down by Pilot Officer 'Johnny' Allen, 54 Squadron, on to the Goodwin Sands, off Ramsgate, Kent. Apart from a broken petrol feed pipe to the fuel tank, D-ASUO suffered no other damage and was towed ashore by the Walmer lifeboat and beached near the lifeboat station. Following this episode, an official Government-backed RAF order was issued which stated that as of 20 July 1940, all Seenotdienst aircraft were to be shot down.

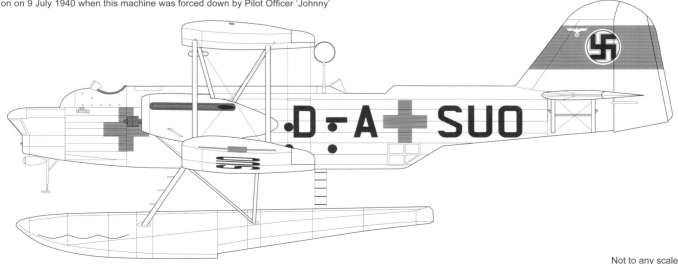

Not to any scale

▲ Defiant Mk.I L7005/PS-X of 264 Squadron, being prepared for take off by groundcrew at Kirton-in-Lindsey, Lincolnshire during early August 1940. (Photo: Imperial War Museum)

situation became infinitely worse from early June 1940 when the use of Sky on Fighter Command aircraft was authorised.

The introduction of Sky to the under surfaces of fighter aircraft can be said to have begun from 6 June 1940. On this date the Air Ministry sent Signal X915 which stated that all under surfaces of fighter aircraft, (that is the mainplanes, fuselage, and tailplanes), were to be Sky. All previous instructions regarding the painting and marking of the under surfaces of fighter aircraft were cancelled.

This immediately caused problems as at that time most fighter squadrons had no idea what colour Sky was. The Air Ministry tried to get around this problem by sending a signal to all concerned on 7 June, which said that, *"The colour of camouflage Sky Type S, repeat S, may be described as Duck Egg Blueish Green..."*, and it would seem that whoever wrote the original signal did not really know whether the colour he was describing was a 'blue' or a 'green'!

The Air Ministry could promulgate what it liked, but it would appear that supplies of Sky (Type S or indeed to DTD 63A with reduced gloss), were difficult to obtain, as, on 10 June, Signal X348 cancelled X915 of 6 June pending further instructions. This signal was followed by Signal X349 a short time later that same day, which stated that due to only limited supplies of Sky Type S to DTD 63A, being available, fighters were to continue to operate with the Night and White under surface colour scheme until supplies of Sky became available.

Following the Signals of 6 June 1940, the fighter squadrons began to indent the stores depots for supplies of 'Sky Type S'. However, as supplies of this colour and material were difficult, if not impossible, to obtain, the squadrons were forced to use something else instead.

Eyewitness accounts for the period June-August 1940, suggest that there were various shades of green, blue, and grey being

▲A formation of Defiant Mk.Is of 264 Squadron, based at Kirton-in-Lindsey in Lincolnshire. N1535/PS-A is pictured leading L7026/PS-V and at least two other aircraft on a cloudy day in early August 1940. (Photo: Imperial War Museum)

Messerschmitt Bf 109E-4, 'Black chevron and disc', Stab III/JG 51, St Omer Nord, France, July 1940.
Pilot: Gruppe's Technical Officer, Oblt Werner Pichon-Kalau von Hofe

Inset: III/JG 51's 'Axt von Niederrhein' (Axe of Niederrhein – a town on the Lower Rhine) emblem.

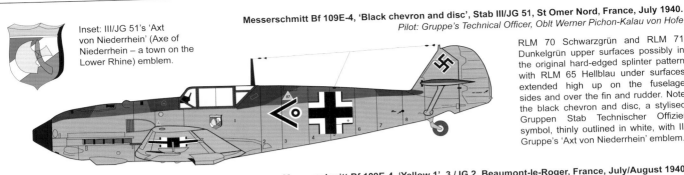

RLM 70 Schwarzgrün and RLM 71 Dunkelgrün upper surfaces possibly in the original hard-edged splinter pattern with RLM 65 Hellblau under surfaces extended high up on the fuselage sides and over the fin and rudder. Note the black chevron and disc, a stylised Gruppen Stab Technischer Offizier symbol, thinly outlined in white, with III Gruppe's 'Axt von Niederrhein' emblem.

Messerschmitt Bf 109E-4, 'Yellow 1', 3./JG 2, Beaumont-le-Roger, France, July/August 1940.
Pilot: Oblt Hanns-Jobst Hauenschild

Inset: 3./JG 2 Staffel's 'Horrido' word on a pennant.

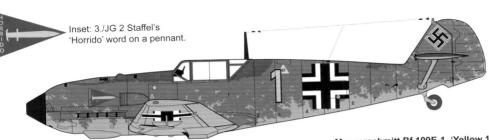

RLM 70 Schwarzgrün and RLM 71 Dunkelgrün upper surfaces possibly in the original hard-edged splinter pattern with RLM 65 Hellblau under surfaces extended high up on the fuselage sides and over the fin and rudder, which have then had a dense stipple of RLM 70/71 applied. Note the white of the fuselage balkenkreuz has been reduced by expanding the black of the outline.

Messerschmitt Bf 109E-1, 'Yellow 11', 9./JG 26, Caffiers, France, August 1940.
Pilot: Fw Artur Beese

Inset: JG 26's black 'Schlageter' script 'S' on a white shield.

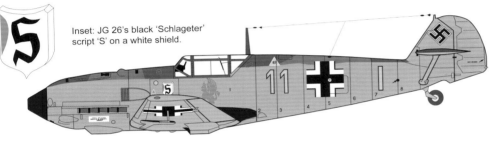

RLM 71 Dunkelgrün and RLM 02 Grau upper surfaces in a soft-edged splinter pattern with RLM 65 Hellblau under surfaces extended high up on the fuselage sides and over the fin and rudder. Note the small size of the fuselage balkenkreuz, numeral '11' and III Gruppe vertical bar and the red 'Hollenhund' (Hell hound), 9 Staffel emblem, under the cockpit. This aircraft force landed in the sand dunes near Calais on 24 August 1940.

Messerschmitt Bf 109E-4, 'Black 1', 5./JG 3, Wierre-au-Bois, France, August 1940.
Pilot: Oblt Herbert Kijewski, the Staffelkapitan

Inset: II Gruppe JG 3's black and white segmented shield with a red outline.

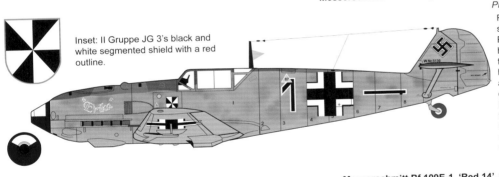

RLM 71 Dunkelgrün and RLM 02 Grau upper surfaces in a soft-edged splinter pattern with RLM 65 Hellblau under surfaces extended high up on the fuselage sides and over the fin and rudder. A sparse mottle of RLM 71/02 has been applied over the fuselage sides, fin and rudder. Note the Staffelkapitan pennant on the radio aerial mast, the white quartered RLM 70 spinner and the name 'Erika' on the cowling, after Kijewski's wife. Naming the aircraft after wives and girlfriends was common in this Staffel. The II/JG 3 shield, was carried on the forward fuselage in front of the cockpit.

Messerschmitt Bf 109E-1, 'Red 14', 2./JG 52, Coquelles, France, August 1940.
Pilot: Uffz Leo Zaunbrecher

Inset: 2 Staffel's 'devil with bow and arrow' emblem.

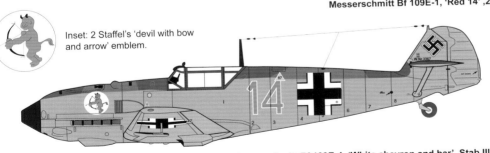

RLM 71 Dunkelgrün and RLM 02 Grau upper surfaces in a soft-edged splinter pattern with RLM 65 Hellblau under surfaces extended high up on the fuselage sides and over the fin and rudder. Note the Staffel's 'devil with bow and arrow' emblem on the cowling side. This aircraft was crash landed by Uffz Zaunbrecher at Selmeston, Sussex on 12 August 1940.

Messerschmitt Bf 109E-4, 'White chevron and bar', Stab III/JG 54, Guines-sud, France, August 1940.
Pilot: Oblt Albrecht Drehs

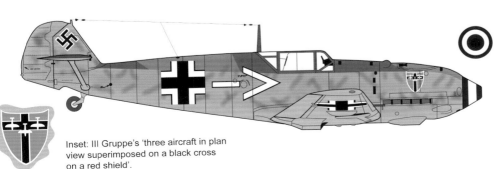

Inset: III Gruppe's 'three aircraft in plan view superimposed on a black cross on a red shield'.

RLM 71 Dunkelgrün and RLM 02 Grau upper surfaces in a soft-edged splinter pattern with RLM 65 Hellblau under surfaces extended high up on the fuselage sides and over the fin and rudder. A sparse streaky mottle of RLM 71/02 has been applied over the fuselage sides, fin and rudder. Note the white band around the RLM 70 spinner, and JG 54's III Gruppe shield emblem on the cowling side. This aircraft was crash landed by Oblt Drehs at Hengrove, Kent on 12 August 1940.

Not to any scale

Junkers Ju 87B-2, A5+AK, 2./StG 1, based at Angers, France, August 1940.

Despite the introduction of the broader white areas to the balkenkreuze, there were still some aircraft with the earlier style, such as A5+AK illustrated here. Finished in the standard two-tone green RLM 70 Schwarzgrün and RLM 71 Dunkelgrün upper surfaces in a straight-edged 'splinter' pattern with RLM 65 Hellblau undersides. Codes were black with a red (for 2 Staffel) individual aircraft letter 'A' and red tip to the RLM 70 propeller spinner. Note the small 'diving raven' on the nose and the swastika in the earlier central position across the fin and rudder.

Junkers Ju 87B-1, 6G+AT, 6./StG 1, based at Pas-de-Calais, France, August 1940.

There was a great deal of reorganisation within the various Geshwader following the Battle of France where Gruppen and sometimes individual Staffeln, were reallocated to different units, but, initially at least, kept their original codes, as in the case of 6,/StG 1 which carried the 6G codes, and badge, of 9./StG 51 from which it was formed in early July 1940. 6G+AT is finished in the standard two-tone green RLM 70 Schwarzgrün and RLM 71 Dunkelgrün upper surfaces in a straight-edged 'splinter' pattern with RLM 65 Hellblau undersides. Codes were black with a yellow (for 6 Staffel) individual aircraft letter 'A' and a broad white band around the RLM 70 propeller spinner. Note the Staffel's 'devil riding a bomb' badge under the windscreen and swastika in the earlier position across the fin and rudder.

Junkers Ju 87B-2, L1+CU, 10 Staffel IV(Stuka)/LG 1, Tramecourt, France, August 1940.

Finished in the standard two-tone green RLM 70 Schwarzgrün and RLM 71 Dunkelgrün upper surfaces in a straight-edged 'splinter' pattern with RLM 65 Hellblau undersides, codes were black with a white (for 10 Staffel) individual aircraft letter 'C' and a white tip to the RLM 70 propeller spinner. Note the individual aircraft letter 'C' on the front of the spats and the Staffel's 'devil with trident riding a bomb' badge under the windscreen.

Junkers Ju 87B-1, S2+AN, 5./StG 77, Caen-Carpiquet, France, August 1940.

Finished in the standard two-tone green RLM 70 Schwarzgrün and RLM 71 Dunkelgrün upper surfaces in a straight-edged 'splinter' pattern with RLM 65 Hellblau undersides, codes were black with a red (for 5 Staffel) individual aircraft letter 'A' and a red tip to the RLM 70 propeller spinner. Note the swastika in the earlier position across the fin and rudder, the individual aircraft letter 'A' on the front of the wheel spats and the Staffel's variation of the leaping panther design under the cockpit.

Junkers Ju 87B-1, S2+EN, 5./StG 77, the forward airstrip at Brugy, France, August 1940.

Starboard side view of the camouflage pattern of an aircraft finished in the standard two-tone green RLM 70 Schwarzgrün and RLM 71 Dunkelgrün upper surfaces in a straight-edged 'splinter' pattern with RLM 65 Hellblau undersides. Codes were black with a red (for 5 Staffel) individual aircraft letter 'E'. RLM 70 propeller spinner. Note the Staffel's badge in front of the cockpit.

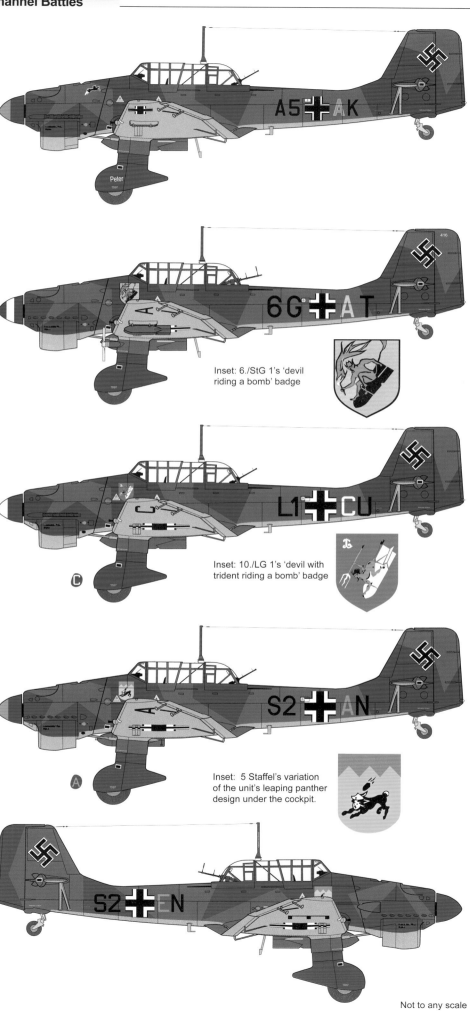

Inset: 6./StG 1's 'devil riding a bomb' badge

Inset: 10./LG 1's 'devil with trident riding a bomb' badge

Inset: 5 Staffel's variation of the unit's leaping panther design under the cockpit.

Not to any scale

Messerschmitt Bf 110C, 2N+GN, 5./ZG 1, Trier-Euren, Germany, June 1940.

Finished in the standard two-tone green RLM 70 Schwarzgrün and RLM 71 Dunkelgrün upper surfaces in a straight-edged 'splinter' pattern with RLM 65 Hellblau undersides. Codes were black with the individual aircraft letter 'G' in the 5 Staffel colour red, outlined in white, and red tips to the RLM 70 propeller spinners. Note the wide spacing of the code letters. This machine was shot down by Swiss Bf 109E fighters whilst escorting He 111s of 4./KG 1 on an attack on Besacon, France, on 8 June 1940. The aircraft crash-landed at Oberkirch, Switzerland.

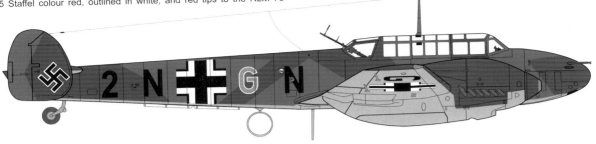

Messerschmitt Bf 110C, A2+BH, 1./ZG 52, Neufchateau, France, June 1940.

Finished in the standard two-tone green RLM 70 Schwarzgrün and RLM 71 Dunkelgrün upper surfaces in a straight-edged 'splinter' pattern with RLM 65 Hellblau undersides. Codes were black with the individual aircraft letter 'B' in the 1 Staffel colour white. Note the white spinners and the unit's 'dragon shield' on the nose.

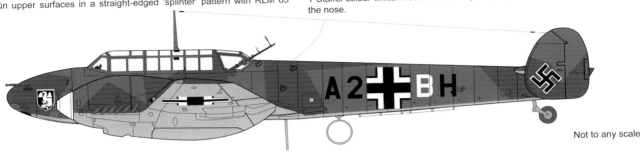

Not to any scale

used on Day Fighter under surfaces before the official shade of Sky became more commonly seen colour from late-August/early September onwards.

In fact evidence has been found of the use of at least five different under surface colours on Fighter Command fighters. These were Sky Grey; BS 381 (1930) No 1 Sky Blue; BS 381 (1930) No 16 Eau-de-Nil; an unidentified blue-grey (possibly Air Ministry Sky Blue?); and the correct colour/shade of Sky.

Sky Grey was an alternative that was readily available at the time as it was the colour developed for Fleet Air Arm aircraft which has already been mentioned, and Sky is the colour which was supposed to be used. The use of the other three colours however is particularly interesting.

Two other standard colours which might possibly have been used, which would account for the colloquial descriptions of the under surfaces reported by eyewitnesses at the time of 'duck egg blue', and 'a rich duck egg green', were BSS 381 (1930) No 1 Sky Blue, a light blue-green colour which could be described as a 'duck egg blue' and BS 381 (1930) No 16 Eau-de-Nil which could be considered to be a 'duck egg green' and was actually the sort of colour actually required.

When faced with demands for Sky which could not initially be met, both the Service and aircraft paint industry supplied what was available. Sky Grey could have readily been drawn from existing service stocks and the use of the two BS 381 colours, No 1 Sky Blue and No 16 Eau-de-Nil, is possibly connected with the decision to use DTD 63A specification finishes as both these colours might well have been available to this specification. In the case of Air Ministry Sky Blue, a paint manufacturer faced with a demand for "Duck Egg Blue (Sky Type S) to DTD 63A with reduced gloss" might well have supplied a colour called Sky Blue which actually looked like

a duck egg blue. And it is thought that some fighter squadrons used Aluminium for a time

Besides these colours it is likely that other variations also existed. For example it is known that individual units tried to mix their own matches for Sky. At the time of writing, no official documentation on this subject has come to light, and, as has already been mentioned, the Service was advised not to try mixing paint with dope or materials to DTD 308 with those of DTD 314, although it is quite likely that this did take place but to what result remains unknown.

Colours other than those mentioned above such as Air Ministry Light Mediterranean Blue or BS 381 (1930) No 28 Silver Grey might also have been used. (Azure Blue had not yet been invented). However, no physical or documentary evidence has as yet come to light to confirm or refute the use of any or all of these colours. Technical representatives were sent around the Fighter Squadrons assisting in whatever help was needed, either in the cleaning down to achieve good adhesion or application of the new finish, or in emergency hand mixing of colour on site.

Although Sky Blue, where available, was considered too pale a hue, it could make a reasonable 'Sky' shade by mixing in a little Dark Green, Yellow and White. The result would not be to Type S standard of course, but a quick polish would help. Blue, Dark Green, Yellow and White in the right proportions could also result in a reasonable 'Sky' finish. Even production Sky was a colour that could vary slightly from batch to batch. Mixing Sky in matt and gloss, cellulose, synthetic and distemper in all their forms would no doubt have resulted in a variety of hues.

With such a mixture of official Air Ministry titles and colloquial ones used by the Air Ministry and public alike, is there any wonder that the introduction of Sky under surfaces appears

Messerschmitt Bf 110C, 3M+GK, 2./ZG 2, Amiens-Glissy, France, July 1940.

Finished in the standard two-tone green RLM 70 Schwarzgrün and RLM 71 Dunkelgrün upper surfaces in a straight-edged 'splinter' pattern with RLM 65 Hellblau undersides. All the codes appear to be black with the individual aircraft

letter 'G' thinly outlined in white. RLM 70 propeller spinners. Note this aircraft carried I/ZG 2's 'Hunter of Bernburger' unit badge on the nose under the windscreen, (hidden behind the engine cowling – see inset).

Inset: I/ZG 2's 'Hunter of Bernburger' unit badge.

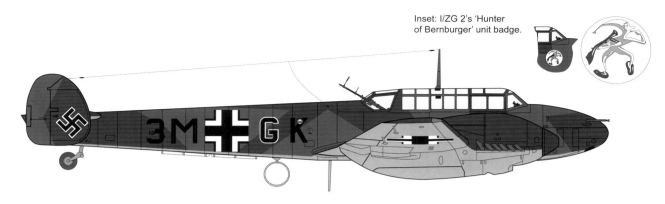

Messerschmitt Bf 110C, 2N+PH, 1./ZG 76, Laval, France, July 1940.

Finished in the standard two-tone green RLM 70 Schwarzgrün and RLM 71 Dunkelgrün upper surfaces in a straight-edged 'splinter' pattern with RLM 65 Hellblau undersides. Codes were black with the individual aircraft letter 'P' in

white, the 1 Staffel colour, and white tips to the RLM 70 propeller spinners. Note the early narrow-bordered fuselage balkenkreuz, swastika in the early central position across the fin and rudder and two narrow white bands around the rear fuselage which may have indicated a Schwarmfuhrer (Flight Leader).

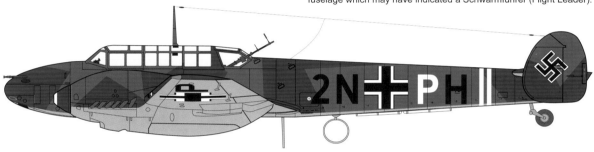

Messerschmitt Bf 110C, 2N+EP, 9./ZG 76, Laval, France, July 1940.
Crewed by Oblt Gerhard Kadow and Gfr Helmut Scholz.

Finished in the standard two-tone green RLM 70 Schwarzgrün and RLM 71 Dunkelgrün upper surfaces in a straight-edged 'splinter' pattern with RLM 65 Hellblau undersides. Codes were black with the individual aircraft letter 'E' in yellow, the 9 Staffel colour, and yellow tips to the RLM 70 propeller spinners. Note

the two white 'kill' bars on the fin. This machine crash landed at Grange Heath, Lulworth, Devon, on 11 July 1940. Pilot, Oblt Gerhard Kadow and Bordfunker, Gfr Helmut Scholz, were both captured wounded.

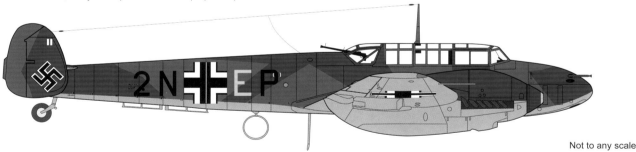

Not to any scale

to have caused more than its fair share of problems over the ensuing decades!

In the final analysis, it is almost impossible to say with any degree of certainty what colour any RAF fighter was on its under surfaces during the period June to August 1940, if some part of it is not obviously in the Night and White scheme, for the simple reason that possibly so many alternative colours appear to have been used as there were insufficient supplies of any one colour.

Luftwaffe

Whilst the new RLM 71 Dunkelgrün/RLM 02 Grau upper surfaces and RLM 65 Hellblau fuselage sides and under

surfaces scheme for fighters was apparently found to be satisfactory during the campaign through France and the Low Countries, during May and June 1940, it was appreciated that further problems with suitable camouflage would arise as they flew across the English Channel, and the unit-applied mottle applications mentioned in Chapter 2 became the norm. Different units adopted different styles and it is understood that these styles were generally decided upon at Gruppe or Geschwader level.

By the time of the opening stages of the Battle of Britain proper in early July 1940, the RLM 70 Schwarzgrün/71 Dunkelgrün upper surfaces were the exception on most Bf 109Es and many Bf 110s, and the RLM 71 Dunkelgrün/02 Grau upper surface scheme was firmly established, albeit with minor variations within the upper surface camouflage patterns which had much 'softer' demarcations and weren't so 'hard-edged'.

Jagdwaffe markings

Further explanation in greater detail of the Jagdwaffe's marking systems might be appropriate here. As briefly mentioned in the introduction, each Staffel was numbered independently within its Gruppe, as were the Gruppen within their Geschwader. When written down for administrative purposes however, the Gruppe number, (identified by Roman numerals), wasn't normally mentioned, because the Staffel number, (identified by Arabic numerals), indicated to which Gruppe the Staffel belonged.
For example:- 9./JG 3 = 9 Staffel, of III Gruppe, of Jagdgeschwader 3.

Individual aircraft within a Staffel were marked with a numeral, (or in some cases a letter), in the Staffel colour, often, but not always, outlined in a contrasting colour. These numerals were generally placed immediately in front of the fuselage cross (both sides), but occasionally were carried on the engine cowling, for example in the cases of 7 and 9./JG 27, or under the windscreen, eg 7 and 8./JG 54.

The Staffel colours were white for the first Staffeln of each Gruppe - ie 1, 4 and 7; initially red for the second Staffeln - ie 2, 5 and 8 - but in mid-1940, an anomaly not only peculiar to the Battle of Britain period but apparent on occasions throughout the war, was the frequent use of black numerals, outlined in either white or red; and yellow for the third Staffeln - ie 3, 6 and 9.

Other exceptions to the rules, include the use of brown numerals by 6./JG 26, 3./JG 51 and 3./LG 2, with light blue and/or light grey numerals being used by 5./JG 53. It must also be added that the use of a single letter, (rather than a numeral), appears to have been confined to 4, 5 and 6, (ie II Gruppe) LG 2, who also marked their aircraft with a black equilateral triangle, invariably outlined in white. The reason for this is that LG 2 had previously been equipped with Henschel Hs 123s in the Schlacht (ground attack) role in the Polish Campaign, and when the unit was re-equipped with Bf 109Es it retained the marking – in front of the fuselage cross, with the letter in the Staffel colour, aft of the cross. Stab machines carried green coloured letters aft of the cross, an example being Oberleutnant Krafft's green 'D' of Stab II/(S)LG 2. I/LG 2 appear to have retained the normal Staffel numeral system.

It had also not been uncommon for the Staffelkapitän to pilot the aircraft marked with the numeral '1', although by July/August this practice tended to be the exception rather than the rule, as did the practice for the Staffelkapitän to carry a metal pennant from the aircraft's radio mast, painted in the Staffel colour, another feature which declined during the course of the Battle of Britain.

Another point worthy of mention, is that Staffel numerals rarely exceeded the numeral '16' – aircraft bearing higher numbers tended to indicate that they belonged to a Training Staffel.

The different Gruppen within a Geschwader were identified by a 'symbol' aft of the fuselage cross, invariably in the same Staffel colour(s) as the numerals. Exceptions to this rule being where second Staffel aircraft had been re-marked with black numerals and had the Gruppe symbol left in the original red.

Stab, (Staff Flight) aircraft used a slightly different system of identification, and the aircraft of these staff pilots and fighter leaders carried distinctive markings for quick identification.

Chevron, bar and/or circle markings were carried in front of the fuselage cross instead of numerals, to denote a particular Stab rank, which actually varied somewhat between units. Also, as mentioned earlier, not all Stab personnel were actually pilots, and it was presumably in such cases where there was insufficient Stab personnel able to fly, that 'normal' Staffel pilots were picked to fly with the Stabsschwarm, in numeral-marked aircraft, (eg Oblt Wilhelm Frönhofer's 'yellow 10' of Stab III/JG 26).

Both Gruppe and Geschwader Stab markings were usually painted in black with white trim, or white with black trim, but other examples have also been recorded. Geschwaderstab aircraft were not allocated any unit i/d markings aft of the fuselage cross, (as they were not directly attached to any particular Gruppe), but some, such as JG 2 Geschwader Kommodore Major Helmut Wick's Bf 109E-4, Werknummer 5344, (in which he lost his life on 28 November 1940), and JG 26 Geschwader Kommodore Major Adolph Galland's E-4, (W.Nr 5819), also used circa October/November 1940, were seen with a horizontal bar aft of their fuselage crosses. However, these were almost certainly part of both commanders' interpretation of their Geschwader Kommodore's Stab rank markings, rather than a III Gruppe symbol, as both aircraft were also marked with a single chevron and horizontal bar in front of the fuselage cross, instead of the double-chevron and bar which was the original pre-war marking for a Geschwader Kommodore.

As a means of developing esprit de corps, aircraft were further frequently embellished by both personal 'artwork' and unit badges and, to a lesser extent by names. Not all the unit badges were identical even within the same units, and even varied in colour between aircraft. As with the unit badges, some of the personal artwork had 'history', having been carried on aircraft active in Spain with the Condor Legion.

Like all Luftwaffe aircraft, Bf 109s were originally delivered from the factory bearing large letters on either side of the fuselage crosses. Known as 'stamkennzeichen', these factory registration letters were generally overpainted or removed prior to the application of Staffel numerals/letters or Stab markings. Nevertheless, some continued to show through on some machines and aircraft are reported to have flown operationally with these factory registration letters still visible.

JG 53 – the Red Ring Geschwader

One of the enduring mysteries involving Battle of Britain period aircraft is the case of JG 53 'Pik As', which, for some reason that has never been fully explained, the Geschwader's 'Ace of Spades' unit badge was painted out for a period between July and September 1940 and replaced by a red band around the cowling.

It has been suggested that it was Göring who ordered the unit's 'Pik As' to be removed or overpainted and replaced with a red band. One reason given was possibly due to some personal dislike between the Reichsmarschall and the then current Geschwader Kommodore, Hans-Jürgen von Cramon-Taubadel. The underlying suggestion being that von Cramon-Taubadel had Jewish relatives in his family. Major von Cramon-Taubadel married Viola von Kaufmann-Asse in November 1933, who was apparently of Jewish ancestry, a fact which came to the attention of Göring during the Battle of France. The consequence was that Göring ordered that the entire JG 53 must remove their 'Ace of Spades' badge and paint a red band around the noses of their aircraft as a mark of shame.

Whatever the real reason, which actually may simply have just been a temporary identification marking introduced by this innovative unit, at the end of September, when Göring replaced many of the older Geshwader Kommodore with younger men, in JG 53's instance by Oblt Günther von Maltzahn, the famous 'Pik As' emblem began to reappear.

Another anomaly related to JG 53 was the overpainting of the swastika on the fins of several II and III Gruppe aircraft around the September to November 1940 period. Whether this was related to the reintroduction of the 'Pik As' emblem, a political gesture, or merely the whims of individual pilots is not known.

Junkers Ju 88A-1, B3+DC, Stab II/KG 54, St André-de-l'Eure, France, August 1940.

Finished in the standard two-tone green RLM 70 Schwarzgrün and RLM 71 Dunkelgrün upper surfaces in a straight-edged 'splinter' pattern with RLM 65 Hellblau undersides. Codes were black with a green individual aircraft letter 'D' in the Gruppe Stab colour. Note green diagonal band around the fuselage just aft of the wings and the white tips to the propeller spinners with a thin green band. This machine crash landed on the beach at Portland Head, Dorset, on 11 August 1940, following an attack on Portland Harbour

Dornier Do 17Z, 3Z+FR, 7./KG 77, Laon, France, August 1940.

Finished in the standard two-tone green RLM 70 Schwarzgrün and RLM 71 Dunkelgrün upper surfaces in a straight-edged 'splinter' pattern with RLM 65 Hellblau undersides. Codes were black with a white individual aircraft letter 'F' in the staffel colour and the white propeller spinners. Note the 'winged eagle' on a banner emblem of KG 77 on the nose.

Inset: The 'winged eagle' on a banner emblem
on a yellow shield outlined in black of III Gruppe KG 77

Junkers Ju 88A-1, 3Z+DK, 2./KG 77, Laon, France, August 1940.

KG 77 was in the process of converting from the Do 17Z to the 'new' Ju 88A during the summer of 1940. I Gruppe was equipped with the Ju 88A-1, as illustrated by 3Z+DK, finished in the standard two-tone green RLM 70 Schwarzgrün and RLM 71 Dunkelgrün upper surfaces in a straight-edged 'splinter' pattern with RLM 65 Hellblau undersides. Codes were black with the individual aircraft letter 'D' outlined in white. Note the red propeller spinners. Flown by Oblt Fritz Oeser this machine was damaged by fighters, 501 Squadron over London on 30 September 1940, and force-landed at Gatwick racecourse.

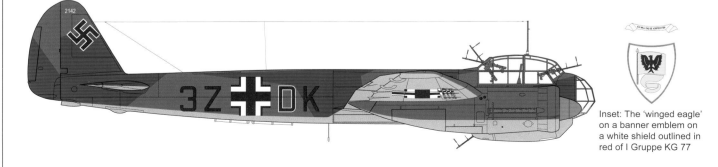

Inset: The 'winged eagle'
on a banner emblem on
a white shield outlined in
red of I Gruppe KG 77

Not to any scale

Messerschmitt Bf 109E-3, 'Black 3', 8./JG 53, La Villiaze, Guernsey, Channel Islands, August 1940.

Towards the end of July, all of JG 53's Bf 109Es started appearing with red bands around their cowlings, covering the unit's 'Pik As' (Ace of Spades) badge. RLM 71 Dunkelgrün and RLM 02 Grau upper surfaces in a soft-edged splinter pattern with RLM 65 Hellblau under surfaces extended high up on the fuselage sides and over the fin and rudder. A densely misted on mottle of RLM 71/02 has been applied over the fuselage sides, fin and rudder. Note the narrow bordered fuselage balkenkreuz, the red band around the cowling and the red tip to the RLM 70 spinner.

Messerschmitt Bf 109E-4, 'Black chevron and bars', Geschwaderstab JG 53, Dinan, France, August 1940
Pilot: Geschwader Kommodore, Maj Hans-Jurgen von Cramon-Taubadel

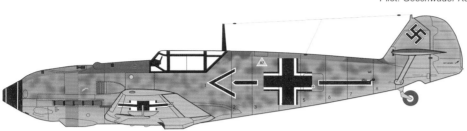

As explained in the accompanying text, it may have been von Cramon-Taubadel's wife's distant Jewish ancestry that caused all of JG 53's Bf 109Es to have red bands painted around their cowlings, covering the unit's 'Pik As' badge. RLM 71 Dunkelgrün and RLM 02 Grau upper surfaces in a soft-edged splinter pattern with RLM 65 Hellblau under surfaces extended high up on the fuselage sides and over the fin and rudder, with a densely applied mottle of RLM 71/02. Note again the narrow bordered fuselage balkenkreuz.

Messerschmitt Bf 109E-4, 'Black double chevron', Stab II/JG 53, Dinan, France, August 1940.
Pilot: II Gruppe Kommandeur, Maj Günther von Maltzahn

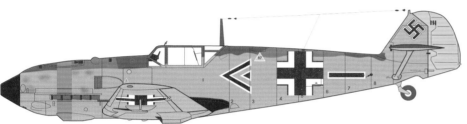

It was von Maltzahn that took over from von Cramon-Taubadel when Göring replaced all the 'older' Geschwader Kommodore at the end of September. RLM 71 Dunkelgrün and RLM 02 Grau upper surfaces in a soft-edged splinter pattern with RLM 65 Hellblau under surfaces extended high up on the fuselage sides and over the fin. Note the yellow rudder, three 'kill' bars on the rudder, (von Maltzahn ultimately claimed 68 victories), and the red band around the cowling.

Messerschmitt Bf 109E-1, 'White outline 12', 5./JG 53, Dinan, France, August 1940.

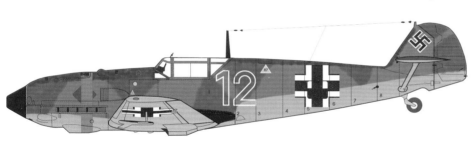

JG 53 were renowned for experimenting with their Bf 109's camouflage schemes as illustrated with this aircraft. RLM 71 Dunkelgrün and RLM 02 Grau upper surfaces in a soft-edged splinter pattern which were extended down the fuselage sides and over the fin and rudder meeting the RLM 65 Hellblau under surfaces midway along the fuselage sides. Note the white outline only numeral '12', the door to the first aid locker which has evidently been fitted inverted and the red band around the cowling. The spinner was RLM 70.

Messerschmitt Bf 109E-3, 'Black chevron', Stab III/JG 53, La Villiaze, Guernsey, Channel Islands, August 1940.
Pilot: Hptm Harro Harder, III Gruppe Kommandeur

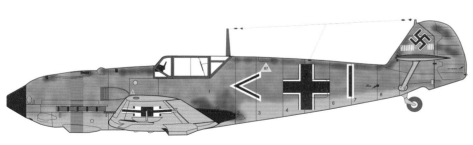

Another experimental camouflage scheme of RLM 71 Dunkelgrün and RLM 02 Grau upper surfaces in a soft-edged splinter pattern with RLM 65 Hellblau under surfaces extended up the fuselage sides and over the fin and rudder, over which a densely misted mix of RLM 71 and RLM 02 was applied. Note again the narrow bordered fuselage balkenkreuz, the red band around the cowling and the twelve white 'kill' bars on the fin. Hptm Harder was killed in action on 12 August 1940, having been credited with twenty-two victories, including eleven in Spain with the Condor Legion.

Messerschmitt Bf 109E-3, 'Black chevron and bars', Geschwaderstab JG 53, Rennes, France, early September 1940.
Pilot: Hptm Wilhelm Meyerweissflog

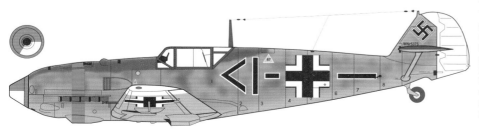

Possibly amongst the first experiments with 'greys', mixed from RLM 66 Schwarzgrau, RLM 71 Dunkelgrün and RLM 02 Grau on the upper surfaces in a soft-edged splinter pattern with RLM 65 Hellblau under surfaces extended high up on the fuselage sides and over the fin and rudder, over which a sparsely misted on 'grey' mottle has been applied. Note the white rudder and wing tips, the red band around the cowling and the white quartered red spinner. Hptm Meyerweissflog was shot down in this aircraft on 5 September 1940, at Monkton, Kent, and taken prisoner.

Not to any scale

▲ A crashed Heinkel He IIIP, 1G+NT of III/KG27, shot down by 92 Squadron's Blue Section at 1800 hrs on 14 August 1940, lying by the side of the road at Charterhouse, Somerset. Note the machine gun projecting from the starboard side of the fuselage as protection from beam attacks. (Photo: Imperial War Museum)

The main attack upon the RAF's defences was code-named 'Adlerangriff' (Eagle Attack), although bad weather over France and the British Isles, which proved such an important factor during the campaign, delayed 'Adlertag', (Eagle Day) until 13 August 1940.

On the previous day, 12 August, the first attempt was made to blind the RDF system when aircraft from the specialist fighter-bomber unit, Erprobungsgruppe 210 (ErprGr 210) attacked four radar stations. Three were briefly taken off the air but were back working within six hours. The raids appeared to show that British radars were difficult to knock out for any length of time. The failure to mount follow-up attacks allowed the RAF to get the stations back on the air, and the Luftwaffe neglected to mount strikes on the supporting infrastructure, such as telephone lines or power stations, which could have rendered the radars useless, even if the towers themselves (which were very difficult to destroy) remained intact.

It was on 13 August, 'Adlertag' (Eagle Day), that the Battle of Britain proper officially began for the Luftwaffe. First there was a series of attacks, again led by ErprGr 210, on coastal airfields used as forward landing grounds for the RAF fighters, as well as satellite airfields including Manston and Hawkinge. Then five waves of bombers with fighter escort were sent against nine airfields – from Eastchurch to Portland.

At times the Luftwaffe threatened to overwhelm the Kent and Sussex sectors, but airfields were rapidly repaired and there was a continuous flow of replacement aircraft and pilots.

On 15 August the Luftwaffe mounted the largest number of sorties of the campaign. Bombers and heavy fighters of Generaloberst Hans-Jürgen Stumpff's Luftflotte 5 based in Scandanavia, attacked the north of England. Believing Fighter Command's strength to be concentrated in the south, raiding forces from Denmark and Norway ran into unexpectedly strong resistance. Inadequately escorted by long-range Bf 110Ds, the first raid's He 111H bombers were shot down in large numbers over the North East, and KG 30's Ju 88A-1 and A-5s suffered a similar fate in a subsequent raid against targets in Yorkshire. As a result of the casualties, Luftflotte 5 did not appear in strength again in the campaign and the day was ruefully named 'Black Thursday' by the Luftwaffe.

Three days later, 18 August, saw the greatest number of casualties to both sides, and has since been dubbed 'The Hardest Day'. Following the grinding battles of 18 August, exhaustion and the weather reduced operations for almost a week, allowing the Luftwaffe to review their performance.

'The Hardest Day' sounded the death knell for the Ju 87 in the Battle. This veteran of the Polish Campaign and the Blitzkrieg was too vulnerable to fighters to operate over Britain, and to preserve the Stuka force, Göring withdrew them from the campaign. This removed the main Luftwaffe precision-bombing weapon and shifted the burden of pinpoint attacks on the already stretched bomb-carrying Bf 110D-0/Bs and Bf 109E-4/Bs of ErprGr 210. The Bf 110C fighters within the Zerstörergeschwader had also proved too vulnerable for dogfighting with single-engined RAF fighters, and the type's participation was scaled back. In future the Bf 110 Zerstörer would only be used when range required it or when sufficient single-engined escort could not be provided for the bombers.

As the week drew on, the airfield attacks moved further inland, and repeated raids were made on the radar chain. However, Göring stopped the attacks on the RDF chain as they were perceived as being unsuccessful. Neither the Reichsmarschall nor his subordinates realised how vital the Chain Home stations were to the defence of the United Kingdom. It was known that RDF provided some early warning of raids, but the belief amongst German fighter pilots was that anything bringing up the 'Tommies' to fight was to be encouraged...

Another of Göring's fateful decisions was to order more Bf 109E bomber escorts at the expense of the free-hunting sweeps. To achieve this, the weight of the attack now fell on Luftflotte 2, and the bulk of the Bf 109Es in Luftflotte 3 were transferred to Kesselring's command, reinforcing the fighter bases in the Pas-de-Calais. Stripped of its fighters, Luftflotte 3 started to concentrate more on night bombing operations.

It was at this stage that Göring, expressed disappointment with the Jagdgruppen's performance thus far in the campaign, and made fundamental changes in the command structure of the fighter units, replacing many of the older Geschwaderkommodore with younger, more aggressive pilots like Adolf Galland and Werner Mölders.

But despite all the problems, the Luftwaffe was actually starting to win the battle of attrition at this stage...

Camouflage and Markings

Problems with Sky

By the beginning of August, Sky, (or one of the alternative/variation colours – see previous chapter) under surfaces on RAF Fighter Command aircraft had finally become well established.

However, if the Service was finding it difficult to get supplies of Sky Type S, it would seem that the aircraft manufacturers were little better off.

Hawker Hurricane Mk.I, P3059/SD-N, 501 Squadron, RAF Hawkinge, August 1940.

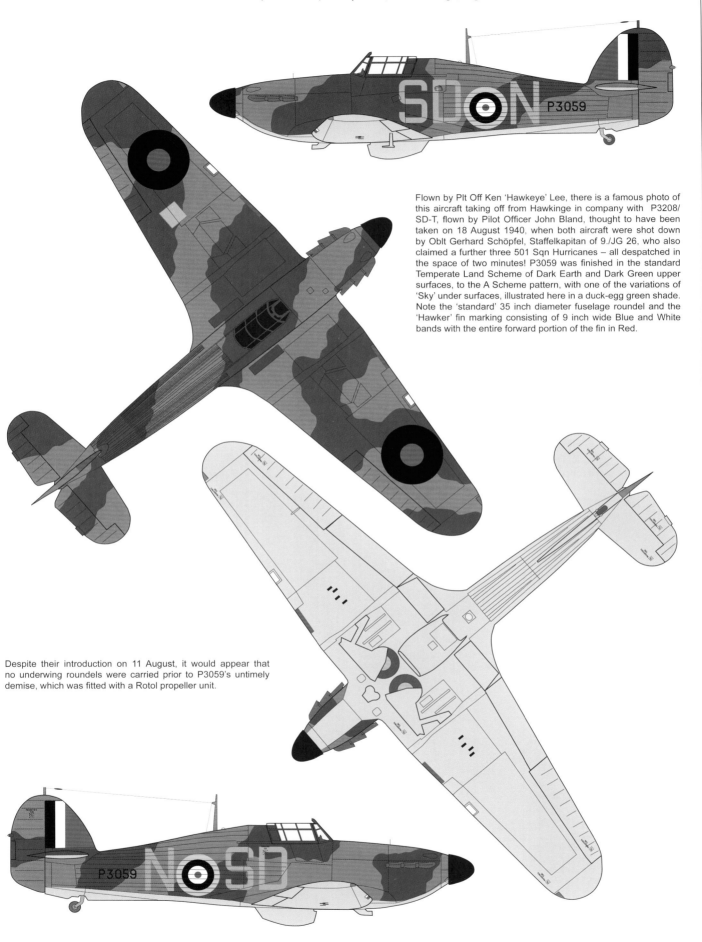

Flown by Plt Off Ken 'Hawkeye' Lee, there is a famous photo of this aircraft taking off from Hawkinge in company with P3208/SD-T, flown by Pilot Officer John Bland, thought to have been taken on 18 August 1940, when both aircraft were shot down by Oblt Gerhard Schöpfel, Staffelkapitan of 9./JG 26, who also claimed a further three 501 Sqn Hurricanes – all despatched in the space of two minutes! P3059 was finished in the standard Temperate Land Scheme of Dark Earth and Dark Green upper surfaces, to the A Scheme pattern, with one of the variations of 'Sky' under surfaces, illustrated here in a duck-egg green shade. Note the 'standard' 35 inch diameter fuselage roundel and the 'Hawker' fin marking consisting of 9 inch wide Blue and White bands with the entire forward portion of the fin in Red.

Despite their introduction on 11 August, it would appear that no underwing roundels were carried prior to P3059's untimely demise, which was fitted with a Rotol propeller unit.

Not to any scale

Hawker Hurricane Mk.I, V7677/GN-N, 249 Squadron, RAF North Weald, Essex, August 1940.

Standard Temperate Land Scheme of Dark Earth and Dark Green upper surfaces, to the A Scheme pattern, with one of the variations of 'Sky' under surfaces. Note the factory applied 'standard' 35 inch diameter fuselage roundel and the 27 inch high 24 inch wide fin flash both of which were starting to be introduced on squadron aircraft in mid-August 1940. V7677 was fitted with a Rotol propeller unit.

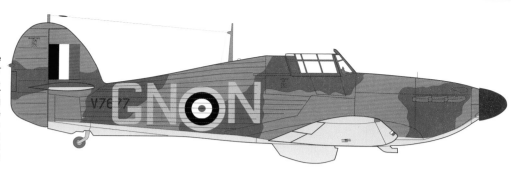

Hawker Hurricane Mk.I, P3110/TP-G, 73 Squadron, RAF Church Fenton, Yorkshire, August 1940.

Standard Temperate Land Scheme of Dark Earth and Dark Green upper surfaces, to the B Scheme pattern, with one of the variations of 'Sky' under surfaces. Note the 'standard' 35 inch diameter fuselage roundel and what is thought to be the Hawker Aircraft Ltd designed fin marking consisting of 9 inch wide Blue and White bands with the entire forward portion of the fin in Red. P3110 was fitted with a Rotol propeller unit.

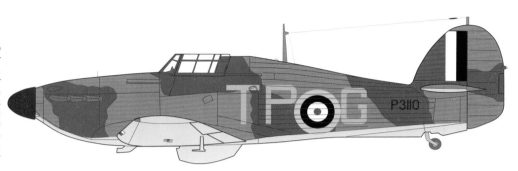

Hawker Hurricane Mk.I, R4224/YB-C, 17 Squadron, RAF North Weald, Essex, August 1940.
Pilot: Squadron Leader A G Miller

Standard Temperate Land Scheme of Dark Earth and Dark Green upper surfaces, to the B Scheme pattern, with one of the variations of 'Sky' under surfaces, which has been extended higher on the nose and scalloped along the leading edges of the wings, a common feature on 17 Squadron aircraft during this period, as was the 'Sky' spinner. Note the 35 inch diameter fuselage roundel and the 'Hawker' fin marking consisting of 9 inch wide Blue and White bands with the entire forward portion of the fin in Red. R4224 was fitted with a Rotol propeller unit.

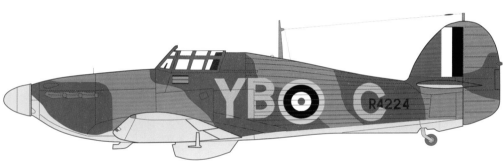

Boulton Paul Defiant Mk.I, N1535/PS-A, 264 Squadron, RAF Hornchurch, Essex, August 1940.

This was the personal aircraft of the unit's CO, Squadron Leader Philip Hunter. Finished in the standard Temperate Land Scheme of Dark Earth and Dark Green upper surfaces, to the B Scheme pattern, with one of the variations of 'Sky' under surfaces, illustrated here in a duck-egg green shade. Note the white tip to the spinner and the standard, factory-applied, 42 inch diameter fuselage roundels and 24 inch wide fin flash that extended the full height of the fin. On 13 August, N1535 was one of four 264 Squadron Defiants to be lost, plus three others damaged. Squadron Leader Hunter and Pilot Officer King his gunner, were both killed in this action.

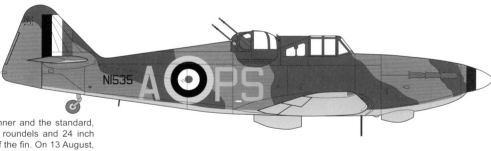

Hawker Hurricane Mk.I, L1829/KW-W, 615 Squadron, RAF Kenley, August 1940.

Whilst being flown by Pilot Officer Anthony Truran, L1829, which was still fitted with fabric-covered wings, was damaged in a dogfight with Bf 109Es off Dungeness on 15 August 1940. A photo of this aircraft after it landed back at Kenley, shows the tattered fabric hanging off the rear fuselage. L1829 was finished in the standard Temperate Land Scheme of Dark Earth and Dark Green upper surfaces, to the A Scheme pattern, with one of the variations of 'Sky' under surfaces. Another fabric-winged Hurricane Mk.I used by 615 Squadron was L1592/KW-Z, which crash-landed at Croydon on 18 August 1940, and is now on display in the Aviation Gallery of the Science Museum in London.

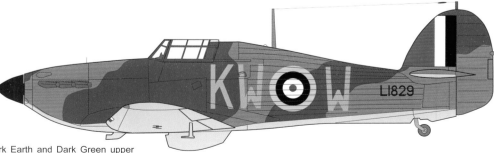

Not to any scale

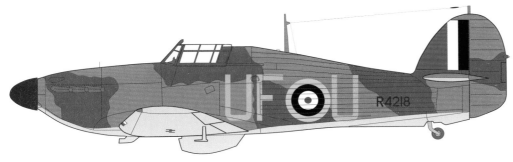

Hawker Hurricane Mk.I, R4218/UF-U, 601 Squadron, RAF Debden, Essex, August 1940.

Finished in the standard Temperate Land Scheme of Dark Earth and Dark Green upper surfaces, to the B Scheme pattern, with one of the variations of 'Sky' under surfaces, illustrated here in a duck-egg green shade. Note the 'standard' 35 inch diameter fuselage roundel and the 'Hawker' fin marking consisting of 9 inch wide Blue and White bands with the entire forward portion of the fin in Red. R4218 was fitted with a Rotol propeller unit.

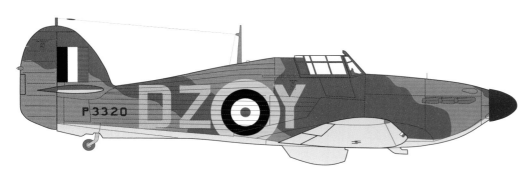

Hawker Hurricane Mk.I, P3320/DZ-Y, 151 Squadron, RAF North Weald, Essex, August 1940.

Finished in the standard Temperate Land Scheme of Dark Earth and Dark Green upper surfaces, to the B Scheme pattern, with one of the variations of 'Sky' under surfaces, illustrated here in a duck-egg green shade. Note the broad Yellow surround to the fuselage roundel and the 27 inch high 24 inch wide fin flash. Although wounded, P3320's pilot, Sergeant L Davis, crash landed the aircraft at RAF Eastchurch, Kent, on 28 August, following combat over the Thames Estuary. The aircraft was severely damaged, but was completely rebuilt and was subsequently transferred to the Fleet Air Arm. P3320 was fitted with a Rotol propeller unit.

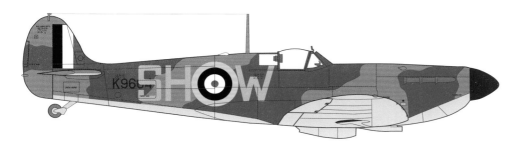

Supermarine Spitfire Mk.I, K9664/SH-W, 64 Squadron, RAF Kenley, Surrey, August 1940.

Finished in the standard Temperate Land Scheme of Dark Earth and Dark Green upper surfaces, to the A Scheme pattern, with one of the variations of 'Sky' under surfaces, illustrated here in a duck-egg green shade. This aircraft was involved in a dogfight over the Channel on 15 August 1940 and crash landed near Calais-Marck airfield in France, and the pilot, Pilot Officer R Roberts was made PoW. K9664 was fitted with a de Havilland/Hamilton propeller unit.

Supermarine Spitfire Mk.I, N3249/QJ-P, 92 Squadron, RAF Pembrey, Carmarthenshire, August 1940.

Finished in the standard Temperate Land Scheme of Dark Earth and Dark Green upper surfaces, to the B Scheme pattern, with one of the variations of 'Sky' under surfaces, illustrated here in a duck-egg green shade, but it may have been a darker duck egg blue shade. Note the dimensions of the fuselage roundel. This machine was seriously damaged in a forced landing back at its home base at Pembrey on 31 August, but was rebuilt. N3249 was fitted with a de Havilland/ Hamilton propeller unit.

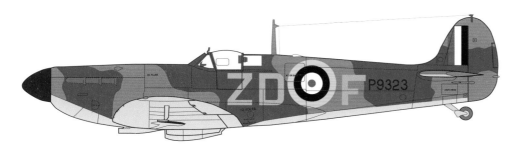

Supermarine Spitfire Mk.I, P9323/ ZD-F, 222 Squadron, RAF Hornchurch, Essex, August 1940.

Finished in the standard Temperate Land Scheme of Dark Earth and Dark Green upper surfaces, to the B Scheme pattern, with one of the variations of 'Sky' under surfaces, illustrated here in a duck-egg green shade, P9323 is finished in a fully updated set of markings for the period and was fitted with a de Havilland/ Hamilton propeller unit.

Not to any scale

It would seem that Air Ministry demands for Sky Type S were also met by the paint manufacturing firms by the closest colours and materials which were available at that time in any quantity – namely BS 381 (1930) No 1 Sky Blue and BS 381 No 16 Eau-de-Nil to 'DTD 63A with reduced gloss', whilst several aircraft manufacturers used Sky Grey.

The correct shade and colour Sky Type S appears to have started to become available about the middle/late August, and from mid-September onwards it appears to have become well established in RAF service and become the predominant colour on the under surface of Fighter Command's fighters. When DTD Technical Circular 144 was issued in March 1941, it cancelled the provisions of all previous DTD Technical Circulars on this subject. In it there is no mention of 'duck egg blue' or 'Sky Type S', but only Sky. This is because that by this time, all camouflage colours were supposed to be of Type S and Sky was firmly established in production, so the term 'duck egg blue' (which probably referred to BSS 381 (1930) No 1 Sky Blue) and/or No 16 Eau-de-Nil, was no longer needed. However, the colloquialism 'duck egg blue' lived on in the minds of the general public who were not privy to the official terms and ultimately came to be associated with Sky.

On the production line

Whilst the fighter squadrons were contemplating the latest changes in their camouflage and markings, the aircraft manufacturers were also being informed of the changes. On 11 June, Glosters were informed that they were to proceed with the painting on the under surfaces of all fighter aircraft with Sky Type S instead of the present Night and White colour scheme. Neither underwing roundels nor underwing serial numbers were required, and the change in colouring was to come into effect on all production aircraft at the earliest possible moment – subject to there being no delay in delivery.

The problems anticipated with new production aircraft notwithstanding, as the new finish would also be applied to aircraft already in service, it was thought that there might be trouble on at least two scores. Firstly how well would the new Sky paint spray over the black Night; and secondly, once again worries were aired about the weight of paint being applied to ailerons upsetting their balance re-appeared. Bearing these points in mind, the RAE was asked for advice as to whether the repainting could be done in service, and if so, what materials would be necessary.

On 14 June, the Air Ministry informed everyone concerned that aircraft which were received from the contractors with Night and White paint schemes could be sprayed over with not more than two coats of Sky Type S. Where this was done, to avoid mass balance problems with the ailerons, the existing paint was to be removed before re-spraying with Dope Solvent. Service units were warned not to try to apply materials to DTD

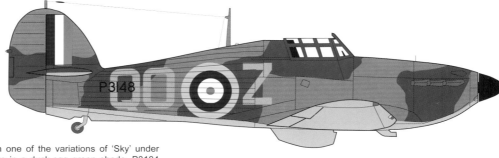

Hawker Hurricane Mk.I, P3148/QO-Z, 3 Squadron, RAF Wick, in the Shetlands, August 1940.

Following its service in the Battle of France, during which it fought furiously, claiming nine enemy aircraft on 12 May alone, 3 Squadron returned to the UK and was posted to Wick for the defence of Scapa Flow where it stayed until September 1940. Finished in the standard Temperate Land Scheme of Dark Earth and Dark Green upper surfaces, to the A Scheme pattern, with one of the variations of 'Sky' under surfaces, which has been illustrated here in a duck-egg green shade. P3184 was fitted with a de Havilland/Hamilton propeller unit.

Hawker Hurricane Mk.I, P3774/TM-V, 504 Squadron, RAF Castletown, in the Shetlands, August 1940.

504 Squadron was another Fighter Command unit that had served and been badly mauled in the Battle of France, and upon its return to the UK was posted 'north of the border' to build up its operational strength, until it also returned south in September 1940. Finished in the standard Temperate Land Scheme of Dark Earth and Dark Green upper surfaces, to the B Scheme pattern, with one of the variations of 'Sky' under surfaces, which has been illustrated here in a duck-egg green shade. P3774 was fitted with a Rotol propeller unit.

Hawker Hurricane Mk.I, P2923/VY-R, 85 Squadron, RAF Martlesham Heath, Hampshire, August 1940.

Finished in the standard Temperate Land Scheme of Dark Earth and Dark Green upper surfaces, to the A Scheme pattern, with one of the variations of 'Sky' on the under surfaces, which has also been extended up the sides of the nose. This aircraft was frequently flown by Flying Officer A G Lewis in August 1940. Note the very non-standard red spinner with two white bands, the way the Yellow outer ring of the fuselage roundel has been truncated along the upper/under camouflage line, and the 'Hawker' fin marking of 9 inch wide Blue and White bands with the entire forward portion of the fin in Red. P2923 was fitted with a Rotol propeller unit.

Not to any scale

Bristol Blenheim Mk.If, L8740/NG-Q, 604 Squadron, RAF Middle Wallop, Hampshire, August 1940.

No 604 Squadron was amongst the first of the Blenheim 'fighter' units to be fitted with Airborne Interception (AI) equipment with which it was working up during the height of the Battle of Britain. Despite its ostensibly Night Fighter role, the aircraft remained in the Day Fighter scheme of Dark Earth and Dark Green upper surfaces, in this instance to the A Scheme pattern, with one of the variations of 'Sky' on the under surfaces. Note the undulating upper/under demarcation and the way the 'Sky' curves up under the tailplane which may be indicative of an in-service repaint job.

Blenheim Mk.If, L8679/BQ-O, 600 Squadron, on detachment to RAF Manston, Kent, August 1940.

Initially designated as a Day and Night Fighter squadron, 600 was sensibly used to fly solely Night Fighter duties by the opening stages of the Battle of Britain. Again, despite its nocturnal role, 600 Squadron's aircraft remained in the Day Fighter scheme of Dark Earth and Dark Green upper surfaces, in L8679's instance to the B Scheme pattern, with one of the variations of 'Sky' on the under surfaces. Note the difference in the upper/under surface colour demarcation to the previous Blenheim Mk.If profile, indicating a factory applied paint finish, and the lack of a serial number on the fuselage, but its retention on the rudder. The dimensions of the fuselage roundel appear to be non-standard and may be the result of the outer yellow ring encroaching on the Blue ring.

Not to any scale

308 on top of materials to DTD 314, or to try mixing these two materials together in an attempt to mix a Sky colour locally.

Problems remained for Fighter Command and the aircraft industry in trying to obtain supplies of Sky over a month after its supposed introduction. On 8 July, the Ministry of Aircraft Production sent a circular to all the Resident Technical Officers in the aircraft factories with regard to the under surface colour of Day Fighters.

The Director of Operational Requirements had ruled in a minute dated 11 June 1940, that the colours used on the under surfaces of Day Fighters were no longer to be of the normal type, but were to be of the new smooth quality. Incorporation of this new requirement was entirely dependent upon stocks of Type S materials becoming available, but when they did become available, the materials were to be introduced on to the production line as soon as possible and the works drawings were to be amended accordingly. The new colour would be known as Sky Type S and be available to specifications DTD 83A, DTD 308, and DTD 314.

The colour of Sky

A Postagram dated 20 July 1940 was sent from the Air Ministry to all home and overseas Commands, the Admiralty, Anti-Aircraft Command and the MAP, which detailed the description of the authorised colours and markings on British aircraft. This same Postagram was apparently circulated to the aircraft manufacturers on 25 July.

In the section which dealt with the under surfaces, fighters were to be... *"Painted duck egg blueish green (Sky Type S); and bombers and torpedo bombers were to be painted black with the exception of Blenheim bombers which were to be painted Duck-egg blueish green."*

Even while the Postagram was being prepared for distribution by the DTD, a conference was held at the Air Ministry on 23 July 1940 to consider aircraft colourings and markings with a view to achieving the maximum degree of standardisation. At this meeting it was pointed out that at that time, the day flying operational RAF aircraft were using two different under surface colours, described as duck-egg blue (ie Sky) and silver (ie Aluminium). It was agreed that 'duck-egg blue' was the better colour for under surfaces than 'silver', and that there was no reason why aircraft (mainly in Coastal Command) with 'silver' under surfaces should not conform to the 'duck egg blue' colour scheme. It was agreed that all types of aircraft whose under surfaces were 'silver' should change over to Sky Type S as soon as supplies of this material became available

That said however, it was also agreed that the colour on the under surfaces of operational types of aircraft should not be rigidly laid down, but that it should be left to the discretion of the Operational Commands to paint the under surfaces of their aircraft either 'duck-egg blue' (Sky Type S) or matt black (Night), according to the operational role of the aircraft.

The decisions made at the conference were circulated to all Commands at home and abroad by a letter dated 11 August accompanied by an appendix.

Paragraph 3 of the appendix dealt with the colouring of the under surfaces s follows...
(i) Operational aircraft. The under surfaces of all operational aircraft were to be either matt black or duck egg blue and could be either one or the other at the discretion of individual Commands to meet operational requirements. The following classes of aircraft were to be produced with duck egg blue under surfaces:- Fighters, Army co-operation, General Reconnaissance, Torpedo bombers, Blenheim bombers, Close support bombers, Troop carriers, and bomber transports.

This appendix was also circulated to the aircraft manufacturers on 23 August. In the accompanying letter, the recipients were asked to note that in paragraph 3(i) *"....provision is made for either matt black or duck egg blue, ie Sky Type S...."*, so there can be no doubt that the colour which was supposed to be applied was Sky.

It can be deduced from the repeated references to Sky Type S being used, when supplies become available, which appear in documents throughout June and July of 1940, that supplies of Sky to either 'DTD 63A with reduced gloss', or DTD 83A, DTD 308, and DTD 314 Type S, were generally not available to fighter squadrons during those months.

Luftwaffe

It would appear that as early as July/August 1940, the Jagdwaffe had been experimenting with 'in the field applied' grey upper surface schemes. Even one of Adolph Galland's aircraft is reported as being so painted.

Apparently a mixed assortment of colours comprising the original RLM 70 and RLM 71 green shades and 'field mixed' grey shades was not uncommon; for example wing and tailplane upper surfaces in RLM 71/02 and the fuselage spine in various shades of grey being a frequently recorded variation.

As air combats got higher over the English countryside, a more suitable 'high altitude' scheme was deemed to be required, and it is believed that the application of grey shades on Luftwaffe fighters, in preference to the green shades, appears to have started to be introduced during this period.

The RLM 74 Dunkelgrau/RLM 75 Mittelgrau/RLM 76 Hellgrau combination has frequently been asserted not to have been introduced before the November 1941 edition of the Luftwaffe's L Dv 521/1 paint chart was released, but examination of Bf 109E wreckage from the Battle of Britain has revealed that a combination of grey paint in shades very similar to, if not the actual, RLM 74/75/76 colours had been applied to several of the aircraft involved.

A plausible explanation for the lack of any Luftwaffe paint charts between 1939 and November 1941, which might have

identified the actual introduction dates of the RLM 74/75/76 greys was that on the acceptance of ultimate defeat in 1945, Göring ordered that all Luftwaffe documentation should be destroyed and it is thought that between 90%-95% was lost within the Luftwaffe – much more than the other services.

Even now, no one appears to be definitely sure when the official RLM 74/75/76 'greys' scheme was actually introduced on to the Bf 109E production line, (as the relevant L Dv 521 paint chart is 'missing' – the only surviving one relates to the above mentioned November 1941 edition) but there is a colour photo of a Bf 109E-7, still with its factory codes in place, which was manufactured in mid-August 1940, sporting a three-tone grey scheme, which would indicate that the RLM 74/75/76 'greys' scheme was being applied. at factory level at least, by then. Obviously, this aircraft and the others on the same production line with it would probably not have been issued to front line units until late September/early October 1940, but it may prove that the RLM 74/75/76 scheme was being applied during the Battle of Britain period.

The actual colours and use of field-applied grey paint shades are anybody's guess – perhaps even ex-Armée de l'Air paints, or more likely mixes of RLM 66 Schwarzgrau, 65 Hellblau, 02 Grau, 71 Dunkelgrün and 70 Schwarzgrün?

Tactical markings

The liberal use of yellow, and to a somewhat lesser degree, white, paint or temporary distemper – removable by washing off with aviation fuel – as an aid to rapid identification of friend from foe, was also starting to gain momentum during August 1940.

Coloured propeller spinners on Bf 109Es and Bf 110s had been recorded as early as July, (and in some cases even earlier during the Phoney War and the Battle of France), but yellow, white or red spinners, sometimes the full spinner, or halved, or quartered or just a segment, or bands of colour, with the remainder of the spinner in the factory applied RLM 70 Schwarzgrün were becoming more and more common.

Examples of tactical markings on the rudders of Bf 109Es

As the tempo of the Battle of Britain increased, so did the need to find a solution to rapid identification of friendly aircraft. Initially propeller spinners were painted, in yellow, white or red, sometimes the full spinner, or halved, or quartered or just a segment, or bands of colour, with the remainder of the spinner in RLM 70 Schwarzgrün. Then, by the middle of August, areas of colour were applied to the rudders of Bf 109Es (and to a lesser extent on Bf 110s).

Initially triangular segments were restricted to the top of the rudder, mainly in yellow, but by the end of August, cowlings and entire rudders, as well as the wing and tailplane tips were commonly painted yellow or, less frequently, white. By no means were all of these recognition features applied to every aircraft, and naturally, there were plenty of anomalies that arose.

Also, some of the air leaders had started to personalise their aircraft for identification purposes during late July. For example Oblt Bartels, and Oberstlt Wick with a yellow rudder and white cowling respectively.

As the tempo of the Battle of Britain increased, so did the need to find a solution to rapid identification of friendly aircraft. The initial Luftwaffe solution, introduced in the middle of August, was to paint a triangular segment on the top of the rudder in yellow. Then, wing and tailplane tips were included.

By the end of August, cowlings and entire rudders, as well as the wing and tailplane tips were commonly painted yellow or, less frequently, white – but by no means were all of these recognition features applied to every aircraft – and naturally, plenty of anomalies arose.

Messerschmitt Bf 109E-4, 'Yellow 1', 9./JG 26, Caffiers, France, August 1940.
Pilot: Staffelkapitan, Oblt Gerhard Schöpfel

RLM 71 Dunkelgrün and RLM 02 Grau upper surfaces in a soft-edged splinter pattern with RLM 65 Hellblau under surfaces extended high up on the fuselage sides and over the fin and rudder. Note the small size of the fuselage balkenkreuze, a feature of many III/JG 26 aircraft, the small numeral '1' and III Gruppe vertical bar, again common on III/JG 26 aircraft. The red 'Hollenhund' (Hell hound), 9 Staffel emblem, was painted under the cockpit. As well as the yellow segment at the top of the rudder, mainplane and tailplane tips have also been painted yellow. On 18 August 1940, Oblt Schöpfel shot down five Hurricanes, 501 Squadron, in the space of two minutes, in the vicinity of Canterbury – his 8th to 12th victims. One of the aircraft was Pilot Officer Ken Lee's, Hurricane Mk.I, P3059, SD-N, illustrated on p84, and another was P3208, SD-TPilot: Pilot Officer John Bland.

Not to any scale

Messerschmitt Bf 109E-4, 'White 3', 7./JG 54, Guines-Sud, France, late August 1940.

RLM 71 Dunkelgrün and RLM 02 Grau upper surfaces in a soft-edged splinter pattern with RLM 65 Hellblau under surfaces extended high up on the fuselage sides and over the fin and rudder. Note the white cowling sides and underside and the small numeral '3' on the forward fuselage in front of the windscreen.

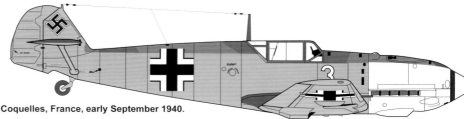

Messerschmitt Bf 109E-4, 'White 12', 1./JG 52, Coquelles, France, early September 1940.
Pilot: Fw Heinz Urhlings

RLM 71 Dunkelgrün and RLM 02 Grau upper surfaces in a soft-edged splinter pattern with RLM 65 Hellblau under surfaces extended high up on the fuselage sides and over the fin and rudder, which have then had a dense mottle of RLM 71/02 applied. Note the white mainplane and tailplane tips, the white ailerons and the majority of the rudder in white, and the unit's 'Running Boar' emblem on the cowling. The spinner was halved black and white with a black tip. Fw Urhlings crash landed 'White 12' at Slurry, Kent on 2 September 1940.

Inset: 1./JG 52 'Running Boar' in a shield emblem.

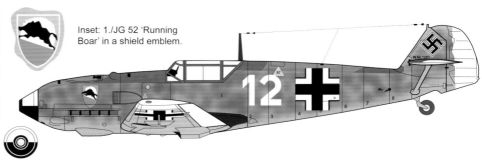

Messerschmitt Bf 109E-4, 'Yellow 10', 6./JG 51, Marquise-West, France, August 1940.
Pilot: Obfw Fritz Beeck

RLM 71 Dunkelgrün and RLM 02 Grau upper surfaces in a soft-edged splinter pattern with RLM 65 Hellblau under surfaces extended high up on the fuselage sides and over the fin and rudder, which have then had a dense mottle of RLM 71/02 applied. Note the yellow mainplane and tailplane tips, the yellow segment at the top of the rudder and the way the swastika has been masked out on the fin leaving the underlying RLM 65 Hellblau. II/JG 52's 'Weeping Woodpecker' emblem was always placed on the rear fuselage of its Bf 109Es. It is thought that the spinner was halved black and white. Obfw Beeck crash landed 'Yellow 10' at East Langdon, Kent on 24 August 1940.

Inset: II/JG 52's 'Weeping Woodpecker' emblem, which was always placed on the rear fuselage.

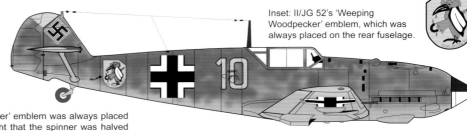

Messerschmitt Bf 109E-1, 'Black 6', 2./JG 3, Colombert, France, August 1940.
Pilot: Obfw Keller
RLM 71 Dunkelgrün and RLM 02 Grau upper surfaces in a soft-edged splinter pattern with RLM 65 Hellblau under surfaces extended high up on the fuselage sides and over the fin and rudder. A varying density mottle of RLM 71/02 has been applied over the fuselage sides, fin and rudder. Note the yellow mainplane tips and the yellow rudder. The I Gruppe 'Tatzelwurm', in the 2 Staffel colour red, is on the cowling side. The black or RLM 70 spinner has a white quarter. This aircraft was retrofitted with a later style heavier-framed canopy. Obfw Keller crash landed 'Black 6' back at his base at Colombert on 15 August 1940.

Inset: I Gruppe JG 3's 'Tatzelwurm', in the 2 Staffel colour red.

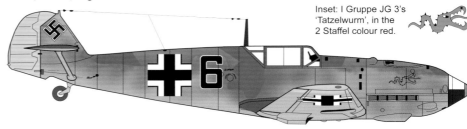

Messerschmitt Bf 109E-4, 'Black 8', 2./JG 3, Colombert, France, August 1940.
Pilot: Obfw Bernard Lampskemper

RLM 71 Dunkelgrün and RLM 02 Grau upper surfaces in a soft-edged splinter pattern with RLM 65 Hellblau under surfaces extended high up on the fuselage sides and over the fin and rudder, with a varying density mottle of RLM 71/02 over the fuselage sides, fin and rudder. A large area of the cowling has been painted yellow, with a 'cut out' for the unit's 'Tatzelwurm', in the 2 Staffel colour red, on the side. The wing tips and rudder are also yellow. This aircraft was crash landed by Obfw Lampskemper near Pevensey Radar Station, Sussex on 29 August 1940. The black or RLM 70 spinner has a white quarter with a red tip.

Messerschmitt Bf 109E-4, 'Yellow 2', 9./JG 2, Le Havre, France, September 1940.

RLM 71 Dunkelgrün and RLM 02 Grau upper surfaces in a soft-edged splinter pattern with RLM 65 Hellblau under surfaces extended high up on the fuselage sides and over the fin and rudder. A sparse mottle of RLM 71/02 has been applied over the fuselage sides, fin and rudder. Note the yellow spinner and cowling with 9 Staffel's 'Stechmücke' (mosquito) emblem on the side, and JG 2's 'Richthofen R' shield under the cockpit.

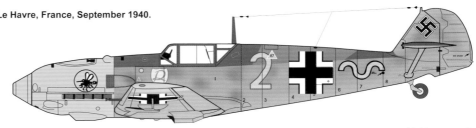

Not to any scale

Messerschmitt Bf 109E upper surface camouflage patterns

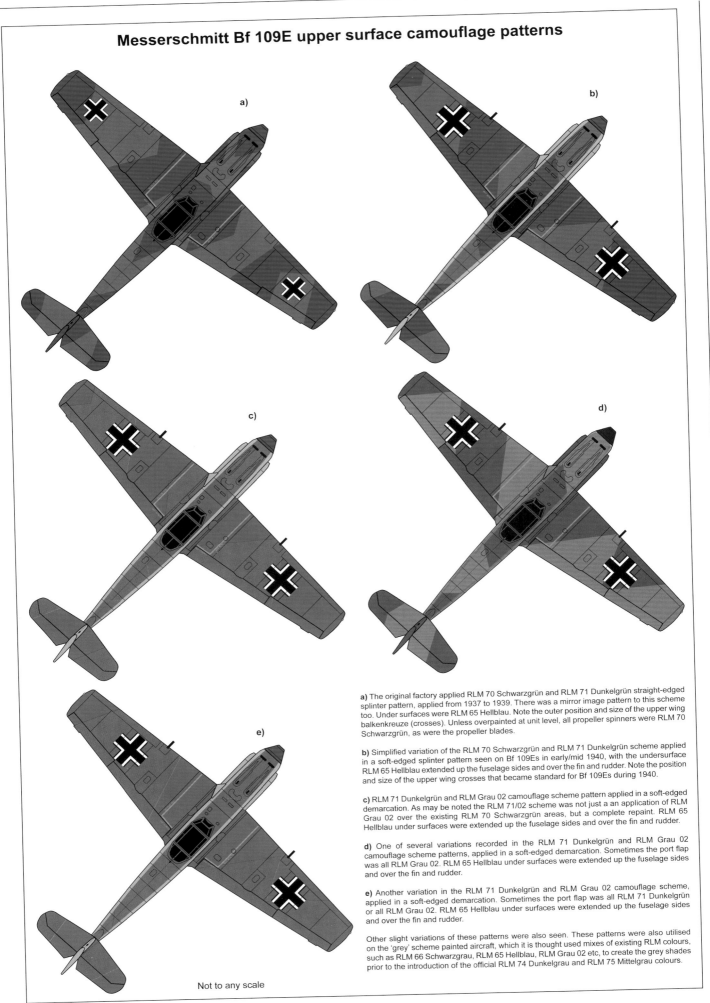

a)

b)

c)

d)

e)

a) The original factory applied RLM 70 Schwarzgrün and RLM 71 Dunkelgrün straight-edged splinter pattern, applied from 1937 to 1939. There was a mirror image pattern to this scheme too. Under surfaces were RLM 65 Hellblau. Note the outer position and size of the upper wing balkenkreuze (crosses). Unless overpainted at unit level, all propeller spinners were RLM 70 Schwarzgrün, as were the propeller blades.

b) Simplified variation of the RLM 70 Schwarzgrün and RLM 71 Dunkelgrün scheme applied in a soft-edged splinter pattern seen on Bf 109Es in early/mid 1940, with the undersurface RLM 65 Hellblau extended up the fuselage sides and over the fin and rudder. Note the position and size of the upper wing crosses that became standard for Bf 109Es during 1940.

c) RLM 71 Dunkelgrün and RLM Grau 02 camouflage scheme pattern applied in a soft-edged demarcation. As may be noted the RLM 71/02 scheme was not just a an application of RLM Grau 02 over the existing RLM 70 Schwarzgrün areas, but a complete repaint. RLM 65 Hellblau under surfaces were extended up the fuselage sides and over the fin and rudder.

d) One of several variations recorded in the RLM 71 Dunkelgrün and RLM Grau 02 camouflage scheme patterns, applied in a soft-edged demarcation. Sometimes the port flap was all RLM Grau 02. RLM 65 Hellblau under surfaces were extended up the fuselage sides and over the fin and rudder.

e) Another variation in the RLM 71 Dunkelgrün and RLM Grau 02 camouflage scheme, applied in a soft-edged demarcation. Sometimes the port flap was all RLM 71 Dunkelgrün or all RLM Grau 02. RLM 65 Hellblau under surfaces were extended up the fuselage sides and over the fin and rudder.

Other slight variations of these patterns were also seen. These patterns were also utilised on the 'grey' scheme painted aircraft, which it is thought used mixes of existing RLM colours, such as RLM 66 Schwarzgrau, RLM 65 Hellblau, RLM Grau 02 etc, to create the grey shades prior to the introduction of the official RLM 74 Dunkelgrau and RLM 75 Mittelgrau colours.

Not to any scale

Messerschmitt Bf 109E-4, 'White 13', 7./JG 26, Caffiers, France, late August 1940.
Pilot: Ltn Walter Blume

RLM 71 Dunkelgrün and RLM 02 Grau upper surfaces in a soft-edged splinter pattern with RLM 65 Hellblau under surfaces extended high up on the fuselage sides and over the fin and rudder. Note the yellow wing tips and triangular segment at the top of the rudder, plus four 'kill' bars. 'White 13' features the small fuselage balkenkreuze and numerals favoured by III/JG 26, the 'Schlageter' script 'S' shield and 7 Staffel's 'red heart' emblem. Lt Blume was shot down in this machine near Canterbury on 18 September 1940. He was severely injured in the crash landing and was later repatriated. When he recovered, he resumed combat operations and claimed a further fourteen victories.

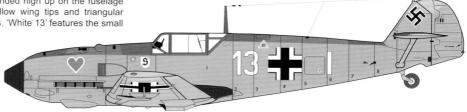

Messerschmitt Bf 109E-4, 'Yellow 3', 9./JG 3, Desvres, France, August 1940.

RLM 71 Dunkelgrün and RLM 02 Grau upper surfaces in a soft-edged splinter pattern with RLM 65 Hellblau under surfaces extended high up on the fuselage sides and over the fin and rudder. Note the yellow mainplane and tailplane tips, and the yellow triangular segment at the top of the rudder. 9 Staffel's 'seahorse shield' was positioned on the fuselage below the rear of the canopy. The spinner was RLM 70 with a white tip.

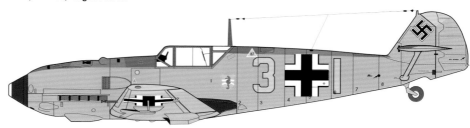

Messerschmitt Bf 109E-3, 'Black 1, 5./JG 51, Desvres, France, August 1940.
Pilot: Staffelkapitän, Hptm Horst Tietzen

RLM 71 Dunkelgrün and RLM 02 Grau upper surfaces in a soft-edged splinter pattern with RLM 65 Hellblau under surfaces extended high up on the fuselage sides and over the fin and rudder, which have then had a mottle of RLM 71/02 applied. Note the yellow mainplane and tailplane tips and the yellow segment at the top of the rudder. II/JG 52's 'Weeping Woodpecker' emblem with a white background, was positioned on the rear fuselage. Note also the eighteen victory bars on the fin partially covering the swastika.

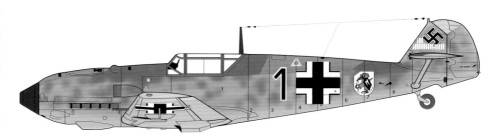

Messerschmitt Bf 109E-4, 'Black 5', 2.(J)/LG 2, Calais-Marck, France, August 1940.

RLM 71 Dunkelgrün and RLM 02 Grau upper surfaces in a soft-edged splinter pattern with RLM 65 Hellblau under surfaces extended high up on the fuselage sides and over the fin and rudder. A varying density mottle of RLM 71/02 has been applied over the fuselage sides, fin and rudder. Note the angled yellow rear section of the rudder and the white 'disc' on the rear fuselage in this instance possibly indicating I Gruppe.

Messerschmitt Bf 109E-3, 'Black 5', Stab I/JG 52, Cocquelles, France, August 1940.
Pilot: Oblt Helmut Bennemann, the Gruppe Adjutant

RLM 71 Dunkelgrün and RLM 02 Grau upper surfaces in a soft-edged splinter pattern with RLM 65 Hellblau under surfaces extended high up on the fuselage sides and over the fin and rudder, with a sparse density mottle of RLM 71/02 over the fuselage sides. A large area of the cowling has been painted yellow with the unit's 'Running Boar', shield on the side. Oblt Bennemann later rose to command the Geschwader and ultimately scored 93 victories.

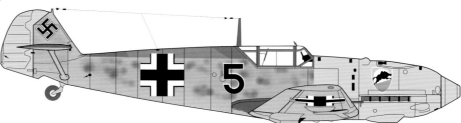

Messerschmitt Bf 109E-4/B, 'Yellow 1', 3./ErprGr 210, Denain but operating from the unit's forward base at Calais-Marck, France, August-October 1940.
Pilot: Staffelkapitän, Oblt Otto Hinze

3 Staffel of Erprobungsgruppe 210 was equipped with brand new Bf 109E-4/Bs, with factory-fitted ETC 500 bomb racks, under the command of the experienced Staffelkapitän Oblt Otto Hintze. RLM 71 Dunkelgrün and RLM 02 Grau upper surfaces in a soft-edged splinter pattern with RLM 65 Hellblau under surfaces extended high up on the fuselage sides and over the fin and rudder, a sparse streaky mottle of RLM 71/02 was applied. Note the 'dark yellow' numeral '1' which may have been RLM 26 Braun, and the yellow tip to the RLM 70 spinner. Oblt Hinze flew this aircraft from early July to 17 October 1940, but was eventually shot down in another Bf 109E-4/B, 'Yellow 6', on 29 October 1940, near Pluckley, Kent, and made a PoW.

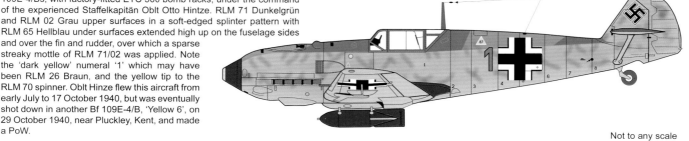

Not to any scale

Messerschmitt Bf 110D-0/B, S9+CB of Stab/ErprGr 210, Denain but operating from the unit's forward base at Calais-Marck, France, August 1940, crewed by the Gruppe Technical Officer, Ltn Karl-Heinz Koch and his bordfunker Uffz Rolf Kahl

Erprobungsgruppe 210, was a specialised experimental test unit, formed at Köln-Ostheim in Germany in July 1940 under the command Hauptmann Walter Rubensdörfer, to develop fighter-bomber techniques with the Bf 110 and Bf 109E. S9+CB was finished in RLM 71 Dunkelgrün and RLM 02 Grau upper surfaces in a soft-edged splinter pattern with RLM 65 Hellblau under surfaces extended high up on the fuselage sides and over the fins and rudders. A varying density mottle of RLM 71/02 has been applied over the fuselage sides, fins and rudders.

Codes were black with the individual aircraft letter 'C' in the Stab colour green thinly outlined in black. Note the extended rear fuselage section of the Bf 110D sub-type which contained a dinghy. Lt Koch and his bordfunker, Uffz Karl, crash landed S9+CB at Hooe, East Sussex, on 15 August 1940, following an attack on RAF Croydon. Koch and Kahl were made PoWs but Kahl was repatriated later due to the severity of his injuries.

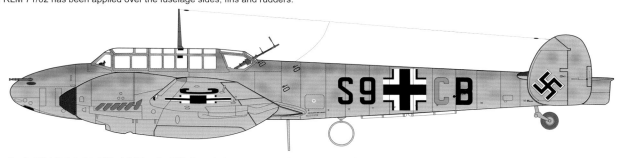

Messerschmitt Bf 110C-6, S9+TH of 1./ErprGr 210, Denain but operating from the unit's forward base at Calais-Marck, France, August 1940, crewed by Lt Erich Beudel and Obgfr Otto Jordan

This was one of twelve, MG 101 30mm cannon-armed, Bf 110C-6 sub-types produced, most of which were issued to 1 Staffel of Erprobungsgruppe 210 for evaluation under operational conditions. Finished in the standard two-tone green RLM 70 Schwarzgrün and RLM 71 Dunkelgrün upper surfaces in a

straight-edged 'splinter' pattern with RLM 65 Hellblau undersides, all the codes were black with the exception of the individual aircraft letter 'T' which was blue thinly outlined in white – an affectation adopted by all 1 Staffel machines during this period. The propeller spinners were also blue with two white bands. This aircraft was also shot down on the 15 August Croydon raid, in which both crew were killed. Note the MG 101 30mm cannon fairing under the fuselage.

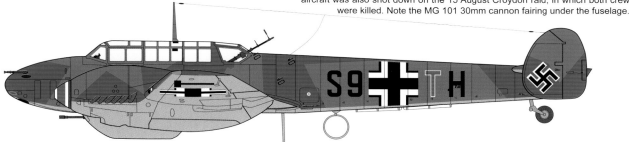

Messerschmitt Bf 110D-0/B, S9+AH of 1./ErprGr 210, Denain but operating from the unit's forward base at Calais-Marck, France, August/September 1940, crewed by Hptm Martin Lutz and his bordfunker Uffz Anton Schön

Hptm Martin Lutz took over command of ErprGr 210 after it's original Gruppenkommandeur, Hptm Walter Rubensdörfer, was shot down and killed. Lutz and Schön usually flew Bf 110D-0/B S9+DH, which was damaged in a heavy landing some days earlier, forcing them to fly S9+AH on a raid against the Parnall Aircraft works near Bristol on 27 September 1940, in which they were shot down and killed. S9+AH was finished in RLM 71 Dunkelgrün and RLM 02

Grau upper surfaces in a soft-edged splinter pattern with RLM 65 Hellblau under surfaces extended high up on the fuselage sides and over the fins and rudders. A varying density mottle of RLM 71/02 was applied over the fuselage sides, fins and rudders. Codes were black with the individual aircraft letter 'A' in blue thinly outlined in white as per all 1 Staffel machines during this period. Note the propeller spinners which were also blue with two white bands and the extended rear fuselage section of the Bf 110D sub-type.

Inset: Erprobungsgruppe 210's 'England in a gunsight' unit marking.

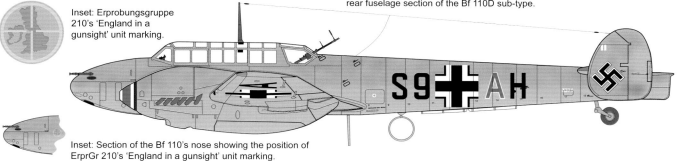

Inset: Section of the Bf 110's nose showing the position of ErprGr 210's 'England in a gunsight' unit marking.

Messerschmitt Bf 110D-0/B, S9+CK of 2./ErprGr 210, Denain but operating from the unit's forward base at Calais-Marck, France, August 1940, crewed by Oblt Alfred Habisch and his bordfunker Uffz Ernst Elfner

S9+CK was finished in RLM 71 Dunkelgrün and RLM 02 Grau upper surfaces in a soft-edged splinter pattern with RLM 65 Hellblau under surfaces extended high up on the fuselage sides and over the fins and rudders. A varying density mottle of RLM 71/02 was applied over the fuselage sides, fins and rudders. Codes were

black with the individual aircraft letter 'C' in black thinly outlined in white. This aircraft was also shot down on the 15 August raid against Croydon, but this time both crew members survived in to captivity. The aircraft was shipped to the USA in 1941 for the US aviation industry to evaluate. Note the RLM 70 spinners and the extended rear fuselage of the Bf 110D sub-type.

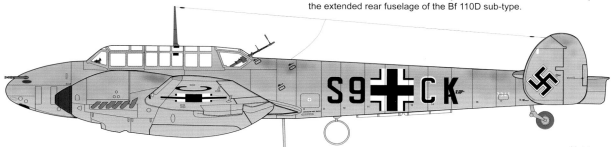

Not to any scale

Messerschmitt Bf 110D-0, W.Nr 3017, M8+MK of 2./ZG 76, Stavanger, Norway, August 1940

I Gruppe of ZG 26 were based in Denmark and were equipped with the long-range 'D' variant of the Bf 110, most of which were fitted with the enormous 'Dackelbauch' (Daschund's belly) fuel tank fairing under the central fuselage. Several 'in-the-field' improvised alternatives were tried, such as this 900 litre (198 gallon) drop tank under the fuselage centreline, but whether it was used operationally is unknown. M8+Mk.was finished in the standard two-tone green RLM 70 Schwarzgrün and RLM 71 Dunkelgrün upper surfaces in a straight-edged 'splinter' pattern with RLM 65 Hellblau undersides. Codes were black with the individual aircraft letter 'M' in the 2 Staffel colour red, outlined in white. The werknummer '3017' in white was applied to the starboard side of the rear fuselage.

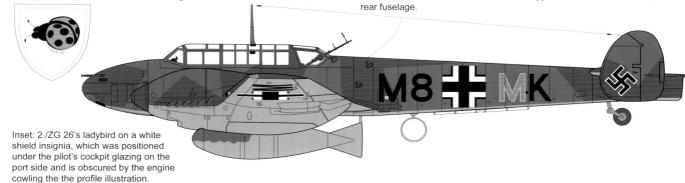

Inset: 2./ZG 26's ladybird on a white shield insignia, which was positioned under the pilot's cockpit glazing on the port side and is obscured by the engine cowling the the profile illustration.

Messerschmitt Bf 110D-0, W.Nr 3497, M8+JK of 2./ZG 76, Trondheim-Vérnes, Norway, August 1940

It would appear that not all I/ZG 76's Bf 110D-0s were fitted with the long range tanks, such as the 'Dackelbauch' or 'in-the-field' improvised alternatives. M8+JK was finished in the standard two-tone green RLM 70 Schwarzgrün and RLM 71 Dunkelgrün upper surfaces in a straight-edged 'splinter' pattern with RLM 65 Hellblau undersides. Codes were black with the individual aircraft letter 'J' in the 2 Staffel colour red, outlined in white. Note the red tips to the propeller spinners and the werknummer '3487' in white on the rear fuselage.

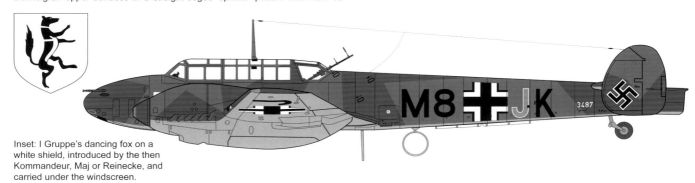

Inset: I Gruppe's dancing fox on a white shield, introduced by the then Kommandeur, Maj or Reinecke, and carried under the windscreen.

Messerschmitt Bf 110D-0, M8+SL of 3./ZG 76, Stavanger, Norway, August 1940

The fuselage-mounted fuel tank could carry some 1050 litres (260 gallons) of fuel and 106 litres (22 gallons) of oil and was covered by the enormous 'Dackelbauch' fairing, which was fixed and couldn't be jettisoned in an emergency. M8+SL was finished in the standard two-tone green RLM 70 Schwarzgrün and RLM 71 Dunkelgrün upper surfaces in a straight-edged 'splinter' pattern with RLM 65 Hellblau undersides. Codes were black with the individual aircraft letter 'S' in the 3 Staffel colour yellow. Note the yellow tips to the propeller spinners.

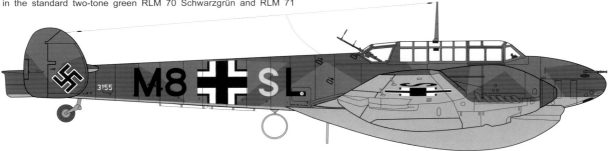

Messerschmitt Bf 110D-0, W.Nr 3155, M8+CH of 1./ZG 76, Stavanger, Norway, August 1940, crewed by Lt Hans-Ulrich Kettling and Obgfr Fritz Volk

The Bf 110D-0s of I/ZG 76 took part in one major raid during the Battle of Britain, escorting the He 111s of KG 26 on a raid against the north-east coast of the UK on 15 August 1940 where they suffered several losses at the hands of the defending RAF fighters. M8+CH was finished in the standard two-tone green RLM 70 Schwarzgrün and RLM 71 Dunkelgrün upper surfaces in a straight-edged 'splinter' pattern with RLM 65 Hellblau undersides. Codes were black with the individual aircraft letter 'C' in the 1 Staffel colour white. Lt Kettling and Obgfr Volk were shot down in this aircraft during that raid and crashed near Barnard Castle in Northumberland and were made PoWs.

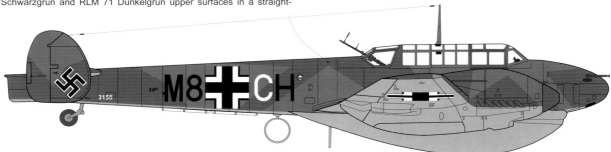

Not to any scale

Messerschmitt Bf 110 upper surface camouflage patterns

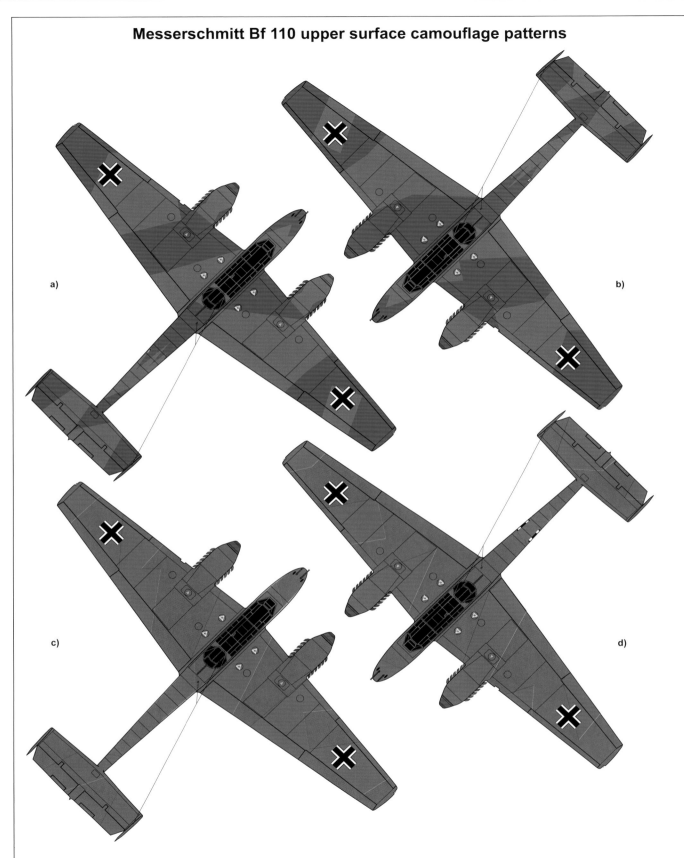

a)

b)

c)

d)

a) The original factory applied RLM 70 Schwarzgrün and RLM 71 Dunkelgrün straight-edged splinter pattern, applied from 1937. There was a mirror image pattern to this scheme too. Under surfaces were RLM 65 Hellblau. Unless overpainted at unit level, all propeller spinners were RLM 70 Schwarzgrün, as were the propeller blades.

b) Variation of the RLM 70 Schwarzgrün and RLM 71 Dunkelgrün scheme sometimes applied in a soft-edged demarcation splinter pattern. Sometimes seen with the undersurface RLM 65 Hellblau extended up the fuselage sides and over the fins and rudders.

c) RLM 71 Dunkelgrün and RLM Grau 02 camouflage scheme pattern applied in a soft-edged demarcation. The RLM 65 Hellblau under surfaces were invariably extended up the fuselage sides and over the fins and rudders.

d) One of the variations recorded in the RLM 71 Dunkelgrün and RLM Grau 02 camouflage scheme patterns, applied in a soft-edged demarcation. Sometimes the starboard flap was all RLM 71 Dunkelgrün, or all RLM Grau 02 as illustrated. RLM 65 Hellblau under surfaces were invariably extended up the fuselage sides and over the fins and rudders in this scheme.

Other slight variations of these patterns were also seen. Patterns 3 and 4 may also have been utilised on the 'grey' scheme painted aircraft, which it is thought used mixes of existing RLM colours, such as RLM 66 Schwarzgrau, RLM 65 Hellblau, RLM Grau 02 etc, to create the grey shades prior to the introduction of the official RLM 74 Dunkelgrau and RLM Mittelgrau colours.

Not to any scale

Messerschmitt Bf 110C, M8+NP, 6./ZG 76, Guernsey, Channel Islands, August 1940.
Crewed by: Staffelkapitän Hptm Heinz Nacke and his bordfunker Ofw Kuehne

II/ZG 76 was based at Laval, France but also operated from forward airfields on the Channel Islands. Carrying the Gruppe's large 'sharkmouth' design on its nose, M8+NP was finished in the standard two-tone green RLM 70 Schwarzgrün and RLM 71 Dunkelgrün upper surfaces in a straight-edged 'splinter' pattern with RLM 65 Hellblau undersides. Codes were black with the individual aircraft letter 'N' in the 6 Staffel colour yellow. Note the six white (abschubalken) 'victory' bars on the fin

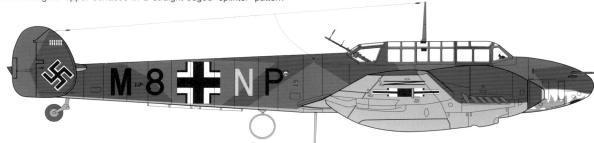

Messerschmitt Bf 110C, U8+BB, Stab I/ZG 26, Yvrench/St Omer, France, August 1940.
Crewed by: Gruppe Adjutant, Oblt Proske and his bordfunker Uffz Mobius

U8+BB was finished in RLM 71 Dunkelgrün and RLM 02 Grau upper surfaces in a soft-edged splinter pattern with RLM 65 Hellblau under surfaces and lower fuselage sides, over which a heavy and dense mottle of RLM 71/02 was applied, including over the fins and rudders. Codes were black with the individual aircraft letter 'B' in the Gruppe Stab colour green. Note I Gruppe's 'Ringelpitz' emblem on the nose and the green and white halved spinners.

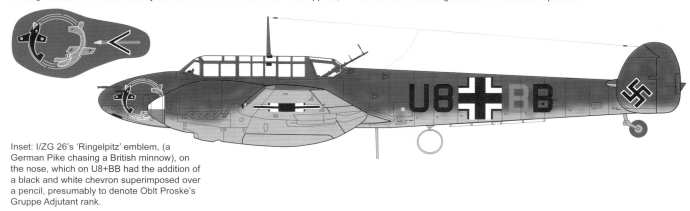

Inset: I/ZG 26's 'Ringelpitz' emblem, (a German Pike chasing a British minnow), on the nose, which on U8+BB had the addition of a black and white chevron superimposed over a pencil, presumably to denote Oblt Proske's Gruppe Adjutant rank.

Messerschmitt Bf 110D-0, 3U+HR, 7./ZG 26, Barley-Arques, France, August 1940.

It wasn't just Bf 109Es that had yellow tactical paint applied to their rudders, as this illustration of 3U+HR shows, albeit in this instance it was restricted to the lower half of the rudders. The rest of the aircraft is finished in what appears to be the 'new' grey shades on the upper surfaces, mixed from existing RLM colours. The under surfaces remained in RLM 65 Hellblau and were extended high up on the fuselage over which a diffused mottle was applied which extended on to the fins/rudders and engine nacelles. Codes were black with the individual aircraft letter 'H' in the staffel colour white. Note the white propeller spinner tips.

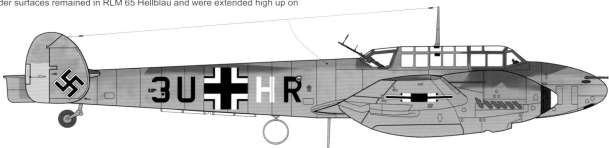

Messerschmitt Bf 110D-0, 3U+LR, 7./ZG 26, Barley-Arques, France, August 1940.

Another one of 7./ZG 26's machines, which had a variation of the yellow tactical paint on the rudders, this time mid chord. Note the white nose, which III/ZG 26 had started applying to its Bf 110s around this time, as a further rapid identification/recognition feature, that extended all the way back to the windscreen in 3U+LR's case. This machine is again thought to have been painted in the 'new' grey shades on the upper surfaces. Under surfaces remained in RLM 65 Hellblau, extended high up on the fuselage over which a diffused mottle was applied. Codes were black with the individual aircraft letter 'L' in the staffel colour white. Note the white propeller spinner tips.

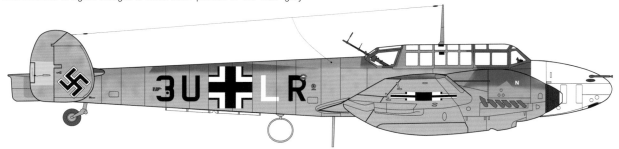

Not to any scale

Junkers Ju 88A-1, B3+BM, 4./KG 54, St André-de-l'Eure, France, August 1940.

Finished in the standard two-tone green RLM 70 Schwarzgrün and RLM 71 Dunkelgrün upper surfaces in a straight-edged 'splinter' pattern with RLM 65 Hellblau undersides. Codes were black with a white individual aircraft letter 'B' in the staffel colour, and the propeller spinners were red with white tips. Note the red diagonal band on the mid fuselage section. Coloured diagonal bands were seen on several aircraft from KG 54 and may have indicated Staffelkapitän status and/or Gruppe or Geschwader leadership. 4./KG 54's 'totenkopf'

(death's head/skull) emblem may have been applied on the forward fuselage under the cockpit glazing of this aircraft but it is unclear from the reference photographs used whether it was carried or not. This particular machine was shot down by a combination of AA and Hurricanes from 17 Squadron during an attack on RAF Brize Norton in Oxfordshire, on 21 August 1940.

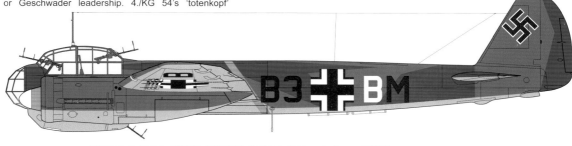

Junkers Ju 88A-5, 4D+DR, 7./KG 30, Aalborg, Denmark, August 1940.
Crewed by: Oblt Werner Bachmann, Fw Georg Henneske, Uffz Werner Evers and Flgfr Robert Walther

Finished in the standard two-tone green RLM 70 Schwarzgrün and RLM 71 Dunkelgrün upper surfaces in a straight-edged 'splinter' pattern with RLM 65 Hellblau undersides. Codes were black with a white individual aircraft letter 'D' in the staffel colour, and the propeller spinners had white tips. Note KG 30's 'Adler' shield positioned behind the nose glazing. This machine was

shot down by a Spitfire Mk.I Pilot: Sergeant Jim Hopewell, 616 Squadron whilst attacking RAF Driffield, Yorkshire on 15 August. Fw Henneske, the wireless operator, was killed, but Oblt Bachmann (pilot), Uffz Evers (observer) and Flgfr Walther (flight engineer/air gunner) all became PoWs.

Inset: III/KG 30's 'Adler' (black diving eagle) shield with III Gruppe's colour pale yellow background.

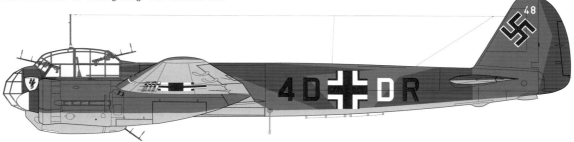

Junkers Ju 88A-1, L1+ER, 7./LG 1, Orleans-Bricy, France, August 1940.

Finished in the standard two-tone green RLM 70 Schwarzgrün and RLM 71 Dunkelgrün upper surfaces in a straight-edged 'splinter' pattern with RLM 65 Hellblau undersides. Codes were black with a white individual aircraft letter 'E' in the staffel colour, and the propeller spinners were white. Note LG 1's 'Griffon' shield positioned behind the nose glazing on the port

side and III Gruppe's 'flying geese' shield behind the nose glazing on the starboard side – see upper inset. Flown by Uffz Fritz Dieter, this machine crashed near Great Ham Farm, Earnley, Sussex, following combat with a Hurricane flown by Flt Lt Stanley Connors, 111 Squadron, on 15 August 1940.

Inset: III/LG 1's Gruppe 'flying geese' shield and LG 1's Geschwader 'Griffon' shield.

Dornier Do 24N-1, D-APDA, Seenotflugkommando 1, Noordwijk, Netherlands, August 1940.

As well as the He 59, (see p81), the Luftwaffe also employed the more modern and very capable Dornier Do 24 on air-sea rescue missions. In accordance with the Geneva Convention, they too were unarmed and painted white overall, with civilian registration markings and red crosses. As mentioned previously, this did not keep them from harm, and this machine was lost on 17 August 1940 during a rescue mission over the North Sea. Despite the danger, the Seenotdienst He

59s (of which at least four were shot down by RAF aircraft) and Do 24s continued to pick up downed Luftwaffe and RAF aircrew throughout the Battle, earning them well deserved praise for their gallantry. Eventually, Seenotflugkommando 1's white Do 24s and He 59s were repainted in RLM 72/73 maritime camouflage colours and armed with defensive machine guns.

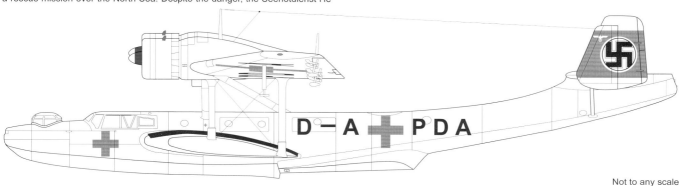

Not to any scale

Battle of Britain Phase 3:
Fight for survival – 24 August - 6 September 1940:
the Luftwaffe targets Fighter Command's airfields

▲ Refuelling a Spitfire of No 19 Squadron at Fowlmere during the Battle of Britain, September 1940. (Photo: Imperial War Museum)

Göring ordered further attacks on aircraft factories on 19 August 1940 and on 23 August 1940 ordered that more RAF airfields were to be attacked, and so, raids on airfields continued throughout August.

From 24 August onwards, the Battle was in essence a fight between Kesselring's Luftflotte 2 and Park's 11 Group. The Luftwaffe concentrated all their strength on knocking out Fighter Command and made repeated attacks on the airfields. Of the thirty-three heavy attacks over the following two weeks, twenty-four were against airfields.

The key Sector Stations were hit repeatedly – Biggin Hill and Hornchurch four times each; Debden and North Weald twice each. Croydon, Gravesend, Rochford, Hawkinge and Manston were also attacked in strength. Coastal Command's Eastchurch was bombed at least seven times because it was believed to be a Fighter Command aerodrome. At times these raids knocked out the Sector Stations, threatening the integrity of the RDF system. Emergency measures had to be taken to keep the Sector Stations operating.

Fighter Command was taking many casualties in the air. Aircraft production could replace aircraft, but replacement pilots were barely keeping pace with losses, and replacement novices were being shot down at an alarming rate. To offset losses, some fifty-eight Fleet Air Arm fighter pilot volunteers

were seconded to RAF squadrons, and a similar number of former Fairey Battle bomber pilots were used.

Most replacements from Operational Training Units (OTUs) had as little as nine hours flying time and no gunnery or air-to-air combat training. At this point the multi-national nature of Fighter Command came to the fore.

Many squadrons and individual personnel from the Dominions were already attached to the RAF, including top level commanders – Australians, Canadians, New Zealanders, Rhodesians and South Africans. They were bolstered by the arrival of fresh Czechoslovak and Polish squadrons. These Polish and Czech squadrons had been held back by Dowding, who thought non-English speaking aircrew would have trouble working within his control system. In addition there were other nationalities, including Free French, Belgian and even a pilot from the British mandate of Palestine.

The Polish and Czech fliers proved especially effective. The pre-war Polish Air Force had lengthy and extensive training, and high standards. With Poland conquered and under German occupation, the Polish pilots of 303 (Polish) Squadron, which was to become the highest-scoring allied unit in the Battle, were strongly motivated. Josef Frantisek, a Czech regular airman who had flown from the occupation of his own country to join the Polish and then French air forces before arriving in

Supermarine Spitfire Mk.I, P9323/ZD-F, 222 Squadron, RAF Hornchurch, Essex, late August/early September 1940.

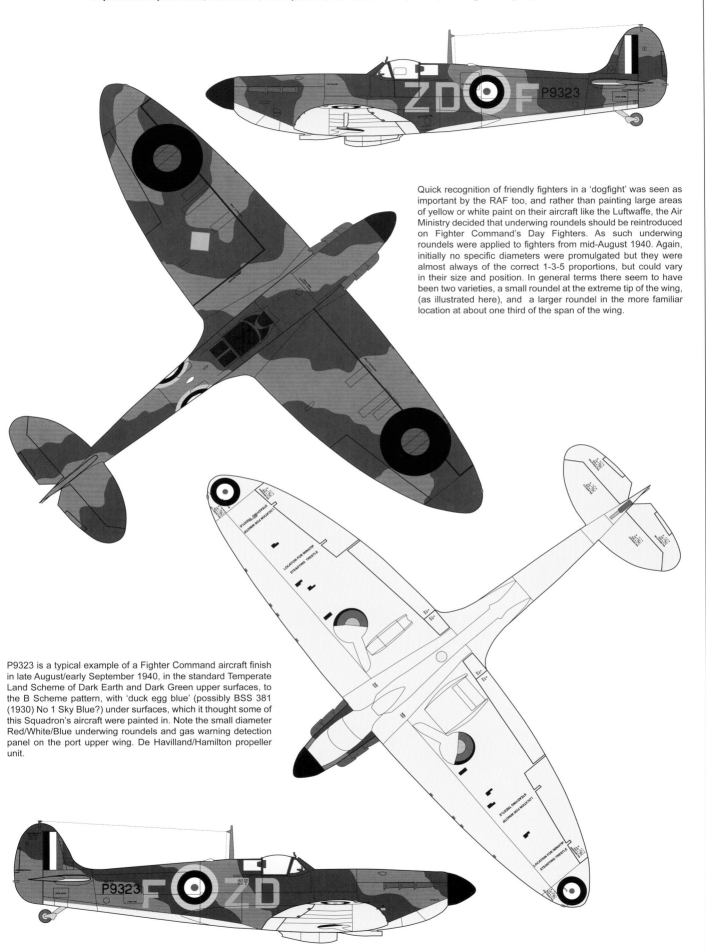

Quick recognition of friendly fighters in a 'dogfight' was seen as important by the RAF too, and rather than painting large areas of yellow or white paint on their aircraft like the Luftwaffe, the Air Ministry decided that underwing roundels should be reintroduced on Fighter Command's Day Fighters. As such underwing roundels were applied to fighters from mid-August 1940. Again, initially no specific diameters were promulgated but they were almost always of the correct 1-3-5 proportions, but could vary in their size and position. In general terms there seem to have been two varieties, a small roundel at the extreme tip of the wing, (as illustrated here), and a larger roundel in the more familiar location at about one third of the span of the wing.

P9323 is a typical example of a Fighter Command aircraft finish in late August/early September 1940, in the standard Temperate Land Scheme of Dark Earth and Dark Green upper surfaces, to the B Scheme pattern, with 'duck egg blue' (possibly BSS 381 (1930) No 1 Sky Blue?) under surfaces, which it thought some of this Squadron's aircraft were painted in. Note the small diameter Red/White/Blue underwing roundels and gas warning detection panel on the port upper wing. De Havilland/Hamilton propeller unit.

Not to any scale

▲ Groundcrew refuelling Supermarine Spitfire Mk.II, P7420, of 19 Squadron from a tractor-drawn petrol bowser at Fowlmere, Cambridgeshire. This newly-arrived example was one of the few Spitfire Mark IIs to fly operationally with a front-line squadron before the end of the Battle of Britain. (Photo: Imperial War Museum)

Britain, flew as a 'guest' of 303 Squadron and was ultimately credited with Fighter Command's highest individual score during the Battle of Britain.

RAF Fighter Command also had the advantage of fighting over home territory. Pilots who baled out of their downed aircraft could be back at their airfields within hours. For the Luftwaffe aircrews, a bale out over England meant capture, while parachuting into the English Channel often meant drowning or death from exposure. As mentioned previously, Luftwaffe morale began to suffer, and 'Kanalkrankheit' (Channel sickness), a form of combat fatigue, began to appear amongst the German pilots. The Luftwaffe's replacement problem was even worse than that of the RAF's. Although the Luftwaffe maintained its numerical superiority, the slow supply of replacement aircraft, and pilots, put increasing strain on the resources of the operational units.

However, on the night of 23/24 August, bombs, which it is thought were dropped by a group of Heinkel He 111s which had failed to find their original target, were dropped on Harrow on the outskirts of London, and on parts of central London and the East End which was set ablaze. There were also raids on Aberdeen, Bristol and South Wales, and Portsmouth was hit by a major attack, the largest raid so far which killed 100.

In retaliation, on the night of 25/26 August 1940, eighty-one Bomber Command bombers were sent out to raid industrial and commercial targets in Berlin, and continued to regularly target Berlin from then on. Cloud prevented accurate identification and the bombs fell across the city, causing some casualties amongst the civilian population as well as damage to residential areas. Göring's pride was hurt, as he had previously claimed the British would never be allowed to bomb the city.

▲ A section of Supermarine Spitfire Mk.Is of 616 Squadron prepare for an evening take-off from Fowlmere, Cambridgeshire during September 1940. Confusion as to the identity of these aircraft has risen from the fact that both 616 and 92 Squadrons shared the same unit code letters 'QJ' at this time. (Photo: Imperial War Museum)

▲ Supermarine Spitfire Mk.I, P9386/QV-K of 19 Squadron, being rearmed between sorties at Fowlmere, Cambridgeshire in September 1940. P9386 was often flown by the unit's Commanding Officer, Squadron Leader 'Sandy' Lane, and was also the preferred aircraft of 'A' Flight commander Flight-Lieutenant W J 'Farmer' Lawson. (Photo: Imperial War Museum)

In spite of the casualties it was inflicting on the RAF, recent research would indicate that the Luftwaffe was perhaps losing this phase of the Battle. Throughout the Battle, the Luftwaffe greatly underestimated the strength of Fighter Command and the scale of British aircraft production, whilst their opposite numbers across the Channel, the Air Intelligence Division of the Air Ministry, consistently overestimated the size of the Luftwaffe and the productive capacity of the German aviation industry.

As the Battle was fought, both sides exaggerated the losses inflicted on the other by a similar, equally large, margin. However, the intelligence picture formed before the Battle encouraged the Luftwaffe to believe that such losses were pushing Fighter Command to the very edge of extinction, whilst the exaggerated picture of German air strength persuaded the RAF that the threat it faced was larger and more dangerous than was actually the case.

This led the British to the conclusion that another two weeks of attacks on 11 Group's airfields might well result in forcing Fighter Command to withdraw its squadrons from the south of England up to airfileds in the north. The German misconception, on the other hand, encouraged first complacency, then strategic misjudgment. The shift of targets from air bases to industry and communications was taken because it was assumed that Fighter Command was virtually eliminated.

Hawker Hurricane Mk.I, P3878/YB-W, 17 Squadron, RAF Tangmere, Sussex, August/September 1940.
Pilot: Pilot Officer Harold Bird-Wilson

Dark Earth and Dark Green upper surfaces, to the B Scheme pattern, with 'duck egg green' (possibly Eau-de-Nil shade?) under surfaces. Note the undulating upper/under colour demarcation line on the wing leading edges (inset) and the nose and the 'Sky' spinner, a common feature on 17 Squadron Hurricanes of this period. P3878 was fitted with a Rotol propeller unit. Pilot Officer Bird-Wilson was shot down and badly burned whilst flying this aircraft, by Maj Adolph Galland, Kommodore of JG 26, on 24 September 1940

Inset: Pilot Officer Harold Bird-Wilson's 'three swords aimed at a German eagle' personal marking painted on the emergency break-out panel door under the cockpit.

Not to any scale

Supermarine Spitfire Mk.I, X4178/EB-K, 41 Squadron, RAF Hornchurch, Essex, September 1940.

Even by early September, RAF Fighter Command aircraft were still to be seen in variations of the 'Sky' under surface scheme. It is thought that Sky Grey was occasionally used as an alternative, as it was readily available, being applied to the undersides of Fleet Air Arm aircraft. Photos, 41 Squadron aircraft during this period are thought to show Sky Grey undersides, as illustrated here, with standard Temperate Land Scheme Dark Earth and Dark Green upper surfaces, to the A Scheme pattern. A de Havilland/Hamilton propeller unit was fitted.

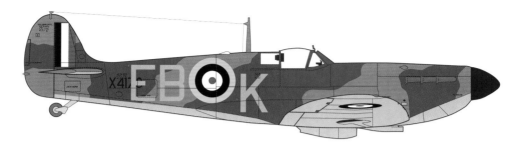

Hawker Hurricane Mk.I, R2689/US-Z, 56 Squadron, RAF North Weald, Essex, late August 1940.
Pilot: Flight Lieutenant Edward 'Jumbo' Gracie

R2689 was finished in the standard Temperate Land Scheme Dark Earth and Dark Green upper surfaces, to the A Scheme pattern. Under surfaces were finished in one of the variations of 'Sky' with a larger style roundel at about one third of the span, and a 'Sky' Rotol propeller spinner. Note the two narrow yellow bands running horizontally across the 'Hawker' style fin marking. Pilot Officer Gracie was shot down in this machine on 30 August 1940, and whilst initially believed to be unhurt, on the following day his neck was found to be broken.

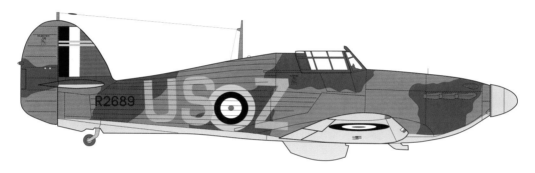

Hawker Hurricane Mk.I, P2798/LK-A, 87 Squadron, RAF Church Fenton, Yorkshire, August/September 1940.
Pilot: Flight Lieutenant Ian 'Widge' Gleed, DFC

Coloured spinners were a rarity within the RAF at this time, but a few aircraft had them, including P2798 illustrated here, when flown by Flight Lieutenant Ian 'Widge' Gleed, DFC, 87 Squadron's A Flight commander. Finished in the Dark Earth and Dark Green upper surfaces, to the B Scheme pattern, with 'Sky' (possibly BS 381 (1930) No 16 Eau-de-Nil) under surfaces, note the pre-war 'bright shades' of Red and Blue on the fuselage roundels and fin marking which some aircraft manufacturers who were then building Hurricanes were still using. Also note the truncated outer yellow ring to the fuselage roundel along the lower demarcation line. Rotol propeller unit.

Inset: 'Figaro' the cat cartoon character from the Walt Disney animated film 'Pinnochio' which was Ian Gleed's personal marking applied on the emergency break-out panel door on the starboard side of the aircraft.

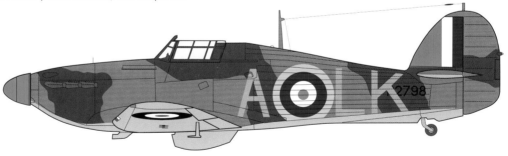

Hawker Hurricane Mk.I, P3462/VK-G, 238 Squadron, RAF Middle Wallop, Hampshire, late August 1940.

Fin markings also continued to be very varied amongst RAF fighters, due to a lack of precision in the instructions which were initially issued for their application. Eventually a conference held at the Air Ministry on 23 July 1940 decided that fin markings were to consist of a Red, White and Blue rectangle, 27 inches high by 24 inches wide applied with the Red leading. By mid-late August 1940 these 'official' fin markings were starting to become more common as illustrated on P3462 here. Dark Earth and Dark Green upper surfaces, to the B Scheme pattern, with 'duck egg green' (possibly Eau-de-Nil shade?) under surfaces. Note the forward angle of the 'V' of the squadron code and the truncated outer yellow ring to the fuselage roundel along the lower demarcation line. Rotol propeller unit.

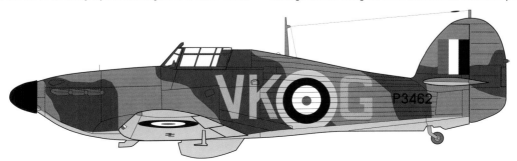

Not to any scale

Yet this analysis ignored the fact that Fighter Command continued to be desperately short of pilots rather than of aircraft, as indeed it had been from the start of the Battle. Incompletely trained recruits, and instructors cannibalised from the training programme, did not augur well for the ability to sustain the defence.

German losses were also severe between the 24 August and 4 September. Luftwaffe serviceability rates, were still just about acceptable at 65-75%, but there was a chronic shortage of spare parts. All units were well below established strength – and the attrition was beginning to affect the fighter units in particular.

Camouflage and markings

RAF – reintroduction of underwing roundels

At an Air Ministry conference on 23 July 1940 it was recognised that due to the importance of quick recognition of friendly fighters in a 'dogfight', underwing roundels should be reintroduced. This decision was circulated in a letter dated 11 August 1940.

In June 1940 the national markings applied to Fighter Command's Day Fighters consisted of Red and Blue roundels on the upper surface of the wings, in which the Red centre was two fifths of the overall diameter of the roundel, and Red, White, Blue and Yellow roundels on the fuselage, supposedly of 1-3-5-7 proportion, and Red, White and Blue fin markings.

All these markings could vary in size from one aircraft type to another or even from one aircraft to another in the following ways. The upperwing roundel varied in size because no regulations were laid down as to what size these markings should be. As a result, each manufacturer decided for themselves how big the roundel should be on their particular aircraft.

The fuselage roundel could also vary in size, proportion and even position depending on where and how it was applied, and which set of regulations were being followed at the time. For example, aircraft manufactured before the Yellow surround to the fuselage roundel was introduced, in May 1940, had the

Yellow surround added by the Service. This might be correctly proportioned and result in a huge roundel which encroached upon the code letters, or alternatively it might not be correctly proportioned resulting in some very odd looking markings with thin Yellow outlines, or a slightly thicker Yellow outline which encroached on the Blue ring in the roundel. Aircraft manufactured after the Yellow ring was introduced could generally be seen with correctly proportioned, but somewhat smaller, fuselage roundels.

When the underwing roundels were reintroduced for fighters from mid-August, they were almost always of the correct 1-3-5 proportions, but could vary in their size and position. In general terms there seem to have been two varieties, a small roundel at the extreme tip of the wing, and a larger roundel in the more familiar location at about one third of the span of the wing. Again these variations are probably the result of the roundels being applied in different places at different times by manufacturers and/or service personnel.

The fin markings also continued to be very varied due to a lack of precision in the instructions which were initially issued for their application. Eventually a conference held at the Air Ministry on 23 July 1940 decided that fin markings were to consist of a Red, White and Blue rectangle, 27 inches high by 24 inches wide applied with the Red leading.

The shades of red and blue paint used in these markings were supposed to be the 'dull' wartime shades, first introduced with the adoption of camouflage in 1937. However, it is known that some aircraft manufacturers, including Glosters who were then building Hurricanes, were still using the pre-war 'bright shades' during the summer of 1940.

On 1 September 1940, the MAP sent a circular to all the aircraft manufacturers with reference to DTD Technical Circular 84 'Identification Colours on Aircraft'. The MAP's Resident Technical Officers were to advise the companies to which they were attached that dull identification colours were required for the national markings on aircraft. The reminder was necessary because it appeared that several companies were still purchasing, or at least using up old stocks of, the pre-war colours which were glossy and bright, but how widespread this practice was is unknown at the time of writing.

Messerschmitt Bf 109E-4, Stab II./JG 3, Wierre-au-Bois, France, September 1940.
Pilot: Oblt Franz von Werra, the Gruppe Adjutant

The one that got way, Oblt Franz von Werra, flew this Bf 109E-4 which was finished in RLM 71 Dunkelgrün and RLM 02 Grau upper surfaces in a soft-edged splinter pattern with RLM 65 Hellblau under surfaces extended up on the fuselage sides and over the fin and rudder. The removable section of fuselage in front of the windscreen appears to be a replacement part and has a faint mottle on its top, whilst the side and lower engine panels appear to have either been recently repainted, or cleaned, and have often been mistaken for being white. Note the white wing tips and rudder, and the black and white quartered spinner

with an RLM 70 backplate. The unit's black and white shield was carried under the windscreen. Franz von Werra was shot down on 5 September 1940, and captured near Marden, Kent. He subsequently escaped from a train taking him to a PoW camp in Canada and returned to Germany in May 1941, where he was awarded the Ritterkreuz. He returned to combat operations on the Russian Front with JG 53 and raised his victory claims to twenty-one, but was killed on 25 October when he lost control of his Bf 109F-4 which crashed in to the North Sea after the unit had transferred to the Netherlands in September 1941.

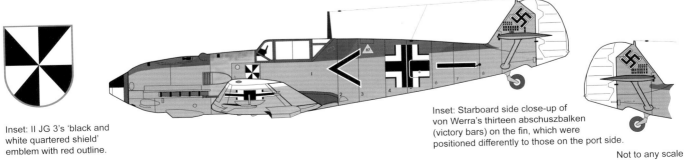

Inset: II JG 3's 'black and white quartered shield' emblem with red outline.

Inset: Starboard side close-up of von Werra's thirteen abschuszbalken (victory bars) on the fin, which were positioned differently to those on the port side.

Not to any scale

Messerschmitt Bf 109E-1, 'Black 2', 8./JG 54, Guines-Sud, France, September 1940.
Pilot: Uffz Heinrich Elbers

RLM 71 Dunkelgrün and RLM 02 Grau upper surfaces in a soft-edged splinter pattern with RLM 65 Hellblau under surfaces extended high up on the fuselage sides and over the fin and rudder, over which a sparse and varied density mottle of RLM 71/02 has been applied. Note the white mainplane and tailplane tips and the white segment at the top of the rudder. 8./JG 54's 'red sparrow' emblem was positioned on the nose as was the aircraft's black numeral '2'. Note the small narrow bordered fuselage balkenkreuze. The balkenkreuze above the wings were in the early outboard position and partially covered by the white wing tip paint. Uffz Elbers was shot down and crash landed this aircraft at Ashford, Kent, on 2 September 1940

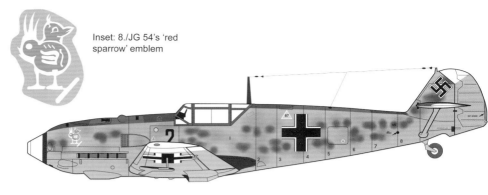

Inset: 8./JG 54's 'red sparrow' emblem

Messerschmitt Bf 109E-3, 'Yellow 7', 3./JG 3, Colembert, France, September 1940.
Pilot: Uffz Heinz Grabow

RLM 71 Dunkelgrün and RLM 02 Grau upper surfaces in a soft-edged splinter pattern with RLM 65 Hellblau under surfaces extended high up on the fuselage sides and over the fin and rudder, over which a varied density mottle of RLM 71/02 has been applied. Note the white mainplane tips and white rudder. For some reason this aircraft sported 1 Staffel's white 'tatzelwurm' emblem which was positioned on both sides of the nose. Note the black disc with a white saltire marking carried only on the starboard rear fuselage and the green and white halved spinner with a yellow tip. Uffz Grabow crash landed this aircraft at Wichling, Kent, on 5 September 1940.

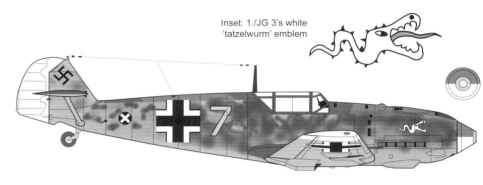

Inset: 1./JG 3's white 'tatzelwurm' emblem

Messerschmitt Bf 109E-4, 'White 12', 7./JG 53, Le Touquet-Etaples, France, September 1940.

Finished in RLM 71 Dunkelgrün and RLM 02 Grau upper surfaces in a soft-edged splinter pattern with RLM 65 Hellblau under surfaces extended up on the fuselage sides and over the fin and rudder, which have then had a very dense application of RLM 71/02 mottle applied. Note how the swastika has been painted out on the fin and reapplied on the rudder. The white numeral '12' and III gruppe vertical bar had no outline and the spinner was all RLM 70 Schwarzgrün.

Messerschmitt Bf 109E-4, 'Yellow 5' , 9./JG 54, Guines-Sud, France, September 1940.

RLM 71 Dunkelgrün and RLM 02 Grau upper surfaces in a soft-edged splinter pattern with RLM 65 Hellblau under surfaces extended high up on the fuselage sides and over the fin and rudder, over which cross-hatch streaks of RLM 71/02 have been applied, carefully masked around the numeral and III Gruppe wavy line. No unit badges appear to have been applied. Note the rearview mirror.

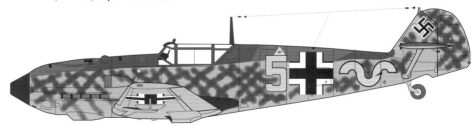

Messerschmitt Bf 109E-4, 'White 6', 6./JG 27, Fiennes, France, September 1940.

RLM 71 Dunkelgrün and RLM 02 Grau upper surfaces in a soft-edged splinter pattern with RLM 65 Hellblau under surfaces extended high up on the fuselage sides and over the fin and rudder, over which a light mottle of RLM 71/02 has been applied. Note the yellow cowling and rudder. II JG 27's 'Berlin Bear' shield was positioned on both sides of the nose.

Inset: II JG 27's 'Berlin Bear' coat of arms emblem

Not to any scale

Messerschmitt Bf 110D, 3U+CA, Geschwaderstab ZG 26, based Boos-Rouen, France, August 1940.

3U+CA was probably finished in the RLM 71 Dunkelgrün and RLM 02 Grau upper surfaces scheme, in a soft-edged splinter pattern, with RLM 65 Hellblau under surfaces, which extended high up on the fuselage sides, along the engine

nacelles and over the fins and rudders, over which a dense mottle of RLM 71/02 had been applied. Codes were black with the individual aircraft letter 'C' in the Geschwaderstab colour blue. Note the also the blue spinners.

Inset: A yellow chevron outlined in black was carried under the windscreen, presumably further denoting a Stab aircraft.

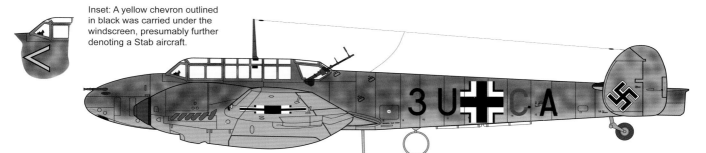

Messerschmitt Bf 110C, U8+AH, 1./ZG 26, Yvrench/St Omer, France, late August 1940.

Finished in RLM 71 Dunkelgrün and RLM 02 Grau upper surfaces in a soft-edged splinter pattern with RLM 65 Hellblau under surfaces, which extended high up on the fuselage sides, along the engine nacelles and over the fins and

rudders. Codes were black with the individual aircraft letter 'A' in the staffel colour white. Note the white tips to the RLM 70 spinners.

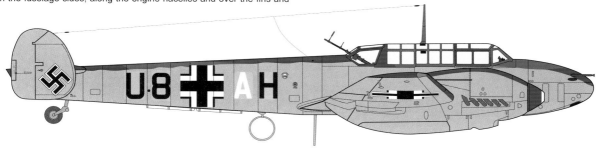

Messerschmitt Bf 110C, U8+HL, 3./ZG 26, Yvrench/St Omer, France, late August 1940.

Even after the introduction of the RLM 71/02 scheme on Bf 110s there were still plenty of examples of machines finished in the two-tone green RLM 70 Schwarzgrün and RLM 71 Dunkelgrün upper surfaces scheme with RLM 65 Hellblau undersides. Codes were all black with the individual aircraft letter 'H' in the staffel colour yellow. Like III/ZG 26, I/ZG 26 started introducing white noses on its Bf 110s as a rapid identification/recognition feature around this time.

Note the thin white band around the rear fuselage, another rapid identification feature, and the narrow white band around the RLM 70 spinners. This aircraft, which carried a steam engine locomotive silhouette on the nose, which had been overpainted with the white tactical paint, crash landed at Cobham Farm, Charing, Kent, on 11 September 1940, its pilot Fw Brinkmann and his bordfunker Uffz Kruesphow being captured.

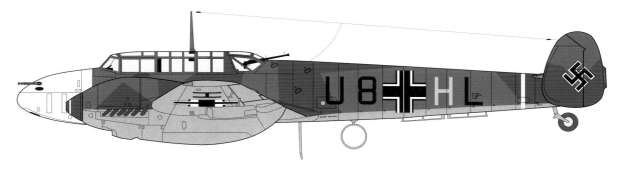

Messerschmitt Bf 110C, U8+GL, 3./ZG 26, Yvrench/St Omer, France, late August 1940.
Crewed by Lt Joachim Koepsell and Uffz Johann Schmidt

Another one of 3 Staffel's machines, which in this instance is thought might have been painted in the 'new' grey shades on the upper surfaces, mixed from existing RLM colours. The under surfaces remained in RLM 65 Hellblau and were extended high up on the fuselage in a undulating demarcation below which a diffused mottle was applied which extended on to the fins/rudders and engine

nacelles. Codes were black with the individual aircraft letter 'G' in the staffel colour yellow. Note the white propeller spinners, white nose and narrow white band around the rear fuselage. This aircraft was shot down over southwest England on 27 September 1940, Lt Koepsell surviving in to captivity but Uffz Schmidt being killed.

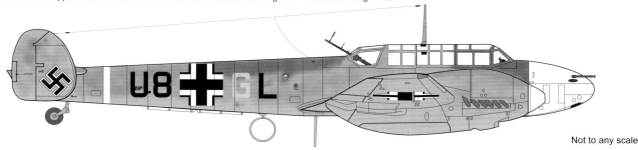

Not to any scale

Messerschmitt Bf 110C, M8+CP, 6./ZG 76, Laval, France, early September 1940.

Known as the 'Haifischgruppe' due to the large 'sharkmouth' design on its nose, this unit tended to retain the 'old' two-tone green RLM 70 Schwarzgrün and RLM 71 Dunkelgrün hard-edged splinter upper surface finish on its Bf 110s. Under surfaces were RLM 65 Hellblau. Codes were black with the individual aircraft

letter 'C' in the 6 Staffel colour yellow. This machine was shot down at Cowden, Kent, on 4 September 1940. Oblt Piduhn and his bordfunker Gfr Odene were both killed.

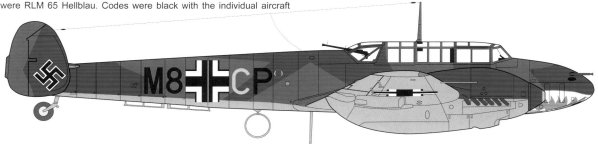

Heinkel He 111H, 1H+LM, 4./KG 26, Amiens, France, September 1940.

Finished in the standard two-tone green RLM 70 Schwarzgrün and RLM 71 Dunkelgrün upper surfaces in a straight-edged 'splinter' pattern with RLM 65 Hellblau undersides. Codes were black with the individual aircraft letter 'L' in the

Staffel colour white, as were the propeller spinners. II Gruppe's 'Vestigum Leonis' insignia was positioned on both sides of the forward fuselage immediately below the pilot's cockpit glazing.

Inset: II/KG 26's 'Vestigum Leonis', black lion sejant on a white shield insignia

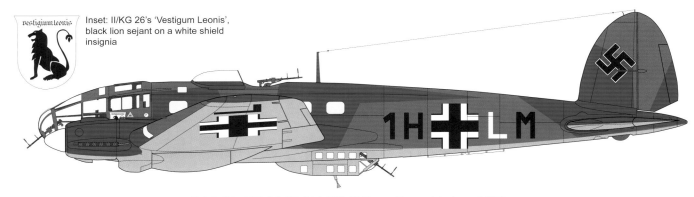

Heinkel He 111P, G1+BB, Stab I/KG 55, Dreux, France, late August 1940.

KG 55 appear to have been mainly equipped with He 111P sub-types during this Battle of Britain period. Finished in the standard two-tone green RLM 70 Schwarzgrün and RLM 71 Dunkelgrün upper surfaces in a straight-edged 'splinter' pattern with RLM 65 Hellblau undersides, the codes were black with a red individual aircraft letter 'B' outlined in white, which was an uncommon colour for a Gruppe Stabskette machine, green being the usual colour, but was recorded as such by the RAF Intelligence Officer who inspected the aircraft.

G1+BB was also fitted with a rearward firing MG15 machine gun in the tail cone. Note the central position of the swastika across the fin and rudder and the white spinners with a red band around them. Piloted by Oblt Ignaz Krenn, this machine made a successful crash landing at Helliers Farm, Wick, Sussex, on 26 August following an attack on Portsmouth Dockyard.

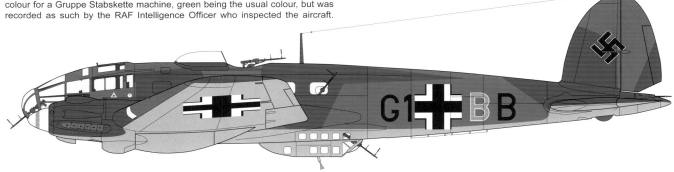

Heinkel He 111H, V4+HV, 11./KG 1, Amiens, France, late August 1940.

Finished in the standard Luftwaffe bomber scheme of two-tone green RLM 70 Schwarzgrün and RLM 71 Dunkelgrün upper surfaces in a straight-edged 'splinter' pattern, with RLM 65 Hellblau undersides, codes were black with a red individual aircraft letter 'H' and red propeller spinners. Note the central position of the swastika across the fin and rudder and the Staffel's red and white 'diamond'

marking to the rear of the cockpit. This aircraft was forced to land at Haxted Farm, Lingfield, Surrey on 30 August 1940, following combat with Pilot Officer John Greenwood, 253 Squadron, after an attack on Farnborough airfield.

Inset: 11./KG 1's red and white 'diamond' marking normally carried on the fuselage to the rear of the cockpit.

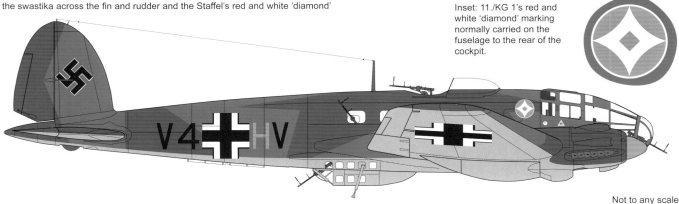

Not to any scale

Messerschmitt Bf 110C, L1+AM, 14(Z)./LG 1, Ligescourt, France, late August 1940.

Finished in the standard two-tone green RLM 70 Schwarzgrün and RLM 71 Dunkelgrün upper surfaces in a straight-edged 'splinter' pattern with RLM 65 Hellblau undersides, note the areas of the fuselage with fresh paint where previous codes, or the factory stammkennzeichen, were painted over. Codes were all black with the individual aircraft letter 'A' outlined in white. Note also the way in which the fuselage balkenkreuze have been 'toned-down' by increasing the width of the black angled borders and the yellow tips to the propeller spinners. This machine was shot down in to the Thames Estuary off Sheerness, Kent, on 31 August 1940. Fw Fritz and his bordfunker Obfw Doepfer were rescued and made PoWs.

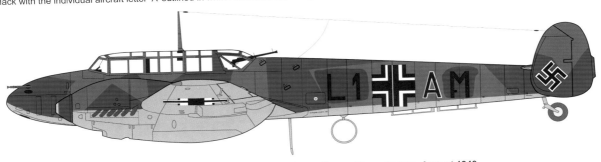

Dornier Do 17Z-2, F1+DT of 9./KG 76, Cormeilles-en-Vixen, France, August 1940.
Crewed by: Hptm Roth (Staffelkapitän), Hptm Peters, Oblt Lamberty, Obfw Geier and Fw Eberhard

Finished in the standard Luftwaffe bomber scheme of two-tone green RLM 70 Schwarzgrün and RLM 71 Dunkelgrün upper surfaces in a straight-edged 'splinter' pattern with RLM 65 Hellblau undersides. Codes were black with the individual aircraft letter 'D' in yellow, the staffel colour, and yellow propeller spinners. The Staffel's red and white shield with three 'Tyr-Runes' was carried under the cockpit. This aircraft was mortally damaged by RAF Kenley's ground defences after attacking the base, preceded by damage inflicted by No 111 Squadron Hurricanes, and crash landed at Leaves Green, near Biggin Hill, Kent on 18 August 1940, where it burnt out.

Inset: 9./KG 76's red and white shield with three 'Tyr-Runes' which in German mythology represent Tyr, the god of war.

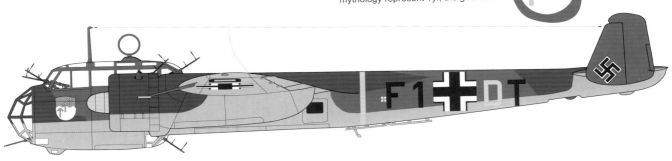

Dornier Do 17Z, U5+ER, 7./KG 2, Cambrai-Sud, France, August 1940.

Standard Luftwaffe bomber scheme of two-tone green RLM 70 Schwarzgrün and RLM 71 Dunkelgrün upper surfaces in a straight-edged 'splinter' pattern with RLM 65 Hellblau undersides. Codes were black with the individual aircraft letter 'E' in white the staffel colour. RLM 70 Schwarzgrün propeller spinners. This machine crash landed at Stodmarsh, Kent, on 13 August 1940, following an attack on RAF Eastchurch.

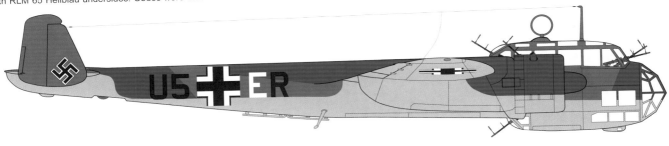

Dornier Do 17P, 4U+BH, 1./(F)AufklGr 123, Toussus-le-Buc, France, August 1940.

The Aufklärungsgruppen were still using the old Do 17P as a reconnaissance platform well in to 1940 as illustrated by this example, finished in the standard Luftwaffe bomber scheme of two-tone green RLM 70 Schwarzgrün and RLM 71 Dunkelgrün upper surfaces in a straight-edged 'splinter' pattern with RLM 65 Hellblau undersides. Codes were black with the individual aircraft letter 'B' in white, the staffel colour. What may have been a personal emblem of a cameraman riding a pencil was applied to the fuselage under the cockpit with the Staffel's 'Knullenkopf' emblem applied to the outer faces of both engine cowlings.

Inset: (near right) Cameraman riding a pencil applied to the fuselage under the cockpit which may have been a personal emblem, and (far right), 1./(F) AufklGr 123's 'Knullenkopf' (a Luftwaffe airman's head and shoulders holding a telescope) applied to the outer faces of both engine cowlings.

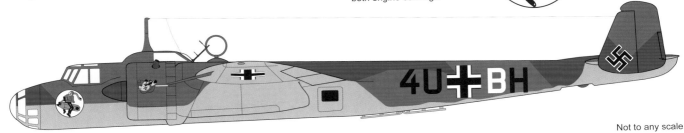

Not to any scale

▲ A fantastic photograph of armourer Fred Roberts replenishing the Browning machine guns on Supermarine Spitfire Mk.I, X4474/QV-I of 19 Squadron, adjacent to Manor Farm at Fowlmere in September 1940. The pilot, Sergeant B J Jennings, can also be seen in conversation with his mechanic prior to another sortie. (Photo: Imperial War Museum)

Despite the raids conducted by RAF Bomber Command against German cities since May 1940, Hitler's Directive No 17, issued on 1 August 1940 on the conduct of war against England, had specifically forbidden the Luftwaffe from conducting 'terror raids' on its own initiative. Hitler had reserved the right of ordering terror attacks as means of reprisal for himself! However, the continuing RAF Bomber Command raids on Berlin led to Hitler withdrawing his Directive 17, and on 3 September Göring made plans to start bombing London, daily, with Kesselring's enthusiastic support, having received reports that the average strength of RAF squadrons was down to six or seven fighters and their airfields in the area were out of action.

Hitler issued another directive on 5 September 1940, ordering attacks on British cities including London. In his speech delivered on 4 September 1940, he threatened to obliterate British cities if British bombing of Germany did not stop.

On 7 September, a massive series of raids involving nearly four hundred bombers and more than six hundred fighters targeted docks in the East End of London during the day – and continued in to the night and for the next fifty-seven consecutive nights.

Despite suffering from shortages, Fighter Command had anticipated further attacks on its airfields and the 11 Group squadrons rose to meet the daylight raid of 7 September – in greater numbers than the Luftwaffe expected.

Next morning, Keith Park flew his Hurricane over London. "It was burning all down the river. It was a horrid sight. But I looked down and said, *"Thank God for that', because I knew that the Nazis had switched their attack from the fighter stations thinking that they were knocked out. They weren't, but they were pretty groggy."*

▲ Spitfire Mk.I of 19 Squadron being re-armed between sorties at Fowlmere in Cambridgeshire during September 1940. (Photo: Imperial War Museum)

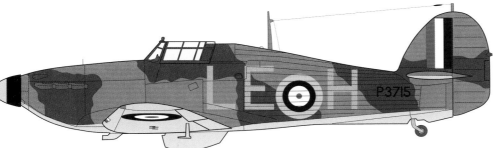

Hawker Hurricane Mk.I, P3715/LE-H, 242 Squadron, RAF Duxford, Essex, September 1940.
Pilot: Pilot Officer Denis Crowley-Milling

During the Battle, 12 Group's AVM Trafford Leigh-Mallory proposed that squadrons be formed into 'Big Wings', consisting of at least three squadrons, to attack the enemy en masse – a method then being pioneered by the legendary Squadron Leader Douglas Bader, the CO, 242 Squadron, in which unit Pilot Officer Crowley-Milling served. His regular aircraft, P3715 was finished in the standard Temperate Land Scheme of Dark Earth and Dark Green upper surfaces, to the B Scheme pattern. Under surfaces were finished in one of the variations of 'Sky' as was the tip of the Rotol propeller spinner.

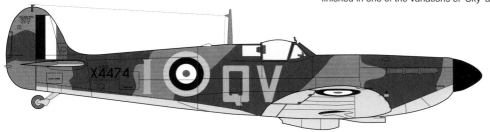

Supermarine Spitfire Mk.I, X4474/ QV-I, 19 Squadron, RAF Fowlmere, Cambridgeshire, September 1940.

Proponents of the 'Big Wing' tactic claimed interceptions in large numbers caused greater enemy losses whilst reducing their own casualties, but opponents pointed out that the 'Big Wings' took too long to form up, and as 12 Group was tasked with protecting 11 Group's airfields, the delay in forming up meant that they often did not arrive until after German bombers had hit 11 Group's airfields. Several squadrons within 12 Group were involved in the Big Wing trials during the late summer and autumn of 1940, including 19 Squadron which was based close to Duxford at Fowlmere in Cambridgeshire. X4474 was finished in Dark Earth and Dark Green upper surfaces, to the A Scheme pattern. Under surfaces were finished in one of the variations of 'Sky'. Note the underwing roundels at the extreme tips of the wings. De Havilland/Hamilton propeller unit fitted.

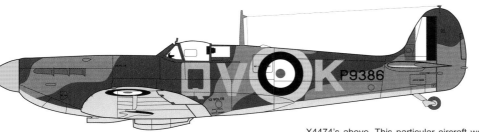

Supermarine Spitfire Mk.I, P9386/QV-K, 19 Squadron, RAF Fowlmere, Cambridgeshire, September 1940.
Pilot: Squadron Leader Brian Lane

There were the inevitable variations in markings even amongst aircraft in the same squadron as illustrated by the difference of the fuselage roundel applied to P9386 compared with that of X4474's above. This particular aircraft was flown by the unit's CO, Squadron Leader Brian Lane, and was finished in the standard Temperate Land Scheme of Dark Earth and Dark Green upper surfaces, to the A Scheme pattern with one of the variations of 'Sky' on the under surfaces. Note again the underwing roundels at the extreme tips of the wings – perhaps a squadron feature at this time? It is also thought that P9386 had a yellow spinner, possibly as a Squadron Commander's recognition feature. De Havilland/Hamilton propeller unit fitted.

Supermarine Spitfire Mk.I, X4329 (overpainted)/QJ-Y, 616 Squadron, RAF Coltishall, Norfolk, September 1940.

One of the squadrons that would be indelibly linked to Douglas Bader's Tangmere Wing during the spring and summer offensive sweeps of 1941, was 616, who were based at RAF Coltishall during much of September 1940, in 12 Group, for a rest after a period of intensive action flying from Kenley in 11 Group during the second half of August. X4329, which appears to have had its serial number overpainted which was relatively rare at this stage of the war, was finished in Dark Earth and Dark Green upper surfaces, to the B Scheme pattern with one of the duck egg blue variations of 'Sky' on the under surfaces. Note again the underwing roundels at the extreme tips of the wings. De Havilland/Hamilton propeller unit fitted.

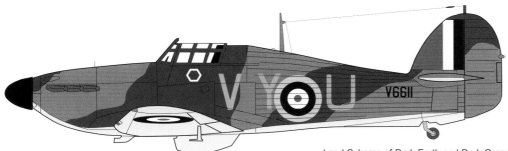

Hawker Hurricane Mk.I, V6611/VY-U, 85 Squadron, RAF Croydon, Surrey, September 1940.

85 Squadron was still in the thick of the fighting through much of August and September, moving from Debden to Croydon and then to Castle Camps, all in 11 Group, before being rested in the north at Church Fenton, where it started to take on more of a Night Fighter role. V6611 was finished in the standard Temperate Land Scheme of Dark Earth and Dark Green upper surfaces, to the A Scheme pattern with a variation of 'Sky' on the under surfaces. The underwing roundels were the larger style located at about one third of the span of the wing. These variations in underwing roundels were probably the result of them being applied in different places at different times by different manufacturers and/or service personnel. Rotol propeller unit fitted.

Not to any scale

Hawker Hurricane Mk.I, V6665/RF-J of 303 (Polish) Squadron, RAF Northolt, Middlesex, September 1940.
Pilot: Flight Lieutenant Johnny Kent

Following a successful engagement by aircraft, 303 (Polish) Squadron out on a training exercise on 30 August 1940, the Polish and Czech squadrons which had been held back to allow the 'foreign nationals' to learn the RAF ways, were declared operational and immediately provided a much needed boost. V6665 flown by one of the 'British' Flight Commanders attached to the Polish-manned squadron, (actually Johnny Kent was a Canadian), was finished in Dark Earth and Dark Green upper surfaces, to the B Scheme pattern with a variation of 'Sky' on the under surfaces. The underwing roundels were the larger style located at about one third of the span of the wing. Note the 'Kosciuszko' coat of arms on the fuselage below the radio mast, and the red diagonal band around the rear of the fuselage which may have indicated a Flight Commander. Rotol propeller unit fitted.

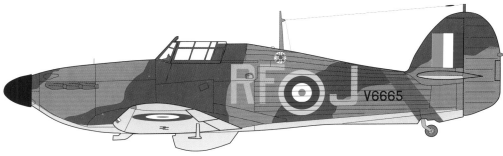

Inset: The official badge, 303 'City of Warsaw/Tadeusz Kosciuszko' (Polish) Squadron, which continued the traditions of the Polish Air Force's 111th Fighter Flight, which was named after General Tadeusz Kosciuszko, a 19th Century Polish national hero.

Hawker Hurricane Mk.I, P3128/RF-A, 303 (Polish) Squadron, RAF Northolt, Middlesex, September 1940.
Pilot: Flg Off Zdzislaw Henneberg

Many of the Polish (and Czech) pilots had had previous combat experience and now, flying modern RAF fighters were able to make their presence felt – Flg Off Henneberg scoring eight 'kills' during the rest of the Battle. P3128 was his regular mount, finished in the standard Temperate Land Scheme of Dark Earth and Dark Green upper surfaces, to the B Scheme pattern with a variation of 'Sky' on the under surfaces. The underwing

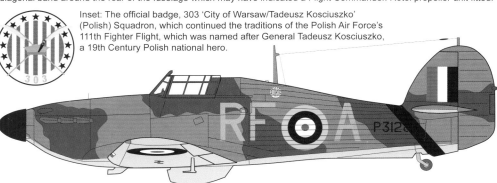

roundels were the larger style located at about one third of the span of the wing. Note the 'Kosciuszko' coat of arms on the fuselage below the radio mast, and the blue diagonal band around the rear of the fuselage which may have indicated some form of formation leader. Rotol propeller unit fitted.

Hawker Hurricane Mk.I, P3143/NN-D, 310 (Czech) Squadron, RAF Duxford, Essex, September 1940.

The success, 303 Squadron on 30 August 1940, prompted the RAF to declare the two Czech-manned squadrons 'operational', and being based at Duxford, 310 (Czech) became part of Douglas Bader's 'Big Wing' formations in September and October 1940. Finished in the standard Temperate Land Scheme of Dark Earth and Dark Green upper surfaces, to the B Scheme pattern with a

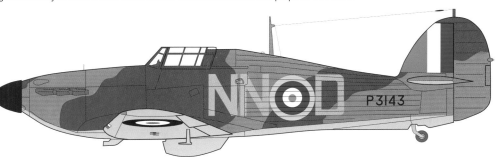

variation of 'Sky' on the under surfaces, P3143 appears to have had its national markings applied in the pre-war 'bright' Blue and Red colours. On 1 September 1940, the MAP sent a circular to all the aircraft manufacturers and the MAP's Resident Technical Officers were to advise the companies to which they were attached that dull identification colours were required for the national markings on aircraft. Rotol propeller unit fitted.

Hawker Hurricane Mk.I, P3148/NN-Q, 310 (Czech) Squadron, RAF Duxford, Essex, September 1940.

Not only were there 'problems' with the colour of some of the national markings, the medium grey squadron code letters could also be seen in a variety of shades, as exemplified by P3148 illustrated here, which had either very pale grey or white codes applied. The rest of the airframe was pretty standard though, finished in the standard Temperate Land Scheme of

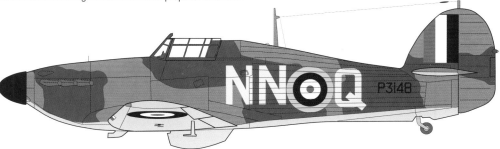

Dark Earth and Dark Green upper surfaces, to the B Scheme pattern with a variation of 'Sky' on the under surfaces. The underwing roundels were the larger style located at about one third of the span of the wing. Rotol propeller unit fitted.

Hawker Hurricane Mk.I, V9845/DU-W, 312 (Czech) Squadron, RAF Speke, Lancashire, October 1940.

The other Czech Fighter unit that had formed in 1940 was 312 Squadron, which also operated Hurricanes in 12 Group, but was based further north at Speke in Lancashire. Finished in the standard Temperate Land Scheme of Dark Earth and Dark Green upper surfaces, to the A Scheme pattern. The national markings on V9845 appear to conform to the Air Ministry standards of the late July AMOs

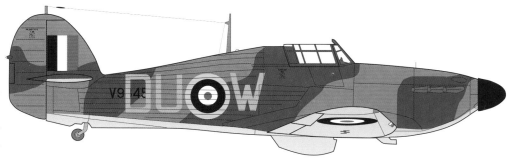

and may be an example of a new factory-fresh production line standard machine with 35 inch diameter fuselage roundels, 24 inch wide by 27 inch high fin marking and underwing roundels of the correct diameter correctly located at about one third of the span of the wing. The under surfaces may even have been the official shade of Sky. Rotol propeller unit fitted.

Not to any scale

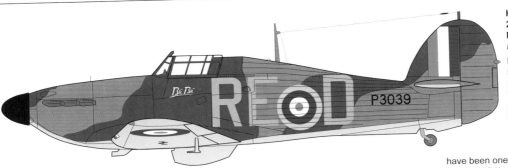

Hawker Hurricane Mk.I, P3039/RE-D, 229 Squadron, RAF Northolt, Middlesex, September 1940/
Pilot: Pilot Officer Victor 'Vicky' Ortmans

Finished in the standard Temperate Land Scheme of Dark Earth and Dark Green upper surfaces, to the A Scheme pattern, the national markings appear to be in the pre-war 'bright' Blue and Red colours, including the underwing roundels, which are of the correct diameter and correctly located at about one third of the span of the wing. The under surfaces may have been one of the subtle variations of 'Sky'. Note the name 'BéBé' under the cockpit canopy. Rotol propeller unit fitted.

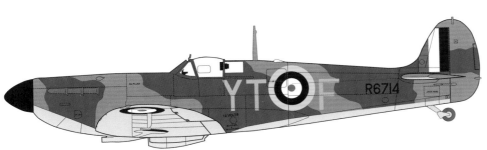

Supermarine Spitfire Mk.I, R6714/YT-F, 65 Squadron, RAF Turnhouse, Midlothian, Scotland, September 1940.
Pilot: Pilot Officer D Glaser

No 65 Squadron was sent north to Turnhouse, where it stayed until November 1940, for a well deserved rest at the end of a two month stint in the thick of the fighting during July and August at Hornchurch. R6714 was finished in the standard Temperate Land Scheme of Dark Earth and Dark Green upper surfaces, to the B Scheme pattern with one of the variations of 'Sky' on the under surfaces. Note the underwing roundels at the extreme tips of the wings. De Havilland/Hamilton propeller unit fitted.

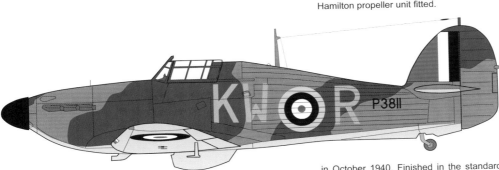

Hawker Hurricane Mk.I, P3811/KW-R, 615 Squadron, Prestwick, Ayrshire, September 1940.

By the end of August, 615 Squadron was another battle weary squadron that was in need of a rest and replacement pilots, and aircraft, having had six destroyed on the ground whilst at Kenley and five others written off in air combat during the month. Its move to Turnhouse was however, brief, as it returned south in October 1940. Finished in the standard Temperate Land Scheme of Dark Earth and Dark Green upper surfaces, to the A Scheme pattern, it probably had one of the variations of 'Sky' on its under surfaces. Note the 'standard' 35 inch diameter fuselage roundel and the 'Hawker' fin marking consisting of 9 inch wide Blue and White bands with the entire forward portion of the fin in Red. Underwing roundels, appear to be of the correct diameter and correctly located at about one third of the span of the wing. Rotol propeller unit fitted.

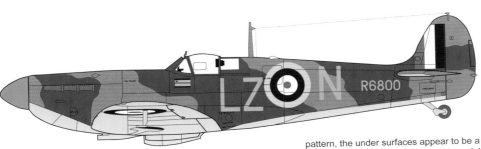

Supermarine Spitfire Mk.I, R6800/LZ-N, 66 Squadron, RAF Gravesend, Kent, September 1940.
Pilot: Squadron Leader Rupert Leigh

Legend has it that after being mistakenly attacked by members of his own squadron, Squadron Leader Leigh had the spinner of his Spitfire painted red so that the error wouldn't be repeated. Finished in the standard Temperate Land Scheme of Dark Earth and Dark Green upper surfaces, to the B Scheme pattern, the under surfaces appear to be a duck egg blue shade. Underwing roundels, appear to be of the correct diameter and located at about one third of the span of the wing. Note the serial number applied in Medium Sea Grey and the Squadron Leader pennant under the cockpit. De Havilland/Hamilton propeller unit fitted.

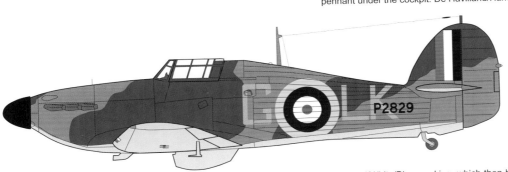

Hawker Hurricane Mk.I, P2829/LK-G, 87 Squadron, RAF Church Fenton, Yorkshire, September 1940.

Finished in the standard Temperate Land Scheme of Dark Earth and Dark Green upper surfaces, to the A Scheme pattern, with Sky under surfaces, the national markings on P2829 reveals how some of the longer-lasting airframes had them updated throughout their service.

The fuselage roundel presumably started life as a factory applied 35 inch diameter Red/White/Blue marking, which then had the outer Yellow ring added at a later date, which was truncated along the upper/under demarcation line. Also revealing that new instructions weren't always acted upon immediately, when photographed, P2829 still hadn't had underwing roundels applied. Rotol propeller unit fitted.

Not to any scale

Hawker Hurricane Mk.I, P3882, DX-L, 245 Squadron, RAF Aldergrove, Northern Ireland, September/October 1940.

Following its return to the UK from operations on the French mainland during the Blitzkrieg, 245 Squadron briefly operated out of Hawkinge, was moved to Turnhouse and then back to Hawkinge again throughout the June and July period, before being transferred to Aldergrove for the defence of Belfast. Finished in the standard Temperate Land Scheme of Dark Earth and Dark Green upper surfaces, to the A Scheme pattern, with Sky under surfaces, the fuselage

roundels feature a narrower than standard outer Yellow ring, although the underwing roundels appear to be of the correct diameter and located at about one third of the span. Rotol propeller unit fitted.

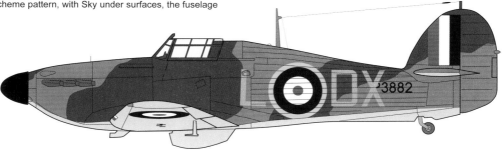

Hawker Hurricane Mk.I, V7434, DZ-R, 151 Squadron, RAF Digby, Lincolnshire, September 1940.
Pilot: Pilot Officer I S Smith

Another Squadron that saw action in the Battle of France and then more in the opening stages of the Battle of Britain, 151 was moved to Digby at the beginning of September for a well-earned rest. Finished in the standard Temperate Land Scheme of Dark Earth and Dark Green upper surfaces, to the A Scheme pattern, with Sky under surfaces, V7434 appears to conform to late Battle of Britain period standard with 35 inch diameter fuselage roundels, 24 inch by 27 inch

fin flash and correct diameter and location underwing roundels. Note the white 'patch' above the port side fuselage roundel which is not a printing error but may be a fabric repair or perhaps the start of some kind of personal marking? Rotol propeller unit fitted.

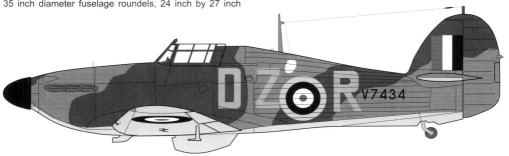

Supermarine Spitfire Mk.II, P7365, UO-, 266 Squadron, RAF Wittering, Cambridgeshire, September 1940.

After a hectic month of operating out of Eastchurch and Hornchurch throughout August 1940, at the beginning of September 266 Squadron was moved to Wittering in 12 Group and became one of the first squadrons to re-equip with the improved Spitfire Mk.II. Finished in the standard Temperate Land Scheme of Dark Earth and Dark Green upper surfaces, to the A Scheme pattern, almost certainly with the official shade of Sky under surfaces applied upon the production line at

the new factory at Castle Bromwich in the Midlands where all the Spitfire Mk.IIs were built, P7365 has 35 inch diameter fuselage roundels, 24 inch by 27 inch fin flash and correct diameter and location underwing roundels. Note the aircraft is still awaiting its individual aircraft letter. Fitted with a Rotol propeller unit.

Hawker Hurricane Mk.I, V6632, UF-L, 601 Squadron, RAF Exeter, Devon, October 1940.
Pilot: Sergeant Frank Jensen

After being heavily involved in the thick of the action, from the Battle of France in May and then throughout June, July and August, operating variously out of Middle Wallop, Tangmere and Debden, 601 Squadron was moved to Exeter in mid-September 1940 for a well-earned rest. Flown by Frank Jensen who was to have a long career rising through the ranks in the RAF, V6632 was finished in the standard Temperate Land Scheme of Dark Earth and Dark Green upper

surfaces, to the B Scheme pattern, possibly with the correct shade of Sky on the under surfaces. It has 'standard' 35 inch diameter fuselage roundels and the 'Hawker' style fin marking. The underwing roundels appear to be of the correct diameter and location at about one third of the span. Rotol propeller unit fitted.

Not to any scale

By mid-September the Luftwaffe's Jagdgeschwader units possessed only 67% of their operational crews against authorised aircraft. For the Bf 110 Zerstörer units it was 46% and for the Kampfgeschwader's bombers it was 59%. On 14 September, due to the failure of the Luftwaffe to establish air supremacy, a conference was assembled with the OKW staff at Hitler's headquarters. Göring was absent, in France, as he had decided to direct the decisive part of the Battle from there, and left Erhard Milch to deputise for him.

At the meeting Hitler raised the question, *"Should we call it off altogether?"* Hitler had accepted that an invasion with massive air cover was no longer possible. Instead he opted to try to crush British morale, whilst still maintaining the threat of invasion. Hitler concluded this may result in *"... eight million going mad"*, (referring to the population of London in 1940), which would *"... cause a catastrophe"* for the British. In those circumstances, Hitler said, *"... even a small invasion might go a long way."* At this point Hitler was against cancelling the invasion as, *"... the cancellation would reach the ears of the enemy and strengthen his resolve."*

The leadership of the Luftwaffe persuaded Hitler to give them a last chance to subjugate the RAF, although they were forced to accept that air superiority had not yet been established.

Hitler decided, *"... to review the situation on 17 September for possible landings on 27 September or 8 October."*

On 15 September two massive waves of German attacks were decisively repulsed by the RAF, with every available aircraft of 11 Group being used on that day. The total casualties on this critical day were sixty German and twenty-six RAF aircraft shot down.

On 17 September, two days after this particular engagement, the Luftwaffe's worst day in the Battle of Britain, when the evidence was clear that the Luftwaffe must have greatly exaggerated the extent of their previous successes against the RAF, Hitler postponed 'Operation Sealion' and the preparations for the invasion of Britain indefinitely. Henceforth, in the face of mounting losses in men, aircraft and the lack of adequate replacements, the Luftwaffe gradually switched from daylight to night-time bombing.

On 16 September Göring ordered the Air Fleets to begin the new phase of the Battle. However, switching to attacks on London took the German fighters to the limit of their range and brought them within range of 12 Group, defending the Midlands.

Hawker Hurricane Mk.I, P3395, JX-B, 1 Squadron, RAF Wittering, Cambridgeshire, October 1940.
Pilot: Flying Officer Arthur V 'Darky' Clowes

Featuring a rather battered fuselage panel below the cockpit, P3395 is none-the-less finished in the standard Temperate Land Scheme of Dark Earth and Dark Green upper surfaces, to the A Scheme pattern, possibly with a duck egg green shade of Sky on the under surfaces. It has the new 'standard' 35 inch diameter fuselage roundels and although the fin flash is the correct 24

inches wide it extends higher up the fin than the required 27 inches. The underwing roundels appear slightly smaller than 'standard' but may be in the recommended location at about one third of the span of the wing. Note the wasp insignia on the nose.

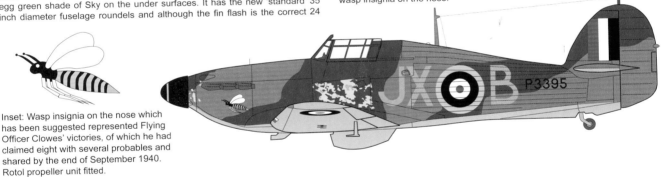

Inset: Wasp insignia on the nose which has been suggested represented Flying Officer Clowes' victories, of which he had claimed eight with several probables and shared by the end of September 1940. Rotol propeller unit fitted.

▲ Pilot Officer A V Taffy Clowes of 1 Squadron climbs into his Hawker Hurricane Mk.I, P3395/JX-B, in one of the numerous revetments at RAF Wittering in what was then Huntingdonshire. The revetments were designed to protect the fighters from blast damage but actually proved to be an even larger target when viewed from the air. Note Clowes' personal 'wasp' emblem under the engine exhausts. (Photo: Imperial War Museum)

▲ Pilot Officer Clowes is pictured here standing by the nose of his Hawker Hurricane at Wittering in late October 1940. The wasp emblem was applied to the cowling during the Battle of Britain and Clowes added a new stripe to the body for each enemy aircraft he shot down. His final score was at least twelve. (Photo: Imperial War Museum)

▲ One of the most infamous characters of the Battle of Britain, Squadron Leader Douglas Bader DSO, DFC, CO of 242 Squadron, seated on the cockpit sill of his Hawker Hurricane in October 1940. (Photo: Imperial War Museum)

Big Wings

The first official deployment of 12 Group's 'Big Wing' took 20 minutes to gain formation, missed its intended target, but encountered another formation of bombers whilst still climbing. 11 Group had had considerable success in breaking up daytime raids. 12 Group repeatedly failed to meet specific requests to protect 11 Group airfields, but their experiments with increasingly large 'Big Wings' did have some successes.

The Luftwaffe began to abandon their morning raids, with attacks on London starting later in the afternoon, but the most damaging aspect to the Luftwaffe's change in targeting London was the increase in range. The Bf 109E escorts had a limited fuel capacity, and by the time they arrived over the capital, had only some 10 minutes of flying time before they had to turn for home. This left many bomber formations undefended by fighter escort. RAF Bomber Command contributed to the problems facing the German naval forces by sinking eighty barges in the Port of Ostend alone.

Luftwaffe raids across Britain continued throughout September, with large attacks on London, mainly targeting the dock area or bombing indiscriminately. Fighter Command had been at its lowest ebb, short of pilots and aircraft, but this sudden break from airfield attacks allowed them to recover...

▲ Pilots of 19 Squadron 'scramble' for the photographer, from the back of a lorry at Fowlmere, Cambridgeshire. The staged nature of the photo is given away by smiles which may otherwise not have been present had this been part of a real 'scramble' to face the enemy. (Photo: Imperial War Museum)

Camouflage and markings

Luftwaffe
Introduction of the bar markings

One of the markings which featured in several RAF Intelligence reports dealing with Dornier Do 17s and Heinkel He 111s was found to be what might arguably be one of the most interesting tactical markings ever employed on Luftwaffe aircraft, the 'bar' markings applied to Do 17s, He 111s and Ju 88s during the period of the big daylight raids on London which took place from the beginning of September 1940.

The earliest recorded use of 'bar' markings on the upper surfaces of the wingtips and sides of the fin and/or rudder, appears to be on a pair of Do 17s of KG 76 recorded during the evening of 7 September 1940. Both the aircraft display a chordwise bar outboard of the national marking on the upper surface of the starboard wing. Another aircraft was seen to be also carrying a single horizontal bar across the fin and rudder on the starboard tailplane.

The date may be significant in that 7 September was the date on which the Luftwaffe shifted the focus of its attacks away from RAF Fighter Command airfields and onto the city of London, for which it employed large formations of bombers in daylight.

It has long been thought that these 'bar' markings were applied as some kind of aid to formation flying, although no really convincing explanation of how the system worked has ever been published.

The widely accepted view is that these markings were white and either used to identify unit leaders or to allow crews to easily identify aircraft of their Gruppe whilst operating in close formation.

From b&w photographs it is difficult to tell exactly what colour the 'bar' markings actually were, other than they were a light colour which stood out clearly from the dark green RLM 70 and RLM 71 camouflage scheme applied to the upper surfaces of Luftwaffe bombers, and the assumption has generally been that they were white. However, there is evidence contained within the RAF Intelligence reports which states that this was not always the case.

Following the onset of the daylight attack on London a number of aircraft carrying such markings were lost over Britain which became the subjects of RAF Intelligence reports, many of which mention the presence of bar markings on the wreckage. Many of the reports were written on aircraft lost during the Luftwaffe's operations on 15 September which is now accepted as the climax of the daylight air battles over Britain in 1940.

For example, a Do 17Z of KG 76 which was lost on the afternoon of 15 September and the subject of an RAF Intelligence report. Werk Nummer 2555 coded F1+FS of 8./KG 76 made a forced landing at Lullingstone Castle, Shoreham, at 1300 hrs. The report recorded that the aircraft was coded F1+FS with the second F outlined in white, that there was a red band around the fuselage, that the spinners were red and

▲ Spitfire Mk.I, X4179/QV-B of 19 Squadron, on the ground at Fowlmere, Cambridgeshire, as the pilot undertakes a cockpit check prior to take off on the 21 September 1940. (Photo: Imperial War Museum)

that there was a horizontal pink band about 12 inches wide on the outside of both rudders. Photographs of the wreck of this aircraft also show a chordwise bar inboard of the national marking on the upper surface of the port wing and the 8./KG 76 emblem applied to the starboard side of the nose with the three Dorniers thereon pointing forward, (although neither of these markings are mentioned in the report).

Another (unidentified) Do 17 which came down on Barn Hurst Golf Course, Bexley, at 1430 hrs on 15 September was found to have similar markings which the intelligence report describes as "... pink stripe on wingtip and rudder." The only other marking which was apparently visible was a white letter 'C' which was presumably found on the upper surface of one of the wings.

Later in the afternoon of 15 September at 1600 hrs, He 111 W/Nr 2771 coded A1+AN of 5./KG 53 came down on West Malling aerodrome. Upon examination this aircraft was found to have red spinners and three vertical pink stripes on what the report calls 'both rudders', presumably meaning both sides of the rudder. No mention is made of any wing markings. Whether this is because none were present, or because the Officer compiling the report simply did not notice them, or alternatively did not think them worth mentioning is not known.

Besides these crash reports, other secondary sources, that is to say the small number of books and magazine articles which have over the years mentioned the use of pink for these markings have claimed the following aircraft also had the following pink bar markings:

- Do 17Z-2 W/Nr 3457, 5K+JM of 4./KG 3 which crashed at Bexley in Kent at 1200hrs 15 September which had a "pink stripe on wingtip and rudder" but which wingtip or which side of the rudder (port or starboard) is not stated.

- Do 17Z W/Nr 2814 coded F1+AT of 9./KG 76 which came down at Rotherfield, Kent during the afternoon of 15 September and was found to have two horizontal pink stripes, each 12 inches wide on the outer faces of each rudder. No mention is made of any wing markings.

- He111 H-2 W/Nr 5718 coded A1+LN of 5./KG 53 which was shot down near Hornchurch at 1435 hrs and found to have three vertical pink stripes on the rudder. Again, no mention is made of any wing markings.

The bar markings appear to have been continued to be used throughout October as shown by the wreckage of Do17 W/Nr 2544 coded 5K+CH of 1./KG3 which crashed at 0200 hrs on 28 October at Boughton Malherbe in Kent. Upon examination, all the codes were found to be black and a large pink horizontal stripe was found on the rudder.

As can be seen, all the RAF Intelligence reports referred to above describe the bar markings as being pink, not white. Whether this is in any way related to the fact that most of the aircraft found to have pink markings were lost on 15 September is not known, nor is the reason why pink was used.

Exactly where this pink paint came from is also unknown as there is currently no known RLM designation for a pink colour. A major problem in carrying out research in to Luftwaffe camouflage and markings is the lack of much documentary evidence, which mainly arises out of orders given in the last days of the war for the Luftwaffe's records to be destroyed to prevent their capture by the Allies. The pink paint could possibly have been mixed at unit level by some means.

The only hard evidence found thus far which sheds any light on the possibly hue of these pink markings is in a report dated 20 November 1940 on an anonymous Do 17 which crashed at 2355 hrs on 15 November 1940 at Rye Hill near Harlow in Essex. The only decipherable marking found on the wreckage was what the report describes as *"a large Salmon Pink square"* on the upper surface of the starboard mainplane.

Whilst on the evidence of the RAF Intelligence reports mentioned above, pink would appear to have been the most commonly used colour for the bar markings applied to Luftwaffe aircraft, white is also known to have been used.

White markings were found on a He 111 of 1./KG 26 which came down at Asplin Head on Foulness Island at 1530 hrs on 15 September. The aircraft was coded 1H+JH with the spinners in white. Two white stripes ran vertically on the starboard side only of the fin and one stripe was found to run vertically on each side of the rudder, each stripe being about 13 inches wide. No mention is made of any wing markings.

White was also said to have been found on the remains of a He111 H-3 W/Nr. 5680 coded 1H+CB of Stab I./KG 26 which came down near Hornchurch at 1620 hrs on 11 September.

▲ Supermarine Spitfire Mk.I, X4474/QV-I taking off from Fowlmere on 21 September 1940 with 19 Squadron's Sergeant B J Jennings at the controls. (Photo: Imperial War Museum)

This aircraft is said to have had two white stripes on the port wingtip and the rudder, although they may have been pink.

It has also been claimed that yellow was also used to apply these bar markings to the wings and tail, but none of the RAF Intelligence reports seen can confirm this. However, if this were true, it would raise the possibility that the markings could have been applied in the three common Staffel colours, if the assumption was made that pink was a more highly visible equivalent to red. This theory breaks down when the colour of the bar markings is compared with the last letter in the code combination which identifies the Staffel to which the aircraft was assigned.

Take for example the two Do 17Zs of KG 76 brought down on 15 September referred to previously. F1+FS belonged to 8 Staffel of III Gruppe. 8 Staffel's assigned colour was red and the aircraft was marked with a pink bar, but F1+AT belonged to 9 Staffel of III Gruppe whose assigned colour was yellow, however it was also marked with pink bars. So, what, if anything, did the use of two, possibly three different colours signify, or indeed the significance of the number of bars which could be applied to an individual aircraft – one, two or three?

From photographic and documentary evidence it is evident that either one, two or three bars could be carried by an individual aircraft. Photographs have been found which show aircraft marked with one and three bars, but aircraft with two bars seem to have been rather camera shy. Fortunately, two of the RAF Intelligence reports referred to above document the use of two bars on two separate aircraft, two pink bars being found on a Dornier and two white bars being found on a Heinkel, so it would appear that some aircraft did indeed carry two bars.
There does not appear to be any relationship between the number of bars applied and the Gruppe to which the aircraft belonged within a Geschwader which has been suggested in the past. For example, the two Dorniers of KG 76 mentioned previously belonged to different Staffels within III Gruppe, but both only carried one pink bar marking on their wings and tail. If the number of bars marked on the aircraft was related to the Gruppe, would not both aircraft have carried three bars? Additionally, two Heinkel He 111s of 5 Staffel, II Gruppe of KG 53 are recorded as having three pink stripes on their rudders.

The location on the airframes of the bars between individual aircraft also varied. It is thought that all three main bomber types carried bar markings on the vertical tail surfaces and the upper surface of the wings. As a general rule, it would appear that Do 17s carried their tail markings horizontally across the outer face of the fin and rudder whilst He 111s and Ju 88s carried their markings vertically either on the fin, on

the rudder or on both the fin and the rudder. There is no record (or photograph) of similar markings appearing on the under surface of the wings of any aircraft at any time.

It would appear that the markings were frequently applied to one side of the aircraft only, and the number of bars on the upper surface(s) of the wing is thought to always correspond to the number of bars marked on the tail. It is interesting to note that where the tail markings were applied to only one side of the tail, this was almost invariably the same side of the aircraft as the wing markings. This would appear to have been done deliberately, but exactly why remains unknown.

Photographic evidence suggests that Do 17s usually carried their wing bars chordwise outboard of the national markings whilst He 111s and Ju 88s carried their wing markings spanwise inboard of the national markings. Inevitably, there were variations and it is possible to find photographs of all these types marked differently. For example the Ju 88 coded 3Z+BB of Stab I Gruppe KG 77 has its upperwing bar applied spanwise outboard of the national marking on the port wing.

Quite how these markings worked has never been satisfactorily explained. Given the three suggested variations in their colour, number and also their differing position on the aircraft one interpretation to explain the purpose of these markings suggests that the number and positioning of the stripes was related to the standard Luftwaffe bomber formation. The basic unit is said to have been some twenty aircraft in a double 'V' formation, each 'V' consisting of ten aircraft. Extended lines of these 'V' formations then made up the mass formation.

This interpretation suggests that three parallel columns might be allocated a colour each and that the leading element would carry one bar, the second element two bars and the rear element three bars. These markings would be changed before every operation.

If this interpretation is correct, it could go some way to explaining the lack of correlation between colour and Staffel, number and Gruppe and the practice of marking just one side of the aircraft according to which side of the formation it was to fly on. The colour assigned to each column could also be changed from one operation to another depending on whether a one, two or three column formation was to be flown.
This raises the possibility that a two column formation was the most common which would explain the lack of evidence for the third colour, ie yellow, being used if this colour was habitually assigned to the middle column.

Thus when the formation as a whole was viewed from above and astern, aircraft with the markings applied to the starboard side would fly in the left hand column and aircraft which were marked on the port side would fly in the right hand column where the markings would be visible to each other and the aircraft in the middle column.

This interpretation is partly supported by one account of the opening attack on 7 September which describes part of the formation as consisting of the Do17s of KG 76 flying in the left hand column, the He 111s of KG 1 in the middle column and the Ju 88s of KG 30 and II./KG 76 in the right hand column, and the fact that the photographs referred to earlier

Dornier Do 17Z, F1+FH, 1./KG 76, Beauvis, France, September 1940.

Finished in the standard two-tone green RLM 70 Schwarzgrün and RLM 71 Dunkelgrün upper surfaces in a straight-edged 'splinter' pattern with RLM 65 Hellblau undersides. Codes were black with a white individual aircraft letter 'F' in the staffel colour, and the propeller spinners were white. 1./KG 76's 'defecating devil' insignia was positioned on the port side forward fuselage behind the nose glazing. Note the 'pink' formation bar partially across the port fin and rudder and the central position of the swastika. A similarly coloured bar was carried above the port wing just inboard of the balkenkreuz. On 15 September 1940,

Sergeant Holmes, 504 Squadron collided with this machine, which was already on fire from previous attacks, causing the Dornier to break up in mid air, the main wreckage falling in to the forecourt of Victoria railway station in London.

Inset: 1./KG 76's 'defecating devil holding a pistol' insignia positioned on the port side forward fuselage behind the nose glazing.

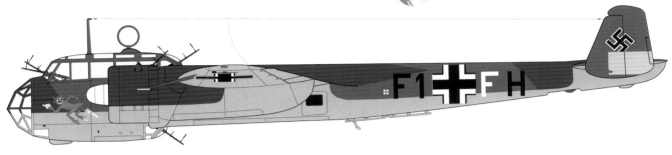

Dornier Do 17Z, W.Nr 2555, F1+FS, 8./KG 76, Cormeilles-en-Vixen, France, September 1940.

Finished in the standard two-tone green RLM 70 Schwarzgrün and RLM 71 Dunkelgrün upper surfaces in a straight-edged 'splinter' pattern with RLM 65 Hellblau undersides. Codes were black with a red individual aircraft letter 'F' in the staffel colour, outlined in white. The propeller spinners were also red. 8./KG 76's shield was positioned on both sides of the forward fuselage behind the nose glazing. Note the 'pink' formation bar across the starboard rudder. A similarly coloured bar was carried chordwise above the starboard wing just inboard of the balkenkreuz – see scrap view. This machine crash landed at Castle Farm, Shoreham, Sussex, on 15 September 1940, following combat with Flg Off John Dundas and Pilot Officer Eugene Tobin, 609 Squadron.

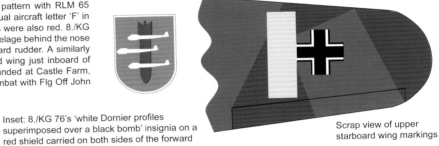

Inset: 8./KG 76's 'white Dornier profiles superimposed over a black bomb' insignia on a red shield carried on both sides of the forward fuselage behind the nose glazing.

Scrap view of upper starboard wing markings

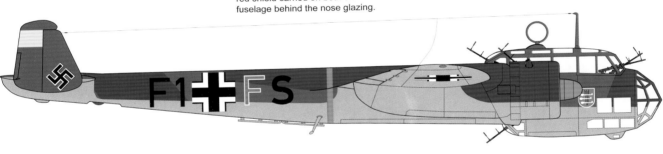

Dornier Do 17Z, 5K+EA, Geschwaderstab/KG 3, Le Culot, France, September 1940.

Finished in the standard two-tone green RLM 70 Schwarzgrün and RLM 71 Dunkelgrün upper surfaces in a straight-edged 'splinter' pattern with RLM 65 Hellblau undersides. Codes were all black with the individual aircraft letter 'E' merely outlined in white. The propeller spinners were in the Stab colour green. The Geshwader's shield was positioned on both sides of the forward fuselage under the cockpit glazing and immediately behind the nose glazing. Note the

'pink' formation bar across the starboard fin and rudder. A similarly coloured bar was carried chordwise above the starboard wing just outboard of the balkenkreuz – see p129.

Inset: Geschwaderstab KG 3's 'Arms of the city of Elbing' insignia (where the unit was originally formed) comprising a red and a white iron cross on a red/white shield

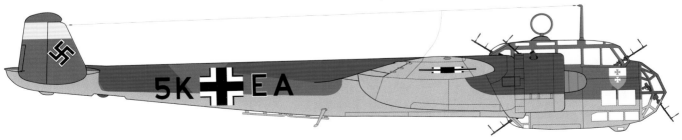

Junkers Ju 88A-1, (W.Nr 4136) 3Z+BB, Stab I/KG 77, Laon, France, September 1940.

Finished in the standard two-tone green RLM 70 Schwarzgrün and RLM 71 Dunkelgrün upper surfaces in a straight-edged 'splinter' pattern with RLM 65 Hellblau undersides. Codes were black with the individual aircraft letter 'B' in Stab green. The propeller spinners were white with green tips. Hit by anti-aircraft

fire, this aircraft crashed near Hertingfordbury on 3 October 1940, following a single-handed attack on the de Havilland factory at Hatfield, in which 21 people were killed, and 70 wounded. The crew were all captured unhurt.

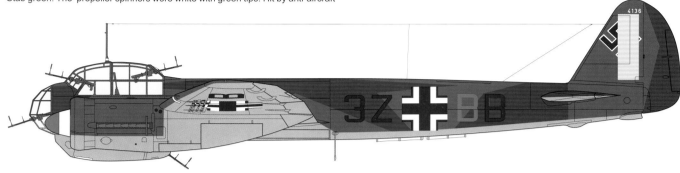

Junkers Ju 88A-1, 3Z+HN, 5./KG 77, Asch-Nord, France, September 1940.

Finished in the standard two-tone green RLM 70 Schwarzgrün and RLM 71 Dunkelgrün upper surfaces in a straight-edged 'splinter' pattern with RLM 65 Hellblau undersides. Codes were black with the individual aircraft letter 'H' in red outlined in white. The tips of the propeller spinners were also red. The II Gruppe

KG 77 shield was positioned on both sides of the forward fuselage immediately behind the nose glazing. Note the 'white' formation bar on the port side of the rudder. A similarly coloured bar was carried spanwise above the port wing just inboard of the balkenkreuz – see p129.

Inset: II Gruppe KG 2s 'black eagle flag' insignia on a red shield. The motto above the shield reads 'Ich will dass si vorfechten' which loosely translated means 'Be my champion' the motto of the German medieval order of Knights.

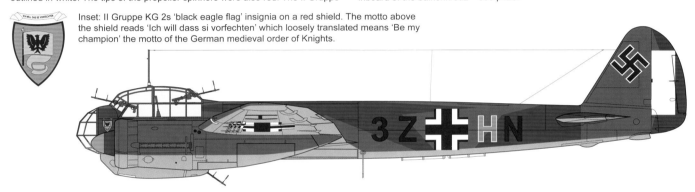

Heinkel He 111H, A1+BH, 1./KG 53, Vitry-en-Artois, France, September 1940.

Finished in the standard two-tone green RLM 70 Schwarzgrün and RLM 71 Dunkelgrün upper surfaces in a straight-edged 'splinter' pattern with RLM 65 Hellblau undersides. Codes were black with the individual aircraft letter 'B' in white and the Staffel letter 'H' outlined in white. The I Gruppe KG 53 insignia was positioned on both sides of the forward fuselage immediately below the pilot's

cockpit glazing. Note the two 'white' formation bars on the port side of the fin. Whether similarly coloured bars were carried above the port wing is unknown.

Heinkel He 111H-2, A1+DA, Geschwaderstab KG 53, Lille-Nord, France, September 1940.

Finished in the standard two-tone green RLM 70 Schwarzgrün and RLM 71 Dunkelgrün upper surfaces in a straight-edged 'splinter' pattern with RLM 65 Hellblau undersides. Codes were black with the individual aircraft letter 'D' in Stab blue. The propeller spinners were also blue. II Gruppe's insignia was

positioned on both sides of the forward fuselage immediately below the pilot's cockpit glazing. Note the three 'pink' formation bars on the port side of the rudder. Similarly coloured bars were presumably carried above the port wing but whether they were span or chord-wise is unknown.

Inset: I Gruppe KG 53's insignia, the white silhouette of a diving eagle carrying a bomb on a black disc outlined in yellow. Why this emblem was carried on this Geschwaderstab machine is unknown.

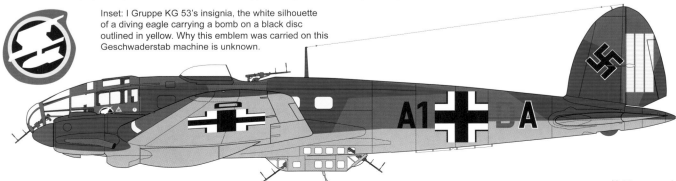

Not to any scale

Schematic view of Luftwaffe bomber formation 'bar system'

Although this is still a speculative theory, it shows how the Luftwaffe bomber formation 'bar system' may have worked. The bar markings could have been used in assisting in the formation-keeping of hundreds of aircraft from many different Staffeln, Gruppen and Geschwader, from different bases in France and Belgium. However, it could be that only a portion of the aircraft within the large September formations were so marked, which might explain why not all the Luftwaffe bombers brought down over the UK during this period carried bar markings.

Port column
Lead element
one bar on starboard side

Middle column
lead element
one bar on both sides

Starboard column
lead element
one bar on port side

Port column
second element
two bars on starboard side

Middle column
second element
two bars on both sides

Starboard column
second element
two bars on port side

Port column
third element
three bars on starboard side

Middle column
third element
three bars on both sides

Starboard column
third element
three bars on port side

allegedly showing two Do 17s of KG 76 show both aircraft to be marked with a bar on the starboard wing.

If the side of the aircraft to which the bar markings were applied signified the column in which the aircraft was to fly then the obvious question arises as to what markings the aircraft in the middle column were to carry. One possibility is that the aircraft in the central column carried markings on both sides of the tail and/or the wings?

The schematic interpretation of how these bar markings might have been applied to a formation in three columns is loosely based on an account of the opening attack on London of 7 September. The formation illustrated overleaf on p115, of aircraft in 'V' formation, is based upon a photograph which shows aircraft in a Staffel formation known to have been used in daylight over the UK towards the end of August.

It would appear that the whole scheme would entail a lot of hard work for the ground staff if the markings had to be changed for whatever reason before each mission. Presumably the material used to apply the markings would have been a water washable distemper. The markings would be very flexible and would allow for casualties inflicted on the Luftwaffe by the RAF and or the periodic unserviceability for whatever reason of an individual aircraft. The markings could be altered to allow

each Geschwader to operate the maximum number of aircraft available or required for each sortie without having to adhere to a rigid system dictated by the Staffel or Gruppe to which the aircraft actually belonged.

Luftwaffe fighters

Although the RLM 71/02/65 scheme was still the predominant scheme throughout the Battle of Britain period, as the summer passed in to autumn, and autumn in to winter, the percentage of 'grey' finished Emils increased.

As mentioned before, much of the Luftwaffe documentation was destroyed by official order in the last days of the Third Reich and what survives is widely scattered and often in private hands.

The extension of the RLM 65 under surface colour up the sides of the fuselage and over the fin and the replacement of RLM 70 with RLM 02 on the upper surfaces were made prior to the campaign through France and the low countries and are thought to have been made on the production line sometime around the end of 1939 and the beginning of 1940, whilst aircraft already in service were repainted in the new scheme by their parent units. This mix of painting methods resulted in many variations of the basic scheme.

Heinkel He 111H, A1+BT, 9./KG 53, Lille-Movaux, France, late August 1940.

Finished in the standard Luftwaffe bomber scheme of RLM 70 Schwarzgrün and RLM 71 Dunkelgrün upper surfaces in a straight-edged 'splinter' pattern. This pattern was similar on all Heinkel He 111 sub-types and could be applied as a mirror image. In this particular instance it represents Scheme A, see pp112-113. Undersides were RLM 65 Hellblau. The codes were black with the individual aircraft letter 'B' in the staffel colour yellow and yellow propeller spinners. Note the early style 'pipe' exhaust manifolds. This aircraft carried three (white or pink) bars above the starboard wing inboard of the balkenkreuz aligned spanwise. (see upper surface view on p129 opposite)

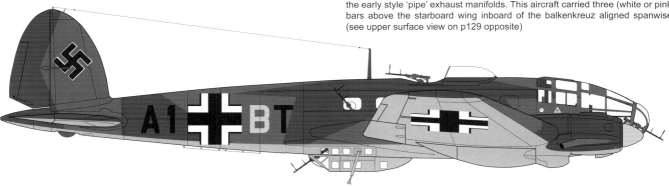

Heinkel He 111P-2, W.Nr 1992, G1+HP, 6./KG 55, Chartres, France, September 1940.

KG 55 were renowned for applying 'graffiti' to their aircraft, invariably in white chalk. Finished in the standard two-tone green RLM 70 Schwarzgrün and RLM 71 Dunkelgrün upper surfaces in a straight-edged 'splinter' pattern with RLM 65 Hellblau undersides. Codes were black with the individual aircraft letter 'H' in the Staffel colour yellow, as were the propeller spinners. It would appear that none of KG 55's Geschwader, Gruppe or Staffel emblems were carried on G1+HP, but

the two 'cartoons' of a man with umbrella on both sides of the rudder must surely make up for their marked absence. Note the swastika in the early central position across the fin and rudder.

Inset: G1+HP's 'graffiti' cartoon on the port side of the rudder.

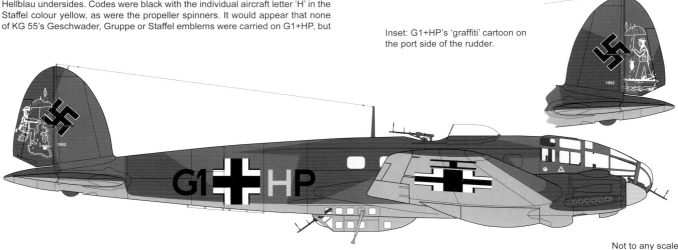

Not to any scale

Upper surface plan views of the RLM 70 Schwarzgrün/RLM 71 Dunkelgrün 'splinter' camouflage pattern applied to Luftwaffe bombers

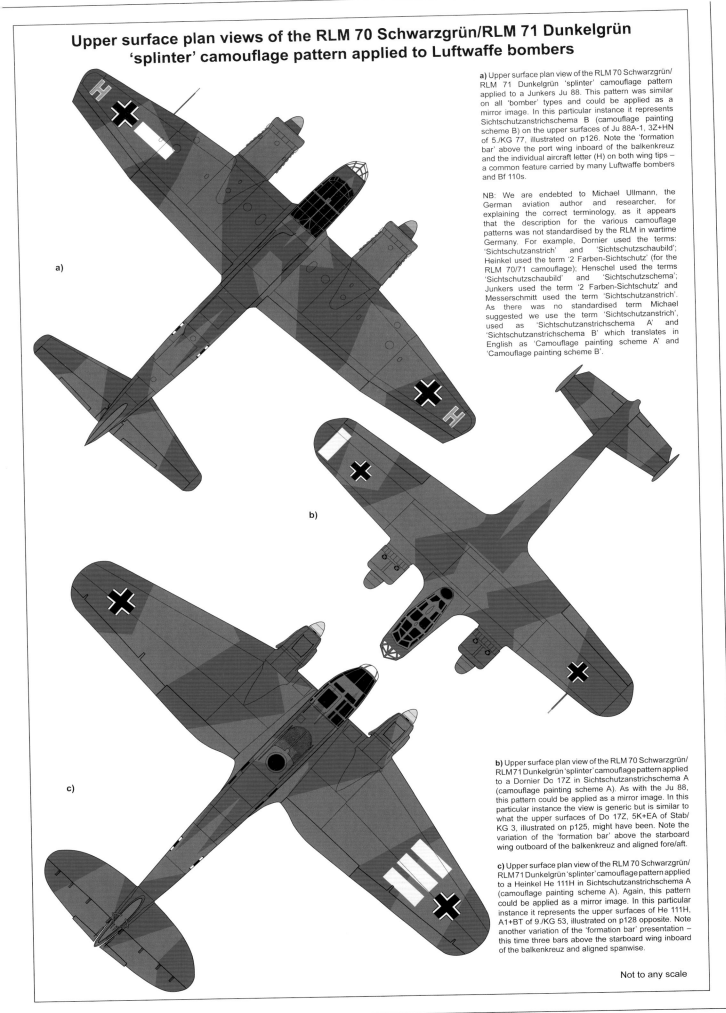

a) Upper surface plan view of the RLM 70 Schwarzgrün/ RLM 71 Dunkelgrün 'splinter' camouflage pattern applied to a Junkers Ju 88. This pattern was similar on all 'bomber' types and could be applied as a mirror image. In this particular instance it represents Sichtschutzanstrichschema B (camouflage painting scheme B) on the upper surfaces of Ju 88A-1, 3Z+HN of 5./KG 77, illustrated on p126. Note the 'formation bar' above the port wing inboard of the balkenkreuz and the individual aircraft letter (H) on both wing tips – a common feature carried by many Luftwaffe bombers and Bf 110s.

NB: We are endebted to Michael Ullmann, the German aviation author and researcher, for explaining the correct terminology, as it appears that the description for the various camouflage patterns was not standardised by the RLM in wartime Germany. For example, Dornier used the terms: 'Sichtschutzanstrich' and 'Sichtschutzschaubild'; Heinkel used the term '2 Farben-Sichtschutz' (for the RLM 70/71 camouflage); Henschel used the terms 'Sichtschutzschaubild' and 'Sichtschutzschema'; Junkers used the term '2 Farben-Sichtschutz' and Messerschmitt used the term 'Sichtschutzanstrich'. As there was no standardised term Michael suggested we use the term 'Sichtschutzanstrich', used as 'Sichtschutzanstrichschema A' and 'Sichtschutzanstrichschema B' which translates in English as 'Camouflage painting scheme A' and 'Camouflage painting scheme B'.

b) Upper surface plan view of the RLM 70 Schwarzgrün/ RLM 71 Dunkelgrün 'splinter' camouflage pattern applied to a Dornier Do 17Z in Sichtschutzanstrichschema A (camouflage painting scheme A). As with the Ju 88, this pattern could be applied as a mirror image. In this particular instance the view is generic but is similar to what the upper surfaces of Do 17Z, 5K+EA of Stab/ KG 3, illustrated on p125, might have been. Note the variation of the 'formation bar' above the starboard wing outboard of the balkenkreuz and aligned fore/aft.

c) Upper surface plan view of the RLM 70 Schwarzgrün/ RLM 71 Dunkelgrün 'splinter' camouflage pattern applied to a Heinkel He 111H in Sichtschutzanstrichschema A (camouflage painting scheme A). Again, this pattern could be applied as a mirror image. In this particular instance it represents the upper surfaces of He 111H, A1+BT of 9./KG 53, illustrated on p128 opposite. Note another variation of the 'formation bar' presentation – this time three bars above the starboard wing inboard of the balkenkreuz and aligned spanwise.

Not to any scale

Heinkel He 111H-2, 1H+CB, Stab I/KG 26, Wevelghem, Belgium, September 1940.

Finished in the standard two-tone green RLM 70 Schwarzgrün and RLM 71 Dunkelgrün upper surfaces in a straight-edged 'splinter' pattern with RLM 65 Hellblau undersides. Codes were black with the individual aircraft letter 'C' in Gruppenstab green. I Gruppe's white 'Vestigum Leonis' shield was positioned on both sides of the forward fuselage immediately below the pilot's cockpit glazing.

Note the two 'pink' formation bars (which may have been white) on the port side of the rudder. It is thought that two similar 'pink' bars were carried spanwise, above the port wing. Stab green spinners. This aircraft was shot down near Hornchurch on 11 September 1940.

Inset: I Gruppe KG 26's white 'Vestigum Leonis' shield.

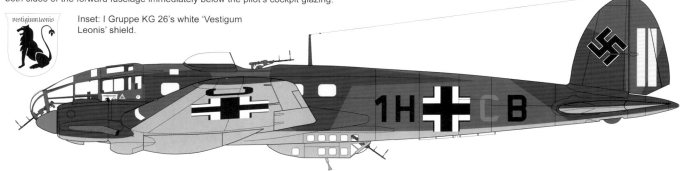

Heinkel He 111H, A1+AC, Stab II/KG 53, Lille-Nord, France, September 1940.

Finished in the standard two-tone green RLM 70 Schwarzgrün and RLM 71 Dunkelgrün upper surfaces in a straight-edged 'splinter' pattern with RLM 65 Hellblau undersides. Codes were black with the individual aircraft letter 'A' in

white rather than the more usual Stab blue or green. The Geshwader's insignia was positioned on both sides of the forward fuselage immediately below the pilot's cockpit glazing.

Inset: KG 53's 'Legion Condor' insignia, commemorating the Geshwader's formation in May 1939 after the Condor Legion's return from the Spanish Civil War

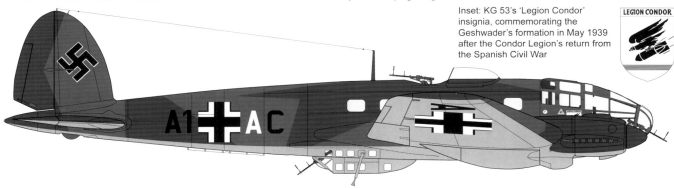

Junkers Ju 88A-5, W.Nr 4547, M7+FH, 1./KGr 806, Nantes, France, September 1940.

Werknummer 4547 was a Dornier Süd-built machine finished in the standard two-tone green RLM 70 Schwarzgrün and RLM 71 Dunkelgrün upper surfaces in a straight-edged 'splinter' pattern with RLM 65 Hellblau undersides. Codes were black with the individual aircraft letter 'F' in the Staffel colour white, as were the propeller spinners. Note the yellow vertical 'bar' that was carried on both

sides of the mid fuselage (which may have originally gone all the way around the fuselage), which is thought to have been a special tactical marking. This machine was shot down by a section of Hurricanes from 312 (Czech) Squadron, which had recently become operational, and were in the process of taking off from RAF Speke. M7+FH crash landed at Bromborough Dock on the Manchester Ship Canal, and the Hurricanes were back on the ground six minutes after take off.

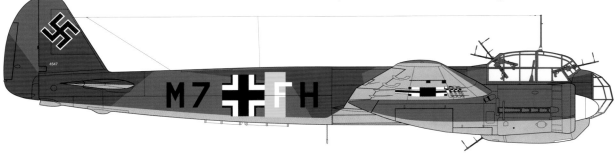

Junkers Ju 88A-1, M7+DK, 2./KGr 806, Caen-Carpiquet, France, September 1940.

KGr 806 started replacing its He 111Js with a mix of Ju 88A-1s and Ju 88A-5s at the end of the 'Blitzkrieg' Campaign in France in May/June and was operational on the type by September 1940. Finished in the standard two-tone green RLM 70 Schwarzgrün and RLM 71 Dunkelgrün upper surfaces in a straight-edged

'splinter' pattern with RLM 65 Hellblau undersides, M7+DK's codes were black with the individual aircraft letter 'D' in the Staffel colour red, as were the tips of the propeller spinners.

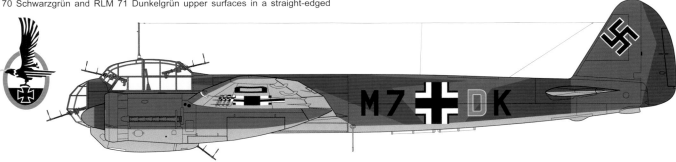

Inset: 2./KGr 806's eagle carrying an iron cross insignia carried on the nose on the port side under the cockpit (obscured by the engine cowling in the side view illustration)

Not to any scale

Junkers Ju 88A-1, W.Nr 0333, 4D+AD, Stab III/KG 30, Amsterdam-Schiphol, Netherlands, September 1940.

Finished in the standard two-tone green RLM 70 Schwarzgrün and RLM 71 Dunkelgrün upper surfaces in a straight-edged 'splinter' pattern with RLM 65 Hellblau undersides. Codes were black with the individual aircraft letter 'A' in the Gruppe Stab colour green, as were the tips of the propeller spinners. III Gruppe's

black swooping eagle on a yellow shield was applied to both sides of the forward fuselage immediately to the rear of the nose glazing.

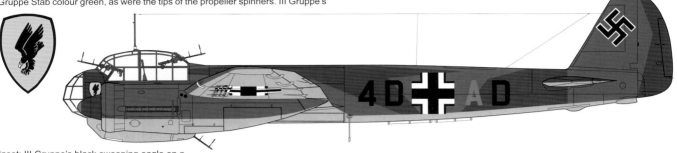

Inset: III Gruppe's black swooping eagle on a yellow shield. Yellow was the III Gruppe colour.

Junkers Ju 88A-5, D7+GA, Wekusta 1, Lichtenfelde, Germany, September 1940.

One very important unit which was operational over the British Isles during the summer and autumn of 1940, was Wettererkundungstaffel 1, (Meteorological Reconnaissance Squadron 1) which provided essential meteorological information to the Luftwaffe High Command. Finished in the standard two-

tone green RLM 70 Schwarzgrün and RLM 71 Dunkelgrün upper surfaces in a straight-edged 'splinter' pattern with RLM 65 Hellblau undersides, the codes were black with the individual aircraft letter 'G' in green. Note the white tips to the RLM 70 propeller spinners.

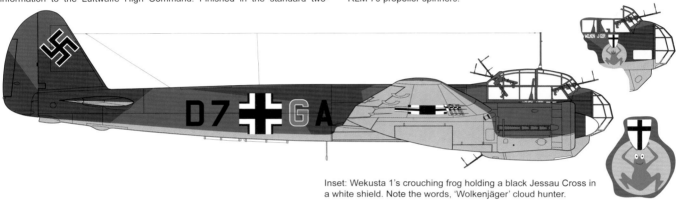

Inset: Wekusta 1's crouching frog holding a black Jessau Cross in a white shield. Note the words, 'Wolkenjäger' cloud hunter.

Junkers Ju 88A-5, 3Z+DC, Stab II/KG 77, Asch-Nord, France, September 1940.

Finished in the standard two-tone green RLM 70 Schwarzgrün and RLM 71 Dunkelgrün upper surfaces in a straight-edged 'splinter' pattern with RLM 65 Hellblau undersides. Codes were black with the individual aircraft letter 'D' in the

II Gruppe Stab colour green, as were the tips of the propeller spinners. II KG 2's black eagle on a yellow banner was applied to both sides of the forward fuselage under the cockpit glazing.

Inset: II/KG 2s 'black eagle flag' insignia on a red shield. The motto above the shield reads 'Ich will dass si vorfechten' which loosely translated means 'Be my champion' the motto of the German medieval order of Knights.

Dornier Do 17Z, U5+FH, 1./KG 2, Epinoy, France, September 1940.

Finished in the standard two-tone green RLM 70 Schwarzgrün and RLM 71 Dunkelgrün upper surfaces in a straight-edged 'splinter' pattern with RLM 65 Hellblau undersides. Codes were black with a white individual aircraft letter 'F'

in the staffel colour, and the propeller spinners were white. Note the additional machine guns in the rear canopy glazing, a regular 'up-gunning' modification on all the Luftwaffe's multi-engined bomber types during this period.

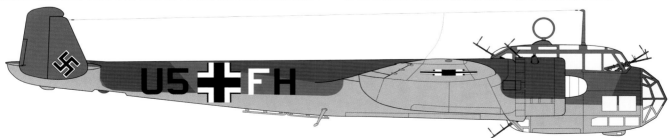

Not to any scale

Then, during the period May to June 1940, and with the commencement of the Battle of Britain, further changes were found to be necessary. It would appear the RLM 65 light blue sides of the fuselage and tail made the aircraft TOO conspicuous when viewed against the waters of the English Channel and that attempts to tone down the blue resulted in a mottled finish being applied to the sides of the fuselage and the fin. The colours usually claimed to have been used for this purpose were RLM 02 Grau, RLM 70 Schwarzgrün and RLM 71 Dunkelgrün, which were applied in a wide variety of styles.

However, by August 1940, various shades of 'grey' were increasingly being reported as being present on wrecked Bf 109s examined by RAF Intelligence officers following their loss over the UK. As there was no standard procedure for recording colours, colloquial terms such as 'battleship grey' and 'cloudy grey' were used in reports. As mentioned in Chapter 5, this has led to speculation that the later grey finish adopted by the Luftwaffe, RLM 74 Dunkelgrau/RLM 75 Mittelgrau and RLM 76 Lichtblau, might have been introduced from the late summer of 1940, although the 'grey' finishes which were being used on Bf 109s at this time were most likely experimental schemes which originated at unit level, ultimately leading to the adoption of the grey scheme proper of RLM 74, 75 and 76 during 1941.

There is also evidence to suggest that a few Bf 109Es were camouflaged in a very dark shade of grey and a dark brown – possibly RLM 66 Schwarzgrau and RLM 61 Dunkelbraun with light blue-grey (RLM 76?) under surfaces. How widespread this RLM 61, RLM 66 and light blue grey (RLM 76?) scheme was and how long it remained in use for is unknown.

As has already been mentioned, it is thought that much mixing of colours was taking place at unit level during this period. It would appear to be possible to mix a variety of grey shades for the so-called 'grey' scheme from readily available colours. For example a good match can be made for RLM 74 by mixing RLM 66 and 70 perhaps with a spot of white, RLM 75 by adding white to RLM 66 and RLM 76 by adding white to RLM 65.

▲ A still taken from gun camera footage captured by Pilot Officer R F G Miller of 609 Squadron during a mission on 25 September 1940. His Supermarine Spitfire Mk.I had closed on the tail of a Heinkel He III of KG 53 or KG 55, which ultimately took hits in the port engine from Miller's machine guns. The aircraft was one of a force which bombed the Bristol Aeroplane Company's factory at Filton, Bristol. Tragically, Miller was killed two days later when he collided head on with a Messerschmitt Bf 110 of III/ZG 26 over Cheselbourne, Dorset. (Photo: Imperial War Museum)

The idea that some Bf 109s were finished in some kind of 'blue' camouflage finish on their upper surfaces appears to have first surfaced in print just after the war. In the years since then the idea that blue schemes of any kind existed have been discredited. However, surviving RAF crash reports contain some interesting anomalies including mention of some Bf 109s which might have had 'blue' camouflage applied on their upper surfaces.

Report No 49 referred to a Bf 109E which crashed at Goudhurst on 2 October. Built in 1940, W/Nr 6370's markings were described as being 3+I in white with a yellow cowling and rudder. Camouflage was described as being dappled dark blue and yellow green on the upper surfaces with light blue on the under surfaces.

Another Bf 109 which is described as having a 'blue' camouflage scheme is identified in report No 74 which concerns an Arado-built Bf 109E-3 W/Nr 3576 of 7./JG 54 which crashed near Lydd on 27 October, its pilot Uffz Arno Zimmerman being captured unhurt. Markings consisted of the numeral 13 on the forward fuselage in front of the windscreen in white with a black outline. The rudder and nose were yellow whilst the spinner was white. A crest in the form of a winged Dutch clog edged in black was found on the engine cowling. The camouflage on the upper surface of the wings was described as being a darkish grey except for a triangle formed from the wing root at the trailing edge to a point half way along the leading edge. This triangle was described as being *"... a dirty light blue."* The fuselage was stated to be *"... a dirty light blue dappled with grey."*

However, before the possibility of a 'blue' scheme can be dismissed it is interesting to note that the Luftwaffe did have two shades of dark blue available to it during 1940. Perhaps the most familiar, if least likely of these to be used for camouflage purposes was RLM 24 Dunkelblau, which was normally used as a code letter/number marking colour.

The second shade of blue and possibly the prime suspect for a blue camouflage finish was Fliegerblaugrau (Air Force Blue-Grey) RAL 840R 7016. This was used by the Luftwaffe for painting its vehicles and ground equipment and was also used by the Wehrmacht as a primer colour. It is therefore possible that this colour was widely available for use at the time.

There were also occasional references to German aircraft having 'pale green' under surfaces in 1940. On the face of it this might be an error of some kind, although mention has already been made of the crash reports written by RAF intelligence officers from August 1940 onwards and their use of colloquial terms to describe the colours of some of the crashed aircraft. Most of the crash reports use the colloquial term 'light blue' to describe the colour of the under surfaces of wrecked German aircraft, a term taken to include both RLM 65 Hellblau and the 'mixed light blue grey' which appears to be very similar to RLM 76. There are however a small number of reports which use the term 'duck egg blue' instead.

Whilst this could also be a reference to either RLM 65 or the lighter 'mixed' RLM 76, the term 'duck egg blue' was usually used colloquially at this time in Britain when referring to the under surface colour of British fighters which were the pale grey green colour officially known as Sky.

Messerschmitt Bf 109E-1, 'White 8', 7./JG 51, St Omer-Nord, France, September 1940.

Inset: III/JG 51's 'Axt von Niederrhein' (Axe of Niederrhein – a town on the Lower Rhine) emblem.

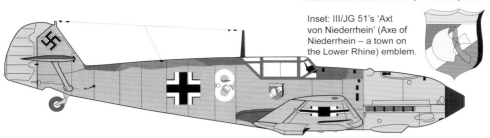

RLM 71 Dunkelgrün and RLM 02 Grau upper surfaces in a soft-edged splinter pattern with RLM 65 Hellblau under surfaces extended high up on the fuselage sides and over the fin and rudder. Yellow cowling and rudder. Note the white numeral '8' without any outline and III/JG 51's 'Axt von Niederrhein' emblem was carried under the cockpit canopy.

Messerschmitt Bf 109E-4, 'Black 4', 8./JG 2, Le Havre-Octeville, France, September 1940.

Inset: 8./JG 52's 'red wolf rampant' emblem, which was the family coat of arms of an earlier Staffelkapitän, Oblt von Winnterfeldt.

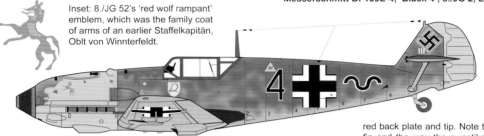

RLM 71 Dunkelgrün and RLM 02 Grau upper surfaces in a soft-edged splinter pattern with RLM 65 Hellblau under surfaces extended high up on the fuselage sides and over the fin and rudder, over which a dense mottle of RLM 71/02 has been applied. Yellow cowling (with the paint wearing off on the front) and rudder. The black numeral '4' and III Gruppe wavy bar were outlined in white. 8 Staffel's red wolf was placed on the cowling. RLM 70 spinner with red back plate and tip. Note the three victory bars (abschuszbalken) on the fin and the way the swastika has been masked out when the mottle was applied leaving an RLM 65 background.

Messerschmitt Bf 109E-1, 'White 7', 1./JG 27, Guines, France, September 1940.

Inset: I Gruppe JG 27's 'Lioness and African's head over a map of Africa' badge.

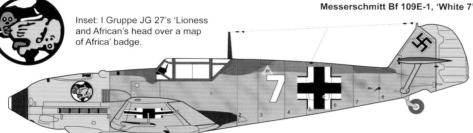

RLM 71 Dunkelgrün and RLM 02 Grau upper surfaces in a soft-edged splinter pattern with RLM 65 Hellblau under surfaces extended high up on the fuselage sides in an undulating demarcation line and over the fin and rudder. Yellow cowling and rudder. RLM 70 spinner with white tip. The white numeral '7' was outlined in black. I/JG 27's 'Afrika' badge was carried on both sides of the cowling.

Messerschmitt Bf 109E-4, 'Yellow 6', 9./JG 3, Desvres, France, September 1940.

Inset: III/JG 3's 'running insect carrying a spear' emblem and 9 Staffel's 'seahorse superimposed on waves' shield, which stemmed from the unit's intended role aboard the unfinished aircraft carrier, Graf Zeppelin.

RLM 71 Dunkelgrün and RLM 02 Grau upper surfaces in a soft-edged splinter pattern with RLM 65 Hellblau under surfaces extended high up on the fuselage sides and over the fin and rudder. Yellow cowling angled back towards the windscreen and rudder. RLM 70 spinner with white segment. The yellow numeral '6' and vertical III Gruppe bar were outlined in black. Both III/JG 3's 'running insect' and 9 Staffel's 'seahorse' badges were carried on the fuselage under the cockpit section.

Messerschmitt Bf 109E-3, 'Yellow 3', 9./JG 2, Octeville, France, September 1940.

Inset: 9./JG 2's 'Stechmücke' (mosquito or gnat) insect on a yellow disc outlined in black applied to the cowling.

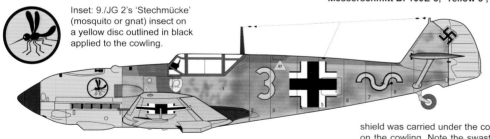

RLM 71 Dunkelgrün and RLM 02 Grau upper surfaces in a soft-edged splinter pattern with RLM 65 Hellblau under surfaces extended high up on the fuselage sides and over the fin and rudder, over which a variable density and random mottle of RLM 71/02 has been applied. Yellow cowling and rudder. RLM 70 spinner fitted with pointed spinner cap. The yellow numeral '3' and wavy III Gruppe bar were outlined in black. JG 2's 'Richthofen R' shield was carried under the cockpit section and 9 Staffel's 'Stechmücke' was on the cowling. Note the swastika in the early central position across the fin and rudder.

Messerschmitt Bf 109E-4, 'White 2', 4./JG 52, Coquelles, France, September 1940.
Pilot: Gefr Erich Mummert

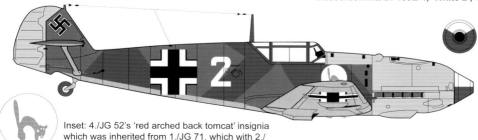

RLM 70 Schwarzgrün and RLM 71 Dunkelgrün upper surfaces in the original hard-edged splinter pattern with RLM 65 Hellblau under surfaces. Yellow cowling (which extends along the top panel to the windscreen) and rudder. RLM 70 spinner with white segment. The white numeral '2' was not outlined. 4./JG 52's 'red tomcat' insignia was carried under the forward cockpit section.

Inset: 4./JG 52's 'red arched back tomcat' insignia which was inherited from 1./JG 71, which with 2./JG 71, the basis of JG 52 was formed in 1939.

Not to any scale

In the light of this, could references in crash reports to German aircraft with 'duck egg blue' under surfaces rather than 'light blue' be taken to mean that the aircraft concerned had a pale grey/green colour similar to Sky applied to their under surfaces?

Whilst this might seem unlikely, it would appear that the Luftwaffe did possess such a pale grey/green colour and there is firm documentary evidence that it was applied to some aircraft. This evidence is contained in Royal Aircraft Establishment Report EA 14/7 issued in October 1940. The report concerned the camouflage scheme which had been applied to a Junkers Ju 88D coded 7A+FM W/Nr 0362 of 4.(F)/121 which was brought down by Hurricanes of 17 Squadron at approximately 11.15hrs on the morning of 19 September 1940.

Entitled 'Examination of Camouflage Scheme' the report called attention to the existence on this aircraft of a camouflage scheme which the RAE thought had apparently been copied in several particulars from British aircraft. All the under surfaces were found to be painted a uniform duck egg bluish-green identical with the Sky colour of British aircraft. The report stated that until this aircraft was seen, the under surfaces of German aircraft examined had been painted a light blue.

On this aircraft however, all the under surfaces of the wings, nacelles, tailplane and fuselage, including the bomb aimer's compartment under the cabin, had been painted with the Sky colour of British aircraft. The usual German light blue colour was still visible on the less accessible parts of the under surface.

The line of demarcation on the fuselage between the pale green colour on the under surfaces and the green camouflage colours on the upper surfaces was found to be in approximately the same position as defined on the British Air Diagrams at the point where a sixty degree tangent with the horizontal meets the fuselage.

Less solid evidence is to be found in Crash Report No 18 which gives details of a Bf 109E which crashed at Ficklephole Farm on 31 August. The report describes this aircraft as being camouflaged on the upper surfaces in grey and green and as having 'duck egg blue' under surfaces.

Report No 26 describes a Bf 109E-4 W/Nr 5567 of 6./II (Schlact)LG 2 which landed at Hawkinge at 0800hrs on 6 September 1940 after its cooling system was damaged in combat. Its camouflage is described as being two shades of grey on the upper surfaces with 'duck egg blue' on the under surfaces.

One final example is provided by a different type altogether, a Messerschmitt Bf 110, 3M+HL of 3./ZG 2, which according to report No 21 crashed on the road to Rye Hill half a mile west of Epping Road at 1100 hrs on 3 September 1940. Carrying the markings with the letter H in yellow the camouflage of this aircraft is described as being dark green on the upper surfaces with light green on the sides of the fuselage whilst the undersurfaces are described as being 'light blue green'.

As a German 'duck egg blue' colour is not positively known to have existed as an RLM colour at any time during the war, what could it be? In 1940 there were perhaps four possible explanations. The first is that the Germans were simply using captured supplies of British paint for trial purposes – Sky or one of its substitute colours, ie BS 381 (1930) No 16 Eau-de-Nil, which had been in use on the under surface of RAF Blenheims from early in 1940 and this type had served with the Advanced Air Striking Force in France prior to the withdrawal from Dunkerque. It is therefore possible that British paint for the maintenance of these aircraft had fallen into German hands and that this is what was being used.

The second possible explanation is that it was a colour taken from RAL 840R which has so far gone undocumented, but without having access to an example of RAL 840R it is impossible to comment further on this possibility. The third possibility is that it was a French colour of some kind, but once again, lack of reliable information on French colours of this period makes further speculation on this possibility pointless.

Finally it is possible that like the 'grey' upper surface colours dealt with previously, the pale blue green was mixed at unit level. It would appear that it might be possible to mix a close match for Sky using RLM 02, RLM 27 and white or possibly some kind of mix based on RLM 65.

Whilst it is impossible to positively identify this German pale green colour today, there would appear to have been such a colour in use in 1940 that might have been well known at one time, but if it was only used in small quantities this might account for its subsequent loss from view. If it did exist, then the question as to how widely it was used and for how long continues to remain unanswered.

Messerschmitt Bf 109E-4, Stab II/JG 54, Camagne-les-Guines, France, September 1940.
Pilot: Lt Bernard Malischewski

Possibly an example of an early 'greys' finished machine with two-tone 'mixed greys' upper surfaces in a soft-edged splinter pattern. The RLM 65 Hellblau under surfaces have been extended high up on the fuselage sides and over the fin and rudder, over which a dense mottle of the 'mixed greys' has been applied. Yellow cowling, (with the top panel extending back to the windscreen), and rudder with just a strip at the base in RLM 65. The RLM 70 spinner had a white quarter and a green tip. The black chevron and bar were bordered in white which was then outlined in black. II/JG 54's 'Lion of Aspern' shield was carried just forward of the cockpit section. Note the four white 'abschuszbalken' (victory bars) at the top of the rudder. Lt Malischewski force-landed this machine at Small Hythe, Kent, on 12 October 1940.

Inset: II/JG 54's 'Lion of Aspern' shield, inherited from the Austrian-manned JG I./134 via I/JG 76 in mid-1940.

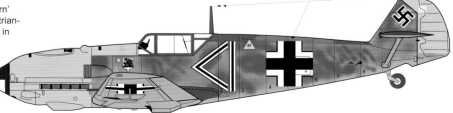

Not to any scale

Messerschmitt Bf 109E-4, 'Red 4' , 2./JG 26, Audembert, France, September 1940.

Inset: 2./JG 26's 'devil's head' emblem applied to both sides of the cowling

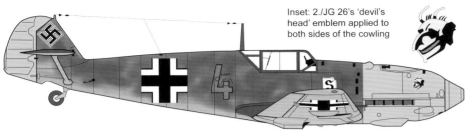

RLM 71 Dunkelgrün and RLM 02 Grau upper surfaces in a soft-edged splinter pattern with RLM 65 Hellblau under surfaces extended high up on the fuselage sides and over the fin and rudder, over which a very dense mottle of RLM 71/02 has been applied. Yellow cowling, spinner and rudder. The red numeral '4' was outlined in black. JG 26's 'Schlageter S' shield was carried just forward of the cockpit section and 2 Staffel's 'devil's head' was on the cowling. Note the way the swastika has been masked out when the mottle was applied leaving an RLM 65 background.

Messerschmitt Bf 109E-4, 'Yellow 13', 3./JG 53, Etaples, France, September 1940.
Pilot: Fw Walter Schulz

RLM 71 Dunkelgrün and RLM 02 Grau upper surfaces in a soft-edged splinter pattern with RLM 65 Hellblau under surfaces. The fuselage sides feature a very dense mottle of RLM 71/02 which terminate in an angled undulating line which rises towards the fin. Yellow cowling, mainplane and tailplane tips and the fin and rudder. The yellow numeral '13' appears paler than the tactical markings' yellow and may have been RLM 27 Gelb. RLM 70 Spinner with yellow tip. Note the swastika across the fin and rudder and the four white victory bars (abschuszbalken) on the fin above the werknummer. Fw Schulz crash landed in this machine at Langley, Sussex, on 30 September 1940 and was captured unhurt.

Messerschmitt Bf 109E-3, 'Yellow 15', 3./JG 52, Coquelles, France, September 1940
Pilot: Uffz Kurt Wolff

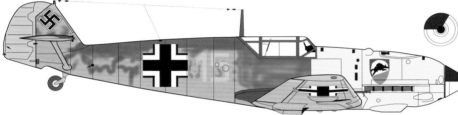

RLM 71 Dunkelgrün and RLM 02 Grau upper surfaces in a soft-edged splinter pattern with RLM 65 Hellblau under surfaces and fuselage sides, over which a very dense mottle of RLM 71/02 has been applied under the cockpit area but which is less dense and more randomly-applied on the rear fuselage and fin. Yellow cowling, mainplane tips, tailplane tips and rudder – note the shade of yellow on the cowling is paler than that of the other tactical painted areas suggesting that either the paler RLM 27 Gelb had been used or the original RLM 04 Gelb

Inset: The slightly stylised variation of I Gruppe JG 52's 'running boar' shield invariably applied to both sides of the cowling.

paint had faded or had been applied more thinly. White spinner with an RLM 70 segment. Note the slightly stylised variation of the I/JG 52 'running boar' shield on the cowling. Uffz Wolff was shot down in this aircraft on 30 September 1940, at Peasmarsh, Sussex, and taken prisoner.

Messerschmitt Bf 109E-1, 'White 2', 6./JG 52, Peuplingues, France, September/October 1940.

RLM 70 Schwarzgrün and RLM 71 Dunkelgrün upper surfaces in the simplified softer-edged splinter pattern variation with RLM 65 Hellblau under surfaces, that may have been extended up the fuselage sides but which were covered in a dense mottle of RLM 70/71 and possibly 02. Yellow cowling and top two thirds of the rudder which fades out along a feathered angled line. RLM 70 spinner. The white numeral '2' was not outlined. Note 6./JG 52's 'winged eagle' insignia which took up most of the cowling.

Messerschmitt Bf 109E-4, 'Blue 1', 5./JG 53, Dinan, France, September 1940.

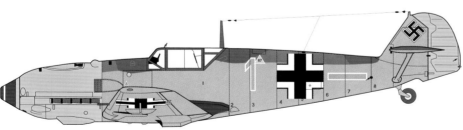

RLM 71 Dunkelgrün and RLM 02 Grau upper surfaces in a soft-edged splinter pattern with RLM 65 Hellblau under surfaces extended high up on the fuselage sides and over the fin and rudder. Note the pale blue numeral '1' and II Gruppe horizontal bar, which should have been red or black for a 5 Staffel/II Gruppe machine, but 'blue' markings were not totally unique to this particular aircraft, being recorded on several other Bf 109Es during the Battle. The yellow cowling has a RLM 70 spinner with a narrow white band and the whole of the rudder is yellow.

Messerschmitt Bf 109E-4, Stab I/(J)LG 2, Calais-Marck, France, late September 1940.

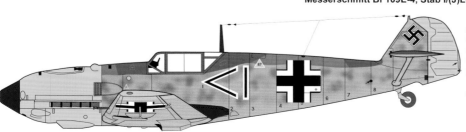

RLM 71 Dunkelgrün and RLM 02 Grau upper surfaces in a soft-edged splinter pattern with RLM 65 Hellblau under surfaces extended high up in an undulating line on the fuselage sides, and over the fin, over which a sparse mottle of RLM 71/02 has been applied. Yellow cowling, mainplane tips and rudder. The black chevron and bar were outlined in white. The spinner was RLM 70 Schwarzgrün.

Not to any scale

▲ A formation of Heinkel He IIIs, a type which went into service in 1937 and of which some 6000 were built. They were found to be a poor match for Hurricanes and Spitfires during the Battle of Britain. (Photo: Imperial War Museum)

The Blitz, as it became known, started during and continued after the Battle of Britain had finished. During the Blitz, between September 1940 and May 1941, the Germans dropped more than 35,000 tons of bombs for the loss of some 650 aircraft. London was attacked nineteen times with over 18,800 tons of bombs dropped.

On 13 October 1940, Hitler again postponed the invasion, "... until the spring of 1941." However, the invasion never happened, and October is regarded as the month in which the regular daylight bombing of Britain ended, but it was not until Hitler's Directive 21 was ordered, on 18 December 1940, that the threat of invasion was finally removed.

Although the campaign of bombing British cities throughout October and December 1940 continued, Hitler had already started to focus his attention on Russia – and on 22 June 1941, he launched the greatest land-air campaign in the history of war, called 'Operation Barbarossa' the invasion of the Soviet Union.

The end of massed daylight operations against the British isles allowed the Luftwaffe just enough time, before the invasion of Russia, to make good some of its losses. However, although it could replace equipment, it could not replace the skilled pilots and aircrew who had been killed or captured.

Hitler and his generals had already made one bad mistake, when they switched the Luftwaffe's tactics from RAF Fighter Command's airfields to focus on the bombing of British cities, just at the time when they were winning the air battle over Britain. Invading Russia was an even worse blunder – and the Luftwaffe that attacked Russia in June 1941 was not the Luftwaffe of the summer of 1940; the RAF had seen to that.

As mentioned previously, both sides in the Battle made exaggerated claims of numbers of enemy aircraft shot down. In general, claims were two to three times the actual numbers lost, mainly because of the confusion of fighting in fast, swirling, three-dimensional air battles. Post-war analysis of records has shown between July and September 1940, the RAF

claimed some 2,698 'kills' against 1,023 RAF fighters lost to all causes, whilst the Luftwaffe fighters claimed 3,198 RAF aircraft downed against their losses of 2,087, split between 873 fighters and 1,214 bombers.

However, to the RAF figure should be added an additional 376 Bomber Command and 148 Coastal Command aircraft conducting bombing, mining, and reconnaissance operations in defence of the country.

There was one final irony though. Having praised 'The Few', Churchill made them one fewer. He sanctioned the RAF's sacking of Air Chief Marshal Sir Hugh Dowding as C-in-C Fighter Command – the man now generally held responsible for the victory...

Camouflage and markings

Luftwaffe night bomber schemes

At this point in the war, the Luftwaffe Kampfgruppen didn't have a specific Night Bomber scheme as such. Aircraft designated to operate at night were finished in the standard Day Bomber scheme of RLM 70 Schwarzgrün (black green) and RLM 71 Dunkelgrün (dark green) on the upper surfaces in a standardised straight-edged 'splinter' pattern, with RLM 65 Hellblau (light blue) under surfaces.

Some attempt at a 'night flying scheme' was introduced as early as July 1940, when the RLM 65 Hellblau under surfaces initially were overpainted with a temporary black paint finish under the RLM specification 7120.22 – a somewhat 'sooty' matt black similar to the RAF's RDM2 Special Night paint (see opposite).

This temporary black paint finish was applied quite crudely, with large brushes, and as the night bombing tempo increased, the variations and the areas where the RLM 7120.22 'sooty' matt black was applied increased, from higher up the fuselage sides and over all the fin/rudder area(s), to over all the airframe, including the upper surfaces – in ether a solid coat or a mottle effect. Even the national markings and unit codes were not exempt in an attempt to 'tone-down' the visibility of the airframe at night, quite often both being totally obliterated under a coat of 'sooty' matt black.

RAF Night Fighter camouflage and markings

As with the Luftwaffe Kampfgruppen, during the summer of 1940, there was no difference in the camouflage and markings of RAF Day and Night Fighters, with all Fighters being camouflaged on the upper surfaces in the Temperate Land Scheme of Dark Green and Dark Earth with whatever colour or colours were required on the under surfaces at that particular moment – which might range from Night, White and Aluminium to Sky, or any of its alternative substitutes!

Markings consisted of the usual national markings of the day with squadron and individual aircraft code letters applied in Medium Sea Grey and serial numbers applied in Night.

Heinkel He 111H, 6N+GL, 3./KGr 100, Vannes-Meucon, France, September 1940.

Finished in the standard two-tone green RLM 70 Schwarzgrün and RLM 71 Dunkelgrün upper surfaces in a straight-edged 'splinter' pattern with RLM 65 Hellblau undersides. Codes were black with the individual aircraft letter 'G' in

the staffel colour yellow. The propeller spinners were also yellow with a black band around the middle. The Gruppe's insignia, a Viking boat, was positioned on both sides of the forward fuselage immediately below the pilot's cockpit glazing, partially hidden by the engine nacelle. Note the ejector exhausts.

Inset: KGr 100's Viking ship, symbolic of the pathfinder role of this specialised unit

Heinkel He 111H-3, 6N+EK, 2./KGr 100, Vannes-Meucon, France, late summer 1940.

Finished in the standard two-tone green RLM 70 Schwarzgrün and RLM 71 Dunkelgrün upper surfaces in a straight-edged 'splinter' pattern with RLM 65 Hellblau undersides. Codes were black with the individual aircraft letter 'E' in the staffel colour red. The Gruppe's insignia, a Viking boat, was positioned on both sides of the forward fuselage immediately below the pilot's cockpit glazing,

partially hidden by the engine nacelle. Note the additional dorsal aerials indicating fitment of the X-Gerät and Y-Gerät radio location equipment for the aircraft's nocturnal pathfinder role. Note the tapered pipe exhaust manifolds.

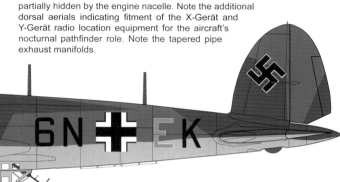

Heinkel He 111H-2, W.Nr 6305, G1+BH, 1./KG 55, Dreux, France, September 1940.

Finished in the standard two-tone green RLM 70 Schwarzgrün and RLM 71 Dunkelgrün upper surfaces in a straight-edged 'splinter' pattern with RLM 65 Hellblau undersides, which had been overpainted in a coat of temporary night camouflage paint, Farbton 7120.22/RLM 22 Schwarz, which was a sooty black finish. Codes were black with the individual aircraft letter 'B' in the staffel colour white. The propeller spinners were halved white and RLM 70. It would appear

that G1+BH didn't carry any Gruppe or Geschwader insignia, but did have a white silhouette of a 'snorting bull' on the port fuselage side. Note the early central position of the swastika across the fin and rudder. This machine, crewed by Fw Fritz Jürges (pilot), Hptm Karl Köthke (navigator), Uffz Josef Altrichter (flight engineer), Gefr Weisbach and Flgr Mueller, was one of four from this unit to be lost during a raid on the Bristol Aircraft Company's aero engine works at Filton on a daylight raid on 25 September 1940, and crash landed Westhill Farm, Studland, near Swanage in Dorset. Uffz Altrichter later died of his wounds. The other aircraft were He 111H G1+DN of 5./KG 55, He 111P G1+EP of 6./KG 55 and He 111P G1+LR of 7./KG 55.

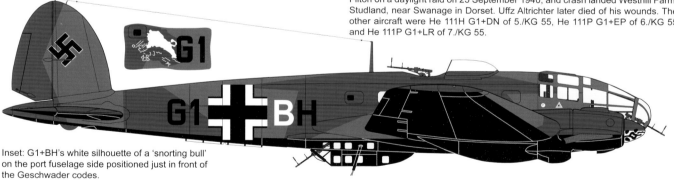

Inset: G1+BH's white silhouette of a 'snorting bull' on the port fuselage side positioned just in front of the Geschwader codes.

Heinkel He 111H, (G1+FM), 4./KG 55, Dreux, France, autumn 1940.

KG 55's penchant for applying 'graffiti' to its aeroplanes is illustrated by this example which had some 78 white 'fish' silhouettes applied down the length of it upper fuselage – presumably representing mission markers? Finished in the standard two-tone green RLM 70 Schwarzgrün and RLM 71 Dunkelgrün upper surfaces in a straight-edged 'splinter' pattern with RLM 65 Hellblau undersides. The undersides and the sides of the fuselage, fin and rudder have been

overpainted in a coat of temporary night camouflage paint, Farbton 7120.22/RLM 22 Schwarz, a sooty black finish, obliterating all the national markings and codes and leaving just the outlines of the fuselage balkenkreuz and the individual aircraft letter.

Inset: 4./KG 55's red griffon with black wings, rampant on a white shield outlined in red

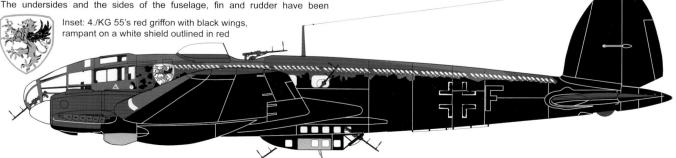

Bristol Blenheim Mk.If, L1327/RO-I, 29 Squadron, RAF Digby, Lincolnshire, October 1940.

As with the Luftwaffe night-operated aircraft, initially there was no difference in the camouflage and markings of RAF Day and Night Fighters, with all Fighters being camouflaged on the upper surfaces in the Temperate Land Scheme of Dark Green and Dark Earth with Sky, or any of its alternative substitutes, on the under surfaces, as illustrated by this Blenheim Mk.If, operated in September/ October 1940. L1327 is finished in the B Scheme pattern and lacks a serial number on its fuselage, but has one on its rudder. Note the non-standard ratios of the fuselage roundel colours.

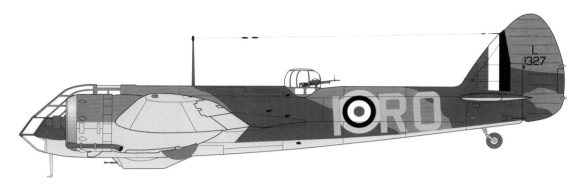

Hawker Hurricane Mk.I, (serial overpainted)/VY-X, 85 Squadron, RAF Kirton-in-Lindsey, Lincolnshire, October/November 1940.

When 85 Squadron was sent north to 'rest' in September, it moved from its initial base at Church Fenton to Kirton-in-Lindsey, to train on night flying techniques before returning south again as an operational Night Fighter unit in November. The overall Special Night RDM2 finish for Night Fighters was introduced in late October. Standard national markings were to be carried with the omission of underwing roundels and the serial number was to be painted in Red. This particular example operated by 85 Squadron retained its Medium Sea Grey codes but had its fuselage roundels toned down by overpainting the White and Yellow areas, and had still to have its serial number reapplied in Red.

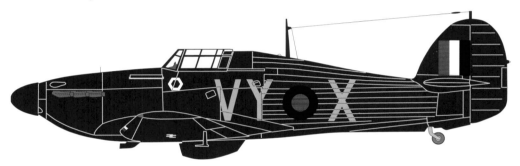

Boulton Paul Defiant Mk.I, N3340/YD-D, 255 Squadron, RAF Kirton-in-Lindsey, Lincolnshire, November 1940.

Following its disastrous performance in daylight operations during the Battle of Britain, a role needed to be found for the Defiant, and Night Fighter seemed to be the one. Finished overall in the sooty Special Night RDM2 again the fuselage roundels had been modified to reduce their perceived brightness at night by over painting the white ring in N3340's instance. Note that the code letters are Medium Sea Grey but the serial number had been reapplied in Red.

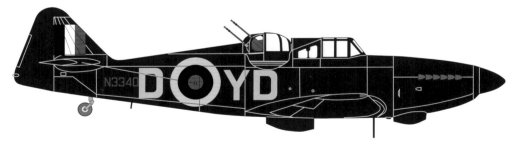

Boulton Paul Defiant Mk.I, V1116/JT-H, 256 Squadron, RAF Catterick, North Yorkshire, December 1940.

Several new squadrons were reformed in November 1940 as Night Fighter units on the Defiant, including 255 and 256 illustrated here. Finish is again the sooty overall Special Night RDM2 but this time the fuselage roundels have not been modified although the ratios are not quite standard. There is some confusion as to whether the code letters were to be Sky Grey or Medium Sea Grey, but it would appear that either colour would have been acceptable – in this case they seem to be Medium Sea Grey. The serial number has been correctly reapplied in Red.

Not to any scale

The introduction of the overall Special Night finish seems to have originated at a meeting held at the Air Ministry in Whitehall on 30 October 1940. At this meeting, the colouring of Night Fighters was amongst the camouflage and markings subjects discussed, presumably on account of the switch in German bombing tactics from day to night operations.

Although the minutes of the meeting do not specifically state why a change in colouring was discussed, it is thought that poor searchlight control by the ground defences was resulting in the pursuing fighter being picked up and illuminated by searchlight instead of the enemy aircraft. Under these circumstances the daylight camouflage which the fighters were finished in did nothing but make them easily visible, both from the ground and also from the bomber they were pursuing.

The introduction of a Night Fighter scheme

For whatever reason, it was agreed that Night Fighters should be coloured black all over and should carry the standard national markings as carried by RAF Night Bombers. The only real difference in markings that this would entail for Night Fighters when compared with Day Fighters would be the use of Red for the serial number on the black finish, (which is thought to have been introduced for Night Bombers already in service), from sometime around 18 October 1940 and the omission of underwing roundels.

There would however, appear to be some question as to the exact colour of the squadron and individual aircraft letters. In theory it is thought that they were supposed to be applied in Medium Sea

Grey, but at least one other source has claimed that they were marked on Night Bombers and Night Fighters in Sky Grey.

From a production point of view, Defiants and DB 7 Fighters, (ie Douglas Havocs and Bostons), would be produced painted black with the standard Night Bomber markings, whilst Hurricanes and Blenheims used in the Night Fighter role, would be painted black under local arrangements at the discretion of Fighter Command. Special arrangements were made for Beaufighters to be produced with only their primary undercoatings applied prior to delivery to Aircraft Servicing Units, (ASUs), where they were to be finished in a colour scheme appropriate to their role.

Night Fighter Beaufighters

This unusual treatment for Beaufighters came about because at this time, Bristols were delivering Beaufighters to the RAF for Service with both Fighter and Coastal Commands. As long as both Commands had the same camouflage requirements, ie Temperate Land Scheme upper surfaces and Sky under surfaces, this posed no problem, but with Fighter Command now requiring a different camouflage scheme, ie overall Special Night, it was thought that delays in production would ensue from having to try to determine where each individual aircraft would eventually go and to finish it in the appropriate camouflage scheme on the production line.

The underlying problem with the Beaufighter was that the equipment standard of the two Commands were widely differing. Fighter Command Beaufighters needed to be

Bristol Beaufighter Mk.If, R2059/A2, Fighter Interception Unit, RAF Tangmere, Sussex, November/December 1940.

Fitting the new Airborne Interception (AI) equipment in to a suitable aircraft which had the space to accommodate it and still retain a credible performance to intercept Luftwaffe bombers at night was going to be a problem – until the Beaufighter came on the scene. Following trials with the Fighter Interception Unit, with which R2059 served, the Beaufighter found a welcome home within

the Night Fighter community. Finished overall in the sooty Special Night RDM2, the national markings were standard for the period. Note Medium Sea Grey FIU 'codes' with the numeral '2' on the outer face of the cowling and the Medium Sea Grey serial number.

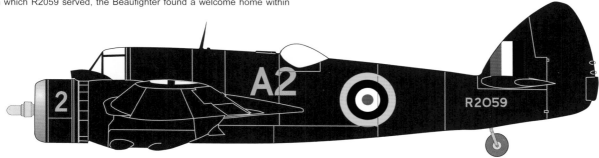

Bristol Beaufighter Mk.If, R2101/NG-R, 604 Squadron, RAF Middle Wallop, Hampshire, November/December 1940.

One of the first front-line squadrons to receive the then new AI-equipped Beaufighter Mk.If, to supplement its Blenheim Mk.Ifs, was 604, who scored its first victory on the type, by Squadron Leader John Cunningham, on the night of 20/21 November 1940, to become the RAF's top-scoring Night Fighter squadron

by the end of the year. Finished overall in the sooty Special Night RDM2, the national markings were standard for the period with Medium Sea Grey codes and serial number. Note the white numeral '3' on the outer face of the cowling

Not to any scale

equipped with airborne radar whilst Coastal Command aircraft needed to be fitted with navigation equipment appropriate to their role as Long Range Fighters. All of this equipment was at this time being fitted by the ASUs once the destination of each individual aircraft had been decided. By requiring the Beaufighter to be delivered in just its primary undercoat colours, it was hoped that no production delays would occur as the aircraft could receive the appropriate camouflage scheme once its final destination was known and it had been equipped for a particular role.

As a result of this decision, Bristols ceased to apply camouflage to the Beaufighter and delivered them instead with Dark Grey Primer on the upper surfaces and Light Grey Primer on the under surfaces along with a full set of national markings which included underwing roundels.

As far as aircraft which were already in service were concerned, these aircraft were to be refinished by Fighter Command units and replacement aircraft which had already been accepted by the service but not yet issued to squadrons would be repainted by ASUs before issue to squadrons.

The idea of supplying Beaufighters in just their primer colours was not well received at HQ 41 Group Maintenance Command, who were concerned that such aircraft would be liable to corrosion during the time between delivery and

final finishing prior to issue to a squadron. They were also concerned that as such aircraft were widely dispersed at the ASUs whilst awaiting the necessary work to be carried out, the grey aircraft would compromise the camouflage of any airfield that they stood on. HQ 41 Group therefore requested that Beaufighters should continue to be delivered in the standard day camouflage.

Whatever colour scheme the Beaufighters were finished in when they arrived at the ASUs, they had to have their Special Night camouflage applied as did the aircraft already finished in the day flying colours. One unforeseen difficulty was apparently a shortage of Special Night paint, presumably due to Bomber Command having first call on the materials as they were in the process of extending the finish up the sides of the fuselages and over the fins of their Night Bombers at just about this time.

On 28 November 1940, the Ministry of Aircraft Production (MAP) made it known that the surfaces of aircraft which were to have the Special Night finish should be first treated with a coat of Night in order to save a coat of Special Night due to the shortage of the pigment required in the production of Special Night.

It may be appropriate here to explain the difference between Night and Special Night. Admittedly the difference is subtle, but it is none the less important. Night was the original night

Dornier Do 17Z (F1+AT), 9./KG 76, St Trond, Belgium, autumn 1940.

Due to being slower and able to carry less of a bomb load, Dornier Do 17Zs were being gradually phased out of front line operational service towards the end of the year although several units soldiered on with the type over the autumn and winter period, such as KG 76. Finished in the standard two-tone green RLM 70 Schwarzgrün and RLM 71 Dunkelgrün upper surfaces in a straight-edged 'splinter' pattern. The original RLM 65 Hellblau undersides have been overpainted in a coat of temporary night camouflage paint, Farbton 7120.22/RLM 22 Schwarz, a sooty black finish, which has been painted around the national markings but over the codes with the exception of individual aircraft letter 'A' which is in the Staffel colour yellow. The propeller spinners were also yellow. Note 9./KG 76's red and white shield with three 'Tyr-Runes' under the cockpit glazing.

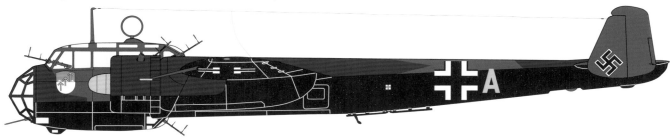

Junkers Ju 88A-5 (V4+HT), 9./KG 1, Bapaume Grevilles, France, late autumn/winter 1940.

By far the best all-round day and night bomber was the Ju 88, especially the A-5 sub-type, with the longer wing span, which was starting re-equip several Gruppen within the various Geschwarden over the winter of 1940/41. Finished in the standard two-tone green RLM 70 Schwarzgrün and RLM 71 Dunkelgrün upper surfaces in a straight-edged 'splinter' pattern, once again the original RLM 65 Hellblau undersides have been overpainted in a coat of temporary night camouflage paint, Farbton 7120.22/RLM 22 Schwarz. The national markings and the codes have been overpainted in the temporary night camouflage paint too but the individual aircraft letter and the staffel letter have been reapplied in small white characters on the rear fuselage.

Inset: Generalfeldmarschall Hindenburg's signature, and it's position on the front fuselage of the aircraft, which was used as KG 1's emblem in 1940, replacing Hindenburg's family coat of arms which had been used on the unit's Ju 86s prior to the outbreak of war.

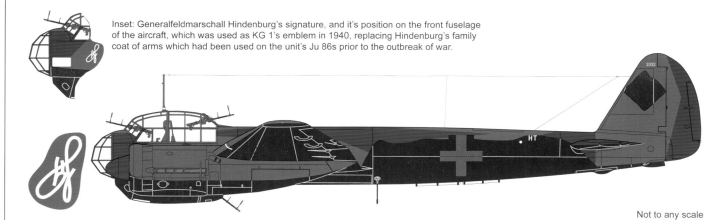

Not to any scale

flying camouflage colour introduced from 1937. It was not so much a true black but a very dark grey, being made up of a mixture of Carbon Black and Ultramarine Blue pigments. It began to be superseded as the under surface finish on the Night Bombers of Bomber Command from September 1939 with the advent of Special Night.

Special Night consisted of only Carbon Black pigment of greater size than the pigments in other camouflage finishes which were intended to bestow on it more of a matt finish. This led to it being described by many who saw it as a 'sooty black'. Throughout its use it was often referred to as RDM 2 Special Night or RDM 2a Special Night. There was no difference in the colour or appearance of these two differing specifications, the difference between RDM 2 and RDM 2a being chemical only.

In service there were found to be two main problems with the Special Night finish. Firstly it tended to come off the aircraft easily, often as a result of faulty application, and secondly, the rough finish proved detrimental to the aircraft's performance. Despite these problems however, Special Night remained in

use as an overall finish on RAF Night Fighters for the whole of 1941 and well into 1942.

During December 1940, questions continued to be raised as to the wisdom of finishing Beaufighters in their primer finish only. An internal MAP memo dated 20 December stated that it had been found impracticable to produce the Beaufighter in undercoating and that Fighter Command had agreed to repaint the small number of Beaufighters it was receiving locally within the units. Thus from early 1941 it would appear that Bristols went back to delivering all Beaufighters in the Temperate Land Scheme with Sky under surfaces which Fighter Command repainted in Special Night following delivery.

In the past it has been noted that several Beaufighters finished in Special Night were received by squadrons still carrying their underwing roundels. This is possibly due to both primer finished and camouflage finished Beaufighters being finished with such markings on the production line which the ASUs preparing the aircraft for front line service failed to over paint for some reason. Such markings were subsequently painted out by the recipient squadrons.

Heinkel He 115C-1, W.Nr 2754, 8L+GH, 1./KFlGr 906, Norderney, Germany, September 1940.

Medium range maritime reconnaissance was always an essential feature of operations against the UK in the first few years of World War Two and several Gruppen equipped with He 115s were tasked with the job throughout 1940 and in to 1941. Finished in the two-tone maritime green shades of RLM 72 Grün and RLM 73 Grün, with RLM 65 Hellblau undersides, 8L+GH was lost on a reconnaissance sortie to Kinnairds Head in Scotland on 16 September 1940. The crew became disorientated in deteriorating weather conditions, and crashed in to a hillside near Aberdeen. The three crew, Hptm Kothe, Lt zur See Aldus and Uffz Meissner were made PoWs. Note the outline of the swastika on the fin which may have been in the process of being 'touched up' (?) when the photo was taken upon which this illustration is based, and the painter has been a little over zealous with the white paint!

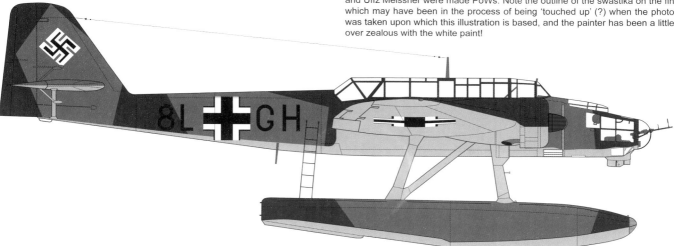

Heinkel He 115C-1, M2+BL, 3./KFlGr 106, Schellingwoude, Netherlands, autumn 1940.

He 115s also undertook nocturnal mine laying operations in the North Sea and had their camouflage scheme suitably modified, like this example, M2+BL of 3./KFlGr 106. Finished in the two-tone maritime green shades of RLM 72 Grün and RLM 73 Grün, the original RLM 65 Hellblau undersides have been overpainted with a coat of temporary night camouflage paint, Farbton 7120.22/RLM 22 Schwarz. The balkenkreuze on the fuselage sides have been overpainted in the temporary night camouflage paint too but the individual aircraft letter which should be yellow appears to have been overpainted in RLM 72? Note how the temporary night paint is wearing off the front of the fuselage and the lower leading edge of the engine cowling.

Inset: The skull and crossbones emblem of 3 Staffel Küstenfliegergruppe 106, which was inherited from 3./KüFlGr 206 in April 1937

Not to any scale

The Regia Aeronautica became involved in the Battle of Britain more for political reasons rather than for any real military necessity, the Italian government merely considering the advantages of sharing a German victory over the United Kingdom. Essentially unprepared and lacking any strategic planning, the Italian Military High Command was totally subjected to Mussolini's personal whims, and Italy's involvement in the Battle of Britain was possibly explained by Mussolini's desire for revenge for the first raid by RAF Bomber Command on the night of 10/11 June 1940, when thirty-six Whitleys bombed Turin on the day after the Italian declaration of war on France and the United Kingdom.

War against France

Airfields at Hyères, Fayance, Cuers-Pierrefeu and Cannet de Mayres, as well as naval bases at Toulon and Fayance, were attacked between 13 and 17 June by CR.42s based in the north-west of Italy, with strafing missions against French airfields in Corsica by CR.32s and Breda 88s based in Sardinia. The French bases in Tunisia at Sidi Ahmed, Korouba, Menzel Temine, El Aouina, Kassar Said, El Djem and the port of Bizerte were also attacked by Regia Aeronautica bombers and fighters from Sicily.

Italy suspended all offensive operations on 24 June, when an armistice was signed between Italy and France. During this brief campaign the Italian Air Force shot down ten French aircraft down, destroying another fifty on the ground. The Regia Aeronautica lost ten aircraft in combat.

The Corpo Aero Italiano

As soon as the Battle of France was over, Mussolini asked Hitler to make some airfields in the Channel area available for an Italian expeditionary force, the Corpo Aero Italiano (CAI). Unfortunately, the Italian Government totally underestimated the problems that would be met by the Regia Aeronautica against a well equipped Royal Air Force as the Corpo Aero Italiano would be equipped with a limited number of, (unsuitable), aircraft types in an alien environmental and with very different operational conditions to the Mediterranean Theatre in which all their units had been trained.

Initially, the Italian request received a polite, 'no thanks' from Hermann Göring, however, due to further political lobbying, on 15 August he finally had to accept the Italian proposal, on the condition that it would be placed under the operational control of Kesselring's Luftflotte 2. Consequently, the Corpo Aero Italiano was officially established on 10 September in Milan, led by General Rino Corso Fougier.

This special unit included two Stormi BT (Bombardamento Terrestre - Land Bomber Wings), 13° and 43°, with eighty twin-engined Fiat BR.20M bombers, and a specially established 56° Stormo CT (Caccia Terrestre - Land Fighter Wing) incorporating two existing fighter groups, namely 18° Gruppo, (previously attached to 3° Stormo), with fifty Fiat CR.42 biplanes, and 20° Gruppo (formerly part of 51° Stormo) with forty-five Fiat G.50 fighters. A single squadron of five

Cant Z.1007bis bombers fulfilled the strategic reconnaissance role and a few more transport and liaison aircraft completed the force.

Further types deployed to the Channel area were a single SIAI Marchetti S.75, (General Fugier's personal aircraft), twelve Caproni Ca 133s as transport aircraft to all fighter squadrons, (two each), and nine Caproni Ca 64s used for liaison, (three attached to CAI HQ and two each to the operational Stormi). Even a single militarised Ala Littoria Junkers Ju 52 was used, to regularly link Italy and Belgium three times a week.

The Italian Air Staff had to accept having all its air units based in Belgium as all the French airfields were fully occupied by Luftwaffe units, and it was obviously illogical for them to be moved whilst fully engaged in the Battle of Britain to accommodate the Italian forces. Only at a later stage, after much Italian insisting, did the Germans hand over the airport at Brussels-Melsbroek, which had a paved runway.

Ferry flight problems

Even the transfer flights to Belgium of the Corpo Aero Italiano were troubled, mainly due to the lack of experience of the pilots in instrument flying and the adverse weather conditions of Northern Europe which grounded the aircraft for many days before they could overfly the Alps and proceed to their destination. As a result, the CAI units were not deployed on their Belgian bases before 19 October, when five Cant Z.1007bis of 172ª Squadriglia RST (Ricognizione Strategica Terrestre -Strategic Land Reconnaissance), arrived from their home base at Bresso (Milan).

The ferry flights demonstrated just how unprepared the Italian crews were, especially in respect of the lack of blind flight training in bad weather and inadequate radio assistance. The problems of flying in the typically overcast winter weather Northern European skies, together with the lack of suitable radio communication and a proper ground control system, would prove to be an equal enemy to that of the British defenders!

Operations

After some training flights to become acquainted with the surrounding area, the first bombing raid was against Harwich on the night of 24/25 October, which highlighted how limited the Italian bombers' night capability was. Four of the seventeen aircraft of 43° and 98° Gruppo were lost in this first operation, none due to enemy action. One crashed soon after take-off killing all the crew; the crews of another two aircraft had to bale out on their way back, not having been able to locate their own base; whilst another machine made an emergency landing at Lille-Seclin. As a consequence of that first 'unlucky' mission, it was agreed with the Germans that the CAI units would operate in daylight.

On 27 October, sixty-two fighters of 18° and 20° Gruppo were sent to escort a bombing raid over Ramsgate, but they missed the rendezvous with the bombers. Two days later a similar mission was successfully accomplished by thirty-nine CR.42s and thirty-four G.50s escorting fifteen BR.20s of 43° Stormo, meeting no British fighter opposition. On 1 November, an offensive sweep was carried by thirty-six CR.42s and thirty-six G.50s against targets between Dover and Canterbury, later repeated on 8 November by twenty-two G.50s between Ramsgate and Folkestone. A successful bombing raid on Harwich was carried on 5 November by eight BR.20s of 3ª Squadriglia, whilst further bomber raids on Ramsgate and Ipswich had to be cancelled on 9 and 10 November due to extremely bad weather conditions.

On 11 November forty CR.42s and twenty-four G.50s escorted ten BR.20s raiding Harwich and five Cant Z.1007s on a diversionary attack over Great Yarmouth. However, the G.50s missed the rendezvous with the bombers and the Hurricanes of Nos 46 and 257 Squadrons intercepted the main attack force over Harwich. In the resulting dogfight two escorting fighters and three Italian bombers were shot down, plus another CR.42, whose pilot, thinking he was on the other side of the English Channel, force-landed on the beach at Orfordness, when he became disoriented in the fog and ran out of fuel. He was captured and his machine is now displayed at RAF Hendon Museum today. But, the worst had yet to come. Due to the deteriorating visibility and aircraft running out of fuel, nineteen other fighters had to land all along the French and the Belgian coast, whilst another eleven pilots crash-landed damaging or destroying their aircraft.

After that disastrous raid, daytime bombing raids were abandoned and the G.50s, due to their shorter range, saw their sorties limited to air patrols over the Dutch and Belgian coast, whilst the CR.42s continued flying offensive raids against coastal targets off Kent, eventually resulting in another clash with RAF fighters on 23 November, during a sweep between Margate and Folkestone, when twenty-nine CR.42s were 'bounced' by the Spitfires of No 603 Squadron, resulting in another two biplanes being shot down.

The following days saw little action due to bad weather, except for the resumption of night bombing raids on Harwich, Ipswich, Great Yarmouth and Lowestoft, carried 'on chance' between 17 November and 3 January by small formations of up to ten unescorted BR.20s each time, mainly belonging to 13° Stormo, as 43° Stormo's operational capability had been severely compromised after the 11 November raid, when that unit had lost at least seven bombers. That evening, the Fleet Air Arm crippled the Italian Fleet at Taranto. At the end of December 1940, the order to return back home was received, and the whole Corpo Aero Italiano force had flown back to Italy by 20 January 1941.

Camouflage and markings

New national tail markings were introduced soon after war was declared. The previous red, white and green rudder stripes were replaced with a white 'Savoy Cross', from the House of Savoy's

---

Fiat G.50bis, MM.5543/352-5, 352ª Squadriglia, 20° Gruppo CT, 56° Stormo, shortly after arrival at their new base at Ursel, Belgium, October 1940.

20° Gruppo's Fiat G.50s were all new aircraft, finished in the standard factory three-tone camouflage scheme of Giallo Mimetico 3 (Camouflage Yellow No 3) a sandy/tan colour base, over which a dense soft-edged mottling of Verde Mimetico 3 (Camouflage Green No 3) a dark olive green and Marrone Mimetico 2 (Camouflage Brown No 2) a reddish brown, was applied. Under surfaces were Grigio Mimetico (Camouflage Grey), a medium gull grey. National, triple fascio, roundels with a white background were carried under wing surfaces only, this being a trademark of all early CMASA-built machines, with the white House of Savoy cross extending over the fin and rudder. The Squadriglia number '352'

in black and the red individual aircraft numeral '1' were applied to the fuselage sides, with the single fasci on a blue disc under the cockpit. No dedicated Stormo badge was carried by the newly formed 56° Stormo and consequently all the G.50s continued to display the badge of their previous parent unit, the distinctive black cat catching three mice of 51° Stormo on the fin. All 20 Gruppo's G.50s were fitted with radios and spinner caps to the propellers. Note that the yellow tactical cowling band had not yet been applied to 352-1, and the tailwheel spat was still fitted.

Inset: The House of Savoy's coat of arms which was displayed on the top of the vertical bar of the Savoy Cross on the rudder of all Regia Aeronautica aircraft.

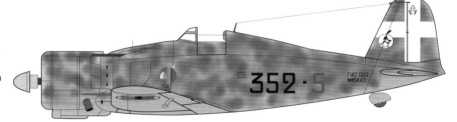

Fiat G.50bis, MM5372, 20° Gruppo CT, 56° Stormo, based at Ursel, Belgium, October 1940.
Pilot: Maggiore Mario Bonzano, unit CO

Despite being new aircraft, the Italian paint on the G.50s soon weathered in the harsh northern European winter climate, as illustrated by the Stormo CO's machine, which had paint flaking off all around the cockpit and mid fuselage area. Finished in the standard factory three-tone camouflage scheme of Giallo Mimetico 3 with a dense, soft-edged mottling, of Verde Mimetico 3 and Marrone Mimetico 2, Maggiore Bonzano's aircraft simply carried the 20 Gruppo numeral

'20°GR' instead of the Squadriglia number and individual aircraft numeral. A blue and red Comandante di Gruppo pennant was also carried on the fuselage side. Under surfaces were Grigio Mimetico and national, triple fascio, roundels with a white background were carried under wing surfaces only. The 56° Stormo badge was carried on the fin and the yellow tactical cowling band had been applied.

Inset: The distinctive black cat catching three mice emblem of 51° Stormo, which was used by 56° Stormo during this period was applied to the fins of all the unit's G.50s.

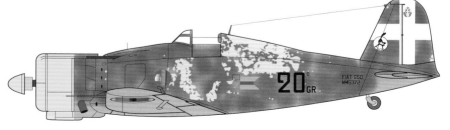

Not to any scale

coat of arms. Initially, this cross was painted just on the rudder, maintaining the central vertical white stripe of the original tricolour rudder stripes, and crossed by a same-width horizontal white band. A lot of variations could be observed during its early use due to different interpretation of the orders at unit level. The national insignia was carried as previously, including the two colour fasci on the fuselage sides and four triple fascio wing roundels, on a white (or sometimes black) disc.

Both Regia Aeronautica fighter types operating in Belgium displayed their standard factory finishes, ostensibly consisting of a mottled camouflage scheme of a sandy/tan Giallo Mimetico 3 (Camouflage Yellow No 3) base with soft-edged dark olive green Verde Mimetico 3 (Camouflage Green No 3) and reddish brown Marrone Mimetico 2 (Camouflage Brown No 2) blotches. However it might be that the CR.42s only had olive green Verde Mimetico 3 blotches over the sandy/tan Giallo Mimetico 3 base, a theory apparently borne out by contemporary photographs of the aircraft taken in Belgium and crash-landed in the UK, but whether this was in fact, or merely the reddish brown Marrone Mimetico 2 blotches subtly blending in to the Giallo Mimetico 3 base is open to

interpretation. The Fiat G.50s upper surfaces certainly look different and somewhat darker than those of the CR.42s lending credence to the single-colour mottle theory.

Similar colours were also used to paint the Fiat BR.20M bombers, whilst the five Cant Z.1007bis carried a very distinctive densely mottled scheme of the dark olive green Verde Mimetico 3 but with medium tan Bruno Mimetico (Camouflage Brown) blotches over a medium sand Giallo Mimetico 2 (Camouflage Yellow No 2) base. All under surfaces, regardless of type, were supposed to be painted in the medium gull grey Grigio Mimetico (Camouflage Grey), but again there is the possibility that silver or aluminium paint may also have been used.

All the aircraft were quite new as 18° Gruppo had been totally re-equipped in August with brand new CR.42s, incorporating a modified armament of a 7.7mm and a 12.7mm calibre machine-gun instead of the usual twin 12.7mm application. Only three aircraft per Squadriglia were fitted with a receiving-only wireless set, whilst only the squadron leaders' machines had received complete receiving/transmitting sets.

Fiat CR.42, MM.5701/13-95, 95ª Squadriglia, 18° Gruppo CT, 56° Stormo, Ursel, Belgium, November 1940.
Pilot: Sergente Pietro Salvadori

The other Regia Aeronautica fighter type operating in Belgium was the Fiat CR.42. Again all the aircraft were fairly new as 18° Gruppo had been totally re-equipped in August with brand new CR.42s, incorporating the modified armament of a single 7.7mm and one 12.7mm calibre machine-gun instead of the usual twin 12.7mm application, in an attempt to gain a few mphs against faster enemy types. Only three aircraft per Squadriglia were fitted with a receiving-only wireless set, whilst only the squadron leaders' machines had complete receiving/transmitting sets. All the 'Falcos' were ostensibly in the standard Fiat factory finish, of a Giallo Mimetico 3 base with a sparser but larger, soft-edged mottling, of Verde Mimetico 3 and possibly Marrone Mimetico 2 on the upper surfaces,

although use of this colour on the CAI's CR.42s is open to question. Under surfaces were the medium gull grey Grigio Mimetico, but could have been silver or aluminium paint on some machines. As no dedicated badge was carried by the newly formed 56° Stormo all the CR.42s continued to carry their traditional 18° Gruppo badge, displaying three arrows on a fascio, on the fuselage sides flanked by the Squadriglia number, (95ª in this case) and the individual aircraft number, 13 in this case – in yellow with a black drop shadow. This machine force landed on a beach at Orfordness, Suffolk, on 11 November 1940, having broken an oil feed line, and Sergente Salvadori was captured.

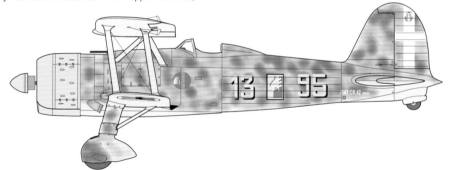

Inset: 18° Gruppo badge, featuring three arrows and the motto 'ocio che te copo!' on a fascio, carried on the fuselage sides of the CR.42s

Fiat CR.42, MM.6976/85-16, 85ª Squadriglia, 18° Gruppo CT, 56° Stormo, Ursel, Belgium, November 1940.
Pilot: Sergente Antonio Lazzari

The CR.42s carried the national, triple fascio, roundels insignia above the upper and below the lower wing, with a white background surrounded by a thin black trim. Propeller spinners (of both the CR.42 and the Fiat G.50) had been painted at factory level in a distinctive bluish-light grey, protective varnish which also extended on to the front face of propeller blades. The rear face of the propeller blades were painted matt black for anti-glare purposes. The CR.42s invariably carried the white Savoy Cross on the rudder only with the House of Savoy's

coat of arms displayed oat the top of the vertical bar. Temporary yellow paint of German origin, which appears to be a lightish shade of yellow suggesting it could have been RLM 27 Gelb, rather than the more usual RLM 04 Gelb, was applied to the cowling and propeller spinner. 85•16 force-landed at Corton railway station, Suffolk, also on 11 November 1940, when its variable pitch propeller mechanism failed and Sergente Lazzari was subsequently taken prisoner.

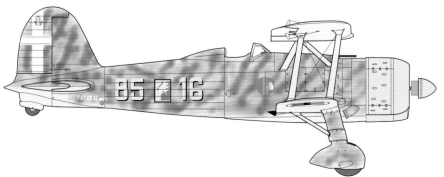

Not to any scale

20° Gruppo, flying Fiat G.50s, had also received new aircraft to operate on the Channel Front, in the usual factory finish. National triple fascio roundels with a white background were carried on under wing surfaces only; this being a trademark of all early CMASA-built machines up to the fourth production batch, as well as the white House of Savoy cross extending over the whole tail surface. Another feature of the type was a red solid disc painted on the mainwheel covers of these early production machines, whose meaning is still uncertain today. Again, just a few machines were fitted with radios, externally recognised by the aerial. New aircraft also had a propeller spinner, later to be adopted as standard by all G.50bis variants.

The CR.42s carried the national insignia both above the upper wing and below the lower one. These national wing roundels always had a white background with a black trim, except on Cant Z.1007s and Ca.133s, which carried a reversal of this practice, with black background and white trim, under the wings. It should also be noted that upper surface camouflage of the wings and tailplanes, (upper wing only on biplanes), along the leading edges, also extended a few inches on to the under surfaces. This was standard practice on the majority of the Italian aircraft of the period. Demarcation between the upper and under surface camouflage colours was normally 'soft'.

Propeller spinners of both fighter types were in a distinctive bluish shade of light grey protective varnish which was also extended on to the front face of the propeller blades. The rear face of the propeller blades were painted anti-glare matt black.

The BR.20 bombers were also quite new as all the aircraft of earlier production batches had been handed over to other units before 13° and 43° Stormo BT were posted to Belgium in order to standardise all squadrons on the latest BR.20M version. The Cant Z.1007s were also essentially brand new, as the unit had been re-equipped only a few weeks before being transferred to Belgium, but in spite of the effort to operate only 'modern' equipment, neither the fighters nor the bombers were really adequate to match modern RAF combat types.

No dedicated badge was carried by the newly formed 56° Stormo and consequently all the CR.42s continued to carry their traditional 18° Gruppo badge of three arrows on a fascio, whilst the G.50s displayed the badge of their previous parent unit, the black cat catching three mice of 51° Stormo. Additionally, all squadron leaders within 18° Gruppo carried a thin fuselage band of the appropriate Squadriglia colour, painted around the rear fuselage. The Gruppo CO's aircraft carried a broad white fuselage band. The 20° Gruppo leader's aircraft carried the numeral/letters '20GR' on fuselage sides in black.

The bombers of 13° Stormo carried colourful squadron insignia on their fuselages, each representing a different Walt Disney cartoon character, eg the 'Donald Duck' of 1a Squadriglia, 'Peg-leg Pete' for 3ª Squadriglia and 'Pluto' for 4ª Squadriglia. Even 172ª Squadriglia carried its own badge on its CANT's fuselages, depicting two dwarfs flying on the back of a goose. However, 43° Stormo's BR.20s had no time to paint any insignia due to their very recent establishment, and only featured standard black and red unit codes on their fuselages, occasionally repeating the individual number in white or red on nose.

Tactical markings

As soon as the Italian aircraft arrived in Belgium, they adopted 'tactical markings' like the Luftwaffe. All the CR.42s and G.50s received yellow cowlings and spinners and the bombers adopted a wide yellow band around their fuselages, painted just behind the wing trailing edge. These 'tactical markings' were painted in temporary yellow paint of German origin which was a lighter shade than any corresponding Italian colour, suggesting it could have been RLM 27 Gelb, rather than the more usual RLM 04 Gelb. The paint itself was easily removable and not very resistant to weathering, as was later confirmed when the British captured a CR.42, and were able to remove the yellow paint from its nose without having to re-touch the original underlying Italian camouflage paint. There are photos showing some G.50s and at least one CR.42 wearing the same broad yellow fuselage band as used on bombers. Its operational use on fighters was limited to a very few days, due to their late arrival in Belgium and that all yellow bands were removed from every Italian type, (except for the Ca.133s), by the end of October, whilst the yellow noses were retained on fighters during all their deployment in the Channel area.

Fiat BR.20M, MM.22267/242-3, 242ª Squadriglia, 99° Gruppo BT, 43° Stormo, Chievres, Belgium, November 1940.

The BR.20 bombers were also quite new as all the aircraft of earlier production batches had been handed over to other Regia Aeronautica units before 13° and 43° Stormo BT were posted to Belgium in order to standardise all CAI squadrons on the latest BR.20M version. All were painted in the factory finish of a medium sand, Giallo Mimetico 2 (Camouflage Yellow No 2), base with a fairly sparse, soft-edged mottle, of Verde Mimetico 3 and possibly the medium tan Bruno Mimetico (Camouflage Brown). Under surfaces were again either Grigio Mimetico ot one of the silver/aluminium alternatives. The upper surface camouflage colours extended a few inches on to the under surfaces of the wings and tailplanes – which was standard practice on the majority of the Italian aircraft of the period – and the demarcation between the upper and under surface camouflage colours was 'soft'. Triple fascio roundels, sometimes with a white background, sometime without, were carried above and below the wings, with the white House of Savoy cross on both faces of the rudders. 43° Stormo's bombers had no time to paint any colourful insignia due to their very recent unit establishment, and only featured the standard black Squadriglia codes and red individual aircraft number on their fuselages, occasionally repeating the individual number in white or red on nose.

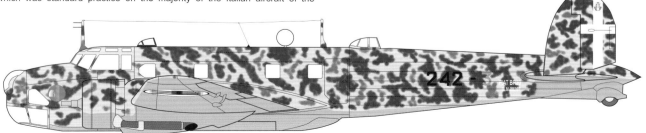

Not to any scale

It is a testament to the courage of the men of the Bomber, Reconnaissance and Coastal Command units that they continued to operate throughout 1940 with little respite and with little of the publicity accorded to Fighter Command. In his famous 20 August 1940 speech about 'The Few', praising Fighter Command, Churchill also made a point to mention Bomber Command's contribution, adding that bombers were even then striking back at Germany. This part of the speech is often overlooked. From July 1940 to the end of the year, Bomber Command lost nearly 330 aircraft and over 1,400 aircrew killed, missing or PoW. The Battle of Britain Chapel in Westminster Abbey lists in a Roll of Honour 718 Bomber Command crew members, and 280 from Coastal Command who were killed between 10 July and 31 October.

At the start of World War Two, Bomber Command was a relatively large force, but equipped with aircraft that had been designed more as tactical support medium bombers, without the range or ordnance capacity for anything more than a limited strategic offensive. Also the Command's lack of technology, specifically in navigational aids, did not allow it to accurately locate targets and thus bomb them successfully.

The UK's policy was to restrict bombing to purely military targets and infrastructure, such as ports and railways which were of military importance. As it was acknowledged that bombing Germany would cause civilian casualties, the British government resisted the deliberate bombing of civilian property, outside combat zones, as a military tactic. However, this policy was abandoned at the end of the Phoney War, after the Luftwaffe had bombed Rotterdam.

Bomber Command's other main problem was the lack of good enough aircraft. The main twin-engined workhorses at the start of the war were the Vickers Armstrong Wellington Mk.I, Handley-Page Hampden Mk.I, Armstrong Whitworth Whitley Mk.V and the smaller 'medium' bombers, the Bristol Blenheim Mk.IV and the single-engined Fairey Battle Mk.I.

After the initial disasters of the war, with Wellington bombers shot down in large numbers attacking Wilhelmshaven and the slaughter of the Battle and Blenheim squadrons sent to France, it became clear that Bomber Command would have to operate mainly at night to achieve any results without incurring very high losses, so from 15 May 1940, a night bomber campaign was launched against the German oil industry, communications, and forests/crops, mainly in the Ruhr area.

The problems of enemy defences were then replaced with the problems of simply finding the target. It was common in the first year of the war for bombers, relying on dead reckoning navigation, to miss entire cities. Surveys of bombing photographs and other sources published during August 1941 indicated that less than one bomb in ten fell within 5 miles (8km) of its intended target. One of the most urgent problems of the Command was thus to develop technical navigational aids to allow accurate bombing.

Bomber Command changed its targeting priority on 3 June 1940, to attack the German aircraft industry. On 4 July, the Air Ministry gave Bomber Command orders to attack ports and shipping. By September, the build up of invasion barges in the Channel ports had become a top priority target. On 7 September, the government issued a warning that an invasion could be expected within the next few days, and attacks were launched against the Channel ports and supply dumps. On 13 September, they carried out another large raid on the Channel ports, sinking some eighty large barges in the port of Ostend. Eighty-four barges were sunk in Dunkerque after another raid on 17 September and by 19 September, almost 200 barges had been sunk. The loss of these barges may well have contributed to Hitler's decision to postpone 'Operation Sealion' indefinitely.

As mentioned in Chapter 1, the Blenheim Mk.IV medium bomber units also raided German-occupied airfields throughout July to December 1940, both during daylight hours and at night. Although most of these raids were unproductive, there were some successes, although there were some missions which produced an almost 100% casualty rate amongst the Blenheims. As well as the bombing operations, Blenheim-equipped units carried out long-range strategic reconnaissance missions over Germany and German-occupied territories. In this role, the Blenheims once again proved to be too slow and vulnerable against Luftwaffe fighters, and they took devastating casualties.

Coastal Command generally directed its attention towards the protection of British shipping, and the destruction of enemy shipping, but as invasion became more likely, it also participated in the strikes on French harbours and airfields, laying mines, and mounting numerous reconnaissance missions over the enemy-held coast. In all, some 9,180 sorties were flown by British bombers from July to October 1940, and although this was much less than the 80,000 sorties flown by Fighter Command's fighters, bomber crews suffered about half the total number of casualties borne by their fighter colleagues. The bomber contribution was therefore much more dangerous on a loss-per-sortie comparison.

Bomber Command organisation

Like Fighter Command, Bomber Command was made up of a number of Groups, Nos 1, 2, 3, 4 and 5, however it was effectively reduced in size after the declaration of war. 1 Group, with its squadrons of Fairey Battles, left for France to form the Advanced Air Striking Force, to give the British Expeditionary Force some air striking power and to allow the Battle to operate against German targets, since it lacked the range to do so from British airfields.

No 2 Group consisted of medium bombers, mainly Blenheim Mk.IVs which, although operating both by day and night, remained part of Bomber Command until 1943, when it was removed to the control of Second Tactical Air Force, to form the light bomber component of that command. Nos 3, 4 and 5 Groups, operated the 'heavy' bombers – the Wellington, Hampden and Whitley.

Armstrong Whitworth Whitley Mk.V, N1428/GE-B, 58 Squadron, RAF Linton-on-Ouse, North Yorkshire, June 1940.

From the outbreak of war in September 1939, 4 Group's Whitleys had invariably operated by night, due in no small part to the type's relatively low performance. Finished in the standard Temperate Land Scheme of Dark Earth and Dark Green upper surfaces, to the A Scheme pattern, N1428 still had the low demarcation with just the under surfaces in Night. Red/White/Blue/Yellow fuselage roundels were carried, no doubt having been progressively updated over the previous months, with no underwing roundels as befits its nocturnal role. Note the Red/White/Blue fin stripes extending the full height of the fin.

Armstrong Whitworth Whitley Mk.V, P4938/KN-C, 77 Squadron, RAF Linton-on-Ouse, North Yorkshire, October 1940.

By the late summer/early autumn of 1940, most Whitleys had had their Night under surfaces extended up the fuselage sides, including the fins/rudders, often in the sooty Special Night RDM2 paint, and invariably terminating in an undulating or scalloped demarcation line. Although serial numbers were promulgated to be in Red, Medium Sea Grey was a readily available alternative as there would have been a plentiful supply of the colour in the squadron's stores, as it was also used for the code letters. P4938 is finished in the standard Temperate Land Scheme of Dark Earth and Dark Green upper surfaces, to the A Scheme pattern. Note the 'standard' 24 x 27 inch fin flash.

Armstrong Whitworth Whitley Mk.V, P5005/ DY-N, 102 Squadron, RAF Linton-on-Ouse, North Yorkshire, November 1940.

Pilot: Pilot Officer Leonard Cheshire, DSO

Destined to become one of the country's best known wartime personalities, and future VC winner, Leonard Cheshire flew many operations in P5005 throughout the autumn and winter of 1940/41. Finished in the standard Temperate Land Scheme of Dark Earth and Dark Green upper surfaces, to the B Scheme pattern, again the under surface colour which would have probably been the sooty Special Night RDM2 has been extended up the fuselage sides, terminating high up in an undulating demarcation, and including the fins/rudders. Note the 'standard' 24 x 27 inch fin flash and the positioning of the individual aircraft letter to clear the fuselage entry door.

Handley Page Hampden Mk.I, L4192/ZN-K, 106 Squadron, RAF Finningley, Yorkshire, April 1940.

Like the Whitley, in the early part of the war Hampdens carried the upper surface Temperate Land Scheme of Dark Earth and Dark Green low down on the fuselage sides. Under surfaces would have been Night during this period. Note that L4192 features Red/White/Blue roundels on the fuselage sides and, despite being on night operations, Red/White/Blue roundels under the wings. No fin markings were carried

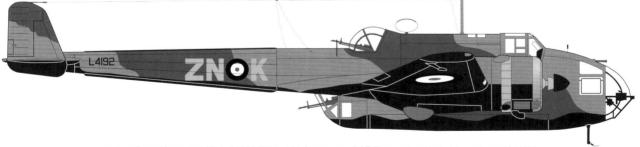

Handley Page Hampden Mk.I, P1228/ZN-L, 106 Squadron, RAF Finningley, Yorkshire, winter 1940/41.

Finished in the standard Temperate Land Scheme of Dark Earth and Dark Green to the A Scheme pattern, the upper/under surface demarcation on this machine also ran midway along the fuselage but this time in a scalloped demarcation. Note how the white of the fuselage roundel and the fin marking have been toned-down with a wash of black. Under surfaces were probably the Special Night RDM2 finish.

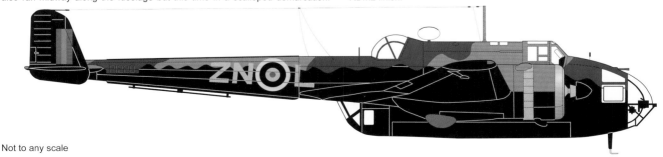

Not to any scale

To some extent, Bomber Command was not 'properly at war' during the first few months of hostilities either. Although it flew many operational missions, and lost aircraft, it did virtually no damage to the enemy. Most of the missions either failed to find their targets, or were propaganda leaflet dropping missions, (the first night flights by RAF bombers over the German homeland were to drop propaganda leaflets at night). The attack in the west on 10 May 1940 changed everything.

The Fairey Battle squadrons of the Advanced Air Striking Force were badly hit by German strikes on their airfields at the opening of the invasion of France. They also proved to be horrendously vulnerable to enemy fighters and ground fire. Many times, Battles would set out to attack, and be almost wiped out in the process. The survivors however, were returned to Bomber Command control after the evacuation of France.

Following the attack on Rotterdam, RAF Bomber Command was authorised to attack German targets east of the Rhine and the Air Ministry authorised Air Marshal Charles Portal to attack targets in the Ruhr, including oil plants and other civilian industrial targets which aided the German war effort. The first attack took place on the night of 15/16 May, with ninety-six bombers setting off to attack targets east of the Rhine, seventy-eight of which were against oil targets. Of these, only twenty-four claimed to have found their targets – but Bomber Command's strategic bombing campaign on Germany had thus begun.

With the collapse of France, invasion seemed a clear and present danger. As its part in the Battle of Britain, Bomber Command was assigned to pound the invasion barges and fleets assembling in the Channel ports. This was much less high profile than the battles of the Spitfires and Hurricanes of RAF Fighter Command, but was still vital and dangerous work.

RAF Bomber Command Night bombers

As mentioned in Chapter 2, camouflage scheme drawings were prepared for Twin Engine Monoplanes - Heavy Bombers; Twin Engine Monoplanes - Medium Bombers; and Single Engine Monoplanes - Medium Bombers. These were illustrated in two disruptive camouflage patterns to be applied to the upper surfaces known as the 'A' and 'B' Schemes, which were the mirror image of each other and were to be applied to alternate aircraft on the production line. (see pp18 and 19)

Initially the demarcation line between the Dark Earth and Dark Green Temperate Land Scheme on the upper surfaces and the Night on the under surfaces followed a line at a tangent of 60 degrees to the horizontal low down on the fuselage side to what would later become known as No 1 Pattern.

Markings

The markings to be carried by RAF Bomber Command aircraft were laid down by AMO A.154/39. Red/Blue roundels were to be located on both sides of the fuselage and on the upper surfaces of the wing tips with Red/White/Blue roundels on the lower surface of the wing tips.

The code letters were to be located either forward or aft of the national markings on both sides of the fuselage and were to be painted in Medium Sea Grey in characters 48 inches high.

Smaller letters were only to be used when the space available made such a course unavoidable. As there was no set style for these markings considerable variation could be seen in how they were actually applied to the aircraft. Some variation could also be seen in the exact shade of grey paint used to apply them. Squadron badges were to be removable at short notice without leaving any trace.

The aircraft's serial number was applied by the manufacturer on the production line but as there was no standard set of characters for this marking, the aircraft manufacturers went their own way. In peacetime, the marking was applied to the rear of the fuselage and to the under surfaces of the mainplanes, although by the outbreak of war the underwing serials were removed from all types except training aircraft. The fuselage serial number was to be 8 inches high, with individual characters not more than 5 inches wide and made up of brush strokes of 1 inch in width. This was to be marked on the fuselage of camouflaged aircraft in Night.

The onset of war however quickly revealed problems. In October 1939, an eyewitness reported seeing some Wellingtons of Nos 149 and 99 Squadrons at Newmarket Heath carrying Red, White and Blue roundels on the fuselage. Whether this was a locally devised and or trial modification to the national markings is unknown, but would appear to have been the result of difficulty being experienced in the positive identification of RAF aircraft as being friendly.

Following the incident over the North Sea later in the month in which a Coastal Command aircraft only narrowly escaped destruction at the hands of an RAF Fighter, (see Chapter 2), Coastal Command undertook some trials to enhance the identification markings applied to RAF aircraft. As a result of Coastal Command's findings, the practice of applying Red, White and Blue roundels to the sides of the fuselage of all RAF aircraft was officially sanctioned by the issue of AMO A.520 which was issued on 7 December 1939.

From day to night

By this time Bomber Command had gone to war in a series of sorties designed to seek out and destroy elements of the German battle fleet in the North Sea, but following the infamous Battle of Heligoland Bight on 18 December 1939, which saw Bomber Command's hopes of daylight bombing quite literally shot down in flames after losing twelve Wellington Mk.Is on an armed reconnaissance of the Wilhelmshaven area, plus three more in forced landings on their return, the Air Staff were forced to acknowledge that even with the much vaunted power turrets, RAF bombers of the day could not survive in daylight over Germany. This event set in motion the conversion of Bomber Command from a predominantly day flying, to a predominantly night flying, force. During most of 1940, Bomber Command found itself diverted from what it considered true strategic bombing by the extenuating circumstances of the war situation. During this period several changes were made to the camouflage and markings applied to the RAF's bomber force.

National markings changes

The first of these changes concerned the national markings. Coastal Command continued to conduct trials to improve the

Handley Page Hampden Mk.I, P4403/EA-M, 49 Squadron, RAF Scampton, Lincolnshire, August 1940.

Finished in the standard Temperate Land Scheme of Dark Earth and Dark Green upper surfaces, to the B Scheme pattern, the under surfaces of P4403 have been extended up the fuselage sides, in either Night or the sooty Special Night RDM2, terminating high up in a relatively straight demarcation. The fins/rudders remained camouflaged. Note the fin marking, applied to both sides of both fins, taking up the whole fin area. Flight Lieutenant Roderick Learoyd was the pilot of this machine and was awarded the VC for his actions on 12 August 1940, during an attack on the Dortmund-Ems canal.

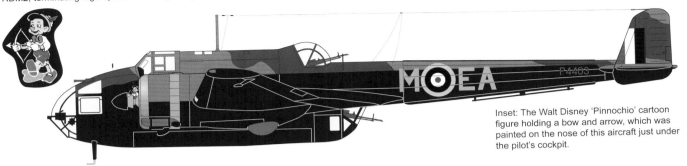

Inset: The Walt Disney 'Pinnochio' cartoon figure holding a bow and arrow, which was painted on the nose of this aircraft just under the pilot's cockpit.

Handley Page Hampden Mk.I, P1355/OL-W, 83 Squadron, RAF Scampton, Lincolnshire, September 1940.

Finished in the standard Temperate Land Scheme of Dark Earth and Dark Green to the B Scheme pattern, despite the date, the camouflaged upper surfaces of P1355 still extend well down the fuselage sides, terminating in an undulating demarcation. The fins/rudders also remained camouflaged, with the fin marking, applied to both sides of both fins, taking up the whole fin area. Under surfaces would probably have been in the Special Night RDM2 finish. Sergeant John Hannah was the Wireless Operator/Air Gunner aboard this machine, and was awarded the VC for his actions on the night of 15/16 September 1940.

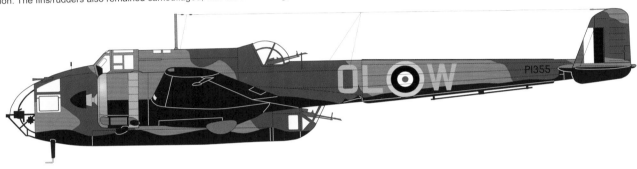

Handley Page Hampden Mk.I, L4070/OL-C, 83 Squadron, RAF Scampton, Lincolnshire, September 1940.

Serving on the same squadron as the previous illustration, at around the same time, L4070 was also finished in the standard Temperate Land Scheme of Dark Earth and Dark Green upper surfaces, to the B Scheme pattern, applied well down the fuselage side and terminating in an undulating demarcation. Under surfaces were either Night or more likely the Special Night RDM2 finish. The fins/ rudders remained camouflaged, with the fin marking, applied to both sides of both fins, taking up the whole fin area. This aircraft was flown by Flight Lieutenant Guy Gibson, DFC, later to earn immortality as the first CO, 617 Squadron of the 'Dam Buster' raid fame.

Inset: Flight Lieutenant Gibson's personal emblem, the name 'Admiral Foo Bang' above a shield surrounding a vertical bomb, which was carried on the aircraft's nose below the pilot's cockpit area.

Handley Page Hampden Mk.I, AE257/KM-X, 44 Squadron, RAF Scampton, Lincolnshire, late 1940/early 1941.

Finished in the standard Temperate Land Scheme of Dark Earth and Dark Green to the B Scheme pattern, the upper/under surface demarcation on this machine ran midway along the fuselage until it met the roundel, then ran higher all the way to the tail. Note how the Dark Earth/Dark Green curves down towards the nose. Under surfaces would have probably been in the Special Night RDM2 finish. The individual aircraft letter is approximately half the height of the squadron codes and the fins/rudders are all Night with a 24 x 27 inch fin marking. Serial number is in Medium Sea Grey.

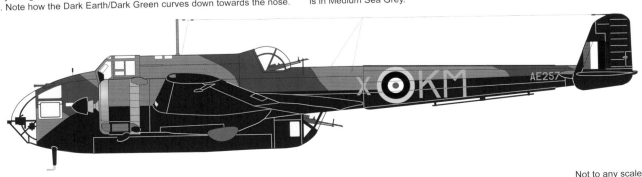

Not to any scale

recognition markings carried by British aircraft as described in Chapter 2. As a result, on 1 May 1940 the Air Ministry sent signal X485 to all Commands at Home and Overseas amending the markings carried by RAF aircraft. Fuselage roundels were now to be encircled with an outer Yellow band the same width of the existing Blue band and vertical stripes of Red, White and Blue, each of the same width, were to be painted on the fins.

Because no detail on the size of the new marking was given, many different interpretations were made by the units themselves as they tried to comply with the new instructions. Roundels were modified with Yellow bands of many different widths to suit the size of the aircraft they were being applied to, whilst the fin flashes were also applied in many different variations.

Aircraft with slim fuselages such as the Hampden were to have the whole roundel reduced in size in order to accommodate the new Yellow outer ring and prevent it encroaching on the upper or under surfaces of the fuselage. As a temporary measure in order to obviate excessive work on operational aircraft, the existing roundels could be outlined with a narrower band of Yellow where the space available made the application of a Yellow band the same width as the Blue band impractical. These instructions meant that Bomber Command Wellingtons, Whitleys and Hampdens could be seen with a wide variety of styles of both fuselage roundel and fin marking throughout the mid to latter part of 1940.

Special Night

The second change was in the type and extent of the black finish applied to the under surfaces. Development of Special Night began before the outbreak of war. The work was carried out by Professor T R Merton, in conjunction with the RAE at Farnborough, and following experiments with different types of materials, by mid-August, trials of the new finish had just started when war broke out. The trials were swiftly completed and as a result, on 25 September 1939, the Air Ministry wrote to the RAE to ask them to forward as quickly as possible 1000 gallons of Special Night to 3 MU for use by Bomber Command who were requesting that this material be adopted forthwith, as a permanent finish rather than the temporary finish originally envisaged.

The initial issue of the new Special Night finish was for the Whitleys of 4 Group as these were the only dedicated night bombers in Bomber Command at this time. It is not clear at what point Special Night was also adopted for the other bombers such as the Wellington and the Hampden but it is thought to have taken place during the first six months of 1940.

However, both Bomber Command and the aircraft manufacturers experienced difficulties in applying Special Night. Bomber Command found that following application on top of an existing finish, the Special Night would crack and peel away after only a very short time. The aircraft manufacturers found that upon application to the aircraft, the Special Night attacked the Primer and both finishes peeled off in big flakes.

Following an RAE investigation of the problems being encountered with Special Night it was decided that the answer lay in revising the chemical formula by using a more volatile chemical base. By the end of September 1940, the formula

had been revised and the nomenclature of the specification for Special Night was changed from RDM2 to RDM2A. Whilst this appears to have made the paint more likely to adhere to the aircraft initially, irrespective of who applied it, Special Night RDM2A quickly gained a reputation for being easily removed from the aircraft by the simple act of touching it by hand!

Whilst the formula of Special Night was being revised during the summer of 1940, the practice of applying underwing roundels to Bombers which operated at night was abandoned. On 23 July 1940 a conference was held at the Air Ministry to consider aircraft colouring and markings. Bomber Command's representative explained that Whitleys, which had the lowest casualty rate of all bombers which were employed on the same duties, were finished in matt black without roundels and therefore asked that the removal of roundels form the under surfaces of all other aircraft might be considered. It was agreed that roundels would not be carried on the under surfaces of aircraft with a matt black finish, except where the aircraft were non-operational and tasked with Searchlight Co-operation duties, from the middle of August 1940.

No sooner had this decision been made, then in early September 1940, Bomber Command also decided to extend the matt black finish applied to the under surfaces up the sides of the fuselage and over the fin to what would later become known as Pattern No 2. No firm instructions appear to have been given as to exactly how this was to be done and once again this resulted in many minor variations on those aircraft which were repainted in service.

A common factor to many bombers which subsequently had the Special Night extended up the fuselage sides on the production line was the use of a wavy or scalloped demarcation line between the upper and under surface colours. As far as is known, such a line never formed part of an official requirement, but appears to have been an interpretation of the instruction that there should be no definite line of demarcation, an instruction which was originally intended to mean a soft sprayed edge.

As no directions appear to have been given as to how the fuselage serial number, which up until this time had been applied in Night, was to be applied following the instruction to extend the matt black finish up the fuselage sides, each squadron came up with its own solution. Some squadrons painted around it, leaving the original Night serial number on a rectangular background of Dark Green or Dark Earth, whilst others reapplied the markings over the Special Night finish using either Medium Sea Grey or Red. Finally, on or about 18 October 1940, Bomber Command instructed that the fuselage serial number should be applied with Red paint.

Coastal Command

Prior to the formation of Coastal Command in 1936, the role of the command was carried out by the Coastal Area organisation. All the other arms of the RAF had priority and Coastal Command had to make do with mostly obsolete aircraft types. At the outbreak of war, of the 224 aircraft nominally on strength, only twenty-four were 'modern types' suitable for all the Command's roles; these were twelve Lockheed Hudson Mk.Is and twelve Short Sunderland Mk.Is. The remaining 200 were mostly Avro Ansons and Bristol Blenheims.

Vickers Wellington Mk.Ic, R3206/OJ-M, 149 Squadron, RAF Mildenhall, Suffolk, August 1940.

Finished in the standard Temperate Land Scheme of Dark Earth and Dark Green to the A Scheme pattern, the upper/under surface demarcation on this machine ran along the top of the fuselage windows then curved up in an undulating line to the leading edge of the fin. Under surfaces would have been the Special Night RDM2 finish. Note how the White of the fuselage roundel has been toned-down by

a wash of black and the small size of the fin marking. The serial number appears to be Medium Sea Grey on the reference photo used for this illustration.

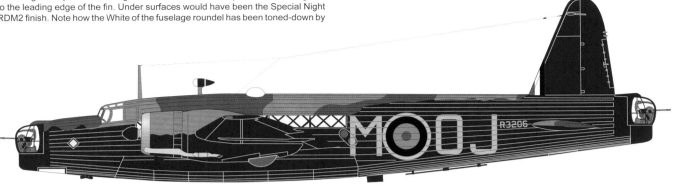

Vickers Wellington Mk.Ic, R1042/JN-A, 150 Squadron, RAF Newton, Nottinghamshire, autumn 1940.

Finished in the standard Temperate Land Scheme of Dark Earth and Dark Green to the A Scheme pattern, the upper/under surface demarcation on this machine also ran along the top of the fuselage windows then continued in an undulating line before curving down to the leading edge of the tailplane and then curving back up from the trailing edge of the tailplane to the rear turret. Note ratios of the fuselage roundel colours with a small Red centre and the 24 x 27 inch fin

marking positioned against the rudder hinge line. Under surfaces were probably the Special Night RDM2 finish.

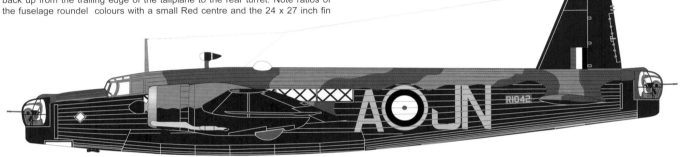

Vickers Wellington Mk.Ic, T2501/LN-F, 99 Squadron, RAF Waterbeach, Cambridgeshire, November 1940.

Finished in the standard Temperate Land Scheme of Dark Earth and Dark Green to the B Scheme pattern, in this instance the upper/under surface demarcation sweeps up from the mainplanes to a position high on the fuselage and runs in an undulating line to the leading edge of the fin. Under surfaces and fuselage sides were almost certainly the Special Night RDM2 finish. Note the diameter of the

fuselage roundel with the extra wide Yellow outer ring, and the 24 x 27 inch fin marking positioned against the rudder hinge line.

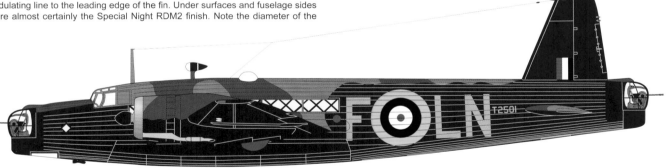

Vickers Wellington Mk.Ic, N2778/BU-R, 214 Squadron, RAF Stradishall, Suffolk, November 1940.

Finished in the standard Temperate Land Scheme of Dark Earth and Dark Green to the A Scheme pattern, the upper/under surface demarcation follows a

scalloped line high up on the fuselage and terminates at the leading edge of the fin. Under surfaces and fuselage sides were almost certainly the Special Night RDM2 finish. Note the 24 x 27 inch fin marking positioned against the rudder hinge line.

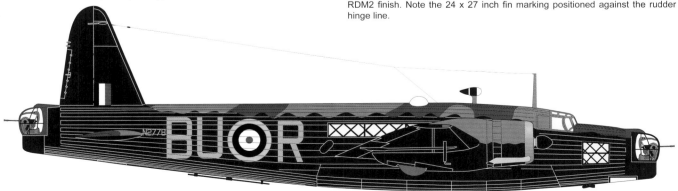

Not to any scale

At the start of the war, Coastal Command had four Groups under its control, Nos 15, 16, 17 and 18, one of which, 17 Group, was dedicated to training aircrews. The other three had responsibility for different geographical sectors of the British coastline.

No 16 Group was responsible for the eastern half of the English Channel and the southern half of the North Sea, and 18 Group covered the remainder of the North Sea and areas to the north and west of Scotland, north of a line running north west from the Mull of Kintyre. 15 Group covered the remainder of the coast of the United Kingdom, principally the South West approaches.

Further important additions were made to Coastal Command's remit when squadrons based outside the UK were also placed under its control. In November 1940, 200 Group at Gibraltar was transferred to the control of Coastal Command, from that of RAF Mediterranean Command.

In 1940, Coastal Command's primary offensive weapon was the small 100lb anti-submarine (A/S) bomb which required perfect accuracy, and did not have enough power to damage a U-boat. Another problem with this weapon was its tendency to skip off the water and in one case hit and destroy the aircraft that dropped it!

Early operations were mostly ineffective, often ending with the U-boat the victor – on the rare occasions they could be found by the aircraft. Even upon finding a submarine the chances of scoring a hit were still low because of the flawed tactics employed. Aircraft were required to get on the stern of the U-boat and make a longitudinal 'along the track' attack. It took too long for the aircraft to get into position and gave the U-boat ample time to quickly dive and change course.

There were also 250lb and 500lb anti-submarine bombs; both still required high accuracy and could only be effectively carried by the Sunderland flying boat.

In 1940, experiments were begun by the Admiralty on a 250lb depth charge, modified to be dropped from the air, for use by the Fleet Air Arm and later Coastal Command. After a successful series of tests, the anti-submarine bomb was replaced with the depth charge in 1941 but due to shortages, A/S bombs were not completely removed from service until 1942.

Coastal Command colours

Previous Chapters have described the ongoing development of the camouflage schemes and markings applied to landplane Coastal Command aircraft, whose squadrons in the summer of 1940, were essentially equipped with Avro Ansons, Bristol Blenheims, Bristol Beauforts, and the first of the Lockheed Hudsons and Bristol Beaufighters – all of which were to be camouflaged on the upper surfaces in the Temperate Land Scheme of Dark Green and Dark Earth.

Under surfaces were to be either Night (black) or Aluminium (silver), including all the Blenheim IVf fighter aircraft in Coastal Command, which had to conform to the standard General Reconnaissance schemes and markings, necessitating the fighter Blenheims having their original Night and White under surfaces replaced with an Aluminium finish.

Coastal Command Fighters

However, whilst the fighter squadrons of Fighter Command were clear on their instructions with regard to repainting their aircraft's under surfaces, the fighter squadrons in Coastal Command might not have been so clear.

Following the original Air Ministry Signal X915 of 6 June, the long range Blenheim fighter squadrons in Coastal Command had thought that the new under surface colouring and marking instructions applied to them as well. HQ Coastal Command however had a different view. On 7 June, Signal ASD/373 was sent to all concerned notifying them that all Blenheim aircraft in Coastal Command would conform to the standard General Reconnaissance markings. This necessitated fighter Blenheims having their Night and White under surfaces removed and replaced by an Aluminium (silver) finish.

As on every Fighter Command squadron, such a change necessitated a great deal of work by the ground crews. Coastal Command seem to have negated this slightly by having a travelling band of aircraft finishers who travelled from station to station carrying out the required changes as they went. For instance, on 18 June, HQ 43 Group wrote a letter to HQ Coastal Command, to inform them that at Bircham Newton, 43 Group had approximately eighteen Blenheim fighters which needed to be camouflaged Aluminium (silver) on their under surfaces. It was requested that the services of a similar party to one which had visited West Raynham be made available to respray them.

Sky for all

Coastal Command retained the Aluminium under surface finish until the end of 1940, when 'Sky' under surfaces for all the Blenheim, Beaufort, Hudson and Beaufighter aircraft was introduced. Special Night could also be applied to the under surfaces of these aircraft at the discretion of the Command or to meet specific operational requirements.

Initially, many of the Flying Boats in Coastal Command such as the Sunderland, Saro Lerwick and Supermarine Stranraer, were also camouflaged in the Temperate Land Scheme, but during the early summer were recamouflaged on the upper surfaces in the Temperate Sea Scheme of Extra Dark Sea Grey and Dark Slate Grey with under surfaces either left bare of any colouring, being protected by a coat of clear Lanolin to prevent corrosion, or Aluminium or Night under surfaces.

Coastal Command's operational role required its aircraft to be flown by day and by night which led to these requirements for different under surface colours. A Command decision was made in mid-1940 in that General Reconnaissance and Torpedo Bomber landplane squadrons would have up to 25 percent of their aircraft finished in Aluminium (and later Sky) and the rest in Night (later Special Night); Long Range Fighter squadrons would have all their aircraft under surfaces finished in Aluminium (and later Sky).

National markings consisted of the usual Red and Blue roundels on the upper surface of the mainplanes, Red, White, Blue and Yellow roundels on the fuselage and Red, White and Blue fin marking. The aircraft serial number was applied to the rear fuselage in Night and the squadron and individual aircraft letters were applied to the fuselage in Medium Sea Grey.

Bristol Blenheim Mk.IV, L8852/LS-Q, 15 Squadron, RAF Wyton, Huntingdonshire, May 1940.

Following its introduction on an experimental batch of Blenheims at the beginning of 1940, in the form of the glossy Sky-coloured Camotint, or possibly the BS 381 Eau-de-Nil shade, 'Sky' in one of its many variations, was rapidly becoming established on Bomber Command's day flying Blenheim force by the time of the Battle of France. Judging by the way the under surface colour curves up to the leading edge of the tailplane on L8852, this would indicate an in-service repaint rather than application at the manufacturers on the production line. Upper surfaces were finished in the standard Temperate Land Scheme of Dark Earth and Dark Green to the B Scheme pattern. By the time this aircraft went missing on 18 May 1940, it might have acquired a Yellow surround to its fuselage roundel and Red/White/Blue fin stripes. Underwing roundels had been applied.

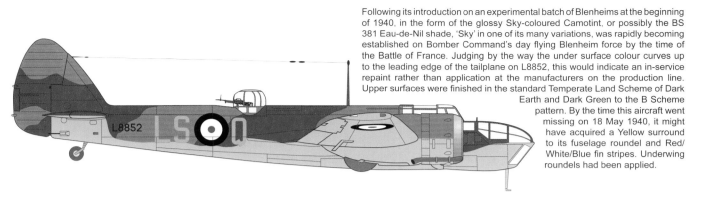

Bristol Blenheim Mk.IV, L8743/YH-P, 21 Squadron, RAF Bodney, Norfolk, June 1940.

Standard Day Bomber scheme of Dark Earth and Dark Green upper surfaces, to the A Scheme pattern, with one of the variations of 'Sky' on the under surfaces. Note the difference in the upper/under surface colour demarcation to the previous Blenheim profile above, still indicating the possibility of an in-service applied paint finish. The fuselage roundel has a Yellow surround of the correct ratio but the fin marking takes up the whole fin area. This aircraft force-landed near Rouen on 11 June 1940.

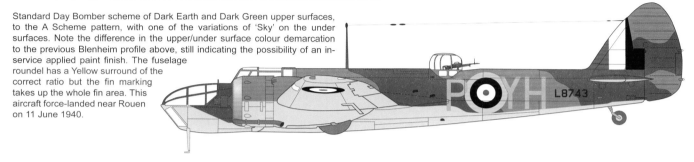

Bristol Blenheim Mk.IV, P4919/OM-J, 107 Squadron, RAF Wattisham, Suffolk, June 1940.

Standard Day Bomber scheme of Dark Earth and Dark Green upper surfaces, to the B Scheme pattern, with one of the variations of 'Sky' on the under surfaces. Again note the difference in the upper/under surface colour demarcation, in this instance possibly indicating a factory applied paint finish as the camouflage starts from under the trailing edge of the wing and continues in a straight line to the rudder hinge. Note the overthick Yellow outer ring to the fuselage roundel, the narrower fin stripes extending the full height of the fin and lack of underwing roundels.

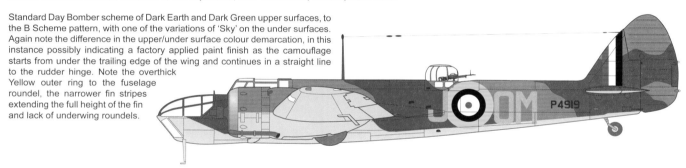

Bristol Blenheim Mk.IV, R3741/VE-A, 110 Squadron, RAF Wyton, Huntingdonshire, July 1940.

This was a Rootes-built machine and was fitted with twin rearward firing 'scarer' guns, encased in a metal fairing, under the nose of the aircraft. Finished in the standard Day Bomber scheme of Dark Earth and Dark Green upper surfaces, to the B Scheme pattern, it is thought that Rootes may have had quantities of a colour very similar to the correct shade of Sky, albeit not to Type S standard, which it used on its Blenheims. Note the slightly smaller white individual aircraft letter 'A', a feature seen on 110 Squadron aircraft at this time, and the even narrower fin stripes extending the full height of the fin.

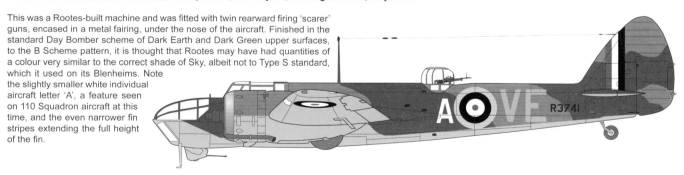

Bristol Blenheim Mk.IV, R3744/BL-K, 40 Squadron, RAF Wyton, Huntingdonshire, July/August 1940.

R3744 was another Rootes-built machine, this time fitted with a single rearward firing 'scarer' gun in a perspex blister. Upper surfaces were the standard scheme of Dark Earth and Dark Green upper surfaces, in this instance to the A Scheme pattern, with the Rootes' version of 'Sky' on the under surfaces. Note the individual aircraft letter 'K', outlined in white, another 'squadron feature' seen on most 40 Squadron's aircraft during this period. R3744 crashed on take-off from Horsham St Faith on 16 December 1940.

Not to any scale

Bristol Blenheim Mk.IV, R3821/UX-N, 82 Squadron, RAF Bodney, Norfolk, August 1940.

Yet another variation in the application of the upper/under surface demarcation saw the Dark Earth and Dark Green upper surface colours run all the way along the fuselage under the mainplane root as on R3821 illustrated here, in the B Scheme pattern. This was another Rootes-built machine with their version of 'Sky' on the under surfaces which was a pale duck egg green shade and slightly glossy. R3821 was reported missing on 13 August 1940.

Bristol Blenheim Mk.IV, R3891/RT-W, 114 Squadron, RAF Oulton, Norfolk, September 1940.

Duck egg blue shades of 'Sky', possibly BS 381 Sky Blue, were also recorded on Day Bomber Blenheims, such as R3891 illustrated here. Standard Temperate Land Scheme Dark Earth and Dark Green upper surface colours, to the A Scheme pattern, and with upper/under fuselage demarcations indicating factory application of the under surface colour. Again no underwing roundels have been applied but the fin marking is the 'official' 24 x 27 inch style.

Bristol Blenheim Mk.If, L1336/WR-E, 248 Squadron, RAF North Coates, Lincolnshire, February 1940.

Coastal Command's Blenheim fighters followed standard Fighter Command camouflage practice until the introduction of Sky under surfaces in June/July 1940. L1336 features typical standard Temperate Land Scheme Dark Earth and Dark Green upper surfaces to the A Scheme, with fighter-style Night and White under surfaces divided centrally down the fuselage centreline. At the beginning of 1940, Yellow outer rings to the fuselage roundel and fin stripes had not been introduced, but the serial number on the rudder had been removed.

Bristol Blenheim Mk.IV, N3537/TR-J, 59 Squadron, RAF Thorney Island, Hampshire, October 1940.

The under surface colouring of all Coastal Command's bomber and fighter Blenheims was ordered to conform to the colours applied to standard General Reconnaissance aircraft and be finished in either Aluminium, or Night as illustrated on N3537. Upper surfaces were the standard Temperate Land Scheme of Dark Earth and Dark Green to the A Scheme pattern in N3537's case. Note the wide fin stripes extending the full height of the fin. N3537 hit some trees overshooting Thorney Island on 1 December 1940.

Bristol Blenheim Mk.IVf, P6957/LA-R, 235 Squadron, RAF Bircham Newton, Norfolk, June 1940.

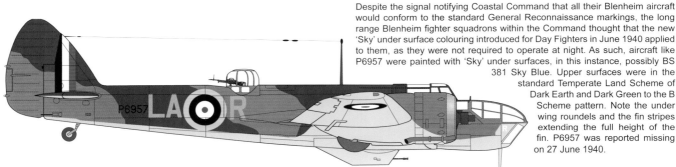

Despite the signal notifying Coastal Command that all their Blenheim aircraft would conform to the standard General Reconnaissance markings, the long range Blenheim fighter squadrons within the Command thought that the new 'Sky' under surface colouring introduced for Day Fighters in June 1940 applied to them, as they were not required to operate at night. As such, aircraft like P6957 were painted with 'Sky' under surfaces, in this instance, possibly BS 381 Sky Blue. Upper surfaces were in the standard Temperate Land Scheme of Dark Earth and Dark Green to the B Scheme pattern. Note the under wing roundels and the fin stripes extending the full height of the fin. P6957 was reported missing on 27 June 1940.

Not to any scale

Lockheed Hudson Mk.I, P5120/VX-C, 206 Squadron, RAF Bircham Newton, Norfolk, May/June 1940.

Coastal Command retained Aluminium under surfaces on its bomber aircraft, such as the Hudson, until the end of 1940. Special Night could also be applied to the under surfaces of these aircraft at the discretion of the Command or to meet specific operational requirements. Being an American manufactured aeroplane, P5120 was finished in shades of brown and green mixed in the USA to match the Air Ministry standards for Dark Earth and Dark Green on the upper surfaces,

in this instance to the A Scheme pattern, with Aluminium under surfaces. Red/White/Blue roundels were carried above the wings, as well as below, which were introduced on all General Reconnaissance aircraft types in lieu of the standard Red/Blue roundel in November 1939. P5120 crashed on landing at Bircham Newton on 20 June 1940.

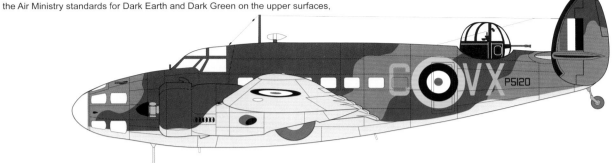

Lockheed Hudson Mk.I, N7266/ZS-D, 233 Squadron, RAF Sumburgh, Shetland Islands, June 1940.

N7266 was one of the Hudsons that had Special Night applied to its under surfaces. Upper surfaces were the American mix Dark Earth and Dark Green shades to the B Scheme pattern. On 21 June 1940, this machine was one of a formation of three aircraft ostensibly from 224 Squadron, (with 233's

N7266 being crewed by 224 personnel) that attacked the German battleship 'Scharnhorst' off Norway. The formation's leader, Squadron Leader D Feeny's aircraft, was shot down and this machine was severely damaged in a crash landing back at Sumburgh. It carried 48 inch diameter Red/White/Blue roundels above the wings which had been modified from the original Red/Blue ones in November 1939 and note how the fin stripes extend below the tailplane tips.

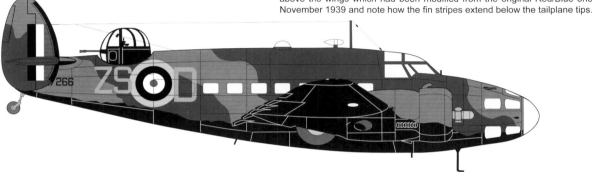

Lockheed Hudson Mk.I, T9277/QX-W, 224 Squadron, RAF Thornaby, North Yorkshire, August 1940.

Another Hudson with Aluminium under surfaces, this aircraft was reported missing on 9 December 1940. Upper surfaces were the American match for the

Air Ministry standards for Dark Earth and Dark Green, to the A Scheme pattern. Note again how the fin stripes extend below the tailplane tips, and in this instance all the way to the top of the fin. By this time Red/Blue roundels would have been carried above the wings.

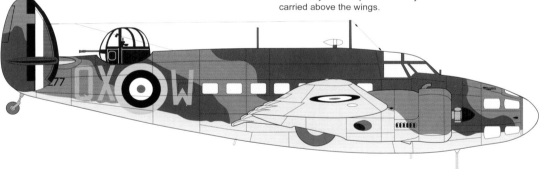

Lockheed Hudson Mk.I, P5117/ZS-S, 233 Squadron, RAF Leuchars, Fife, August 1940.

Finished in the American mixed Dark Earth and Dark Green shades on the upper surfaces, in this instance to the A Scheme pattern, the under surfaces were in the alternative Special Night finish. Note again how the fin stripes extend below the

tailplane tips, and also how the Medium Sea Grey code letters overlap the Yellow outer ring of the fuselage roundel, an indication that P5117 had Red/White/Blue fuselage roundels when they were applied and the Yellow outer had to be painted around them. This aircraft was abandoned in bad weather near Berwick on 5 October 1940. Red/Blue roundels would have been carried above the wings by this period.

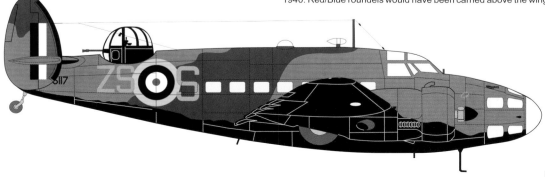

Not to any scale

Bristol Beaufort Mk.I, L4461/OA-U, 22 Squadron, RAF Thorney Island, Hampshire, June 1940.

As with the Hudsons, Coastal Command's Beauforts were required to have either Aluminium or Night under surfaces, but some still managed to be wrongly painted, as in L4461's case which is thought to have had a duck egg green/Eau-de-Nil shade of 'Sky' applied over its original Aluminium undersides in early June 1940. Upper surfaces were the standard Temperate Land Scheme of Dark Earth and Dark Green to the B Scheme pattern. Note the lack of a Yellow surround

to the fuselage roundel and lack of fin markings, presumably added before the month was out? Red/White/Blue roundels would have probably been carried above the wings. L4461 was eventually Struck Off Charge in February 1944.

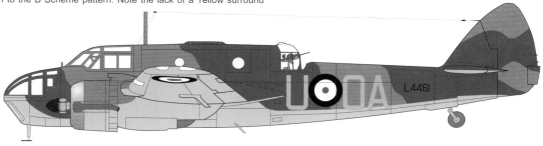

Bristol Beaufort Mk.I, L4448/OA-H, 22 Squadron, RAF Thorney Island, Hampshire, August 1940.

A correctly finished machine of the same squadron, illustrated as it looked circa August 1940 with standard Temperate Land Scheme of Dark Earth and Dark Green to the A Scheme pattern and Aluminium under surfaces. In this instance the Yellow outer ring has been added to the fuselage roundel but note how it

has been painted around the Medium Sea Grey code letters. A Red/White/Blue fin marking has also been added as well as under wing roundels, and Red/Blue roundels would have been carried above the wings. This particular machine was eventually sent to Australia as a Pattern Aircraft.

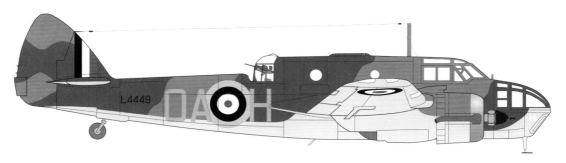

Bristol Beaufort Mk.I, L4491/AW-R, 42 Squadron, RAF Wick, Caithness, June 1940.

An example of a Beaufort with Special Night under surfaces, L4491 had standard Temperate Land Scheme Dark Earth and Dark Green upper surfaces to the B Scheme pattern with Special Night under surfaces. Again the Yellow outer ring had been added to the fuselage roundel by this period as well as fin stripes although Red/White/Blue roundels would still have been carried above the

wings. No under wing roundels were applied, presumably to comply with its 'night operations' scheme? Flown by Pilot Officer G Rooney, L4491 participated in an attack on the Scharnhorst off the Norwegian coast on 21 June 1940. No torpedoes were available at RAF Wick, so a dive bombing attack was carried out using two 500lb (230kg) bombs.

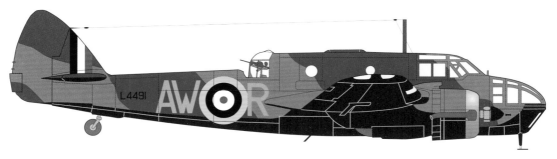

Bristol Beaufort Mk.I, L9965/AW-M, 42 Squadron, RAF Thorney Island, Hampshire, September 1940.

By September 1940 several Coastal Command 'bombers' could be seen with 'Sky' under surfaces and eventually Sky was introduced as the standard under surface colour on Blenheims, Hudsons and Beauforts, as well as the new Beaufighter which starting to enter Coastal Command service at the end of 1940. Upper surfaces initially remained in the Temperate Land Scheme

of Dark Earth and Dark Green, in L9965's case to the B Scheme pattern, with Red/Blue roundels above the wings. Note the name 'Mercury' in red on the nose, the lack of underwing roundels and the width of the fin stripes. L9965 went missing on 24 February, whilst still serving with 42 Squadron.

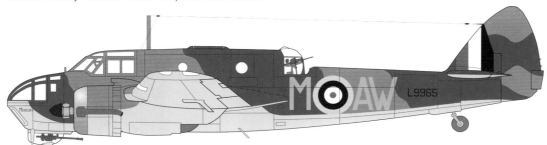

Not to any scale

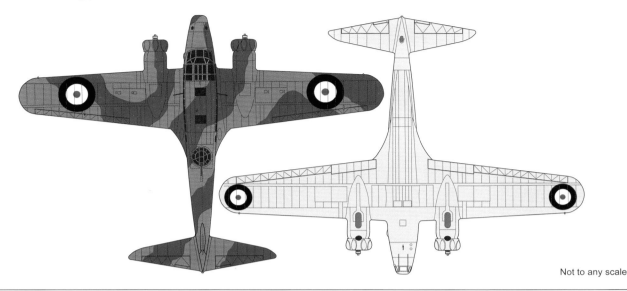

Upper and under surface plan views of a Coastal Command Avro Anson's camouflage scheme, to the B Scheme pattern. Note the Red/White/Blue roundels above the wings, as well as below, introduced on all General

Reconnaissance aircraft types in lieu of the standard Red/Blue roundel in November 1939. Red/Blue upper wing roundels were reintroduced on Coastal Command aircraft on 25 July 1940.

Not to any scale

Avro Anson Mk.I, K6189/VX-R, 206 Squadron, RAF Bircham Newton, Norfolk, May/June 1940.

Although the Anson was getting somewhat 'long in the tooth' for operational work by the start of 1940, several squadrons still operated the type on convoy patrol sorties well in to the summer. K6189 would have probably originally been delivered in overall Aluminium, but would have been camouflaged 'in-service' prior to the outbreak of war. Upper surfaces were the Temperate Land Scheme of

Dark Earth and Dark Green, in the A Scheme pattern, with the original Aluminium finish on the under surfaces. It would have carried Red/White/Blue upper wing roundels. Note the angle of the fin stripes which matched the angle of the rudder hinge.

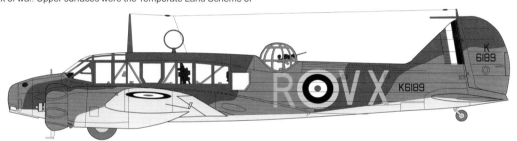

Avro Anson Mk.I, N9732/MK-V, 500 Squadron, RAF Detling, Kent, June 1940.

Temperate Land Scheme of Dark Earth and Dark Green, in the B Scheme pattern, with Red/White/Blue upper wing roundels and the original Aluminium finish on the under surfaces, which also carried Red/White/Blue roundels. On 1

June 1940 this machine was attacked by nine Bf 109Es whilst on convoy patrol and shot down two of them. The pilot, Pilot Officer P Peters was awarded the DFC, whilst the other four crewman received DFMs.

Avro Anson Mk.I, K6285/MW-F, 217 Squadron, RAF St Eval, Cornwall, July 1940.

Temperate Land Scheme of Dark Earth and Dark Green, in the B Scheme pattern, with Red/White/Blue upper wing roundels and the original Aluminium finish on the under surfaces. Although the yellow outer ring to the fuselage

roundel has been added, the fin stripes have yet to be applied. K6285 crashed in a forced landing on 9 August 1940 and was damaged beyond economical repair.

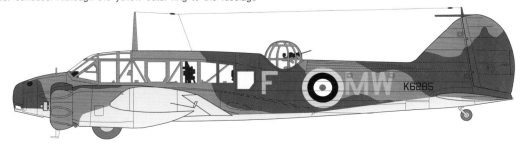

Not to any scale

▲ The first production Blackburn Roc, L3057 which served at the A&AEE until struck off charge in January 1941. Like the RAF's Defiant, the Fleet Air Arm's Roc was fitted with a four-gun, power operated, Boulton Paul turret and no forward firing wing armament, for the intended role of 'bomber destroyer', an outdated concept by 1940, and the type saw little operational action in the Battle of Britain. (Photo: Imperial War Museum)

By 1937, the tragic obsolescence of carrier aircraft had become so scandalous that Parliament finally agreed to remove carrier aircraft from RAF control and return it to the Royal Navy and full Admiralty control in 1938. However, irreparable damage had already been done to Great Britain's Naval aviation that would require years to correct, but the pressure of international tensions would not wait. The outbreak of World War Two found the Royal Navy's Fleet Air Arm ill-prepared with neither the infrastructure, the pilots, nor the necessary training programmes and ground personnel.

Equally unprepared was Britain's aircraft industry where land-based aircraft had been the primary developmental focus since World War One. Under intense pressure to reconstitute itself before becoming enmeshed in World War Two, the service was forced to resort to making-do with improvised redesigns of land-based fighters such as the biplane Gloster Gladiator.

Still holding on to the philosophy of utilising Navalised versions of RAF aircraft, the Royal Navy found its carriers equipped with inferior aircraft that lacked the required performance, reliability and stamina to effectively face the enemy.

At the onset of World War Two, the Fleet Air Arm, consisted of only twenty Squadrons and some 232 aircraft. Typical of these was the disappointingly slow Blackburn Skua dive bomber.

The Blackburn Skua, which entered FAA service in November 1938 as a replacement for the Hawker Osprey and Nimrod biplane fighter aircraft in service at the time, can claim several significant firsts to its name. It was the Fleet Air Arm's first stressed skin monoplane aircraft and also the first British aircraft specifically designed for dive-bombing duties. It was also first British-built dive bomber and the first aircraft to shoot down an enemy aircraft in World War Two – a Dornier Do 18 flying boat on 25 September 1939 – claimed by Lieutenant-Commander B S McEwan RN and Petty Officer Brian Seymour of 803 Naval Air Squadron operating from HMS Ark Royal, whilst on air patrol off the Norwegian coast.

In fact Blackburn Skuas were at the forefront of the Norwegian campaign, often operating at the extreme limit of their range and under gruelling North Sea conditions. Despite these limiting factors, Skuas of 800 and 803 NAS, managed to successfully dive bomb and sink the German cruiser Königsberg, in Bergen Fjord, Norway, on 10 April 1940 – the highlight of the type's career.

No fewer than four front line and twenty-two second line and training Fleet Air Arm squadrons operated Blackburn Skuas between 1938 and 1941.

The Fairey Fulmar Mk.I, which entered carrier service in 1940, was a direct descendant of the 1935 vintage land-based Fairey Battle light bomber – another two-seat fighter saddled with the Naval requirement that all carrier aircraft required navigators. The Merlin-powered Fulmar was built well enough, but was too heavy and lacked the climb ability to successfully engage enemy fighters.

Even though these 'new' designs proved to be barely adequate as land-based military aircraft, it seems that only the obsolete Fairey Swordfish, introduced in 1935, had the structural ruggedness required for sustained carrier operations.

Although the Royal Navy entered the 1930s with six aircraft carriers, they were generally limited in speed, size, range and defensive firepower. On average Britain's pre-war carriers could accommodate only twenty to forty-five aircraft in a mix of Sea Gladiators, Blackburn Skua dive bombers, Fairey Swordfish torpedo bombers and Fairey Fulmar fighters.

The early loss of the carrier HMS Courageous, the first major British warship to be torpedoed and sunk, by U-29 in September 1939 with a loss of more than 500 crew only months after the declaration of war, was an eye-opening blow that caused the Royal Navy to immediately withdraw all fleet carriers from anti-submarine operations.

However, the one major success of FAA operations in 1940 was the Battle of Taranto which took place on the night of 11/12 November 1940. The attack dubbed 'Operation Judgement' was launched from the carrier HMS Illustrious against the Italian fleet anchored in Taranto harbour.

This first all-aircraft naval attack in history, comprised twenty-one torpedo and bomb-carrying Fairey Swordfish biplanes, flying at just 35 feet, in two waves. The torpedo carriers were fitted with specially modified shallow-running torpedoes designed to miss the Italians' torpedo nets. Led in by flare-carrying pathfinders, in the space of a few minutes, half of Italy's battleship force had been sunk, for the loss of only two of the attackers, shot down. By dawn, the low-flying Swordfish were back aboard the Illustrious, little aware that their audacious raid in the black of night had revolutionised naval warfare.

The effect of the British carrier-launched aircraft on the Italian warships foreshadowed the end of the 'big gun' ship and the rise of naval air-power.

Fleet Air Arm camouflage in 1940

Technically speaking, the Fleet Air Arm, (or at least Fleet Air Arm aircraft, as many FAA pilots and aircrew were seconded to operational Fighter Command units during the Battle, and beyond), did not take part in the Battle of Britain as such, although its Skuas and Sea Gladiators were very active during the Norwegian Campaign, the first Martlets and Fulmars to be delivered were defending Scapa Flow, and of course its Swordfish won a tremendous victory at Taranto. When Italy declared war on the United Kingdom on 10 June 1940, the Sea Gladiators of the Hal Far Fighter Flight on Malta also fought their way in to history and legend too... but that's a different story.

In early 1939 the RAE was asked by the Air Ministry to create a camouflage scheme for carrier-based Fleet Air Arm

aircraft. Five colours were developed for what was termed the Temperate Sea Scheme – Extra Dark Sea Grey, Dark Sea Grey, Dark Slate Grey, Light Slate Grey and Sky Grey, for use on monoplane (eg Skua and Fulmar) and biplane (eg Sea Gladiator and Swordfish) aircraft.

Monoplane aircraft were to be camouflaged Extra Dark Sea Grey and Dark Slate Grey on the upper surfaces and Sky Grey on the under surfaces, the upper/under demarcation being half way up the fuselage side to meet the Extra Dark Sea Grey and Dark Slate Grey on the upper half of the fuselage in a wavy line. The fin and rudder were also to be Sky Grey.

Blackburn Skua Mk.II, L2887/(L)6C, 806 Naval Air Squadron, RAF Detling, Kent, May/June 1940.

Although the Fleet Air Arm's fighter squadrons were not directly involved in the day-to-day defence of the United Kingdom, (although many FAA pilots and aircrew were seconded to operational Fighter Command units during the Battle), its Skuas were very active during the Norwegian Campaign – see Chapter 2. Monoplane aircraft, such as the Skua, Roc and Fulmar were camouflaged in the Temperate Sea Scheme, introduced in mid-1939, comprising Extra Dark Sea Grey and Dark Slate Grey on the upper surfaces, in L2887's case to the A Scheme pattern, and Sky Grey on the under surfaces, the upper/under

demarcation being high up on the fuselage sides in an undulating demarcation. The fin and rudder were also Sky Grey. Night and White under surfaces for FAA fighters was promulgated in December 1939. On Skuas this normally took the form of the Night and White being just applied to the mainplane and divided centrally along the centreline. Yellow outer ring to the fuselage roundels, Red/White/Blue fin markings and Red/White/Blue underwing roundels were applied after 30 May 1940. Note the aircraft's code '6C' applied over the fin stripes.

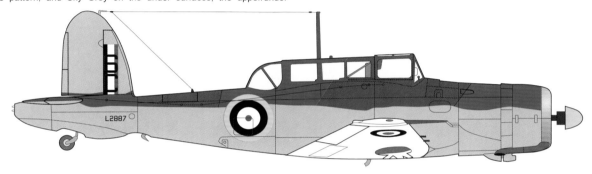

Blackburn Skua Mk.II, L3049/L, 800 Naval Air Squadron, operating off HMS Ark Royal, December 1940 .

Camouflaged in the Temperate Sea Scheme of Extra Dark Sea Grey and Dark Slate Grey on the upper surfaces, L3049 represents the transitional scheme applied to several FAA types following the introduction of Sky under surfaces in September 1940. The original Sky Grey on the under surfaces was overpainted in Sky, but Sky Grey was retained on the fuselage sides and the fin and rudder.

Note the straight demarcation line high up on the fuselage sides, Yellow outer ring to the fuselage roundels, Red/White/Blue fin markings covering the whole of the fin and lack of underwing roundels. The aircraft's full code '6L was applied to the wing leading edges, in white, inboard of the wing fold.

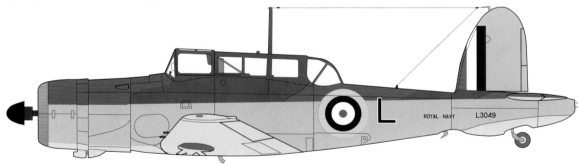

Blackburn Roc Mk.I, L3075/L6R, 806 Naval Air Squadron, operating off HMS Illustrious, mid-1940.

Temperate Sea Scheme of Extra Dark Sea Grey and Dark Slate Grey on the upper surfaces to the A Scheme pattern, and Sky Grey on the under surfaces, with a straight upper/under surface demarcation high up the fuselage sides. The fin and rudder were Sky Grey. The introduction of Sky under surfaces on

RAF aircraft was supposed to take place in June as related elsewhere, but was ordered to take place from September 1940 for all Fleet Air Arm aircraft types hence L3075 still being in Sky Grey. Note the Red/Blue roundel on the fuselage sides and lack of fin stripes, where the aircraft's codes were carried.

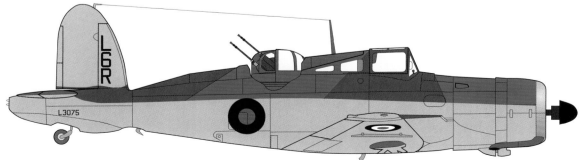

Not to any scale

Biplane aircraft were finished in a variation of the Shadow Compensating Scheme, with the upper surfaces of the upper wing, tailplanes and the top half of the fuselage in Extra Dark Sea Grey and Dark Slate Grey and Dark Sea Grey and Light Slate Grey on the upper surface of the lower wing. Sky Grey was used for the under surfaces which again reached half way up the fuselage side to meet the Extra Dark Sea Grey and Dark Slate Grey on the upper half of the fuselage in a wavy line. The fin and rudder were again to be Sky Grey.

The new Temperate Sea Scheme camouflage scheme was promulgated by the Admiralty in Confidential Admiralty Fleet Order (CAFO) 1213/39 issued on 11 May 1939. The CAFO stated that it had been decided to introduce the Camouflage Scheme as standard for all Fleet Air Arm aircraft except Training aircraft and any aircraft which might be ordered to be painted a different scheme in the future.

The CAFO then stated that whilst new aircraft on the production line would be received from the manufacturers already finished in the Scheme, special arrangements would be necessary to ensure that all aircraft already in service or were in reserve which were not camouflaged, which meant those Fleet Air Arm aircraft which had previously been delivered in the overall Aluminium finish with various metal panels sometimes further protected by an application of Cerrux Grey

paint, would be sprayed the appropriate colour at the earliest convenient date.

CAFO 1213/39 went on to explain that the Admiralty, in conjunction with the Air Ministry, would be issuing the necessary drawings and finishing materials required for each type of aircraft and instructions for its application would be issued in due course.

Two mirror image schemes were shown on the diagram, to be applied to equal numbers of aircraft within each squadron. With the introduction of the camouflage finish the aircraft serial number was to be omitted from the wings and reduced in size on the fuselage to a height of four inches.

The introduction of Night and White under surfaces for fighters was promulgated in CAFO 4021/39 dated 21 December 1939 whilst the introduction of Red, White, Blue and Yellow fuselage roundels, Red, White and Blue fin marking and underwing roundels on the Night and White under surfaces is thought to have been promulgated in CAFO 884/40 issued on 30 May 1940.

The introduction of Sky under surfaces, which was supposed to take place in June 1940 for RAF aircraft, was ordered to take place from September 1940 for all Fleet Air Arm aircraft types.

Gloster Sea Gladiator Mk.II, N2276, 'H', 804 Naval Air Squadron, operating off HMS Furious, September 1940.
Pilot: Lieutenant R H P Carver RN

Sea Gladiators were also very active during the Norwegian Campaign and of course became legendary with the Hal Far Fighter Flight on Malta in June/July 1940. In the UK, in the summer of 1940, 804 NAS was operating off HMS Furious and its Gladiators were finished in a variation of the Shadow Compensating Scheme, with the upper surfaces of the upper wing, tailplanes and the top half of the fuselage in Extra Dark Sea Grey and Dark Slate Grey and Dark Sea Grey and Light Slate Grey on the upper surface of the lower wing, all to the B Scheme pattern. Sky Grey was used for the under surfaces which again reached half

way up the fuselage side to meet the Extra Dark Sea Grey and Dark Slate Grey on the upper half of the fuselage in N2276's case in a straight line. The fin and rudder were again Sky Grey. Sea Gladiator's also had the Night/White under surface scheme applied, in N2276's case under the lower mainplanes, the full length of the fuselage underside divided centrally down the middle, and under the tailplanes. Note the Watts two-blade wooden propeller, a spreadeagled bat on a yellow oval background personal insignia (?) under the cockpit, yellow aircraft letter 'H' and fin stripes over the whole of the fin area.

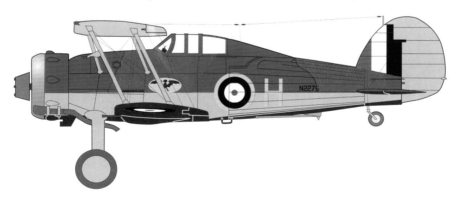

Fairey Fulmar Mk.I, N1881/H, 806 Naval Air Squadron, operating off HMS Illustrious, September/October 1940.

Camouflaged in the Temperate Sea Scheme of Extra Dark Sea Grey and Dark Slate Grey on the upper surfaces, N1881 has full Sky under surfaces introduced on FAA types in September 1940. Note the straight demarcation line half way up the fuselage sides and continuing under the tailplane and

the upper surface camouflage colours on the rudder. Again, the Red/White/Blue fin markings cover the whole of the fin. The aircraft's full code '6H' was applied to the wing leading edges, in white, inboard of the wing fold.

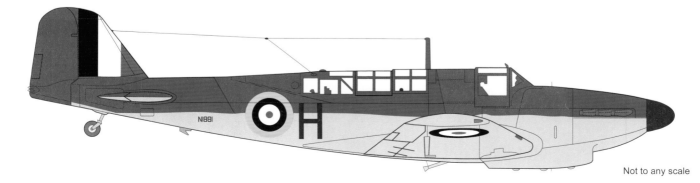

Not to any scale

Fairey Swordfish Mk.I, L2822/A2Q, 810 Naval Air Squadron, operating off HMS Ark Royal, September 1939.

No reference to the Fleet Air Arm in 1940 would be complete without some mention of the Fairey Swordfish. This particular aircraft looks as if it had recently been repainted from the original overall pre-war Aluminium/Cerrux Grey paint scheme in to the Temperate Sea Scheme of Extra Dark Sea Grey and Dark Slate Grey on the upper surfaces of the top wing, the fuselage and the top of the

tailpane, with Dark Sea Grey and Light Slate Grey on the upper surfaces of the lower wings. The under surfaces were Sky Grey which reached half way up the fuselage side in a fairly level line. The fin and rudder were Sky Grey. Fuselage roundels were presumably awaiting replacing. Note the code 'A2Q' on the fin.

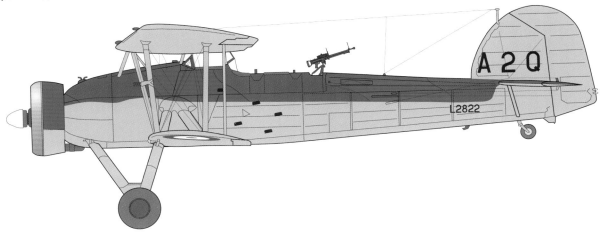

Fairey Swordfish Mk.I, P4085/U3G, 815 Naval Air Squadron, operating off HMS Furious, early 1940.

By the beginning of 1940, the Temperate Sea Scheme of Extra Dark Sea Grey/Dark Slate Grey and Dark Sea Grey/Light Slate Grey upper surfaces with Sky Grey under surfaces was well established within the Swordfish fleet and would remain so for the rest of the year. Again the upper/under surface demarcation

along the fuselage was in a fairly level line and the fin and rudder were Sky Grey. The fuselage and wing under surface roundels were in the pre-war 'Bright' shades as presumably were the Red/White/Blue roundels above the top wing. Note the code 'U3G' on the fin.

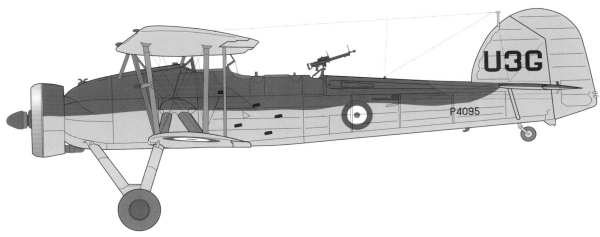

Fairey Swordfish Mk.I, K8418/(E)5K, 824 Naval Air Squadron, operating off HMS Eagle, September 1940.

Of course some mention of the Fairey Swordfish and the famous raid against the Italian fleet at Taranto in November needs to be made. This particualr aircraft, K8418, was aboard HMS Eagle in the late summer/early autumn of 1940 and is thought to have taken part in the action. As such, it may have received black under surfaces, but in September was finished in the temperate Sea Scheme of Extra Dark Sea Grey/Dark Slate Grey and Dark Sea Grey/Light Slate Grey

on the upper surfaces with Sky Grey undersides which reached half way up the fuselage side in an undulating wavy line. The fin and rudder were Sky Grey. This aircraft was flown by Lieutenant Patch who was the senior pilot in the squadron, as denoted by the two black bars on the fin, below which was the aircraft's code, '5K'. Note the angle of the fin stripes against the rudder hinge line.

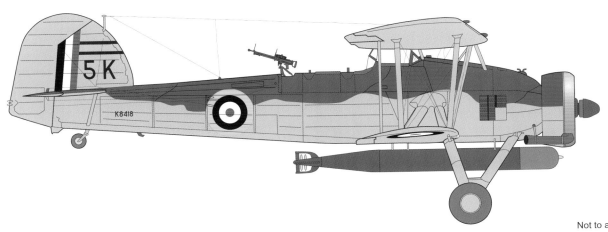

Not to any scale

As the scale of the Luftwaffe's night attacks grew, the Kampfgruppe daylight bomber effort rapidly faded to be replaced by large formation sweeps of single-engined fighters, of which a growing number were converted to carry a 250kg bomb in the fighter-bomber role.

It was Erprobrungsgruppe 210, (ErprGr 210, the specialist test and evaluation unit, whose 1 and 2 Staffeln were equipped with bomb-carrying Messerschmitt Bf 110D-0/Bs), that was the first unit to use single-engined fighters in the 'Jagdbomber' role in July 1940, when 3./ErprGr 210 started operating with its specially adapted bomb-carrying Bf 109E-4/Bs.

Then, during August 1940, Göring ordered that the Bf 109Es of one Staffel in every Gruppe in Luftflotte 2 should be modified to carry bombs and be designated as a Jabostaffel, (fighter-bomber squadron), following what he perceived to be the Jagdverbande's failure to successfully protect the Luftwaffe's bomber force and gain air superiority over the British Isles during the Battle of Britain. Reluctantly, the Jagdgeschwader complied with the order which saw the relatively widespread use of the Bf 109E as fighter-bomber from late September 1940.

The selected units' Bf 109Es were field modified to carry a centre-line mounted bomb rack, either the ETC 500 for a single 250kg bomb, or the ETC 50 for the four smaller 50kg bombs. Examples of Bf 109E-1s, E-3s, E-4s, and the then latest E-7s, were all afflicted, although the vast majority, (at least of those shot down over the British Isles and on which some kind of RAF intelligence report could be made), appear to have been of either the E-1 or E-4 sub-types.

However, a great deal of both factory and 'on-unit' modification and upgrading was undertaken during the early/mid 1940 period, particularly with many of the earlier Bf 109E-1s for example, having their wing mounted MG 17 machine guns replaced by MG FF 20mm cannons, and the later 'square' canopy hoods and windscreens retrofitted, together with the associated head armour, often making absolute identification of the exact sub-type, even if the Werk Nummer is known, almost impossible.

Bomb-carrying Bf 109Es were identified as Jabos by the /B suffix designation, (eg Bf 109E-1/B, Bf 109E-4/B), and operated together with the factory 'wired and plumbed' new Bf 109E-7 variant, which was designed from the start to carry either a centre line bomb or 300 litre fuel tank.

At least nineteen staffeln operated Jabo '109s during the Battle of Britain, ie 3./ErprGr. 210; 2, 3, 4, 5 and 6./LG 2; 7 and 8./JG 3; 3, 4 and 9./JG 26; 2, 3 and 9./JG 27; 1 and 2./JG 51 and 3, 4 and 8./JG 53

However, by the end of October 1940/beginning of November, daylight Jabo operations over the UK also dwindled as the year drew to a close with the worsening weather conditions. Many of the Jabo staffeln remained active well into the new year, but by the spring of 1941, the RAF had gone on to the offensive and the Bf 109s were required in a more defensive role.

This shift in Luftwaffe tactics did serve two purposes though. Firstly, the Jabos could maintain the pressure on the UK's urban population by way of regular, albeit relatively small scale, bombing raids, and secondly, it engaged Fighter Command in a steady war of attrition.

Messerschmitt Bf 109E-4/B, 'Yellow 11', 3./ErprGr 210, Denain, France, autumn 1940.

RLM 71 Dunkelgrün and RLM 02 Grau upper surfaces in a soft-edged splinter pattern with RLM 65 Hellblau under surfaces and fuselage sides, over which a very dense mottle of RLM 71/02 has been applied. The yellow numeral '11' was outlined in white. Yellow cowling, angled back towards the windscreen, and rudder. The yellow spinner had a white tip. No unit insignia appear to have been carried by ErprGr 210's Bf 109Es. Note again the way the swastika was masked out when the mottle was applied leaving an RLM 65 'background'.

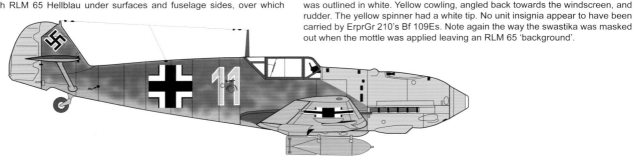

Messerschmitt Bf 109E-7, 'Black 11', 5./JG 52, Peuplingues, France, autumn 1940.

'Black 11' still appears to be in the original RLM 70 Schwarzgrün and RLM 71 Dunkelgrün upper surfaces, albeit possibly in a soft-edged semi-splinter pattern, with RLM 65 Hellblau under surfaces and fuselage sides. Yellow cowling, the side area extending back to the supercharger intake, and rudder. The RLM 70 spinner had a pointed cap. JG 52's winged sword insignia was carried under the windscreen with 5 Staffel's 'rabbatz' emblem applied to the cowling side. Note the four SC 50 bombs on an ETC 50 rack under the fuselage.

Inset: JG 52's winged sword on a black and red shield insignia and 5 Staffel's 'rabbatz' (red devil with bow and arrow) emblem.

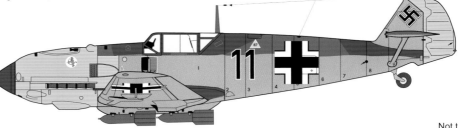

Not to any scale

This strategy only made sense in the light of the continuing Luftwaffe's under estimation of the strength of Fighter Command which continued to believe that Fighter Command was down to its last few hundred fighters and that production was falling under the weight of the German onslaught. In October 253 of these 'nuisance' raids were mounted, followed by some 235 in November.

These raids were carried out at altitudes around 20,000ft where the Bf 109E had an advantage due to its DB 601's two-stage engine supercharger. This forced Fighter Command to switch tactics, as it was now required to once again mount standing patrols at high altitudes as the Chain Home RDF experienced difficulty in tracking aircraft at high altitudes.

RAF Fighter Command changes

Following the introduction of Sky in June 1940, and the reintroduction of roundels in August, the next change in the camouflage and marking of the RAF Day Fighter Force came in November 1940. Large fighter-versus-fighter encounters once again led to an urgent operational requirement for some way of being quickly and easily able to distinguish friend from foe – in the air and from the ground

As has already been described the British Air Ministry had put a great deal of effort into devising what became known as the Temperate Land Scheme on the upper surfaces of most landplanes which consisted of Dark Green and Dark Earth, applied in a disruptive pattern which was intended to break up the outline of the aircraft.

In fact, the only apparent variation to this Temperate Land Scheme is thought to have come about by accident as a result of the incorrect thinning and application of paint on the production line. It is thought that a number of early Spitfire Mk.IIs built at Castle Bromwich were finished in paint which had been over thinned which resulted in a change in observed colour when sprayed. The Dark Earth paint dried as a much lighter colour, something like Light Earth, whilst the Dark Green underwent a change in hue to a more blue-green appearance somewhat reminiscent of Extra Dark Sea Green.

Night port underwing reintroduced

On 27 November 1940, the Air Ministry sent Signal X789 to notify all Commands that the under surfaces of the port wing of Day Fighters were once again to be given a black finish. All Day Fighters were ordered to be coloured Night (or alternatively Special Night) on the under surface of the port wing by Aircraft Storage Units before delivery to Fighter Command units.

Generally, roundels were only carried on the under surfaces of operational Day Fighters, which were to carry Red, White and Blue roundels, in the 1-3-5 proportions. The roundel on the new black (Night/Special Night) under surfaces of the port wing of Day Fighters was to be given a Yellow surrounding ring, which was not supposed to overlap on to the aileron.

To further assist in rapid air-to-air recognition, Day Fighters were also to carry an 18 inch wide band of Sky right around the fuselage immediately forward of the tailplane, and were to have the airscrew spinner painted Sky too.

Supermarine Spitfire Mk.II, P7666/EB-Z, 41 Squadron, RAF Hornchurch, November/December 1940.
Pilot: Squadron Leader Donald Finlay DSO, Squadron CO

P7666 was amongst the first few hundred Castle Bromwich-built Spitfire Mk.IIs that were being issued to Fighter Command's squadrons in the last three months of 1940. This particular machine was also a presentation aircraft and had the legend 'Observer Corps' on the forward fuselage. Finished in the standard Temperate Land Scheme of Dark Earth and Dark Green upper surfaces, to the B Scheme pattern, it would almost certainly have had the 'standard' Sky shade applied to the under surfaces, on the production line, with Night/Special Night RDM2 applied under the port wing. Note the light blue Air Ministry Sky Blue shade spinner and rear fuselage tail band that was terminated along the upper/under demarcation line. Note also the two swastika 'kill' markings under the windscreen and the full height fin stripes.

Supermarine Spitfire Mk.Ib, X4272/QJ-D, 92 Squadron, RAF Biggin Hill, December 1940.

X4272 was one of a batch of Spitfire Mk.Is that had been returned to Supermarine for fitting with the improved 20mm cannon armament following the earlier disappointing trials with cannon-armed Spitfires operated by 19 Squadron in August 1940. Termed Spitfire Mk.Ib, to differentiate them from the standard eight 0.303 inch machine gun-armed Spitfire Mk.I, which were then retrospectively re-termed Spitfire Mk.Ia, these aircraft proved their efficiency and paved the way for the cannon-armed Spitfire Mk.Vb. Standard Temperate Land Scheme of Dark Earth and Dark Green upper surfaces, to the A Scheme pattern, with standard Sky shade, or at least a close approximation to it, under surfaces with a Night/Special Night RDM2 port under wing. The 'Sky' spinner and 18 inch wide rear fuselage band appear to be in the light blue/Air Ministry Sky Blue shade. Note the small underwing roundels positioned at the extreme tip and the fin stripes extending the full height of the fin.

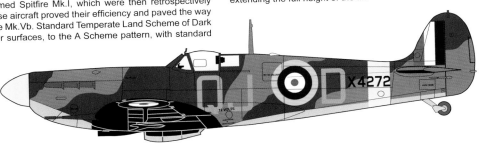

Not to any scale

However, the description of these new identification markings were described as "... a vertical duck egg blue band 18 inches wide which was to be painted completely around the fuselage immediately in front of the tailplane and a coloured spinner which was also to be painted duck egg blue".

Although the fact that the term 'duck egg blue' was a colloquialism for Sky appears to have been well understood by 3 Maintenance Unit at Milton, which is thought to have been the main Stores Depot responsible for supplying the RAF's paints and dopes at this time, on 18 December 1940, 3 MU sent a signal to the RAE advising them that the Maintenance Unit did not have a Vocabulary of Stores reference number for Sky, and enquired which shade of Sky – Sky Grey or Sky Blue – was required!

This is probably the reason why there are eyewitness accounts of RAF Day Fighters with 'light blue' spinners and tailbands well into the summer of 1941, and the difference in tone often visible in photographs between the spinner and tailband and the under surface colour.

How widespread the use of Sky Blue for spinners and tailbands was, and for how long it actually continued, is currently unknown, but it is thought that any use of Sky Blue for such markings finally ceased in the summer of 1941 with the introduction of the 'grey/green' Day Fighter Scheme when the aircraft manufacturers began to apply such markings on the production line instead of leaving the job to Maintenance Units.

Luftwaffe greys

As detailed in Chapter 5, the Jagdwaffe had been experimenting with 'in the field applied' grey upper surface schemes as early as July/August 1940, apparently by mixing an assortment of the available RLM 70 and RLM 71 green shades and RLM 02 Grau (a grey-green shade) and RLM 66 Schwarzgrau (black-grey) to produce 'field mixed' grey shades.

As the air combats of late September and early October began to reach heights in excess of 20,000 feet, a more suitable 'high altitude' camouflage was required, and it appears that it was

Messerschmitt Bf 109E-7, 'Black 6', 5./JG 51, Mardyck, France, autumn 1940.

RLM 71 Dunkelgrün and RLM 02 Grau upper surfaces in a soft-edged splinter pattern with RLM 65 Hellblau under surfaces and fuselage sides, over which a very dense mottle of RLM 71/02 has been applied. Note the removable fuselage

panel just in front of the windscreen which appears to be in a primer grey shade? The black numeral '6' was outlined in white and 5 Staffel's green woodpecker or parrot with umbrella insignia was carried on the rear fuselage. Yellow cowling and rudder. RLM 70 spinner. Note the motto 'Achtung Anfänger!' (beware the avenger) under the cockpit area.

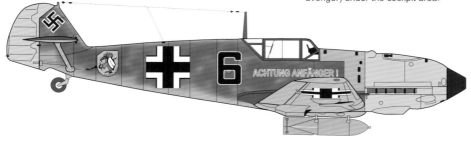

ACHTUNG ANFÄNGER !

Inset: 'Achtung Anfänger!' (Beware the Avenger) in white outline under the cockpit area.

Messerschmitt Bf 109E-7, 'Black 1', 2(J)./LG 2, Calais-Marck, France, November 1940.

RLM 71 Dunkelgrün and RLM 02 Grau upper surfaces in a soft-edged splinter pattern with RLM 65 Hellblau under surfaces and fuselage sides, over which

a very dense mottle of RLM 71/02 has been applied. Yellow cowling, which extends back to the windscreen along the top, and rudder. RLM 70 spinner. The black numeral '1' was thinly outlined in white and note the position on the rear fuselage of the black top hat in a white disc which may have been a personal rather than a unit marking.

Inset: Black 1's 'top hat' emblem

Messerschmitt Bf 109E-4, 'Yellow 1', 6./JG 77, Brest-Guipavas, France, November 1940.

RLM 71 Dunkelgrün and RLM 02 Grau upper surfaces in a soft-edged splinter pattern with RLM 65 Hellblau under surfaces and fuselage sides. Yellow cowling,

spinner and rudder. The yellow numeral '1' and II Gruppe horizontal bar was outlined in black. No unit insignia appears to have been carried.

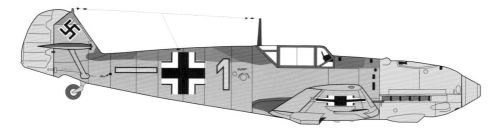

Not to any scale

Hawker Hurricane Mk.I, V6873/DT-O, 257 Squadron, RAF North Weald, December 1940.

Standard Temperate Land Scheme of Dark Earth and Dark Green upper surfaces, to the B Scheme pattern, with a duck egg blue shade of 'Sky' (possibly BS 381 Sky Blue?) under surfaces that was recorded on several, 257 Squadron's Gloster-built Hurricane Mk.Is. Port wing under surface in Night, introduced in late November 1940, at the same time as the 'Sky' spinner and 18 inch wide rear

fuselage band which were in the light blue/Air Ministry Sky Blue shade. Note how far back the tailband is, being truncated at the base of the fin. All other markings are standard for the period including 49 inch diameter upper wing roundels, 35 inch diameter fuselage roundels, 45 inch diameter under wing roundels and the 24 x 27 inch fin flash.

Hawker Hurricane Mk.I, (serial unknown)/SD-O, 257 Squadron, RAF North Weald, December 1940.

Despite being in the A Scheme pattern, the areas of Dark Earth and Dark Green on the upper surfaces appear to have been transposed, perhaps indicating a complete repaint at squadron level? The under surfaces appear to be the standard Sky shade or at least a close approximation to it. However, the

propeller spinner and the rear fuselage tail band appear much darker and may be an in-service mix resulting in a rich duck-egg blue shade. All the other national markings appear standard for the time period.

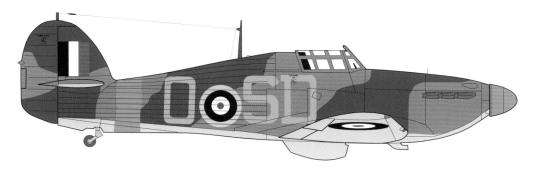

Hawker Hurricane Mk.I, V6732/TM-J, 504 Squadron, RAF Exeter, December 1940.

Standard Temperate Land Scheme of Dark Earth and Dark Green upper surfaces, to the B Scheme pattern, with 'Sky' starboard under surfaces and what appears to be Night/Special Night RDM2 applied under the whole of the port underside, divided centrally down the aircraft's centreline similar to the previous Night/White

scheme. The spinner and rear fuselage tailband appear to be 'Sky'. Note how the tailband is truncated on the upper/under surface demarcation line. All other markings are standard for the period including the 35 inch diameter fuselage roundels and the 24 x 27 inch fin flash.

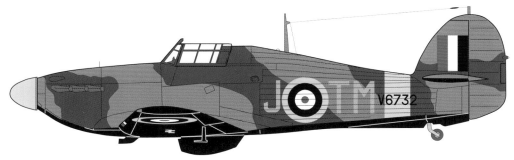

Hawker Hurricane Mk.I, V7104/UF-B, 601 Squadron, RAF Northolt, December 1940.

Standard Temperate Land Scheme of Dark Earth and Dark Green upper surfaces, to the B Scheme pattern, with a duck egg green shade of 'Sky' (possibly BS 381 Eau-de-Nil?) under surfaces. Port wing under surface in Night/Special Night RDM2. The propeller spinner and the rear fuselage tail band again appear much

darker than usual and may be an in-service mix resulting in a rich duck-egg blue shade. Note how the tailband is truncated around the serial number. All the other national markings appear standard for the period including 35 inch diameter fuselage roundels and the 24 x 27 inch fin flash.

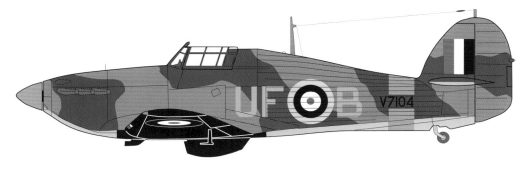

Not to any scale

during this period that the application of 'grey' shades on Luftwaffe fighters, in preference to the then standard RLM 71/02 scheme, seems to have increased, eventually resulting in the new standard fighter scheme of RLM 74 Dunkelgrau/RLM 75 Mittelgrau/RLM 76 Hellgrau recorded in the November 1941 edition of the Luftwaffe's L Dv 521/1 paint chart.

It now looks as if this 'standard' scheme may have been introduced much earlier on to the production line, if the colour photo of the Bf 109E-7, still with its factory codes in place, mentioned in Chapter 5 is anything to go by. This late-series 'Emil', was apparently manufactured in mid-August 1940, and was finished in a three-tone grey scheme, which would indicate that the RLM 74/75/76 'greys' scheme was being applied. at factory level at least, by then.

That this aircraft, and others on the same production line, would probably have been issued to front line units in late September/early October 1940, which might well indicate that the standard RLM 74/75/76 scheme was actually being applied to front-line Bf 109Es during this period. Wreckage, consisting of various earlier and mid-production sub-types of the 'Emil' from this later stage of the Battle of Britain, has also revealed that combinations of grey paint in shades very similar to, if not the actual RLM 74/75/76 colours, had been applied to a growing number of the Bf 109Es examined.

However, it should not be construed that ALL Bf 109Es were finished in 'shades of grey' by the end of the year, as the predominant 'fighter scheme' still appears to have been the standard RLM 71/02 scheme introduced at the beginning of 1940.

Junkers Ju 87B-2, J9+BL, 9./StG 1, based either at St Pol, France, or Ostende, Belgium, as the unit moved during November 1940.

At first look this aircraft is a bit of an enigma. Listed as a 9 Staffel machine, the Staffel letter 'L' is usually associated with 3 Staffel and the 'devil with torch riding a bomb' badge, is 6./StG 1's emblem! However, the codes J9 originally belonged to I/StG 186 which was re-designated III/StG 1 in July 1940 but the Gruppe continued to use the J9 code and their original I Gruppe staffel letters, B, H, K and L – hence J9+BL being a 9 Staffel machine. Why it carried 6./StG 1's emblem though is anybody's guess! Finished in the standard two-tone green RLM 70 Schwarzgrün and RLM 71 Dunkelgrün upper surfaces in a straight-edged 'splinter' pattern, the original RLM 65 Hellblau undersides were overpainted with

a temporary black wash for nocturnal operations when III/StG 1 was operating against south-east coast targets over the winter of 1940/41. Codes were black with a yellow individual aircraft letter 'B' which, like the national insignia, had been toned-down with black temporary paint. Note the yellow tip to the RLM 70 propeller spinner, which had also been toned-down with black paint and the 'devil with torch riding a bomb' badge, (6./StG 1's emblem), under the windscreen.

Inset: 6./StG 1's 'devil with torch riding a bomb' emblem.

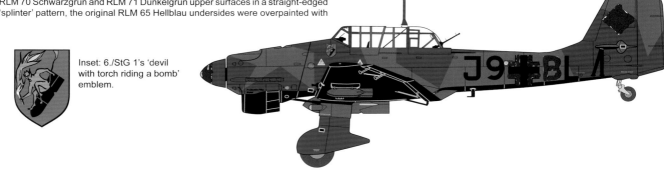

Messerschmitt Bf 109E-4/B, 'Yellow 1', 9./JG 54, Guines, France, October 1940.

An example of the early 'greys' finished machine with two-tone 'mixed grey' upper surfaces in a soft-edged splinter pattern. The RLM 65 Hellblau under surfaces have been extended up the fuselage sides and over the fin and rudder, over

which a dense mottle of the 'mixed greys' has been applied. Yellow cowling and rudder. The spinner is white with a pointed spinner cap. The yellow numeral '1' is outlined in black. This aircraft carried 9 Staffel's 'grinning red devil's head' in a yellow shield just forward of the cockpit section and for some reason 7./JG 54's 'winged clog' on the cowling side. Note the way the swastika was masked out when the mottle was applied leaving an RLM 65 'background'.

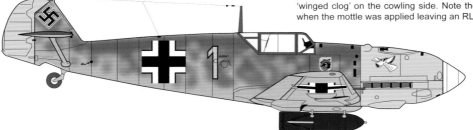

Inset: 9./JG 54's 'grinning red devil's head' in a yellow shield and 7./JG 54's 'winged clog' emblems.

Messerschmitt Bf 109E-1/B, W.Nr 6313, 'White G', 2./JG 27, based at Calais-Marck, France, November 1940.
Pilot: Uffz Paul Wacker

Another possible example of a 'greys' finished machine, with two-tone 'mixed grey' upper surfaces in a soft-edged splinter pattern. The RLM 65 Hellblau under surfaces have been extended over the fuselage sides and over the fin and rudder. The cowling was yellow, RLM 04 Gelb, as was the rudder and the spinner. This aircraft had only recently been transferred from 4.(Schlacht)/LG 2 to 2./JG 27 and still retained many of its previous owner's markings, including a black 'schlacht' triangle and a white individual aircraft letter, (rather than JG 27's more usual numeral), at the time it made a forced landing at Woodyhyde Farm, Worth Matravers, Dorset on 30 November 1940 after suffering engine malfunction. Uffz

Wacker became a PoW. W.Nr 6313 had been retrofitted with the later heavier framed 'square' canopy, with head armour, and had an ETC 500/IXb bomb rack for the carriage of an SC 250 bomb – although it may not have been so fitted when the aircraft crash-landed, as it was apparently on a reconnaissance sweep. Note the three red bars (abschuszbalken) on the rudder, which may have been the 'victories' of the aircraft's previous 4.(Schlacht)/LG 2 pilot.

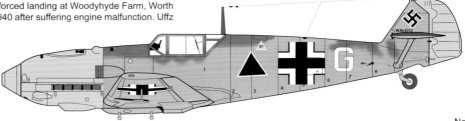

Not to any scale

Hawker Hurricane Mk.I, V7462/JU-T, 111 Squadron, RAF Dyce, Aberdeenshire, November/December 1940.

On 27 November 1940, the Air Ministry informed all Commands that the under surfaces of the port wing of Day Fighters were once again to be given a black finish, in either Night or Special Night. The roundel on the new black (Night/Special Night) under surfaces was to be given a Yellow surrounding ring, which was not supposed to overlap on to the aileron. To assist further in rapid air-to-air recognition, Day Fighters were also ordered to carry an 18 inch wide band of Sky right around the fuselage immediately forward of the tailplane, and were to have the propeller spinner painted Sky too.

However, there is photographic evidence to suggest that RAF Day Fighters were painted with 'light blue' spinners and tailbands well into the summer of 1941. How widespread the use of this 'light blue', which may have been Air Ministry Sky Blue, for spinners and tailbands was, and for how long it actually continued, is currently unknown, but it is thought that the use of 'Sky Blue' for such markings only ceased in the summer of 1941 with the introduction of the 'grey/green' Day Fighter Scheme, when the aircraft manufacturers began to apply such markings on the production line instead of leaving the job to Maintenance Units. V7462's upper surfaces are in the standard Temperate Land Scheme of Dark Earth and Dark Green to the B Scheme pattern. Note how far back the Sky Blue tailband is, being truncated at the base of the fin. All other markings are standard for the period including 49 inch diameter upper wing roundels, 35 inch diameter fuselage roundels, 45 inch diameter under wing roundels and the 24 x 27 inch fin flash. V7462 was finally Struck Off Charge in October 1944.

Not to any scale

Colour Chart

Dark Earth	Dark Green	Sky Type S
BS381 (1930) No1 Sky Blue	BS381 (1930) Eau-de-Nil	Air Ministry Sky Blue
Red (wartime dull)	Blue (wartime dull)	Red (pre-war bright)
Blue (pre-war bright)	Yellow	Extra Dark Sea Grey
Dark Slate Grey	Dark Sea Grey	Light Slate Grey
Sky Grey	RLM 02 Grau	RLM 04 Gelb
RLM 23 Rot	RLM 24 Dunkelblau	RLM 25 Hellgrün
RLM 26 Braun	RLM 27 Gelb	RLM 61 Dunkelbraun
RLM 62 Grün	RLM 63 Hellgrau	RLM 65 Hellblau
RLM 66 Schwarzgrau	RLM 70 Schwarzgrün	RLM 71 Dunkelgrün
RLM 72 Grün (maritime green)	RLM 73 Grün (maritime green)	RLM 74 Dunkelgrau (mixed)
RLM 75 Mittelgrau (mixed)	Giallo Mimetico 3 (camo yellow 3)	Giallo Verde 3 (camo green 3)
Bruno Mimetico (camo brown)	Grigio Mimetico (camo grey)	Chocolat
Vert Emaillite	Gris Bleu Fonce (Dark blue grey)	Terre Fonce (Dark earth)
Terre de Sienne (Light earth)	Kaki	Sable
Gris Bleu Clair (Light blue grey)	Rouge	Bleu Brillant